# The Assassination of D'Arcy McGee

BOOKS BY T. P. SLATTERY, Q.C.

*Loyola and Montreal*
*The Assassination of D'Arcy McGee*

# The Assassination of D'Arcy McGee

## T. P. SLATTERY, Q.C.

*with illustrations by the author*

1968
Doubleday Canada Limited, Toronto
Doubleday & Company, Inc., Garden City, New York

Library of Congress Catalog Card Number 68–13134
Copyright © 1968 by T. P. Slattery, Q.C.
Printed in the United States of America
First Edition

*To the Youngest*

# FOREWORD

Luck, it seemed, was there from the start. Sitting in the sun of Bermuda, the year before he died, Thomas Costain happened to say that he admired D'Arcy McGee and had often thought of writing a book on him. When I made an idle remark about collecting material on McGee as a kind of hobby, George Nelson of Doubleday invited me to do something about it. Soon after that I happened to be with the late Dr. Emmet Mullally when he opened a brown paper bag to find forty-four original, unpublished letters by McGee and members of his family. That put me to work.

Providence permits me now, almost four years later, to thank my three children, Maureen, Brian and Patricia, for their priceless help in this undertaking. But there is more to it than this. What still fascinates us is the mystery of McGee's assassination, and a second book is now partly written on the murder trial. No passage of arms is more absorbing for me than a family discussion on who killed McGee—which, to use an understatement, is endless. And through all this, as ever, my wife "sustains, believes, hopes and endures to the last."

*T. P. Slattery*

# ACKNOWLEDGMENTS

For their kind assistance, I wish to express my gratitude to Mr. E. A. Anglin, Q.C., Mr. M. G. Ballantyne, Mr. George Broderick, Q.C., Mr. Robin B. Burns, Bishop Emmett G. Carter, D.D., Mr. Justice P. C. Casey, Miss Agnes Coffey, Mr. E. A. Collard, Senator John J. Connolly, Dr. J. I. Cooper, Mrs. J. Cornellier, the late Msgr. H. J. Doran, the late Mr. Justice Guy Favreau, Rev. J. P. Finn, Rev. Gordon George, S.J., Senator Allister Grosart, Mr. Matthew Harris, the late Rev. W. H. Hingston, S.J., Sister St. Ida, Mr. William Kehoe, Mr. John D. King, Dr. W. Kaye Lamb, Msgr. E. J. LaPointe, Mr. J. J. Lefebvre, Mr. George L. Long, the late Mr. John Loye, Mr. Daniel C. Lyne, Mr. T. D. MacDonald, Q.C., Mr. W. A. McFaul, Judge Emmett J. McManamy, Mr. K. F. McNamee, Q.C., Mr. W. J. McQuillan, Q.C., Rev. Patrick G. Malone, S.J., Mr. David Manuel, Mr. John N. Mappin, Mr. Dominic Martini, Sister St. Mary Assumpta, Mr. Louis Melzack, Miss Kathleen O'Brien, Mr. Justice J. B. O'Connor, Mr. Dermot O'Gallagher, Miss Marie O'Kelly, Senator Grattan O'Leary, Mr. W. G. Ormsby, the late Mr. D. F. Pepler, K.C., Mr. Arthur Perrault, Mrs. George B. Roche, Miss Grace Slattery, Mr. S. Triggs, Mr. George Trowsdale, Mr. H. J. Walker, Mr. Charles H. Wayland and many others.

*T. P. Slattery*

# CONTENTS

tion of Upper and Lower Canada. Reciprocity and depression, 1857. McGee's *New Era*. Early editorials on Confederation. Political parties, Clear Grits, old Reformers, *Rouges*, Tories, *Bleus* and Coalition. McGee, Independent warrior. His campaign and first election. First Session in Parliament. Murder in Toronto. Triumph in Montreal.

## PART TWO: STRUGGLE

## PART THREE: SACRIFICE

## PART FOUR: MURDER

# LIST OF ILLUSTRATIONS

The dead have their rights as the living have; injustice to them is one of the worst forms of all injustice.

*Thomas D'Arcy McGee*

# PART ONE

# OMENS

The like of me has a store of knowledge
that's a weight and a terror.
*John M. Synge*
DEIRDRE OF THE SORROWS

# I

## THE SCHOLAR AND THE SWORD

His heart hums within him, for he has distinguished himself at public assemblies for his eloquence.

My mother said when he was born, he would be a great man yet, with the help of God, and to the day of her death, she lived in that belief.

*Dorcas McGee, describing her sixteen-year-old brother, Thomas D'Arcy McGee, in a letter to her aunt*

Hate, not love, was born blind.
*Thomas D'Arcy McGee*

Thomas D'Arcy McGee was born on Wednesday, April 13, 1825, in Carlingford, Ireland, on the Rosstrevor coast along an arm of the green waters of the Irish Sea. There the rain is soft, and sunlight comes in patches. When it comes, they say you can hear the sound of bees.

His formal instruction in school was scanty. But more important than that, his pious dark-haired mother, the intelligent daughter of a Dublin bookseller, was very fond of books and ballads and had a charming voice. His father, James McGee, an Irish coastguard, was lively, steady enough and clearly a man of spirit. Together they trained him in the habit of work and touched him with their love.

An upward view from his native cottage gave it its Gaelic name, *Radharc An Tsleibhe,* or "Sight of the Mountain," which led him to romantic paths, and hid the hard road just ahead. When D'Arcy was eight, the family moved south to Wexford. On their way his mother was the victim of an accident and died soon after, on August 22, 1833. This was a heavy blow. But a hedge schoolmaster, an extraordinary man named Michael Donnelly, helped him along with his books and fertilized his dreams; "the brightest scholar I ever taught" was Donnelly's memory of McGee in 1891, when the venerable schoolmaster was over a hundred years old. As a mere lad, D'Arcy (or Tommy, as he was then called) had to work for his living, and later his employer in Wexford remembered him as "full of intellect, gentle and amiable."

D'Arcy McGee was both proud and troubled to recognize that he came "of good rebel blood." Almost all the men on both sides of his family had been out in the rising of 1798, and his mother's father, the bookseller, had fought with the United Irishmen, been imprisoned and then ruined. D'Arcy heard of atrocities from his earliest years. His own hedge schoolmaster would often tell how the elder Donnelly, his father, had been hanged at Ross in '98; and in Wexford, where the fiercest fighting had taken place, there were endless tales of carnage.

While McGee was a growing boy, four Irishmen influenced him deeply—the first two through his reading, and the latter two personally: Edmund Burke as a wise statesman, and Thomas Moore, his mother's favourite minstrel; then Father Theobald Matthew, the Franciscan apostle of Temperance, and Daniel O'Connell, Ireland's unrivalled leader, who gloried in Lord Shrewsbury's gibe as "king of the beggars." Something else left an indelible mark on his young mind, which became the irony of his career: the ugly results of secret societies. There were many, and on all sides. Foremost in his abhorrence, however, was the Orange Lodge.

Orangemen, he was taught, represented the aggressors who directed the Penal Code against the Catholics of Ireland. On this Penal Code, he accepted Edmund Burke's stern judgement:

> It was a machine of wise and elaborate contrivance and as well fitted for the oppression, impoverishment and degradation of a people, and the debasement in them of human nature itself, as ever proceeded from the perverted ingenuity of man.

In Wexford, D'Arcy had a boyish moment of triumph when he gave a speech before the Juvenile Temperance Society, and Father Matthew, who happened to be there, reached over as a sign of praise and tousled his hair. In the long evenings he would often ramble from house to cottage and sit in the circle around a blazing turf fire, listening in the half-light to the old men telling their tales, some as old as a thousand years.

His father as a widower in Wexford had a young and very active family under his care, so he married again. D'Arcy's sister Dorcas did not hide the wounded feelings of the older children, and in a letter to her Aunt Bella in Rhode Island she wrote: "From the day of my father's making a second choice the shock was given."

So on April 7 (the ominous date of his death) in the year 1842, when D'Arcy McGee was not yet seventeen, he left Ireland with his sister Dorcas to go and live with that aunt, their mother's only sister, Mrs. Charles Morgan, in Providence, Rhode Island. Their older brother Lawrence was then working as a hand on the brig *Leo,* sailing under Captain Robert Murphy in the lumber trade between Wexford and Quebec City, bearing white and red pine from the St. Lawrence valley, and returning with Irish emigrants in the hold. So they sailed with him, each paying $8.40 for their passage of six weeks. It was thus by chance that D'Arcy McGee's first impression of the New World came from Canada, with its grand sweep of the St. Lawrence River and the expanse of a whitish blue sky over the Quebec Citadel. Disembarking with his sister at Quebec, he went on, as he said, "to Providence in America."

But Providence did not provide the opening he was seeking, and he was soon in Boston looking for work. He applied first at several newspaper offices, but as he discovered, "they want small boys to do dirty work." Then he tried the shops. Finally, with the aid of Mr. A. McEvoy, one of his first friends in America, he obtained a modest job with the Irish Catholic newspaper the Boston *Pilot,* and the promise of a three-year contract paying him "$50 for the first year, $75 for the second and $100 for the third," this grand total of $225 to be supplemented by his "board, washing and mending" at the home of Patrick Donahoe, the owner of the newspaper and later a successful publisher and banker. As D'Arcy explained in detail to his aunt, he managed, beyond his "scribbling," to earn some extra money "lecturing," enough to buy "a pair of thick boots, an outside coat and other items—value about $30."

He was a good correspondent—"I have a round dozen of letters to answer today," he notes one busy Wednesday. But because the cost of postage was so high, the charge for the short distance from Boston to Providence being twelve and a half cents, he asked his friends to deliver most of his letters by hand.

In the evenings he attended Temperance meetings in Father Matthew's movement, and Repeal meetings to support O'Connell's cause. He was hardly in Boston before he was on his feet speaking at an Irish assembly urging Repeal of the Legislative Union which had merged Ireland into England. The president of the Repeal Association invited him back to speak on the Fourth of July. "Ought I to address them?" he asks his aunt, and, without waiting for a reply, he did. And his next letter followed promptly:

> The fourth of July was about the finest sight I ever saw. The Repealers met in the Marlboro Chapel, where I was introduced, well received and highly complimented. But you will perceive this by the liberal newspapers, if they do me justice.
>
> I have been requested to go with one or two others to the State of Maine to arouse the Repealers there. Now if nothing else offers, I should not refuse a six weeks tour, as our expenses will be decently discharged. Mr. McEvoy has been very kind and has introduced me to about half the population of Boston.

Five days later he wrote:

> The Boston *Pilot* contains the best report of my speech. But the *Reporter* is rascally, it is not the same at all. I sent Saturday's *Pilot* to Wexford, and you may perceive by it that Donahoe has appointed me his agent. You shall see occasional articles from me in his paper, all on National subjects, whether prose or verse.

His speeches were almost always on Irish topics. If he touched on American politics, he was quick to explain his neutrality to his aunt:

I have attempted, without anything of party in my words or thoughts, to speak on the broad principles of Democracy, the same which form the political creed of O'Connell and Jackson. Ahem! A very elaborate disquisition indeed.

The exchange of news with his family in Wexford was far from dull, as this letter from his father revealed:

Wexford, Ireland
July 26, 1843

My dear Son:

I received your letter dated 15th of May. It was only 15 days coming to hand.

I think you must have had a letter from me about this time giving all particulars about Lawrence. My mind was so agitated from the news that came from the *Leo*. She had an excellent passage of 30 days, but orders came to stop Lawrence's market money and two others. I did not know what to think.

I heard the *John Bill* of Ross brought word that Lawrence was in gaol in Quebec for beating the mate, Tom Codd. I then gave expression to my sentiment in the Custom House and before Div Clarks, that I was satisfied for him to get a month's incarceration, providing he beat the scoundrel well, for Codd is a horrid character.

It seems it was all about navigation, and Lawrence has proved himself to be more competent and fitter to be mate than Codd; which Captain Murphy's letter today testified. So Codd is discharged, and Lawrence is made Chief Mate. So much for one of the "Macs."

My dear fellow, circumstances so combined this day to hear of Lawrence's promotion, and of you as secretary to the Boston Repeal Association, held in the Miller Tabernacle (and Annie's birthday into the bargain)—we rejoice and bless God for giving such two sons—you employed for the regeneration of our long misgoverned and oppressed country under the tyranny of the truculent Saxon yoke.

Your articles which appear in the papers are read with much interest by your old friends.

Jimmy and Rosy are kept constantly at school. He will be another clever fellow—Jimmy is a very fine boy, and he says he is one of the "Macs." There was a gentleman here from London that much admired him. He asked would we allow him to take his likeness. We did so, and he drew one for us, a most splendid thing valued to 5 guineas.

My dear fellow, I will write to you shortly and let you know more particulars about Lawrence. We expect his arrival every tide. As I mentioned, in my former letter the best 4 months he ever spent both for soul and body was last winter.

Your affectionate father,
James McGee

This letter with all its news from home must have been read many times over and even dreamt about, for written vertically across his father's writing on its first page, in young D'Arcy's unfaltering hand, in pencil but still legible, are the first sixteen lines of what he published later as a "Song of the American Repealers." A comparison of this first draft with its final form shows that only a few changes were made later. And indeed some of them may not have been for the better.

That year romance probably cast its spell over his work for Reform, for on September 30, 1843, he could not refrain from telling his Aunt Bella:

I have a long story to tell you about a fair Georgian whom I met in New Haven. She was at a Boarding School there and attending my lecture on Temperance, and took the pledge. She also came to the Repeal meetings and subscribed handsomely. But I must wait till further opportunities for the particulars.

Ambition was also stirring within him, and early in 1844 he wrote to his aunt that he was coming down some Sunday to consult her

upon a project which I have entertained for some time past. Don't be startled. It isn't to marry or become a Methodist preacher, but to study the law of the land.

Amongst my many good qualities, heaven has blest me with a bold face, a fluent tongue and a love for argument—in plainer words, with impudence, volubility and combativeness, the life and soul and fortune of ten thousand lawyers.

On the 13th of April next I shall be nineteen. One month later I hope to be in Cincinnati studying law with an excellent Irish Counsellor of good standing there, named Gallagher.

Why I prefer the West you may yourself guess: less prejudice and more room for rising.

A month later, a second letter came from Boston:

Two years, Mr. Gallagher informs, is the only time laid down for law students by the constitution of Ohio. That's short enough, and a fellow must use much industry to make it serve for a vigorous examination.

Early in April with the opening of the Spring, I, T. D. McG., God willing, will shake off the dust of this puritanical city from my shoes, and following the evening sun, will settle down in the West.

But D'Arcy's sister Dorcas needed financial help and he had to forego his plan to be a lawyer. He remained with the Boston *Pilot*, devoting himself day and night to the skills of writing and speaking. In fact, by the age of nineteen, though rhetoric was outstripping his thought, he had become one of its editors.

At this stage Daniel O'Connell was unquestionably young McGee's hero; and that year he published his first book, *O'Connell and his Friends*, which had a very encouraging sale through three editions.

The distress which followed upon the French Revolution and the Irish Rising of 1798 had taught O'Connell to distrust physical force and oppose secret conspiracy. O'Connell's method, though simple to describe, was practically impossible for lesser men to imitate. It consisted in relentless agitation, as open and as forceful as possible, with bloodshed banned. O'Connell was able to mount this as a movement to such a height of fervour that in the end only he could control it and avert violence. To do that he relied on the restraint which he wielded over the masses through his eloquence. By forcing the issue to the point of a moral threat, a large measure of emancipation was finally granted to the Catholics in 1829. By this Act, Catholics were released from their abject state and allowed to own property, to practise law, to obtain commissions in the Army and Navy, to sit in Parliament and to exercise their religion without serious disability.

In 1843 Daniel O'Connell was almost seventy years old, but there was still "sedition in his very walk," as he displayed incredible energy and gave spirit, heart and unity to the tired masses in a ceaseless clamour for his next objective. Here his aim was the Repeal of the Legislative Union of Ireland with England. Compared to Protestants, Catholics were still pariahs in Ireland; and it was only by establishing their own Irish Parliament, O'Connell maintained, that the harsh laws on education, taxes and precarious land tenure could be abolished.

Those were the years of O'Connell's tremendous mass meetings, which were the origin of those vast and peaceful devices, later refined by men like Gandhi, designed to achieve lasting political results by bloodless revolution. His greatest meeting had been the one at Tara in August of 1843 where at least a quarter of a million persons, each paying his penny to the Repeal Rent, came to hear, or hear repeated, what O'Connell was saying on the summit of the sacred hill. Irishmen were also holding large meetings in America, and sending money and messages back to Ireland; one envelope, for example, contained $2000 and ten words: "Whilst we say little, we are prepared to do much."

Then it happened that one of McGee's editorials in the Boston *Pilot*, a buoyant one on the future of Ireland, was shown to O'Connell, who publicly referred to it at a Repeal meeting as "the inspired writings of a young exiled Irish boy in America." Such a compliment from the Irish Liberator was likely to bring renown.

Soon enough it did, when another of his editorials, "of singular sensibility and power, on periodical famines in Ireland," attracted the attention of Dr. John Gray and Moses Wilson Gray, the principal proprietors of the *Freeman's Journal*. This Dublin paper was an able supporter of O'Connell and Repeal, liberal in tone, yet practical and mindful of the interests of the commercial classes; it was probably then the most powerful organ of opinion in Ireland. The Grays made an offer to McGee to return to Dublin and join their staff "at quite a liberal salary." Excited and honoured, McGee accepted.

When he arrived back in Ireland, he promptly wrote to Rhode Island on August 3, 1845:

> My reception at home was everything that could gratify and inspirit. In Wexford I was munificently feasted. From O'Connell, from Dr. McHale, from Young Ireland and all, my reception has been most cordial. I found my father's family all well, the step-mother behaving herself very well, though more from policy than affection, of course.

That first summer in Dublin he met Charles Gavan Duffy, Thomas Davis and John Dillon, the founders of a new journal, youthful, literary, and patriotic in spirit, called *The Nation*. McGee was deferential and awkward then; they were accomplished and sure. Yet from the beginning, notwithstanding their differences in age, class and manners, he felt that these three men were his congenial leaders. And he was full of ambition. Besides writing for the *Freeman's Journal*, he was planning to continue his night courses in Latin and then go on to seek a bachelor of arts degree at Trinity and later qualify himself as a lawyer. But again his legal plans were disrupted.

In September he was sent as the Parliamentary correspondent of the *Freeman* to London. There he turned somewhat from what he called the "drudgery" of a journalist to the ways of a student, as he spent every available hour in the British Museum studying old Irish manuscripts. Meanwhile he was finishing his second book: *The Irish Writers of the Seventeenth Century*, and preparing a third: *The Life and Conquests of Art MacMurrough, King of Leinster*.

McGee's remarkable literary achievements before the age of twenty-one were a natural part of the new movement of youth. Irish lore, ballads and antiquities were their inspiration, or, as McGee expressed it, the "memory in the night that lies behind the hills of day." Though not prominent, the most enterprising and persevering man in the movement was James Duffy, the publisher. Aiming to supply good quality at a cheap price, he succeeded in publishing a book for a shilling each month on Irish history, literature or the arts. This became his *Library of Ireland*, the best national series of small books issued, and it introduced McGee to the public with his two books on *Irish Writers* and *MacMurrough*.

But in the spring of 1846, McGee reawakened to modern Irish politics with something of a bardic pride. Dr. Gray discovered that McGee was contributing anonymous articles to *The Nation*, and he told him that he could not permit the practical interests of the *Freeman* to be sacrificed to McGee's research or opinions. So McGee quickly found that the *Freeman* was too cautious to suit him.

What followed was warmly recounted in a letter to his aunt in Providence:

> 32 Blackhall Street
> Dublin, October 3rd 1846

My very dear Aunt—

Your letter of August, so full of your usual kindness and intelligence, only reached me yesterday—by what chance detained, I know not. You judged rightly when you suspected me in *The Nation*. I have been one of the writers of that paper since June, and to that office, or to the above address, you must send my letters in future.

In May I left the *Freeman*. Doctor Gray I found to be a trimmer, and rather than share that character with him, I would quit the country.

Mr. Gavan Duffy, whom I met soon after my return, had been in the interim most intimate with me, and no sooner had I left the *Freeman* than he secured me for *The Nation* at the same salary.

Since July we have had not only to battle with the English enemy, but, strange to say, with Mr. O'Connell himself. For this, and for all the recent trouble, he and his son John are answerable. John is ambitious to succeed to the leadership, but as we have a score of men superior to him in mind and standing, they would not hear it.

All the claims of the father are and will be allowed, but not one of the pretensions of the son. He has attempted to force the obedience of his superiors, to browbeat his equals, and to stifle remonstrance, and has thus damned forever his own prospects of leadership. He will be reduced in time to his proper mediocrity, and then we will have Union once more in our National Association.

The terms on which I stand with Donahoe are not of the most cordial. He allowed poor Dr. O'Flaherty (God rest his soul!) to attack me, and never said a word in my defence. From the *Pilot* I did not deserve this. I have not remonstrated with him. But as he is respectful to you, you may explain to him the cause of my displeasure, when you next meet him in Providence. Do so kindly, my dear aunt, for, after all, it may have been less from want of heart than of brains that he overlooked his duty to his then correspondent and former co-laborer.

I regret you did not get my book, which I sent out by Harden's Dublin agent. But as the Rev. Mr. Hardy is here I have taken the opportunity of sending one to you and one to Mr. Wiley. You will get yours by calling on him. Is not this a safe way to send it?

Dorcas lives with me, and does business as a silk milliner at Johnston's in Sackville Street—the first house in Dublin.

Lawrence has become a teetotaller, keeps his ship, and has taken to save money. He is the first of the family, I imagine, who undertook such a feat as that. James, at the last College examination in Wexford, carried off two-thirds of the prizes. Anne and Rose are well, and at home. They are waiting until Lawrence and I set up Dorcas and them next year in Wexford. My father is wonderfully fresh and stout. His good woman thrives and is civil. And the little "half," John, goes to school daily, but pays more attention to his lunch than to the other contents of his satchel. However he will improve.

Such is our family picture in October 1846.

As for my uncle and you and my dear girls, Sally and Isabella, you have not said to me half enough. I declare to you, aunt, without the least affectation, that my thoughts and wishes are as often at Providence as in Wexford. To Sally especially (don't tell Bella so) I feel an indescribable fondness, only equalled by what I feel for my delicate Anny.

If in my lifetime Ireland becomes free, I will go to America to see all my friends—and you and these little cousins of mine first and foremost. If not, aunt, God knows whether we shall meet or not.

But "I do not despair for Ireland," as I said in a late letter to the Repealers of America, which by this time, I take it, you have read. The reasons wherefore, I have briefly set down in that letter. Live seven years, dear aunt, to join me at Providence in the Jubilee for Repeal.

Tell all my friends whom you may see in Providence or from any other locality that I am well—right well.

Tell them too that I am one of those who are called Young Ireland —a body of men whose worth will be better known ten years hence than it is now. Tell them we will not see Ireland sold or swapped to any English factions for any boons whatever. Bid them watch us, and wait.

My dear aunt, present my best regards to Father Wiley, to Mr. McCarthy, to John Benins and anybody or everybody worth mentioning. Don't forget Arthur Morgan and Mrs. Barnes from your catalogue.

I hope my uncle's health is tolerably good. He continues, I trust, to keep the pledge. I have resumed mine, or I would have been killed by hospitality here.

The moderate weather, I trust, will agree with you better than the summer. Ah! many a hot day I panted up Constitution Hill! Well. Well.

Give my fondest love and that of Dorcas and all our loves to the girls and to my uncle; and accept, my dear aunt, for yourself, all the love I would give my mother if she were living.

Yours ever the same,
Thos. D. McGee

What was happening then in Ireland cannot be understood without knowing something of two immense popular movements among the poorer classes; and McGee's letter to his aunt reflected something of both.

The pledge he mentioned was, of course, the central act of Father Matthew's great Temperance movement, which was sweeping through the country. The number of persons who had taken the pledge in Ireland, and in England, Scotland and the New World as well, was running into the millions, and it had already cut down the consumption of alcohol in Ireland by half.

The other extraordinary movement stemmed from Daniel O'Connell. But something seemed to be draining away its strength. In 1844 O'Connell had been jailed by a verdict from a packed jury. Although he had asked the people of Ireland in a short, earnest letter to remain firm and quiet while he was in prison, the blow had broken his own inner spirit. Imprisoned with him at the same time were Dr. John Gray of the *Freeman's Journal* and Gavan Duffy of *The Nation*. O'Connell appealed the verdict to the House of Lords, and finally had it reversed in terse language from the Chief Justice which became famous:

> If such practises continue, trial by jury would become a mockery, a delusion and a snare.

O'Connell was released with Gray and Duffy. But he was not the same man, except in flashes when he showed his old fire. He was losing his power to fascinate and stir the young men; and those who had founded *The Nation* in 1843 were soon criticizing him.

*The Nation* was a new journal, brimming over with the talent, the confidence and frequently the defiance of youth. Conceived in Phoenix Park "under a noble elm, to foster a public opinion in Ireland and make it racy of the soil," it grew quickly from a literary to a militant organ for a variety of young idealists, some steadfast, others fitful, who yearned for freedom and went together under the casual name of Young Ireland. In that era of romantic nationalism, with revolutions in Italy, France, Austria, Hungary and Germany, Mazzini's Young Italy was typical; and Young Ireland sounded up to date. But it took O'Connell's retort to make the name stick:

> Young Ireland may play what pranks they please. I do not envy them their name. I shall stand by old Ireland, and I have some slight notion that old Ireland will stand by me.

The ranks of O'Connell's Repeal Association were beginning to split into the Federalists, on the one hand, who advocated a subordinate Irish Parliament with Irish members who would also sit in the English Parliament, and the Nationalists or Young Ireland, on the other hand, who were shocked by O'Connell's off-hand remark:

> It is no doubt a very fine thing to die for one's country, but, believe me, one living patriot is worth a whole churchyard of dead ones.

O'Connell's constant policy of agitation strictly within the law and his condemnation of violence were not realistic enough for Young Ireland. Yet the coarse strength of O'Connell's oratory, his shrewd tactics and his common sense were, paradoxically, too realistic for their more refined literary tastes and visions. The truth was the young men were sick of delays, and their indignation was giving way to scorn.

Yet there was no one in Young Ireland who had that insight into human nature that O'Connell was canny enough to cover with his hearty manner. The inspiration of Young Ireland and *The Nation* had come from Thomas Davis: short in stature, of fresh complexion, he was simple, spontaneous, selfless and also humourless; he died "when the bud was on the tree," soon after McGee first met him in Dublin. The pivot was Charles Gavan Duffy, with his dome-like brow, his lustrous eyes, his generous ways, his clear quick voice and his inner balance. He was the natural leader, and in later life he was to rise the highest of all in the political realm. But he never could mix with the people as "Cheerful Dan" O'Connell did, nor could he speak Irish as the native tongue like O'Connell, who spoke only in that language until the age of four. John Dillon, the last of the trio who founded *The Nation,* was the balance wheel, calmly averse to force yet drawn finally by honour into the field of arms.

Among all the members of Young Ireland the one most noted in England, because of his ancestors, was William Smith O'Brien. Aristocratic, well poised and gracious, but not genial, a diffident speaker who held himself aloof, he exercised a deep personal influence. He also enjoyed special prestige, having served as deputy leader of the Repeal Association on the direct nomination of O'Connell. Ranking next came Thomas Francis Meagher, who, notwithstanding his English Stonyhurst accent, became famous overnight for his impassioned speech in Conciliation Hall on the patriot's sword, and who was known thereafter as "Meagher of the Sword." Then came John Mitchel, the fiery son of a Unitarian minister from County Derry; vitriolic Devin Reilly; Michael Doheny, sensitive and sturdy, and quiet Richard O'Gorman.

In the field of poetry they ranged from that shy, vague genius, always clad in a plain brown garment, with his blanched hair and unearthly moods, James Clarence Mangan, to Denis Florence McCarthy, a graceful lyricist with sensitive religious feeling, an industrious collector of old ballads and a competent Spanish scholar. Young Thomas D'Arcy McGee was a poet too, but as practical as a secretary; which, in fact, was soon recognized when he was appointed Secretary of the Young Ireland Confederacy. Nearly all of them, except McGee and of course poor Mangan, were relatively well off and came from prosperous sections of the cities or from the landowning class.

The early need to earn his own living had taught McGee the simple lesson of getting on with the job and doing it well; yet by temperament he retained the detached, conservative inclinations of a scholar, open to the other man's view, and much more interested in the ballads of the past than in the harsh politics of the day. Of all his confederates he was the slowest to espouse their restless, radical methods, and he was known as much for his moderation as for his eloquence.

Soon after his return from London to Dublin, D'Arcy McGee met Mary Teresa Caffrey at an art exhibition. She was hopeful, humane and under the spell of a new author, Charles Dickens, sharing his cheerful, romantic confidence in the careless common men. No one matched D'Arcy's soaring patriotism, poetic moods or sudden spurts of fantastic fun in a more congenial way than Mary. They were married in Dublin in the fall of 1847.

Their bright first days together in the hills of Wicklow were full of wonder and delight. In D'Arcy's eyes Mary was as "artless as the very word of truth," and he often wrote of her in verse—"hair like midnight, eyes like morning, and that voice like music sighing." When those rare autumn evenings "faded from golden into grey," they strayed together in the hollows and moonlit haunts of Wicklow "under trees that glowed like diamonds" as he "chanted young love's hymn":

> I may reveal it to the night,
> Where lurks around no tattling fairy,
> With only stars and streams in sight,
> I love, I love thee, Mary.

John Mitchel was becoming very aggressive as a radical, and McGee stood up against him. Like Gavan Duffy, McGee was never in favour of a republic as the future for Ireland. He preferred a monarchy controlled by an Irish parliamentary government, because he believed in the value of continuity. The Crown, he held, had once been the "golden link" between the two countries and could, under freedom, resume that historic role once again. With that hope for home rule and respect for tradition, he held out to the last for the force of opinion as against the force of arms. He was still faithful to the ideal he had learnt earlier from O'Connell—in those better days when, in McGee's words, O'Connell's "judgement and courage were equal to his eloquence." The associations between them, however, were growing thinner every month, although their differences never degenerated into malice. Indeed, O'Connell's last letters, written with an unusual spirit of personal humility, were pleas for reconciliation with Young Ireland.

But the tragic course of events had taken over. The truth was that an undiagnosed disease was gnawing away within O'Connell, resulting in a slow softening of the brain. No one knew it, however, and certainly no one foresaw how abrupt, how soon and how total his fall would be. But Gavan Duffy had grown so impatient with the aging, ailing ways of O'Connell that he had finally led *The Nation* and Young Ireland to break away completely from him. More reluctant to abandon O'Connell than others in Young Ireland, McGee left him nonetheless, scarcely realizing, however, how decisively O'Connell's principles would later guide him on such matters as religious and racial toleration, the extension of freedom to dissenters, the admission of Jews to Parliament or opposition to slavery in America.

Daniel O'Connell, described by Gladstone as "the greatest popular leader the world has ever seen," died, a pitiful spectre, in May of 1847.

DANIEL
O'CONNELL.

That was the darkest of those years, known as "Black '47," when coercion was rampant and the total number of deaths from famine and disease mounted to one fourth of the Irish people, with millions obliged to leave their homeland for the United States and Canada. Eventually the earlier Irish population of over eight million was practically cut in half.

"My heart is sick at daily scenes of misery," McGee wrote. "I cannot endure this state of society longer. Nothing green, nothing noble will grow in it. The towns have become one universal poorhouse and fever shed, the country one great graveyard." Across the Irish Sea, the London

*Times* was coldly calculating: "In a few years more, a Celtic Irishman will be as rare in Connemara as is the Red Indian on the shores of Manhattan. . . . Now for the first time England has Ireland at her mercy, and can deal with her as she pleases."

The Young Ireland party moved one step closer to revolt. Their leaders spoke no longer against resort to violence; now they said they did not exclude resort to violence. Even McGee, in a report of October 4, 1847, to Smith O'Brien, indicated that, without directly advocating force, he was fully prepared to see it erupt:

> In Wexford I established a committee of 13, who are to meet regularly once a week. They promise to get 50 or 60 by our next meeting. On the whole I think I may safely say the County Wexford is more with us, socially, than with the others. A little more success in other quarters, a little more violence on the part of Dr. Synnott, and it will break out as suddenly and strongly as it did in '98.

But such an attitude was too supine for John Mitchel and Devin Reilly. "Humbug," Mitchel called it. When the English Government passed the Coercion and Disarming Bill, Mitchel publicly declared that "the Government which called on the people of Ireland to deliver up their arms must be the mortal enemy of the people, their rights, their liberties and their lives," and he pressed for an open recognition by Young Ireland of an actual state of war.

McGee opposed Mitchel's ultimatum in these terms:

> not because it is treason against the law, but because it is treason against common sense.

McGee grew more disturbed as the statements from Mitchel and Reilly became more inflammatory. On January 20, 1848, he wrote to Smith O'Brien protesting against Mitchel and Reilly remaining within the party:

> I intend to resign my place as Secretary of this Association. I am obliged now to be tongue tied and hand tied while nonsense and mischief are saying and doing all around me. It is my place to be silent. Yet I cannot look upon such scenes as I see, and do so. Mr. Duffy wishes me to cast in my lot with him in *The Nation*. I intend to act for a month from Monday to give time for the right choice of a successor.

That same month Gavan Duffy formally excluded Mitchel and Reilly as writers from *The Nation*. "Rosewater revolutionists" was the taunt Mitchel threw back at Duffy, O'Brien and McGee.

Mitchel founded a new journal, the *United Irishman,* and there "in plain English" he preached "holy hatred and open warfare." Within three months the English had Mitchel in fetters on board the *Scourge* bound for Bermuda, and then on to Australia and the gum trees of Van Diemen's Land.

The English Government continued to act quickly. To ward off a sudden surge for independence, it arrested Duffy, Meagher and others. When McGee protested in a stirring speech at Roundwood in Wicklow, he was also arrested. But soon all except Gavan Duffy had regained their freedom.

In early July there were heated debates within the ranks of the Young Ireland party for an immediate appeal to arms. Delay was counselled: wait until after the harvest; then the country would be ready, it was hoped, to strike for freedom with them. Was this wisdom or weakness? Or were they playing with words? For desperation and death were on all sides, and in command. Even McGee was writing: "Farewell sickle. Welcome sword."

On the morning of July 22, 1848, William Smith O'Brien secretly went to Wexford to try and prepare the people for an eventual outbreak. And McGee opened his personal narrative that same day:

Early on Saturday, the 22nd of July, I left my pleasant home in Cullenswood near Dublin, to which I was never to return.

That night under orders from Young Ireland, McGee left Dublin on his dangerous mission to Scotland, to gather the Irishmen around Glasgow together and prepare them for armed action.

Then came a startling alarm. The *Habeas Corpus* Act had unexpectedly been suspended, and warrants were out for the arrests of the leaders of Young Ireland. *The Nation* was suppressed. The die was cast, and a collision of force was inevitable. To arm quickly against great odds was the desperate prospect. And in their passionate code of honour, however unprepared they were to meet the British Army, there was no turning back. But revolt did not come as the orator and poet had envisioned it. It came, not as a golden cloud of glory, but in the drab browns and dry greys of this earth.

Imagine those ranks of volunteers with their swords glittering in the setting sun, gallant pikemen singing, banners waving and pipes playing, columns of peasants filing through gap and glen, camp fires glimmering in the mist with shanachies telling stories of the old warring athletes, and then, with the fires on the hilltops going out one by one, with the

stars appearing among the tall trees, and the rising of the moon . . .
But where were they, those resolute men of action who peopled the
poems, the orations and the illusions of Young Ireland?

In fact, when the lone flag of insurrection was raised that pale noon
of July 29 by William Smith O'Brien in the small town of Ballingarry,
a motley group of four hundred hungry men stood by him; twenty perhaps had firearms, twice as many held pikes and pitchforks, and the rest
were there with their bare hands. There was no contest against the
English soldiers. The priest of Ballingarry and his curate finally intervened and called on the rebels to desist. Many did; and within two hours
it was all over. Those who could took to the hills.

Two of the fugitives were then scarcely known (but were to be encountered often later on). One, an engineering student with a solitary,
proud and somewhat sinister temperament, had been wounded in the
thigh and managed to crawl away. He covered his disappearance by
the clever ruse of inserting his own obituary in the Kilkenny *Moder-
ator* of August 19, 1848:

The untimely and melancholy fate of James Stephens will be much
regretted by a numerous circle of friends.

Stephens came to be known as "The Hawk." He linked up with Michael Doheny; and for two months they were hunted over mountain and
moor, hiding in huts or in the bogside, and then, after wading through
a mountain torrent, they shivered in a choir loft of the Trappist monastery at Mount Melleray "while vespers were being sung." Stephens finally got off to France disguised as a lady's maid, while Doheny drove
some bullocks on board a boat at Cork and made his way over to Paris,
where he again joined Stephens.

The other fugitive was John O'Mahony, a different stamp of a man.
Tall, stern and solemn, with shaggy hair, a splendid physique and
great prowess, a dreamer by disposition with a slight cast in one eye,
and a poor judge of men, he was one of the few who sustained his spirit
and attracted followers after the disheartening show at Ballingarry. On
the night of September 12, signal fires were lit on the slopes of Slievenamon. Alarms spread and he led some sporadic attacks. But they were
soon put down. Such was John O'Mahony, gentleman farmer from Tipperary, a distinguished Gaelic scholar and a student of Hebrew and
Sanskrit. Haggard and troubled, he narrowly escaped to Paris, where he,
too, met James Stephens.

Meanwhile what had happened to D'Arcy McGee, who as a youth had been repelled by secrecy and violence?

It was late in July of 1848, really too late. The secret work he was doing to raise men and arms for the Young Ireland Confederacy was moving far too slow for an impetuous scholar driven to the sword by a hunger and a thirst after justice which had grown wild within him. His cause was simple. In his land, for years before he was born, there had been callous misrule by the English Government and absentee landlords. And now there was famine. He had seen it like a plague all around him. That year there were no dark green, crispy leaves nor yellow and purple blossoms in the potato-fields. And the abandoned cottages nearby he described as "lifeless homes staring like skulls aghast."

Leaving Dublin for the North that Saturday of July 22, 1848, he slipped through a network of detectives and informers and arrived by stage-coach the next day at Londonderry in the North of Ireland. On Monday he managed to send a letter back to his wife in Dublin, while he waited for the "night to cast her shadows" to let him sail for Glasgow. From Glasgow he went on to Edinburgh and two nearby towns. There he worked until he had a list of nearly four hundred men "pretty well equipped, ready for the risk." Plans were made for them to sail from Greenock and to ship their arms ahead to the remote glens of Sligo on the North-west Irish coast. He was recording his activities with care: "These arrangements occupied from Tuesday till Friday of the last week of July. In the meantime London journals arrived."

Dishevelled and lonely, he entered a public reading room in Paisley, Scotland, and was turning the pages of a government gazette called *The Hue and Cry* when he saw this police notice offering $1500 for his capture:

Thomas D'Arcy McGee—Connected with the Nation newspaper—Twenty-three years old—Five foot three inches in height—Black hair, dark face—Delicate, thin man—Dresses generally black shooting coat, plaid trousers, light vest.

Glancing around, he slipped away as a felon with a price on his head in that busy city of threads.

Warned when he was recognized on the streets in Glasgow, he decided to take his chances that some of his followers would join him in Sligo, and made his escape through the North of England. Saturday night he slept in Newcastle. "The next day between Newcastle and Carlisle," he continued, "I had a fellow passenger, the Rev. Thresham Grigg who was on a lecturing excursion against the Pope in the north of England." He went on to Whitehaven, where he had to wait over for the Belfast steamer.

"On Tuesday morning, August 1, I arrived in Belfast, and at 8 o'clock I was safely embarked on the Ulster railway for Armagh. At Aughnacloy a detective gave me a light; and before I went to bed at Enniskillen I had read the proclamations against the leaders of the Southern movement on the gates of the Barracks."

The next morning I reached Sligo—by the Leitrim road. . . . For the first time in ten days I saw the Irish papers. I read the list of clergymen by whom the Southern movement had been "denounced" on Sunday, July 23, and Sunday, July 30. The same paper contained Lord Clarendon's wily letter to Archbishop Murray. The game of the Government was clear, it was to separate the clergy from the people in the coming struggle.

Posing as a sickly Dublin student on a holiday, McGee lodged under the legendary heights of Ben Bulben, while he assessed the strength of the Sligo garrison at only ninety men. Here he waited restlessly for his arms and men from Scotland, relying, too, on a promise from the local rebels, the Molly Maguires, to provide two thousand men, if he could guarantee a general uprising.

Guarantee? The news from the South of Ireland went from bad to worse. Word of O'Brien's failure at Ballingarry was followed by the report of his arrest one week later. McGee was at his wit's end as he wrote:

For ten dismal days I remained in this neighbourhood, hoping against hope and endeavouring to make others do the same. The proposals I then made, the result of desperation, I will not repeat. I confess they look wild and extravagant.

Finally a message came that Meagher of the Sword had been arrested near Holycross in Tipperary on August 12. "Then indeed," McGee conceded "I knew all was up." The inglorious rising of Young Ireland had failed, and he had to escape.

The men of Young Ireland were scattered everywhere in 1848. Among them was a fiery twenty-six-year-old schoolmaster from Cork, Timothy Anglin, who left Ireland to settle in Saint John, New Brunswick. During the twenty years to follow, the paths of the Young Ireland men would cross and criss-cross in strange designs. And the secret doings of the two fugitives in Paris, Stephens and O'Mahony, the founders of the Fenians, would become a seed-plot of suspicion.

TP5

**THE COLOURS OF THE TWELVE WINDS OF IRELAND**

N

BLACK

GREY — SPECKLED

DARK BROWN — DARK

W — PALE — PURPLE — E

GREEN — YELLOW

GREYISH GREEN — RED

WHITE

S

FROM THE SALTAIR NA RANN

DISGUISED AS A PRIEST, WITH A PRICE ON HIS HEAD, D'ARCY McGEE, 23, FLED FROM THE COAST OF DERRY ON THE "SHAMROCK", BOUND FOR PHILADELPHIA ON SEPTEMBER 1 1848

Now they ride the wintry dawn Where Ben Bulben sets the scene...

DERRY

BELFAST

BEN BULBEN

SLIGO

ARMAGH

CARLINGFORD

DUBLIN

LIMERICK

BALLINGARRY

SLIEVENAMON — WEXFORD

CORK

IN CARLINGFORD BY THE CASTLE OF KING JOHN WHERE

*Life lingers latest in those blustery stone tunnels*

THOMAS D'ARCY McGEE WAS BORN ON WEDNESDAY APRIL 13 1825

Long, long ago, beyond the misty space
Of twice a thousand years,
In Erin old there dwelt a mighty race,
Taller than Roman spears;
Like oaks and towers they had a giant grace,
Were fleet as deers.
With wind and waves they made their 'biding place,
These western shepherd seers.

— THE CELTS, THOMAS D'ARCY McGEE —

FROM WEXFORD AS AN IMMIGRANT BOY OF 16 — D'ARCY McGEE SAILED ON THE BRIG "LEO" FOR QUEBEC CITY ON APRIL 7 1842

"Sad and eager," McGee's young wife, Mary, bearing their unborn child, came up furtively from Dublin to Derry, where after too brief a meeting near the River Foyle he had to leave her. "God be with you, love" were her words that he remembered as he left her "like the dawn."

On September 1, 1848, he secretly boarded a ship, the *Shamrock*, sailing off the coast of Derry under Captain John Moore of Galway. And so it was. Not as a scholar nor as a soldier, D'Arcy McGee, in the disguise of a young priest but not in that spirit, sailed alone for America.

# 2

## HOME-SICKNESS

The birds have a foreign tongue; the very trees, whispering
to the wind, whisper in accents unknown to me, for your
gum tree leaves are all hard, horny and polished as the
laurel; they can never, never whisper, quiver, sigh or sing,
as do the beeches and the sycamores of old Rosstrevor.

JAIL JOURNAL: John Mitchel

But our faith is all unshaken
Though our present hope is gone.
*Thomas D'Arcy McGee*

Life did not begin anew for D'Arcy McGee in the New World. His young wife, his friends, his interests and his longings were still back in Ireland. So he did what many a homesick man has done: he tried to lose himself in his work.

Crossing the Atlantic with his few belongings, disguised as "Father John," he landed in Philadelphia on October 10, 1848. He then had fifty-two dollars. Yet he succeeded, within the amazingly short period of sixteen days, to bring out the first issue of his own newspaper, published simultaneously from three offices, one at 151 Fulton Street in New York City, another at 8 Atkinson Street in Boston and the third at 9 South Eighth Street in Philadelphia. It was similar to the Dublin *Nation* and was called the *New York Nation*. He described it as "a weekly devoted to Ireland and her emigrants, and the European democracies." He did not mention the United States, which was a symptom of his state of mind.

Without any capital or dependable advertising, he relied for his revenue on whatever circulation his reputation as a writer and a rebel could draw from the Irish Americans. But he was rushing into a well-occupied field.

His two former newspapers, Donahoe's Boston *Pilot*, and the Grays' *Freeman's Journal* through its New York edition, remained faithful to the tradition of O'Connell and satisfied most of the available American readers with their moderate views. For these publishers, Young Ireland was a fiasco of political adolescents, and McGee was not merely an intruder but a dangerous agitator. From the opposite side, the extreme *Irish American*, which followed the radical separatism of John Mitchel and Devin Reilly, was hurling abuse at McGee to the point of stupefaction; he was "a horrid, hunchbacked, halfbreed specimen of a viperous, slanderous lying race," and so on.

Actually McGee was the first of the leaders of Young Ireland to arrive in America, and he did have many exciting tales to tell and strong opinions to air. These he exploited to the full to push his circulation, and unfortunately he forced even his best points. In seven months his gross income was $5000, but he had to sink all of it back into his venture. "*The Nation* is going on gloriously; we publish seven thousand this week," he said, but it was a brave front for his creditors. He had no real stake in the United States. In his heart, he was "a camper," a restless exile.

Nor was he ready to forget. In his new journal, he hastened to judge the past before it came into focus, and he was bitter enough to blame the clergy for the collapse of the revolution in Ireland. Here he roused the ire of Bishop John Hughes of New York. The Bishop was a generation older than McGee. A kind, severe man, aggressive under attack, he was a towering character with a genius for administration. While no one could question his attachment to his native soil of County Tyrone, he was actively opposed to any nationalist movements in America that would perpetuate racial differences or fan old hatreds. He believed in the melting pot.

Bishop Hughes had supported the Young Ireland movement at first, and had even assisted at a public meeting in New York to raise funds for it. "My contribution shall be for a shield, not for a sword" was his explanation. But when the insurrection broke out, he was mortified: "a movement so nobly conceived but so miserably conducted." Plainly, he fastened the blame indiscriminately on O'Brien and Mitchel, on Duffy and Reilly and on Meagher and McGee, without stopping to distinguish between the differences in their ideas and the conflicting roles they had played. Now, when he found McGee newly arrived in his own diocese and assailing the clergy for what he saw as Young Ireland's own "futility," the Bishop decided to act. He condemned McGee's *New York Nation* and banned it from the parishes in New York City.

McGee was inexperienced enough not to have anticipated this blow, yet bold enough to feel he was equal to it. He was baffled and hurt that Bishop Hughes could criticize him, from the right, for his "red-hot Irishism," while the *Irish American* could attack him from the left, as a cold skeleton of O'Connell. He turned for consolation to his friend Gavan Duffy, in Ireland, who had just been released from prison and was then attempting under great difficulties to start up the suppressed *Nation* once again. Duffy, who was older, urged McGee to return to Dublin and offered him a partnership in reviving the original *Nation;* then he added this home truth:

You do not act wisely in attacking the bishops and priests in that style. You are angry and therefore unreasonable.

McGee answered with a touch of grandiloquence:

I will not go back to Ireland. I have thrown myself on the race in America. I aspire to be the Duffy of our emigrants. I have provoked their attention to projects and themes which I am bound to see out.

But his words, puffed up with pride, scarcely hid his worries over the mounting debts and the crushing opposition.

He was lonely, too, and it showed in his writings:

> I left two loves on a distand strand,
> One young and fond and fair and bland,
> One fair and old and sadly grand,
> My wedded wife and my native land.

But ambitions were burning in his brain like passions, and he became transparently immoderate, saying too much and, as often happens under that stimulus, drinking too much. As a young man of twenty-three, he had come face to face with failure, and it seemed to have such a desolate finality about it: "for I'm lonely, very lonely, and longing to be dead." Such was his "unstrung harp," and drink became his solace. Yet he was not a negligible person whose failing can be stated without involving fine qualities. Highly talented, tender-hearted and fiercely independent, he was sociable and quarrelsome to excess, and all his life these excesses would pursue him. That year in New York, however, after several bad weeks, D'Arcy McGee came back to more temperate habits; but a weakness had been revealed that was to recur later, and in critical periods.

His personal troubles brought him closer to the emigrants, and he felt all the stronger that his place was with them in their plight. Nearly a million wasted people were cleared off their land by eviction or emigration in the years following the Irish famine of 1847. They arrived, unwanted and uncounted, in seaports like Boston, Philadelphia and particularly New York. Most of them were uninstructed peasants, cast into surroundings that were strange and often hostile. So they herded together, making a distinct Irish quarter in every city where they settled. Their generosity and kindred easy-going rural habits, when transplanted and contaminated by the manners of the back alleys and the groggeries, too often turned into improvident and garrulous ways; and the broth of a boy from Ballyhooly became a Bowery slack-jaw. Where, as peasants, they had been victims of wholesale expulsion back home, now many were to be victims of clannish blindness and wholesale exploitation in America.

New York quickly became the most overcrowded area in the Western world; and an inspector's report on its "Fourth Sanitary District" described a typical dwelling of poor Irish immigrants.

The inspector told how he left the street on a sunny day, walked through a dismal alley under the tall front tenements and entered a yard filled with wet wash overhanging the garbage cans in the atmosphere of a dank well. Going down some broken steps to the cellar of a rear tenement, he reached a low room with a smoke-blackened ceiling and damp discoloured walls. It had two small windows set in a depression covered with green mould, which let in a faint twilight. A door at the back of this room led to another, which was completely dark. Both rooms together formed an abode which was eighteen feet square and "served to immure" six persons. The father, a day labourer, was absent. The mother, a crone at the age of thirty, was rocking a pallid infant in her arms. Two older children were playing in the street. A fourth child, a victim of marasmus, sat on a rickety chair under the open windows breathing the air laden with all the effluvia of the slums. Yet sometimes in such a hovel on a Sunday evening the father could relax with his family and light up his pipe and speak of Shanagolden and a blue sky over it.

Parents had disappeared by the thousands in this great dispersion, and their orphans grew up, many as urchins. Blocking their way in the better districts was the Nativist sign "No Irish wanted." With a half-shrug, a canal digger could stack his spade by his shanty near Albany, look up from under his caubeen and respond: "I work here from early morning and by night I dream of Ireland." His reverie was that last look down the native valley: a lone hawthorn, a quiet lake, a stile, a brake, a brawling stream, a thatch roof and blackberries on the hedge. . . . The Irish worked hard for their daily bread and beer, digging the Erie Canal to establish the supremacy of New York State or laying the early railroads of the New York Central to link the Atlantic with the Great Lakes and the Mississippi. And as they laboured for low wages, they felt they deserved better from the native ascendancy than to be called "the low Irish."

One Thursday a few months after his arrival in New York, McGee sat down "in haste, of course, as always" and wrote to his aunt in Rhode Island to give her the news from Ireland:

> I have not heard from home this week but I had two letters last. Everything is going on well with my folk and Mary had "engaged a doctor for next week." The next mail I suppose will bring me good news.

The good news came "from God's pocket" that he was the father of a baby girl, Martha Dorcas. Then on June 28, 1849, carrying his added

family responsibilities and struggling harder than ever to keep his newspaper alive, he wrote again to his good aunt:

> Many thanks for the $75 which came all safe and in time.
>
> My poor girl is still in Ireland. Her last letter told me she would
> leave on the 1st of July. She has been rather ill with a sore breast,
> and Mrs. Auticell who saw her early in May tells me she looked thin
> and anxious. I begin to be rather uneasy about her, but I hope to
> take her under my own care by the 1st of August, as nearly all our
> affairs in Dublin have been arranged. James by this time is in Dublin
> with her, and in charge of his niece who has been weaned.
>
> My fatherly and husbandly anxieties are not a few, neither, you
> may guess, are my editorial. However I like plenty of labour and
> exertion, and the heat of the day makes the repose of the evening
> the more comforting.

Finally his wife Mary, his infant daughter Martha Dorcas and his
younger brother James landed in New York. They were just in time
to witness the collapse of his *New York Nation,* and to listen as he talked
of the necessity of returning to Ireland. He moved on to Boston planning
to sail back when a warning came from Ireland that if he did, he would
run the risk of arrest on his arrival.

So he had to postpone his return to Ireland and remain with his young
family in Boston. There he picked up a few fees lecturing, and as he
moved from meeting to meeting he gathered together some hazardous
financial backing for a new newspaper. His supporters were young,
mostly Irish workmen who were irritated by the unexciting views of the
Boston *Pilot,* and took it for granted that McGee would be more to their
taste as a rebel. By the end of August 1849 he started his second newspaper, the *American Celt.* But it soon became evident, to the dismay
of his backers, that his views were changing.

Family life gave him a quieter balance. Up to now excitement had
hidden the deeper effects of his loneliness from him, and he was not
conscious of the usual morbid anatomy of young rebels as outcasts.
He mistook his intense reactions for independent strength and indulged
in his forlorn moods as if they were serious thoughts. Nor did he yet
have that insight, which dawns with maturity, to unmask his pride in
its clever postures. Now that he was united with his wife and child, he
began to see himself less dramatically, and he uncovered some uncouth
motives. It was chastening.

His letters and particularly his verses during that trying phase are revealing. There was his deep affection for his wife, "pure as martyr's mem-

ory and warm as convert's zeal," and there was the abiding memory of
his mother, who was, as he had described the maternal influence over
Edmund Burke, "one of those mothers who make men." The days of his
"saucy doubts" were on the wane.

A time comes when someone who feels he has been wronged will ask
himself if he intends to persist in nursing his resentment on the same
low level as the wrong itself, or to rise above it and forget. McGee could
stay there, shut in as he was, and harden as a prisoner of his pride, or
he could climb up the path of humility. "Knowledge," he wrote, "comes
painfully and in bits, through experience." D'Arcy McGee finally expressed his reconciliation with his religion in a forthright letter:

> I cheerfully said to myself: "You are on the wrong track. You think
> you know something of human affairs but you do not. You can put
> sentences together, but what does that avail you? You have a soul.
> What will all the fame of talents avail you, if you lose that?"
> A man who has grown to years of discretion, and has not become
> wedded to one idea, should be as ready to regulate his conduct as
> to set his watch when the parish clock declares it wrong. He must
> be ready to be taught by the high as well as by the low.

The sudden pressures in the past two years had been too strenuous
for his neglected boyhood faith. What he had suffered was a common
religious hernia. Now he saw, as he expressed it, that what protruded
was an inflamed radical liberalism, with "its own kind of faith, to believe
in nothing but its own superiority." Four lines wrttien on New Year's Day
expressed his renewed aspiration:

> God in his goodness give us strength
> And time and courage to recover,
> Let us look forward now at length
> And cease to live the poor past over.

On Friday, March 29, 1850, "a brave, fine day," D'Arcy McGee had
more good news. Writing from 35 High Street in Boston to his aunt in
Providence, he told her of his *alanna aroon:*

> I would have written to you a fortnight ago, but daily expecting
> Mary's confinement. The event took place yesterday at 5 o'clock, and
> we have another little girl. She is the image of Martha, as far as I
> can guess.
> Mary passed a very comfortable night and feels easy this morning.
> Little one, ditto.

Martha did not at first much incline to the stranger, but she is in better humour today and orders us all "not to noise the baby."

My dear aunt, I want you to do me a favour, which is to be God-mother for this little Christian, somewhere about a week from now. Can you possibly come? As the child is healthy, any time within a fortnight, perhaps, would do. Fix your own day and we will arrange accordingly.

I will look out for Sadlier and let you know in due time. We are all glad to hear of Bella's progress. I have an invitation to Canada, and may go there with you this summer.

This was his second child, baptized Mary Euphrasia and known as "Fasa."

Shortly afterwards McGee led an Irish delegation to President Fillmore of the United States, urging him to seek an amnesty for William Smith O'Brien and other Young Ireland rebels who had just been banished for life to Van Diemen's Land in Australia. Millard Fillmore was hardly the man to respond to such an appeal (as later support from the Know-Nothing Party demonstrated), but McGee did win warm praise for his address from Daniel Webster, a member of Fillmore's Cabinet.

While in Washington McGee met a Canadian delegate, James G. Moylan, who aroused his interest in Canada, and later came to work closely with McGee. Through this meeting with Moylan in 1850, McGee made two lecture tours of the principal Canadian cities: Montreal, Quebec, Toronto, Peterborough and Ottawa. From that time, too, McGee began his friendship with James Sadlier, an enterprising publisher in Montreal and New York, and his wife, the author Mary Anne Sadlier.

Meanwhile, though in no way prosperous, the *American Celt* became more solidly and broadly based than the *New York Nation;* and it meant much to McGee to have as a sympathetic subscriber a cousin of his aunt, Bishop Fitzpatrick of Boston.

As an editor McGee was facing the Know-Nothing movement, which was in full blast. This was a secret Nativist organization which spread out from New York City, and was directed mainly against the Irish-Catholic immigrants. As part of its rigmarole of secret signs, grips and passwords, each member was under oath to reply, when questioned about his activities: "I don't know." This gave birth to its nickname of the Know-Nothings. As aggressive as buck teeth, it became a political party of menacing strength. Through waves of riots and repeated burnings of

Catholic churches and convents, it grew to the point where in 1855 it had elected Know-Nothing governors in New Hampshire, Connecticut and Rhode Island and had carried the elections in nine different states.

While sharpening his powers of invective against the Know-Nothings, he made a reputation for himself, but no money. Forced as he was to supplement his uncertain income as a journalist, he had no cause to be "purse-proud". Travelling almost constantly and living beyond his means, he delivered hundreds of addresses for whatever fees were available. These speaking tours were often extensive, leading him to Philadelphia, Baltimore, Washington, Cincinnati, St. Louis and points in the Middle West. His lectures then served as material for more books. In the winter of 1850 and 1851 he completed his *History of the Irish Settlers in North America*, which was reprinted with additions in 1855. Then in 1853 he published five of his discourses as *The Catholic History of North America*, followed two years later by *The Attempts to Establish the Reformation in Ireland*. With all this travelling, lecturing and writing, McGee kept up a wide correspondence, responding promptly to every letter (except those from his creditors).

The more traditional the tone of the *American Celt* became, the more it duplicated the appeal of the Boston *Pilot*, which had grown, under Donahoe's sense for business, into the largest paper of national influence for Catholic and Irish interests in America. But the *Celt* resolutely abstained from "the advocacy of any special Irish American organization," and continued to stress the state of affairs in Ireland. Inevitably, its circulation dwindled.

Visions of improving his financial situation and of reaching the rapidly increasing numbers of Irish workers who were drawn westward by the public works of the Erie and Genesee Valley Canals made McGee move the editorial office of the *American Celt* in 1852 to Buffalo. So he made the journey with his young family to Albany and from there set off on the long, rough trek into the pioneering diocese of Bishop John Timon.

On August 2, 1852, his wife wrote a newsy letter from their new home on Franklin Street in Buffalo to his aunt in Providence:

> Since I am here my time has been occupied a good deal between arranging house matters and not getting a good servant. The first I got I was obliged to part with, but I think I now have got one that will answer me, as she is a steady old maid who has given up all ideas of matrimony—at least she says so.
>
> We have a very comfortable house and a large garden with my favorite vegetable, cabbage, down in it, as it was too late to plant

any other vegetable. The neighbourhood is very pleasant, and our neighbours are all holy people. We have the Sisters of Mercy quite close to us—they have charge of an hospital. And a short distance we have a Convent of the Sacred Heart—they keep a school for educating young ladies, and also a school for poor children.

The Bishop has called several times. I never saw one who so completely gave me the idea of what a Bishop should be. Nothing can exceed his humility and charity.

Sometimes I feel very lonely here and miss my old friends. I had a letter from Bella which indeed gave me great pleasure. Her first attempt at poetry is very good. But tell her that Thomas will review it, and will be a better critic than I possibly could be.

I had a letter from Dublin. I hope my mother will now make up her mind and come to us as she has no inducement to remain in Dublin.

You must come to see the world's wonder, the Falls. Thomas' health is improving. He eats Stirabout every morning which has greatly improved his appetite. Fasa has grown so much that her Godmother would scarcely know her. I was very sick for two days last week with a sort of cholera, but am now, thank God, quite recovered.

But financial troubles again caught up with poor "Thomas" (his wife never called him "D'Arcy"). Bishop Timon could help McGee only for a while, and before two years were up, McGee had moved back to New York City. In 1854 James Moylan found McGee in a small office in New York City, sheltering his wandering *American Celt*. Moylan was introduced to James McGee, his younger brother, who was working as D'Arcy's assistant editor; and he also met another writer on the *Celt*, the tense, impulsive Bernard Doran Killian, who will reappear later in the most quixotic of the Fenian ventures.

During these years McGee gained in stature and influence—but not in all circles. The split in the ranks of Young Ireland had never closed. When Gavan Duffy and D'Arcy McGee reverted to their original positions in favour of constitutional and parliamentary policy, they were bitterly scorned by the partisans of force.

To trace the vagaries followed in later years by the men of '48, one basic difference must be kept in mind. In Ireland there were the Constitutional Nationalists who looked back a generation to Henry Grattan as their eloquent source. These were the men in favour of peaceful agitation, and Daniel O'Connell had led their followers to the heights. Apart from them, sometimes running a parallel course but more often a diverging one, were the Revolutionary Nationalists who took Wolfe Tone and the agitators of '98 as their passionate inspiration. These were the Separatists, "the men of a noble rage," and one romantic example was that unaccountable celebrity of "The Wearing of the Green," Napper Tandy.

Nearly all of the men of Young Ireland were now banished or outlaws, and most of them finally found their way to the United States. Devin Reilly, always personally jealous of McGee, was the first after him to arrive. With John Mitchel, he had broken away to the left, far apart from Gavan Duffy and D'Arcy McGee in their *Nation,* to become a Jacobin extremist. Then came a very different person and a man of much higher calibre, difficult, brilliant and fiery, Thomas Francis Meagher. Later there arrived that fascinating, brooding genius of violence, John Mitchel. In the shadows, working mysteriously, were James Stephens, John O'Mahony and Michael Doheny. Their paths are worth following to understand McGee's future.

The case of Devin Reilly was as sad as it was simple. He was suffering from a mania. As wild as his red hair, Reilly "drove the knife up to the handle" into McGee as often as he could. He spared no one; "Gavan Duffy" he added, "is Give-in Duffy. About the 'priests and the holy wells,' all I say is: pray God to sink the first to the bottom of the second." Far off in Australia, as a felon, John Mitchel received long, troubled letters from Reilly which led him to observe:

> I pity Reilly. He needs a ticket of leave and a gum-tree hut here in the forests as an escape from the turmoil, or he will perish.

Poor Reilly did perish, later in Washington, D.C., by his own hand.

Early in 1852 Thomas Francis Meagher made a sensational escape from the penal colony of Van Diemen's Land and arrived in New York. McGee welcomed him in verse: *"Cead Mille Failthe, O'Meagher.* Beyond hope, beyond warning, our lost star appears." But Meagher soon grew angry with McGee for criticizing the policy of insurrection, and McGee in an open letter criticized Meagher for attacking the clergy:

> Permit me as one who has been over the ground to tell you what I discovered at the very outset of the inquiry, my own ignorance. This I discovered in a way which, I trust in God, you will never have to travel—by controversy, and bitterness, and sorrow for lost time and wasted opportunities. Had we studied principles in Ireland as devoutly as we did an ideal nationality, I might not now be labour-

ing double tides to recover a confidence which my own fault forfeited.

There is a Christendom.

There is in our own age, one of the most dangerous and general conspiracies against Christendom that the world has ever seen. It is the highest duty of a Catholic man to go over cheerfully, heartily, and at once to the side of Christendom—to the Catholic side, and to resist with all his might the conspirators who, under the stolen name of Liberty, make war upon all Christian institutions.

Restless, well groomed and buoyant, Meagher decided that he, too, would try his hand as a journalist. A visitor found him in an old section of New York, at the top of a crooked stairway in a dingy double room covered with Irish maps, editing the first issue of his short-lived *Irish News*—with D'Arcy McGee as one of his targets.

Back in Dublin, Gavan Duffy was saddened:

It seems the eternal fate of unsuccessful revolutionists to fly at each other's throats.

He chided Meagher and rallied to the side of McGee:

To forty political prisoners in Newgate, when the world seemed shut out to me forever, I estimated McGee as I do today. I said, if I were about to begin our work anew, I would rather have his help than any man's, of all our confederates. He could do more things like a master than the best amongst us since Thomas Davis.

But Meagher, too, changed. It was Meagher who then said:

If Ireland is to have a new birth she must be baptized in her old holy wells.

McGee had yet another journalist to contend with, the most indomitable and unpredictable of them all. John Mitchel had also escaped from Van Diemen's Land; and he ended his *Jail Journal*, a literary masterpiece of its kind, with a final entry on November 29, 1853, when he sailed into New York and Meagher stepped on board to welcome him.

Though his health was bad and his eyesight dimming, Mitchel also started his own newspaper, *The Irish Citizen*. His pen was still the trenchant blade, and his style, though shot through with colourful curses, showed flashes of rare beauty. As expected, he continued to deride McGee and Duffy for their "peaceful agitation." "Flatulent pabulum," he mocked. But Mitchel had lost his constancy, and was about to do some unexpected things.

Word came to D'Arcy McGee that perhaps he could now return to Ireland in safety, as he had been "thinking long to do." So in February of 1855 he took the risk, left his family in Brooklyn and after two weeks of stormy weather on the North Atlantic, reached Liverpool. A few thousand Irishmen met him on the dock—quietly, as he asked. This peaceful reception was taken as a pledge, and the English authorities decided not to arrest him. "I parted with all my bile on the Atlantic" was the way he explained it in a letter to his wife. In Dublin he met his old friend Gavan Duffy. But Duffy was downhearted and was talking of migrating to Australia.

Then he paid a visit to Wexford where he gave a lecture in aid of charity. His father was in good health, he found, but his younger sister, Rose, was "very tall and not looking well." An hour before sunset, he walked down by the harbour where "the blue hills shade the amber air." The men were sitting on the sea-wall as usual, smoking their pipes and gazing out at some "white ships on the distant, silent, silver ocean." That evening they talked of his older brother, Lawrence, who had risen to become captain of *The Dora,* and then had lost his life when he went down with his ship in mid-Atlantic.

After a filial visit to his mother's grave "covered with more than twenty summers' faded grass," he set off under the guidance of Doctor O'Brien of Dublin to deliver a series of lectures on "The Social and Religious Results of Irish Emigration to America," visiting Cork, Limerick, Galway and Dublin. His native skies were clouded and cheerless. Shocked by the way emigration was draining the Irish countryside dry, and distressed by the abject conditions which he knew awaited the emigrants in American seaports, McGee did not advocate emigration to the United States:

> I visited Canada last autumn and sought carefully for information useful to our people, and my judgment was more favourable than otherwise to the choice of Canada by Irish settlers.
>
> The colony is as free as the neighbouring Republic; its proximity to the Republic is the best guarantee against English oppression.
>
> Lower Canada is three-quarters and Upper Canada one-third Catholic; its school system is more parental and less objectionable than the system of the Union; the rates of wages as high as on the other side of the line; the wear and tear of human life is thirty per cent less, and the possibility of any such wholesale proscription as Know-Nothingism is entirely chimerical in Canada.

His talks in Ireland stirred up bitter winds against him in America. John Mitchel in his *Citizen* imputed base motives to McGee for praising Canada at the expense of the United States, and denounced him for "truckling to British rule." Then the Boston *Pilot*, moderately but firmly, joined with the *Citizen*. What McGee had first intended to be a candid statement of the better opportunities for rural settlement for Irish emigrants in Canada, rather than the United States, became, in the eyes of many Irish Americans, a disguised attempt to weaken American democracy and to strengthen British monarchy in North America.

In a way, it was a sad journey for McGee, and what made him saddest were "the anxious children of the poor." Ireland was "the crushed Dark Rose." He found it in a state of lethargy, and leaderless. Looking at the United States again with this longer perspective, he felt out of step with the money-making rush in the booming cities on the Eastern seaboard, and yearned rather idyllically for the quiet of the country farther west. Within three months McGee was back with his family in their small house on Duffield Street in Brooklyn. He knew now that his future was irrevocably in the New World. Yet he was restless.

Nor was Ireland as inert as it appeared to McGee and his weary friend Gavan Duffy. Beneath a languid surface there was a strange movement. Yet if someone had asked where were James Stephens and John O'Mahony, could anyone have answered?

JOHN
O'MAHONY

Michael Doheny had left them in Paris, and had gone on to New York
to write his own adventurous story, *The Felon's Track,* and to study law.
James Stephens and John O'Mahony remained unnoticed in Paris, adopting the manners of Continental revolutionists. But it was more than a
matter of manners. In fact, they were plotting and preparing a subtle
conspiracy, with their labours divided between them. As fields of action,
Stephens took the Old World and O'Mahony took the New.

Their early movements are still shrouded in mystery, but this much
is known. In 1855 a clandestine meeting was held in Doheny's cramped
law office on Centre Street in New York City. John O'Mahony was present. And it was there that the plans for their secret society in America
were first unfolded. It was O'Mahony as the Irish scholar, who was the
first to call the organization the Fenians, named after the *Fianna Eirinn,*
the storied military legion of ancient Ireland under its leader "Finn, the
father of the Bard." The name was at first resisted by his American followers; but O'Mahony forced it on them. Then it took hold and spread.
Circles were formed, each around a leader called a *Centre,* and all
around O'Mahony as the *Head Centre.*

Stephens, it appears, stayed on in Paris eking out a poor living teaching
English, and biding his time. Then, penniless, he made some appearances in the South-west of Ireland. Whispers spread. Were young men
drilling? What was this oath-bound society called? The Phoenix, re-
named the Irish Republican Brotherhood and later called the Fenians?
The scope of this intrigue only came to light much later.

D'Arcy McGee was now thirty-one. A decade of his years had been
spent in the United States. Yet he remained aloof from the life of the
nation. He never, for example, took out any papers for American citizen-
ship, nor did he engage in American party politics, not even to obtain
the support he needed for his newspapers. In the hurried affairs of business, he was an alien and unconcerned. Even in his own literary sphere
he felt apart from writers like Emerson, Holmes and Whittier. More to
his liking were Longfellow and Thoreau. But his conversation kept turning back to the perspectives of Burke, the music of Moore, the warmth
of Burns, Scott and Goldsmith or the melancholy wit of Dean Swift, and
further back to the days of Shakespeare, and then beyond into his own
realm of the ancient Irish bards. Contemporary American literature did
not attract him. He was dismayed by the freakish preachers and by
bosses of all kinds, especially those in the Irish wards. He remained an

exile. Yet lately he had come to realize that he was permanently up-rooted from his native land.

Freedom in the United States had first enchanted him, but then he saw some blemishes. Jefferson's glowing statements on liberty contrasted strangely with the hard Yankees who dealt so harshly with him in the East. Further west, in Cincinnati, where ten years earlier he had thought of becoming a lawyer, he was repelled in 1855 by a notice that no Cath-olic would be permitted in the public procession on the Fourth of July. "I am for progress with all my heart," he wrote, "but I want to know who is at the helm."

While he lived in the United States, all his attention was turned towards Ireland and the Irish. Help Newman's Catholic University in Dublin, he urged; aid the ancient missionary schools; assist the Irish linen, lace and muslin trade in America; encourage Irish industrial enterprise; de-velop literature; revive the music of Ireland—these were his themes in the *American Celt.*

Probably his most meritorious work was with the poor Irish immigrants. At first it expressed itself in founding night schools for them. Later it was conceived as a vast project to lead them out of their crowded ten-ements in the Eastern slums, and to settle them on the prairies in the West. To advance this work, McGee initiated the Buffalo Convention, which sat as a senate of a hundred Irish-American and Irish-Canadian leaders. Their task was to entice those who had struggled for conacre and cabin in Ireland to cultivate the new land as farmers; and in that rustic spirit he wrote such ballads as "St. Patrick's of the Woods," "The Army of the West," and "Irish Homes in Illinois."

Early in 1856 delegates began to arrive in Buffalo for the Convention, registering at the chief hotels, the Clarence, the American and the Man-sion House. Two delegates, elected on January 13, came from Montreal, and both, as it turned out, were to play a part in McGee's future. One was Bernard Devlin, a forceful member of the Bar of Montreal. He had started to study medicine in Dublin when he emigrated with his father to Quebec City. There he applied to continue his medical studies, but was deferred because he was under twenty-one. After ed-iting a small newspaper for a few months, he moved to Montreal where he studied law and was admitted to the Bar in 1847 at the age of twenty-three. The other was George Edward Clerk, an austere Catholic convert, a member of a titled Scottish family, and now the editor of the Montreal weekly *True Witness,* the best Catholic newspaper in Canada.

On Wednesday, February 12, the Convention assembled in the Dudley House. Vicar General McDonnell from Kingston of Upper Canada was elected as chairman, and the committee was composed equally of Americans and Canadians. On this committee, McGee again met James Moylan, one of the Canadian delegates, who served as its secretary and observed McGee at work:

I had a good opportunity to form an estimate of McGee's grasp of mind and analytical powers. He listened in silence to all that was said. As a rule he reserved his own remarks till the last. They were practical and to the point. Along with his own views, he would give in a condensed and tangible shape, whatever had fallen in a desultory and undigested way from previous speakers that was deserving of notice.

After four busy days D'Arcy McGee, with Clerk's assistance, composed the final "Address to the Irish Catholics of the Continent." It was adopted by acclamation and called for sustained action on a vast scale. The plan was to ask an estimated one hundred thousand Irish immigrants, who had means but were unsettled, to invest in co-operatives organized to take up land in selected sections of Canada and the United States. Then a further estimated two hundred thousand, who were without means, would be settled on grants of land, relying on the strength of their personal undertakings to pay back the advances in five, seven or ten years as they became self-sustaining farmers.

Wide support was promised, particularly from the clergy, since one third of the delegates were priests. But outside the Convention, voices of dissent were heard. The Buffalo *Sentinel* printed a series of resolutions from some hostile Irish groups. Then came an attack from Canada. It was the strident voice of George Brown in his Toronto *Globe,* which would challenge, rise and then change, but continue to resound in McGee's future. Brown was very blunt about the Buffalo Convention:

A deep scheme of Romish Priestcraft to colonize Upper Canada with papists . . . a movement to swamp the Protestantism of Canada by bringing into the Province 800,000 unenlightened and bigoted Romanists . . . a device to plant a second Connaught, a second district of Quebec, a second Naples—with no schools, no roads and no progress; a new scheme of the Roman hierarchy to unite the Irish Roman Catholics of the continent in a great league for the overthrow of our common school system so fatal to popery.

This opposition may well have been expected. But the next voice was not. An old opponent of McGee had yet to be heard from. He had become the first Archbishop of New York, John Joseph Hughes, at the height of his command. Clearly and directly, he spoke out against the Buffalo Convention. It was based on "pessimism," he declared; it would lead to "segregation," and there was no place in America for "separate Irish towns."

The Archbishop had touched upon a weak spot in the project. Optimistic as he was by temperament, McGee viewed the future of the Irish in the great American cities with a curious tinge of pessimism. Otherwise, the prelate's judgement was too hasty, and his concept of the full purpose of the Convention was too restricted. This, in fact, would be demonstrated twenty years later by the successful work in rural settlement around St. Paul in Minnesota under Archbishop John Ireland.

Withal, the plans of the Buffalo Convention made little headway against the august prelate's opposition, and for the second time Archbishop Hughes had prevailed over D'Arcy McGee. In this encounter, McGee decided not to reply. Instead, McGee turned and looked towards Canada, where he was invited to settle. And there, notwithstanding George Brown's Toronto *Globe*, such work as he had in mind seemed more promising.

There was a sequel after Archbishop Hughes died in January 1864, which can be related here. The Archbishop, however rash he was, had never underestimated McGee's talents, which he had assessed at the time in a letter to Archbishop Connolly of Halifax:

McGee has the biggest mind and is unquestionably the cleverest man and the greatest orator that Ireland has sent forth in our time.

Before that was ever published, when McGee heard of the death of Archbishop Hughes, he wrote a private letter from Ottawa to James Sadlier:

So the poor Archbishop is dead.

I heard the news suddenly at Brockville, the other day, and felt it most sincerely. God rest his soul! With all his shortcomings, a gifted man, and a great worker. I had almost concluded to write some tribute to his character—not in verse, for it had not to me the song-yielding qualities, but in good oratorical prose. However, at the Saint Patrick's Society's Festival on the 19th instant in Montreal, I may probably contribute my quoit to his cairn. Exaggerate I shall not; but a hearty, honest though modulated testimony would perhaps from me, be not only fit and proper now, but a debt due to the proprieties of the past.

There were many reasons which prompted D'Arcy McGee to adopt Canada as his new country. When he moved north, he stepped out of the shadow of Archbishop Hughes, which, as he admitted later, "in great measure led me to leave the United States." Then there were his repeated financial setbacks; there were insults from old colleagues; and a dread of a new power, what he called "the common mind of mushroom millionaires." Underneath and unspoken, there was also personal sorrow.

By this time D'Arcy McGee and his wife had four children. Martha Dorcas, the first child, was born in Ireland, and her exiled father had written about her before he saw her as "a little life I have not seen." But she died before she was four years old. The second was also a daughter, Fasa. Then came their only son, christened with such hope, Thomas Patrick Bede. Rose was the fourth, their baby.

One hot July night in 1856, Mary McGee sat at D'Arcy's desk in their Brooklyn home and wrote to Aunt Bella in Providence. In her fine, rapid script revealing her energy and poise, she quickly sketched in the news of her active family:

> About a fortnight ago, Fasa fell from the piazza at the back of the house, and hurt her head very severely. It was a miracle she was not killed. Patty had his old complaint, the croup, six weeks ago but is now quite well. Rose is well and beginning to walk.
>
> Thomas as usual is away from home. He is at present in Montreal. I do not expect him home before the beginning of August. As for my mother's health, the excessive warm weather does not agree with her at all.

A few months passed swiftly. Then suddenly that anxious, happy pattern was shattered. Patrick, their only son, and their baby, Rose, died of scarlet fever. Only Fasa was left to console them.

In that clouded year of 1856, D'Arcy McGee was invited to settle in Montreal. It came like a turning at the top of the road where a bright gap opens. Spread out ahead was a new country of the North, glistening with promise. With that prospect of splendour, he was still young enough to think, if not to dream, of a new beginning.

# 3

## OVERTURE OR INTERLUDE?

> Doors of hope fly open
> When doors of promise shut.
> *Thomas D'Arcy McGee*

> Montreal is remarkable for many things—for long winters,
> sudden springs and rapid vegetation.
> Its character is in the crucible.
> *Thomas D'Arcy McGee*

That hot summer night in Brooklyn when Mary McGee was writing to their Aunt Bella, she casually mentioned that her husband, "Thomas," was "at present in Montreal." But it was not just a casual trip. Nor was Montreal the uncomplicated city it had first appeared to be from afar to McGee. Actually the ground was being carefully tested in 1856 for a possible permanent move to Montreal.

Most active in this plan was James Sadlier. Operating the publishing house of D. & J. Sadlier with his brother, who ran the New York business from Barclay Street, he managed the Montreal branch at the corner of Notre Dame and St. Francis Xavier streets, with the aid of his wife, the author. James Sadlier was in touch with Bishop de Charbonnel of Toronto about the need of a newspaper centred in Montreal which could take an independent, strong stand in politics and advance the interests of Irish Catholics without involving the hierarchy.

On the other hand, George Edward Clerk, the confidant of Bishop Bourget of Montreal and the editor of the *True Witness*, Montreal's weekly Catholic newspaper, was perturbed. There were several reasons. To appreciate them, the sources of strife in Montreal must be considered. Differences arising from language, race and religion were profoundly felt, and they were openly aggravated by the newspapers. Montrealers adjusted themselves to these rifts, mainly by keeping apart and silent. When they did not, there was trouble; which was frequent.

Montreal had always been a garrison town—at least the smoke-grey houses with their iron shutters behind its walls gave that appearance. But its military history was not the gallant one of Quebec City.

Twice Montreal had surrendered without a battle: in 1760, when the Marquis de Vaudreuil capitulated to the English General Amherst, and in 1775, when Sir Guy Carleton abandoned its fortifications to the American General Richard Montgomery. Both times the victorious invaders marched through the West Gate on Notre Dame Street at McGill, under the venerable elms of the Récollet Church. The first time, they were the British redcoats with the Union Jack; the second time they were Americans in motley dress, bearing long-barrelled rifles, tomahawks and scalping knives, wearing deep ash-coloured hunting shirts, leggings and moccasins, an carrying an early Congressional flag of plain crimson with a black border.

For seven months, Montreal was an American city under Congress. Benjamin Franklin, Samuel Chase of Maryland and Charles Carroll of Carrollton—with his brother John, the future Archbishop of Baltimore—were its American Commissioners established at the Château de Ramezay. The mission collapsed, and "the Fourteenth Colony" was abandoned. Yet that brief American occupation of Montreal represented something unique at the heart of Canada's history.

The British had failed, through the American Revolution, to keep within one natural, political society those very people of their own race and language who had settled overseas in the American colonies. Yet by the Quebec Act of 1774 the British Government with the astute guidance of Carleton, managed to bind the French Canadians, despite their different language, religion and political heritage, together with the people of the British Isles in a heterogeneous Imperial structure. It was accomplished by the expedient of granting a calculated measure of religious freedom. A contradiction in principle was apparent, and the exasperated Americans were quick to seize upon it as "intolerable." Catholics in Canada, which meant the French, were now free, under the Quebec Act, from the legal disabilities which remained imposed on the Catholics in the British Isles. The latter had to endure the Penal Code for more than another half century until O'Connell pushed the Catholic Emancipation Act through the British House of Commons in 1829.

When the Americans failed to win over Canada to the cause of the American Revolution, and Benjamin Franklin, the "liberator of Montreal," withdrew, it was plain that the unexpected had survived. At the very time that the Thirteen Colonies peopled by Anglo-Saxons had severed their natural ties with Britain, the colony to the north, peopled by French Canadians and taken by force of arms from France, cautiously began a new life of cold allegiance to the British Crown.

As the nineteenth century opened, everyone in Montreal was acutely conscious of the political aspects of language and of religion. Politicians in their unprogressive way automatically labelled every man who touched politics as either "English-Protestant" or "French-Catholic." There were also the Scots, some being staunch Catholics, but they were hardly counted. The broad, simple classification, though unrecognized, was really based on language rather than religion, and was part of the sad racist blunder of trying to confine a religion within a language. When the Irish arrived, they, of course, entered politics; and they were quickly distinguished either as "Irish-Catholics," who were much more numerous, or as "Irish-Protestants," who were wealthier. The simplism of the old pattern broke down into a puzzle, and the hyphen became the overworked trademark of local politics. Being so openly based on race and religion, politics were bound to be extreme, and they took this course.

While Montreal was always overshadowed by Quebec City in military exploits, it grew steadily with the nineteenth century to surpass Quebec City in trade to become the chief inland port of Canada. The vigorous commercial character of Montreal produced its own spirit of compromise, if not of tolerance. Yet no one would call it placid, particularly in the years approaching the Rebellion of 1837.

This Rebellion was not a simple clash of races. What came to a head around Montreal in French-speaking Lower Canada had much in common with the Rebellion which gathered around Toronto in English-speaking Upper Canada. Bad times and lack of responsible government were causes of disaffection in both. And both were reactions of a majority drawn from the frustrated agrarian and poorer classes against the minority composed of officials and merchants who were viewed as an oppressive oligarchy. But there was also in Montreal the insidious irritant of different languages and beliefs with their increasing misunderstandings and prejudices. And added to that, if often overlooked, was a mixed stream flowing from Ireland.

There were Irish Catholics like Michael O'Sullivan, the first Chief Justice of the Court of King's Bench at Montreal, Irish Protestants like John Samuel McCord whose son founded McGill's McCord Museum, or James O'Donnell, the architect of Notre Dame Church who was born a Protestant in Wexford and died a Catholic in Montreal. They were Constitutionalists. But there were others like two physicians, Dr. Daniel Tracey and Dr. Edmund Bailey O'Callaghan, who were very active as rebel *Patriotes*. Somehow, nearly all of these Irishmen came together in the founding of Saint Patrick's Society on Monday, March 17, 1834, the oldest of the national societies in Montreal, which was started three months before *La Société St. Jean Baptiste,* and almost a year before St. Andrew's Society and St. George's Society.

Nothing revealed what was going on in Montreal at that time so clearly as its newspapers. Though much smaller than modern newspapers, they were more numerous, more personal and much more outspoken. Editors did not mince their words, and with the approach of the Rebellion, the bluntest (for none were dull) became sharper.

The oldest and the strongest of Montreal's newspapers was the *Gazette* founded on June 3, 1778, by a sprightly, unhappy printer from Lyon, Fleury Mesplet, who came to Montreal with Benjamin Franklin. First it was a weekly, issued "for two and a half Spanish dollars per annum" or "ten *sous* per copy." Then it was developed as the bi-weekly organ of commercial interests by enterprising Scots who soon gave it a permanent financial stamp. Conservative and commanding in its ways, with a steady circulation extending beyond Montreal, it was proud to be called loyal and Imperial.

The *Herald* was started as its rival. A printer, William Gray, from Aberdeen sold its first issue on October 19, 1811, to 170 persons, and within three years had over a thousand subscribers. It was liberal, daring and satirical, and often at odds with the *Gazette*. But in the Rebellion of 1837, the *Herald* united with the loyalist stand of the *Gazette*, which branded the rebel leader of *Les Patriotes*, Louis Joseph Papineau, as a "demagogue," and openly declared that force was justified and must be used to suppress the uprising.

Pitted directly against the *Gazette* and the *Herald* were the two fiery papers of *Les Patriotes: La Minerve* in French and the *Vindicator* in English.

Founded in 1826 and supporting Papineau, *La Minerve* as a tri-weekly, was the best edited of all the French newspapers. "Immediate separation from England is the only means of preserving French-Canadian nationality" was its program in 1837. At that time it was *Rouge* (inaccurately translated as "liberal"), with its editor Ludger Duvernay ardently supporting Papineau and his young, almost unknown lieutenant, the vibrant and talented George Etienne Cartier. *La Minerve* lasted for seventy years and changed later with Cartier as he became decidedly *Bleu* (badly translated also as "conservative").

Then there was the bi-weekly *Vindicator*. Dr. Daniel Tracey of Dublin's Royal College of Surgeons started it in 1828, three years after his arrival in Montreal. The *Vindicator* gained greatly in circulation when Tracey, attacking the *clique du Château*, was arbitrarily imprisoned with Duvernay early in 1832 by the Legislative Council. Immediately on his release from prison, Tracey was elected as a member for Montreal. But the election was marred when three French Canadians were killed by gunfire from the British troops. This became the "Massacre of Montreal" in the passionate speeches of Papineau, and from then on rebellion became inevitable. Tracey died in the cholera epidemic that same summer before he took his seat, and the new editor of the *Vindicator* became Dr. O'Callaghan, who exercised a special influence because he was in touch with Daniel O'Connell. It was through O'Callaghan that O'Connell was moved, with David Hume, to support the cause of *Les Patriotes* in the British House of Commons.

From then on, the *Vindicator* was more than the paper of the Irish immigrants in Montreal. It became the organ of the English-speaking radicals in the Assembly at Quebec, strongly supported by Dr. Wolfred Nelson. "Henceforth there must be no peace in the Province—no quarter for the plunderers. Agitate! Agitate! Agitate!" wrote O'Callaghan.

When Papineau wavered on the eve of the Rebellion, it was Nelson who deliberately laid down the policy: "The time has come to melt our spoons and make them into balls." Fighting broke out in 1837, and the Loyalists immediately attacked and destroyed the printing press of the *Vindicator* on old St. Lambert Hill near Fortification Lane. O'Callaghan managed to escape, and although he was granted an amnesty in 1843, he never returned to Canada. The *Vindicator* disappeared, and O'Callaghan settled down as the sedate historian of the State of New York.

Journalism was intense and rugged and, in the days of the Rebellion, fatally hot-headed. In fact, during the nineteenth century, 800 journals in the French language and 681 in the English language died in Montreal. But D'Arcy McGee, having buried two newspapers of his own, would not feel perturbed by such a well-filled journalistic cemetery.

There was another link with Ireland which McGee would find in Montreal. In the years leading up to the Rebellion of 1837, Daniel O'Connell exercised an extraordinary influence on the French Canadians; and even in the remote homes of the habitants, his picture was frequently seen. At least three of Papineau's Ninety-two Resolutions of 1834 praised and thanked O'Connell for his support. Then on May 7, 1837, when *Les Patriotes* adopted the final Twelve Resolutions, O'Connell was proclaimed in the tenth Resolution as the ideal political chief—"all should rally around a single man following the example of Ireland"— and Papineau was urged to organize and collect small contributions on the vast scale of "O'Connell's Tribute."

Lord Durham, known as "Radical Jack" in his youth, was very direct as Governor General in his famous Report of 1839 on the Affairs of British North America:

Deadly animosity now separates the inhabitants of Lower Canada into the hostile divisions of French and English.

I believe that tranquillity can only be restored by subjecting the Province to the vigorous rule of an English majority; and that the only efficacious government would be that formed by a Legislative Union.

French Canadians were deeply hurt when Durham described them as "a people with no history and no literature." His solution was the fusion of the French Canadians into the English-speaking majority, which he foresaw would grow with the mass of immigrants arriving "either from the middle classes of Great Britain or the poorer classes of Ireland; the latter almost exclusively Catholics, and the former in a great proportion either Scotch Presbyterians or English dissenters."

Durham balanced his criticisms by adding a scathing denunciation of Orangeism in Upper Canada, where "the Catholics constitute at least a fifth of the whole population . . . and the Irish Catholics complain very loudly and justly." He spoke plainly about what he saw of the nature and objects of Orangeism in Canada:

It would seem that their great purpose has been to introduce the machinery rather than the tenets of Orangeism, and the leaders probably hope to make use of this kind of permanent conspiracy and illegal organization to gain political power for themselves.

Orangemen were in the eyes of Durham a rowdy conspiracy of professional Protestants, and through them:

at the last general election, the Tories succeeded in carrying more than one seat by means of the violence of the organized mob, thus placed at their disposal.

Durham's Report was broader than these excerpts would suggest, yet these are the parts that have lived in the memory of the Canadians affected. There was no doubt that Durham recommended a course whereby the French Canadians would be absorbed and amalgamated, but he believed it should be done through a process of Representation by Population.

The British Government acted quickly on Durham's Report, and in so doing oversimplified it and dropped his plan of Representation by Population. The Act of Union of the two Canadas was introduced in 1840 in the Imperial Parliament. The only notable person who opposed it was Daniel O'Connell. He protested that by granting the same representation to 450 thousand people in Upper Canada, which was largely English-Protestant, as it did to 690 thousand people in Lower Canada, which was predominantly French-Catholic, the Union was flagrantly un-just. But the Bill was easily carried through the British House of Commons, with only O'Connell and five others voting against it; and the two Canadas were united in 1841.

Seven years later in 1848, when the Young Ireland Insurrection was failing, Papineau wrote in a despondent mood from Lower Canada to his fellow rebel Dr. O'Callaghan, then exiled in New York:

> In a few years from now we shall stand in the same relation to Upper Canada as Ireland to England.

The Irish were relatively new arrivals in Montreal. In 1817 they were merely a handful. But in the thirties and forties they were arriving by the thousands each year, and in May 1842, Charles Dickens, noting "the bursting out of spring" in Montreal, saw "vast numbers of emigrants who have newly arrived from Ireland with their chests and boxes on the granite quays." Those who could afford it crossed the ocean in six weeks, carrying hardened loaves of barley bread for food, and some bringing their own goat for milk.

Labour was cheap, with wages as low as fifty cents a day for unskilled workers and a dollar a day for mechanics. Yet so was food: milk could be had at five cents a quart, butter at fifteen cents a pound, a dozen eggs for ten cents, a pair of chickens for twenty-five cents and beef or some other cuts of meat at five cents a pound. Rents ran from two to four dollars per month. Working in these conditions of the forties, Irish labourers in their thong-stitched brogues, wearing "moleskins" in the summer, and *bawneens* of thick homespun in the winter, deepened the Lachine Canal in Montreal to double its draft.

In 1847 however, the year of the great famine, one hundred thousand starving Irish immigrants arrived in Canada. A narrative of one of these crossings has survived. It was written on a small ship which left Ireland on May 30, 1847, with more than a hundred emigrants from County Meath in steerage, and one passenger in cabin class.

On the tenth day out, two women had severe attacks of fever. Two days later several more were ill, and the supply of water "was very scanty, two casks having leaked." By June 14 there was more fever "of a peculiar character, and very alarming." Two nights later the sea was very rough, and two new cases of fever were announced next morning, and several passengers were delirious.

On June 19 a shark was seen following the boat; "a forerunner of death," the mate observed. One of the women became worse, "her feet swollen to double their natural size, and covered with black putrid spots." The following day she died and was dropped into the sea. By June 28 there were thirty cases of fever, and one was described in detail:

A mother, her head swollen to a most unnatural size and her face hideously deformed, had been nearly three weeks ill, and was dying. Her husband stood by her, holding a blessed candle in his hand, awaiting the departure of her spirit. As the sun was setting, he said a prayer over her corpse, which, as he said "Amen," was lowered into the ocean.

Early in July, a dense fog enveloped the ship off the Grand Banks of Newfoundland. On July 6 two of three brothers died, and "were consigned to the deep covered by an old sail." By the ninth, fifty emigrants were sick. The third brother died and was cast into the sea in two weighted meal-sacks. He left two orphan boys, and "the next day one boy was seen wearing his father's coat."

On July 15 a child was born. There was another burial on the nineteenth. Three days later one of the orphan boys died. Water was no longer available; the passengers were forced to use salt water from the Gulf of the St. Lawrence; and three new virulent cases of fever broke out.

At last on July 27 fresh water was reached. On the following day, after more than eight weeks at sea, anchor was dropped off Grosse Isle below Quebec City, but so many other fever-laden ships were also waiting, that two entire days passed without attention. Then two French-Canadian priests came aboard, followed the next day by a doctor, who had to inform them that only one half the sick could be admitted to hospital:

A husband was taken from his emaciated wife and small family, and a mother was dragged from her children, as she was lifted over the bulwarks.

On August 1 those passengers who remained were transferred to a steamship which went direct to Montreal, and some of those who left relatives in the hospital at Grosse Isle never saw them again.

Most of the Irish immigrants, who were stricken with typhus, called "ship fever," came through Montreal. The healthier ones, who survived the epidemic, went on up the Ottawa Valley to the lumber camps, or across to Peterborough or the Niagara Peninsula and beyond Detroit, or down by Lake Champlain and the Hudson River towards Albany. The sick and the dying and the orphans were housed in twenty-two sheds in Point St. Charles on the river bank in Montreal, and cut off in strict quarantine from the frightened city. More than six thousand of them were buried in an open pit of quicklime near the sheds. It was worse than the Black Hole of Calcutta.

That winter of 1848 a sudden deep thaw set in. Many of the ailing Irish immigrants who were still housed with a hundred orphans in the freezing fever sheds on the river bank watched as the ice broke up in Lake St. Louis and was swept through the Lachine Rapids downstream, passing them at Point St. Charles and into the narrows at St. Helen's Island. They welcomed the warmer weather as a blessing, and were enthralled by the pushing, packing and piling of the ice as it froze again in a new barrier. But to Montrealers this was danger. Overnight, the ice jammed and solidified twenty feet thick, directly across St. Mary's Current. In the morning there was a green mountain of ice rising from deep purple to crests of white, sometimes thirty feet high. It extended right across the St. Lawrence and the blockage caused the river to rise. Hourly everyone waited, hoping for the great ice shove, when like unannounced thunder there would be a quake and a great booming sound as the mass of ice would break and move downstream beyond Longueuil. But the ice shove did not come. The water continued to rise steadily until Point St. Charles and then Griffintown were flooded for three days with icy water rising in some areas up to ten feet.

Then came a series of almost annual civic disasters. In 1849 the Canadian House of Parliament housed in St. Ann's Market was burnt down by a mob. In 1850 a fire started in McNiven's carpenter shop in Griffintown and left five hundred homeless. Two years later the great fire occurred destroying eleven thousand houses in Montreal. In 1853 forty persons were injured or killed in the Gavazzi Riot. But of all these, the most significant was the gutting and destruction in 1849 of Canada's House of Parliament, then situated on Youville Square in Montreal.

Six years before, in 1843, an amnesty had been granted to the rebels of 1837 and a committee was established to study the claims of those who had suffered losses by the Rebellion in Lower Canada. Citizens in Upper Canada were already being indemnified for damages suffered there; but racial differences made it a very different and provocative matter in Lower Canada.

Finally the Reform Ministry of Lafontaine and Baldwin introduced the Rebellion Losses Bill in January of 1849 as one of the first measures of that Session in Montreal. Over two thousand claims had been received from those who suffered losses in Lower Canada through the Rebellion of 1837, and after months of study the committee had scaled them down and recommended an appropriation of a half million dollars. These claims included not only the claims of Loyalists, but inevitably those who had rebel sympathies, because the only ones who could be excluded were those who had been convicted of treason or had been banished to Bermuda.

The Rebellion Losses Bill was explosive from the start. "Did the Ministry actually intend to reward the rebels?" This question provoked fist fights in Parliament, and the climax came on February 16 when William Blake, an Anglo-Irish Reformer and a follower of Baldwin, made a long and blistering attack on the Tory Loyalists. Among the Tories and strongly opposing the Bill "as most shameful" was a young lawyer from Kingston, then thirty-four years old. Roused to such a fury, he wrote Blake a note in the heat of the moment challenging him to a duel. It was John Alexander MacDonald. Blake and MacDonald left the Assembly to find their seconds; but friends finally intervened, and the extremity was averted. John A. MacDonald would soon learn slower and better-humoured ways of handling opponents.

That stormy Session of Parliament was the first of many famous ones for George Etienne Cartier; yet, strangely enough for this rebel of '37, there is no record that he participated in this fiery debate. But there was no doubt about the outcome. The Rebellion Losses Bill received its final reading on March 9, 1849, with a clear majority from the representatives of both the Canadas. Then it lay dormant for more than a month, unsanctioned, while the fury of the Opposition mounted. Violence broke out in Toronto where the homes of Baldwin and Blake were attacked by Tory Loyalists, and the Reform leaders were burnt in effigy.

D'Arcy McGee was then in New York City, having arrived there only six months before following the failure of the Young Ireland Insurrection of 1848. His mind was still inflamed, and he was writing under great emotional stress for his very partisan *New York Nation*. When he heard of these wild scenes in Montreal and Toronto, he dashed into the fray with this diatribe as an "open letter" to Canadians:

> Brethren! The question of your independence of Britain—the common oppressor of our native and adopted countries—is again being entertained. . . . We look to you to protect yourselves and avenge the famines of '46, '47 and '48 on their heartless authors. We expect you to remember Mitchel and the rest. We do not counsel you to

originate a revolution. But if a struggle must come in Canada, we ex-
hort you to be prepared to act a prompt and powerful part. Do not
suffer yourselves to be cajoled by words or caught with promises.
Canada had never a better opportunity. England has ruled you for
a century, and at the end of it you find yourself ruined. Are you content? Are you happy? Are you not slaves?

You strike at the empire in the name of all its victims. Strike but
a blow for each of them, and that empire will plunder round the
globe no longer.

Brethren! We need say no more. Prepare, arm and organize.

What D'Arcy McGee wrote in March 1849 from New York would have
been read by very few Canadians. He incited no one. But one person
in Montreal who would have been shocked was the staunch Loyalist
George Edward Clerk.

Meanwhile word was spreading that Governor General Elgin, although
he personally disliked the Rebellion Losses Bill, had decided that he had
no choice but to sanction what the unquestioned majority of the House
had adopted.

The merchants of Montreal were in a frenzy, and great pressure
was put on Lord Elgin to withhold royal assent. The Montreal *Gazette*
called Elgin "the last Governor of Canada" and wrote in fury:

Anglo-Saxons! You must live for the future; your blood and your race
will be henceforward your supreme law, if you are faithful to yourselves. You will be English, if you no longer may be British.

Then it happened. It was a Wednesday evening; and an eye-witness,
Rev. W. R. Seaver, a Congregational minister living near Youville Square,
wrote to his wife and told her what he saw:

Montreal, April 25, 1849.

My dear wife,

Today the Governor came to town on horseback attended as usual.
It was rumoured that the Bill for indemnifying the Rebellion losses
was now to be sanctioned. On the report spreading through town
(which it did like wildfire) an immense mob assembled and surrounded the Parliament House. When it was finally announced that
he had really given the Royal Sanction to the Bill, then there was
trouble.

As His Excellency left the House for his carriage at the door, he
was assailed with stones, clubs, and rotten and good eggs by thousands. He was struck in the face with an egg and his carriage win-

dows broken. But by the speed of his horses, he was enabled to escape with no injury. . . .

I stop here for the cry is raised that the Parliament House is on fire—red flames light up the heavens. More later—

April 26

Tis too true. Last night about 8 o'clock while Parliament was still sitting, a mob (it can be called nothing else, though composed of some of our most worthy citizens) commenced the destruction of the Building. The gas pipes were fired in a dozen places and the building wrapped in flames. That splended building with its rare paintings, all the records of the Provinces from the first settlement, all the Acts of Parliament, that Library, worth alone £100,000, all, all are destroyed.

Not only a mob acted. Two days later, St. Andrew's Society of Montreal expelled the Governor General, for "his insult and outrage," as "unworthy" of their membership.

But what happened in Montreal was no mystery to the Governor General Lord Elgin. His explanation to Earl Grey on April 30, 1849, was simple:

The whole row is the work of the Orange Societies, backed by the commercial men who desire annexation, and the political leaders who want places.

It was bound to come. Within six months the desperate Annexation Manifesto was issued in Montreal, urging "separation from British connection" and "a union upon equitable terms with the great North American Confederacy of Sovereign States."

It was signed by members of Montreal's most prominent families, like the Molsons, the Redpaths, the Workmans and the Torrances, by future Cabinet Ministers like John Rose, Q.C., and by a future Chief Justice. Within ten days they obtained the signatures of a thousand persons—a large number in a town of fifty-seven thousand. Of all the signatures on that dismal document, the most surprising to find were those of a future Father of Confederation, Alexander Tilloch Galt, and of a future Prime Minister of Canada, John J. C. Abbott.

The Vermont Legislature then supported Annexation with a similar resolution, and all moves were styled as "friendly and peaceful." But Lord Elgin thought otherwise, and within the circle of his family the destinies of colonies were being shaped. As the son-in-law of Lord Durham, and now writing as the Governor General of Canada to his uncle,

Earl Grey, the British Colonial Secretary, he felt unusually free to be outspoken:

> If things remain on their present footing there is nothing before us but violent agitation, ending in convulsion. Canada is gravitating pretty surely towards the United States.

In England, Grey was unperturbed and privately said that "the loss of Canada would be the loss of little but a source of heavy expense and great anxiety"; and the *Morning Advertiser* published a similar statement with an air of authority:

> We speak advisedly when we say that this country would be no loser by the secession of the Canadas. That is certainly the conclusion at which Ministers have arrived.

Then Lord John Russell, as the Whig Prime Minister with a reforming policy of Free Trade, openly intimated that Britain was about to sever her connection with Canada. At the head of the Canadian Ministry, Robert Baldwin was stung. He had worn himself out in his Ministry with Lafontaine building a responsible Parliament in Canada, and could contain himself no longer. So he lodged his complaint with the Governor General, Lord Elgin:

> If the British Government has really come to the conclusion that we are a burden to be cast off whenever a favourable opportunity offers, then surely we ought to be warned.

Elgin, too, was exasperated, as he wrote:

> The English Government thought it necessary in order to give moral support to their representative in Ireland, to assert in the most solemn manner that the Crown never would consent to the severance of the Union; although according to the O'Connell doctrine, the allegiance to the Crown of the Irish was to be unimpaired notwithstanding such severance.
>
> But when I protest against Canadian projects for dismembering the Empire, I am always told the most eminent statesmen in England have over and over again told us, that whenever we chose we might separate. Why, then, blame us for discussing the subject?

On the eve of McGee's arrival in Montreal, disquiet and turbulence were everywhere.

These causes of strife in Montreal were to affect D'Arcy McGee and George Edward Clerk, the editor of the *True Witness*, in different ways.

Something in the temperament and training of Clerk made him feel instinctively that he would find it difficult to get along with McGee. He was the second son of the sixth Baronet of Peneciuk near Edinburgh. Leaving Eton, he joined the Royal Navy and later lived for ten years in Australia. Taking shelter from a storm one night in a cabin of an Irish family he passed the time away reading a book by Cardinal Wiseman. It led him to return to Scotland and be received into the Catholic Church. His father, a Presbyterian, was deeply disturbed.

So he left home again and arrived in Montreal with little means on October 7, 1847. Well educated and scholarly, he tried to gain entry into the notarial profession but did not meet with success. Meanwhile he had married Marie Louise Dupuis of Laprairie. The following year, one of his earliest friends in Montreal, Msgr. Joseph La Rocque, co-adjutor to Bishop Ignace Bourget of Montreal, arranged a series of meetings for Clerk, with Bishop Bourget, James Sadlier, the publisher, and John Gillies, the printer. The result was a new Catholic weekly, the *True Witness*. Its first issue appeared on Friday, August 16, 1850, edited and owned by Clerk, with private financial backing from the Bishop's Fund, which fluctuated greatly but managed to sustain this journal for sixty years.

In those days, it was hardly possible to read a newspaper without being confronted by some form of religious attack expressed in aggressive, if not offensive, terms. The French press in Montreal, with a few articulate exceptions, was Catholic. The English press, without exception since the death of the *Vindicator*, was Protestant. So Catholics who spoke English in Montreal often had the feeling of being calumniated and undefended.

This sentiment had been aggravated since 1846 when John Dougall, a man of rigid religion and strict temperance, started the *Witness*, first as a weekly and later as a successful daily, which was often truculent in the Protestant cause. Clerk's *True Witness* was the immediate answer to Dougall's *Witness*, and was equally fearless, unreserved, outspoken and too often over-provocative. The *True Witness* was ultramontane, and faithfully reflected the mind of Bishop Bourget, but its loyal conservatism did not respond to the views of the bulk of its readers, who were Irish.

Clerk felt this isolation, worked hard over long hours, worried, took long walks around Montreal, and managed, with agents in twenty-one towns, to bring the circulation of the *True Witness* up to twenty-eight hundred. Many of his readers lived beyond Montreal, particularly in Quebec City and Upper Canada, with quite a few in the Maritimes and

New England. Clerk described his journal as "essentially though not exclusively religious." He aimed "to avoid politics." But, because of his strong stand in support of Catholic Separate Schools in Upper Canada, and of his open battles with the Orange Lodges, he never could avoid them. He was particularly opposed to the Conservative *Bleu* Government, then called the "Ministry," of John A. MacDonald and George Etienne Cartier.

As a fervent British Loyalist, Clerk had been greatly disturbed by D'Arcy McGee's diatribe against Canada's British connection, which McGee wrote in March of 1849 in his *New York Nation*. Three years later, however, when he heard of McGee's return to an orthodox position in his *American Celt*, Clerk turned to praise McGee in an editorial:

> Seldom have we seen a nobler instance of candor, and acknowledgment of past error, than he has of late manifested, and we cannot but hope that Catholics—Irishmen—will show their appreciation of his conduct by giving a liberal support to his paper.

Clerk was then writing from Montreal in 1852 about McGee in Boston, and he was quietly trying to melt some of the opposition from Donahoe of the Boston *Pilot* towards McGee. But four years later when McGee was in Montreal, it was not quite the same. Subconsciously at least, McGee was on Clerk's mind, as he prepared his issue for August 15, 1856.

It marked the opening of the seventh year of publication of the *True Witness*. In it Clerk condemned "the unparalleled treachery of the present Ministry for their failure to grant freedom of education to the Catholic minority in Upper Canada such as granted to the Protestant minority in Lower Canada." At the same time he announced a new policy and changed the format of his paper:

> We have perchance trod upon some corns and perhaps shocked some morbid sensibilities. We remain thoroughly Catholic and perfectly independent.

Then for a reason that soon became apparent, he widened the appeal of the *True Witness* towards the lay and Irish readers by adding more secular news, foreign views and a new feature: "Irish Intelligence." The explanation was not hard to find. Clerk had just privately heard that D'Arcy McGee had been invited as an Irish journalist to come to Montreal. In his diary Clerk revealed more of what was going on:

> 1856, August 11, Monday: Heard through Mr. Sadlier that

T. D'Arcy McGee is in town and has received Msgr. de Charbonnel's letter of 18th instant which he approves of.

August 31, Sunday: Called at Mr. Sadlier's where McGee arrived yesterday.

September 1, Monday: D'Arcy McGee called at the office with Sadlier. Both in favour of a tri-weekly paper, which I doubt. Spoke to Bishop Bourget about it; to have an answer in a few weeks. Tonight was McGee's lecture on the Colonisation business, but I was too busy to attend.

Clerk had relied heavily on James Sadlier, so he interpreted Sadlier's sponsorship of McGee's journalistic project in Montreal as a withdrawal of support for the *True Witness*.

Then there was another point. Two years before, in July of 1854, Clerk had privately corresponded with Bishop de Charbonnel of Toronto, telling the Bishop of his eventual plan to run for Parliament with the support of the Catholics in Montreal. McGee's arrival in Montreal as a likely political candidate could readily put an end to that. And lately Bishop de Charbonnel had made some suggestions to Clerk about bolstering his paper, which Clerk had chosen to disregard; so a coolness was growing between them.

Financially, Clerk was worried. His newspaper had never emerged from pecuniary difficulties, and he had to rely on subsidies from the Bishop's Fund, which was handled by Bishop Bourget; and these payments were irregular and dwindling. Clerk was not a man of worldly ambition. But he had a growing family, and he was not making ends meet. Then, too, he was personally reluctant to call upon his father in Scotland for any help.

Clerk gave a sparse account of his activities in his diary. He was fearful that D'Arcy McGee would be more of a racial than a religious leader. Yet underneath this, he knew the Bishops were divided, and he had a natural, subconscious fear of a rival:

September 11: Received a note from T.D. McGee who is to be here on the 29th upon the subject of a tri-weekly paper. His remarks I will lay before the Bishop. I still adhere to my opposition in favour of a weekly paper.

September 23: Called on the Bishop of Alexandria about the McGee business, which will come to naught.

October 3, Friday: Spoke to Msgr. La Rocque about the D. McGee business. He seems to be of the same opinion as the Quebec authorities.

October 7, Tuesday: Wrote to McGee enclosing final reply of Bishops as to a tri-weekly paper.

What that "final reply" was and the effect it had on D'Arcy McGee, are revealed in a confidential letter McGee then wrote from New York to James Sadlier in Montreal on October 14, 1856:

Day before yesterday I got a letter from Mr. Clerk with an enclosure from Msgr. La Rocque adverse to the proposed tri-weekly. As to a weekly I quite agree with you that it could not be expected to give both parties a decent subsistence, so I must either give up Canada, or at least give up Montreal for the present.

One thing might still be done. If you know a man with some experience of the Province who would go half-partner with me in an independent tri-weekly, Catholic only on Catholic questions, as the *Celt* is, but Irish and Canadian on all others, I would like in November to treat with him. If a business man, standing tolerably well with all parties could be got, the enterprise might be made mutually beneficial. Otherwise I shall return from Montreal in November convinced that that City, at least, is impracticable.

In his letter Mr. Clerk indirectly cautions me not to make known the result of our request to the Bishops. In reply I stated that, as you were my confidant in the whole case, I should make it known to you alone—at present.

But the project did not die. Help came from Toronto, mainly through John O'Donohue, later a Senator, and Thomas Devine, an engineer of long standing with the Canadian Government, whose topographical maps and field-book were well known to surveyors. In Quebec City, support was organized by John O'Farrell, a lawyer and Member of the Assembly for Lotbinière. But the principal backing was in Montreal. By this time there was considerable wealth among the Irish Catholics in Montreal, which added to the strength of their numbers. They were conscious of their power and felt a need for more leadership.

It was mainly due to the annual arrival of large numbers of Irish Catholic immigrants that the population of Montreal grew from 40,500 in 1840 to 90,000 by the end of 1856. This vast tide of immigration was unprecedented, and a comparison will illustrate what it meant in the history of the country. For the whole period of 150 years of the French Regime, which closed with a Canadian population of 65,000 in 1760, the total immigration from France to Canada amounted to 10,000 persons; that is to say, an average of only 66 persons left France to settle in Canada

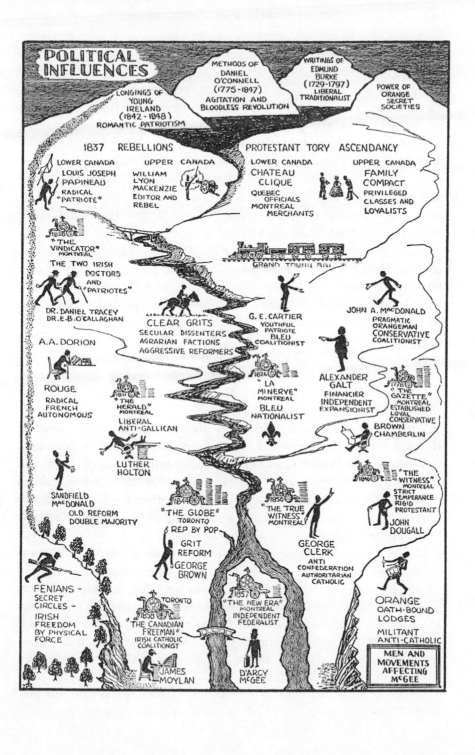

POLITICAL INFLUENCES

LONGINGS OF YOUNG IRELAND (1842-1848) ROMANTIC PATRIOTISM

METHODS OF DANIEL O'CONNELL (1775-1847) AGITATION AND BLOODLESS REVOLUTION

WRITINGS OF EDMUND BURKE (1729-1797) LIBERAL TRADITIONALIST

POWER OF ORANGE SECRET SOCIETIES

1837 REBELLIONS

PROTESTANT TORY ASCENDANCY

LOWER CANADA
LOUIS JOSEPH PAPINEAU
RADICAL "PATRIOTE"

UPPER CANADA
WILLIAM LYON MACKENZIE
EDITOR AND REBEL

LOWER CANADA
CHATEAU CLIQUE
QUEBEC OFFICIALS
MONTREAL MERCHANTS

UPPER CANADA
FAMILY COMPACT
PRIVILEGED CLASSES AND LOYALISTS

1826 "THE VINDICATOR" MONTREAL

THE TWO IRISH DOCTORS AND "PATRIOTES"

DR. DANIEL TRACEY
DR. E.B. O'CALLAGHAN

GRAND TRUNK LINE

CLEAR GRITS
SECULAR DISSENTERS
AGRARIAN FACTIONS
AGGRESSIVE REFORMERS

G. E. CARTIER
YOUTHFUL PATRIOTE
BLEU COALITIONIST

JOHN A. MACDONALD
PRAGMATIC ORANGEMAN
CONSERVATIVE COALITIONIST

A.A. DORION

ROUGE
RADICAL FRENCH
AUTONOMOUS

1811 "THE HERALD" MONTREAL
LIBERAL ANTI-GALLICAN

1826 "LA MINERVE" MONTREAL
BLEU NATIONALIST

ALEXANDER GALT
FINANCIER
INDEPENDENT EXPANSIONIST

1778 "THE GAZETTE" MONTREAL
ESTABLISHED LOYAL CONSERVATIVE

BROWN CHAMBERLIN

LUTHER HOLTON

SANDFIELD MACDONALD
OLD REFORM
DOUBLE MAJORITY

1844 "THE GLOBE" TORONTO
REP BY POP

GRIT REFORM
GEORGE BROWN

1850 "THE TRUE WITNESS" MONTREAL

GEORGE CLERK
ANTI CONFEDERATION
AUTHORITARIAN CATHOLIC

1846 "THE WITNESS" MONTREAL
STRICT TEMPERANCE
RIGID PROTESTANT

JOHN DOUGALL

FENIANS -
SECRET CIRCLES -
IRISH FREEDOM BY PHYSICAL FORCE

1858 TORONTO
"THE CANADIAN FREEMAN"
IRISH CATHOLIC COALITIONIST

JAMES MOYLAN

1857 "THE NEW ERA" MONTREAL
INDEPENDENT FEDERALIST

D'ARCY McGEE

ORANGE
OATH-BOUND LODGES
MILITANT ANTI-CATHOLIC

MEN AND MOVEMENTS AFFECTING McGEE

each year. Yet in two years, 1833 and 1834, 80,000 Irish immigrants arrived in Canada, and in the one year of 1847 the number of Irish immigrants rose to 100,000.

Montreal was an older city than Boston, but only half its size in 1856. Yet it suddenly found itself, like Boston, to be notably Irish. They made up one third of the population of Montreal. They were clustered around the two large transportation developments, the Lachine Canal and the Grand Trunk Railway, which cut across Montreal like a giant cross and marked off the two adjacent Irish centres of Point St. Charles and Griffintown. Then they were constructing Victoria Bridge as a marvellous new iron tube two miles long that would carry the Grand Trunk Railway across the St. Lawrence River.

Three parishes were organized for the Irish Catholics by 1856. Two of them were strong: St. Patrick's, with Father Joseph Connolly as pastor, but in reality run by the remarkable Father Patrick Dowd (who had already declined an offer to be Bishop of Toronto and another offer to be Bishop of Kingston); and St. Ann's, with Father Michael O'Brien as pastor. The third, St. Bridget's, had just that year been opened in the east end of the city, known then as the Quebec suburbs. St. Patrick's Hospital had been founded two years before, situated on Guy Street at Dorchester, where Dr. Henry Howard, then president of St. Patrick's Society, was one of the active founders.

Within this closely knit community there was a firm determination to bring McGee to Montreal. Like all minorities, it was self conscious, and just like the French Canadians, it tended to turn in upon itself; and because it had suffered as a racial group for its religion, it was inclined to identify its race with religion. In such a situation, Clerk, being British and a Catholic convert, did not feel at ease with either the Irish Catholics or the French Catholics.

McGee returned to Montreal early in November of 1856 to fulfil some speaking engagements at the Mechanics Institute. But the editors of Montreal's newspapers viewed McGee with suspicion, and none of them, except the *Herald*, would report his lectures, even when his topics were literary—such as those on Edmund Burke or Thomas Moore. Meanwhile Clerk got in touch with Bernard Devlin, the lawyer who had accompanied Clerk as a delegate to the Buffalo Convention, who was then in favour of McGee's project.

What Clerk heard from Devlin was not revealed, except by this puzzling entry:

November 16, Sunday: Called at Sadlier's where I met Mr. Bernard Devlin from whom I heard news that caused me much pain.

Then Clerk recorded the events of the next three days, all too tersely:

November 17: Mr. McGee called at the office and wrote some copy. Attended McGee's lecture on "Tom Moore and his Poetry." Lecture and attendance good. He will call tomorrow, I suppose, finally to announce the new arrangement.

November 18: Mr. McGee called at the office, and announced the design of a new paper. I said little as he starts today for Quebec.

November 19: Spoke to Mr. Sadlier and Dr. Henry Howard on the McGee scheme, upon the advantages of which I am by no means sanguine.

Nonetheless, conclusive steps were being taken, which were unconcerned with Clerk's disturbed state of mind, to establish McGee as a journalist in Montreal.

The year 1856 was one of those hectic years when "railroads were politics," and Montreal was the railway centre of the North. It was in that month of November, in the city's full tide of prosperity, that a gala celebration was held in Montreal for the opening of the Grand Trunk Railway between Montreal and Toronto, which attracted visitors from across Canada and the United States and reached its climax in a banquet at Point St. Charles with four thousand present. It provided the occasion for a meeting of leading Irishmen at the Franklin House at the corner of William and King streets in Griffintown. What was needed, they decided, was "a newspaper, independent and liberal in politics, and particularly devoted to the expression and advancement of Irish feeling and interest in the community."

D'Arcy McGee was still in Montreal lecturing, and his interest in the proposal was explained. So he was formally approached. He replied that he was ready to accept, provided, he added, that this was not a "sectional invitation," and that he could be assured it represented "a general expression of opinion from all his countrymen in Canada."

A second and more enthusiastic meeting was then held at the Franklin House. This time D'Arcy McGee himself attended; and after he had expressed his views, and James Sadlier was appointed treasurer, the record read that "$2500 was subscribed on the spot as an inducement to him to undertake the project."

The narrative was continued under another light in Clerk's diary:

November 21: Heard of a meeting on the McGee business at the Franklin House in which Mallon, M.P. Ryan *et hoc genus omne* were conspicuous; "promises" to pay $1300 handed in. Spoke to Bishop who is of my opinion that to engage in secular politics would be to compromise independence.

November 22, Saturday: Spoke to Rev. Mr. Michael O'Brien at Sadlier's . . . *all* are against me.

November 23: Heard contradictory rumours of McGee scheme . . . spoken to in the streets and dissatisfaction therewith expressed. To D'Arcy McGee's lecture on "The Irish Brigade" at the Coté St. Theatre. House crowded. Devlin made announcement which seemed dubiously received, and contradicted McGee who said publicly he had given no authority to Devlin.

Clerk's next entry marked the small beginning of what became very significant some years later:

November 27: Heard of misunderstanding between Devlin and McGee.

The next day Clerk saw Dr. Henry Howard, who was also a convert to Catholicism, and, like Clerk, somewhat of an outsider when it came to politics:

November 28: Saw Dr. Howard, and from what he says I cannot but think that Rev. Mr. O'Brien (pastor of St. Ann's Church) and perhaps Rev. Mr. Patrick Dowd (of St. Patrick's) are for McGee.

Meanwhile a committee composed of Matthew P. Ryan, Marcus Doherty, Henry Kavanagh and James Donnelly had been formed, and as a result of a letter sent to prominent Irishmen in Upper Canada on November 27, financial backing seemed assured. D'Arcy McGee's project was adopted at a final meeting in Montreal on December 16, 1856.

These were some of the realities in Montreal at the close of the year 1856. Early in 1857 D'Arcy McGee would arrive as a journalist with the prospect of entering public life. He was induced by the pledges of Canadian Irish Catholics to leave the United States and come to Montreal, at the climactic point when many Irishmen, and many more French Canadians, were quitting Canada for the United States.

McGee arrived in bad weather. And some of those around Bishop Ignace Bourget were hoisting storm-signals. At home in his study that New Year's Eve, Clerk completed his diary:

Summary of the year, 1856:

In our Canadian parties nothing has been gained for the Catholic cause owing to the treachery of *soi-disant* Catholic ministers and the venality of their Catholic supporters. I fear that the advent of McGee will tend still more to divide and accordingly to weaken. He can succeed only as a distinctly Irish organ and as such his policy must be injurious to Catholic interests.

Was this an overture, setting the mood for a coming conflict? Or merely an interlude, as a mimic pause between acts?

# 4

## WHEN THE NORTH WAS YOUNG

The one thing needed for Canada is to rub down all sharp
angles, and to remove those asperities which divide our
people on questions of origin and religion. The man who
says this cannot be done with the charity of the Gospel is a
blockhead.

*Thomas D'Arcy McGee*

I have put away sorrow like a shoe that is worn out and
muddy.

*John M. Synge*

D'Arcy McGee moved to Montreal in 1857, during a year of great economic depression and at a time when the value of British North America as a zone of Empire was questioned.

That year any schoolboy in London or Bombay, drawing a map of the world, would have placidly coloured the immense northern half of the American continent a solid red. But a realist in the Colonial Office would not have been misled by such a cover-all. Conventional maps had created the illusion that British Imperial power lay in the control of land, and revealed nothing of its strength as the empire of oceans.

What appeared as British North America on the map as one unbroken mass of colour did not portray the tenuous hold over those vast, uncharted territories nor the wilderness and emptiness that separated nine distinct regions, each thinly peopled and isolated as a colony. Once they had been fishing stations, trading posts, forts, islands or coastal strips, and their settlers had spread up the river valleys, with some of them reaching into the shallow back country. In 1857 Governor General Head could report with accuracy: "This country is all frontier."

In their true situation and scale these nine colonies of British North America were scattered across the vast table of the continent like pockets. In sentiment they were like parishes, and in spirit raw and turbulent.

The important line, then as now, was not a natural one. The natural folds of the continent ran north to south, like lanes, it would seem, of geographic predestination. Yet the line that made history was from east to west, marked by lakes and vaguely by rivers, sometimes contested, mostly invisible, and at each extremity resented. This was the southern boundary line with the United States. Along it, like odd beads, with a central double one almost pinched in half, the British colonies were sparsely strung, with wide gaps between them.

The wealthiest of these nine colonies were the two central Provinces, Lower Canada and Upper Canada. Their populated areas were not extensive. In shape they resembled twin Indian arrowheads pointing away from each other. The western tip of one was at Detroit, with its northern barbed flange at Owen Sound and its southern at Buffalo; and the eastern tip of the other was at Rivière du Loup, its northern flange

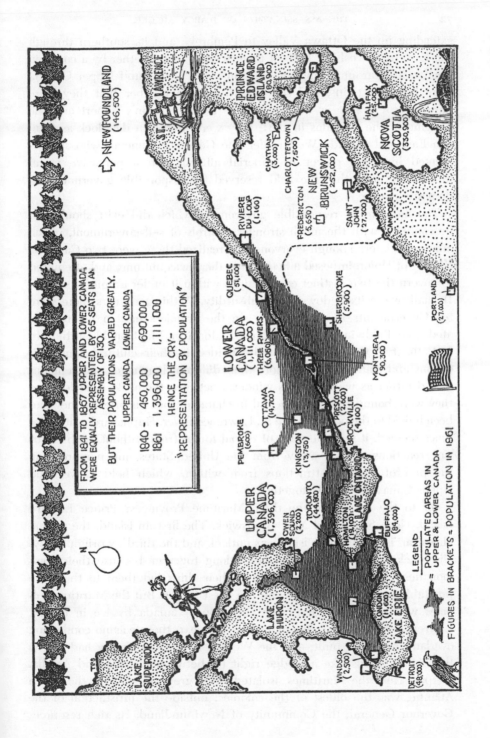

FROM 1841 TO 1867 UPPER AND LOWER CANADA WERE EQUALLY REPRESENTED BY 65 SEATS IN AN ASSEMBLY OF 130.

BUT THEIR POPULATIONS VARIED GREATLY.

|  | UPPER CANADA | LOWER CANADA |
|---|---|---|
| 1840 - | 450,000 | 690,000 |
| 1861 - | 1,396,000 | 1,111,000 |

HENCE THE CRY—
"REPRESENTATION BY POPULATION"

NEWFOUNDLAND (146,500)

ST. LAWRENCE

PRINCE EDWARD ISLAND (80,900)

CHATHAM (3,000)
CHARLOTTETOWN (7,500)
NEW BRUNSWICK (252,000)

NOVA SCOTIA (330,900)

HALIFAX (25,000)

RIVIERE DU LOUP (1,160)
FREDERICTON (5,650)
SAINT JOHN (27,300)
CAMPOBELLS

QUEBEC (51,100)

SHERBROOKE (5,900)

PORTLAND (27,000)

LOWER CANADA (1,111,000)

THREE RIVERS (6,050)

MONTREAL (90,300)

OTTAWA (14,700)

PEMBROKE (600)

PRESCOTT (2,600)
BROCKVILLE (4,100)

KINGSTON (13,750)

UPPER CANADA (1,396,000)

OWEN SOUND (2,300)

TORONTO (44,600)

HAMILTON (19,100)

LAKE ONTARIO

BUFFALO (84,000)

LAKE HURON

LONDON (11,600)

LAKE ERIE

WINDSOR (2,500)
DETROIT (48,000)

LAKE SUPERIOR

N

LEGEND

= POPULATED AREAS IN UPPER & LOWER CANADA

FIGURES IN BRACKETS = POPULATION IN 1861

extending up the Ottawa Valley to Pembroke and its southern through
the Eastern Townships. Both of them were joined together by a common
slender shaft around Kingston. But, in truth, Lower and Upper Canada
were far from twins, and so distrustful of each other that they were
hardly recognizable as brothers. Since Lord Durham's Report and the
merging of the Canadas in 1841, they were united in deadlock as Canada East and Canada West under one Governor General, who supplemented his legal power in imperial affairs, with a pervasive moral
influence even within the field reserved for responsible government in
domestic matters.

The measure of responsible government which did exist should not
be confused with the much stronger controls of self-government, which
only came later. Though everyone still realized there were two Canadas,
the Act of Union imposed a fiction that there was but one, and attempted
to govern the two distinct communities within it under a unitary system.
It finally wore itself down to an absurdity. Within ten years there were
ten Governments in office, and even the Premiers had to be hyphen-
ated, like Baldwin-Lafontaine, Hincks-Morin or MacDonald-Cartier. In
fact, the two Canadas were sadly divided in their cultural communications and spiritual communion; their different languages and religions
served rather as walls than as windows between them. By their location
they were bound to be continental in character, but historically they had
been linked to the ocean by the St. Lawrence River. Haphazard as it sometimes seemed, it was the push of casual forces from without, with recurring reactions of fear away from the United States, much more than
the pull of mutual attractions from within, which held Lower and
Upper Canada strangely together.

Off to the east were the three Maritime Provinces: Prince Edward
Island, Nova Scotia and New Brunswick. The first an island, the second
almost an island with an islander's outlook and the third by origin a Loyalist enclave, they cautiously went along together because their common destiny was on the ocean and their ships led them to the same
profitable markets of Europe and the West Indies. But the Maritime colonies were cut off from Lower and Upper Canada by ice in the St.
Lawrence River during five months of the year; there was no connecting
overland route yet built; and the Webster-Ashburton Treaty had driven
the Maine woods like a wedge right up between Canada and Acadia.

Apart from the Maritimes, isolated in its grey grandeur in the North
Atlantic, was the oldest of the colonies: outside the jurisdiction of the
Governor General, the Community of Newfoundland. Its rich resources

were then hidden, except for the cod on the Grand Banks. But what were they in the eyes of Imperial adventurers compared with the dazzling wealth of India?

Then, far across the North American continent, in another climate and basking on another ocean, with neighbours only on the south who listened to the same exotic tales from the Far East and who shared the same fever for gold in California as they did on the gravel bars of the Fraser, were the colonies of Vancouver Island and the vaguely defined region of British Columbia, each technically separate but with a single governor. Their excitement that year was the reputed wealth of the Couteau mines.

Finally, there were the lonely expanses of the prairies, those luxuriant undulations of rich loam almost untouched by the American desert but cut off by the giant barriers of the Rocky Mountains in the West, by the colossal shield of prehistoric granite, scrub and muskeg in the East, and in the silence of the North, by the frozen tundra and the snows. Only to the South were there inviting openings, merging imperceptibly with the Great American Plains. For the American settlers thrusting up from Minneapolis and St. Paul, this was the coveted heartland of the enormous domain of the Hudson Bay Company, administered as it was from Fort Garry on the Red River but controlled directly from London. The boundary line drawn at the forty-ninth parallel was scarcely more accepted by the Western pioneers as a geographical reality than by the herds of buffalo as they thundered across the rich lands stretching north and south.

A small Canadian Party on the Red River became noisy enough to provoke an opposing American Party to urge Annexation to the United States. This led the new legislature in Minnesota to pass a resolution in 1858 in favour of annexing the Red River District. While it amounted to nothing more than a resolution, it did indicate that the Western Prairies felt they had no real ties of common interest and few of sentiment with the settled colonies in the East.

The cities of the British North American colonies, such as they were, could still fairly be described as urban centres or even market towns; for Halifax, Quebec, Montreal and Toronto were not far from their fisheries, their forests and (if no longer their fur trading posts) their farms. Yet good arable land, once granted lavishly for fifty cents an acre, was no longer available in the East. And the West was beyond reach because of one thousand miles of the impassable Shield. Water and wind had served as the first roads and the early power of Canada, but with fur and timber they were losing their importance to steam, iron, grain, coal and lately the gambles of the money market.

Upper Canada had suddenly outgrown Lower Canada in population; and a Census indicated that the outnumbering was by about one fifth. This marked the watershed in the historic debate in Canada on Representation by Population. In 1841, when Lower Canada outnumbered Upper Canada by almost one third, the representation in Parliament was nonetheless maintained as strictly equal. Now with the positions reversed, Upper Canada Reformers saw the coincidence of justice with their interests in the doctrine of representation proportionate to population. It seemed, too, that Upper Canada was continuing to grow faster than Lower Canada, and forecasts were already being made as to what the Census of 1861 would show.

Yet these British colonies, each within its own confines, were lagging badly behind the United States, where, as Lord Durham had earlier observed, all was "activity and bustle." New York had taken a lead that kept on increasing as the Erie Canal drained the richest trade away from the St. Lawrence River. Buffalo, though younger, was much larger than Kingston. And in the Midwest a railroad had reached Chicago before Canada had more than fifty miles of rail.

The total number of people living in all the settled areas of the British North American colonies was still well below three million. Great distances separated them, but worse than that were the strong dislikes which held them apart.

The United Empire Loyalists nursed bitter memories of the United States and were more vehement in their attachment to England than to Canada. French Canadians, "their vain hopes of nationality" seemingly subdued by Durham's Report and the proclamation of the Union Act in 1841, were more nationalist than ever. Baffled when extremists under Papineau urged them to join the United States, they revived their patriotism only to have the *Rouges* divert it dangerously inward, while their economic pursuits, rudimentary enough, remained ingrown. Then migration to the United States, particularly to New England, started in alarming numbers. French Canadians spoke of 1857 as *"l'année terrible."*

A few years before, Lord Elgin as Governor General had depicted a distressing picture of the races:

Firstly we have the Irish repeal body. They are here just what they are in Ireland. Secondly we have the French population. Their attitude as regards England and America is that of armed neutrality. . . . The British, though furiously anti-Gallican, are with some exceptions, the least loyal.

With all that distance, diversity and sparsity, did anyone in 1857 dream of unity?

A Federal Union of the British North American Provinces was "no remedy"; such had been the flat statement in 1849 of leading Montrealers in their Manifesto in favour of Annexation to the United States. But in that same year Elgin made a private plea to the British Colonial Office which was to change the course of history in North America:

> You have a great opportunity before you—obtain reciprocity for us.
> . . . Canada cannot be saved unless you force the selfish, scheming
> Yankees to concede reciprocity.

Five years later, in 1854, Elgin himself, working in masterful fashion under the shadow of war, as British and American naval ships threatened each other in Maritime waters, negotiated the celebrated Reciprocity Treaty with the United States. Elgin's secretary mildly conceded that champagne "in the hands of a skilful diplomatist" is "a beverage not without its value," and thus was the Reciprocity Treaty floated in. It had just that effect on Canada, too.

Prosperity sparkled for a few years and went to everyone's head. There was an orgy of public expenditure. Railways were built with dazzling speed—and with the wrong gauge—as the staggering amount of one hundred million dollars was poured into them. For three years the different races and factions in the colonies of British North America floated above most of their quarrels and weaknesses, and forsook their habit of brooding. They also overlooked the fact that the boom was artificially prolonged by the Crimean War.

The collapse came as a shock. After so many bubble schemes had broken, which should have served as warnings, the sharp depression of 1857 set in. Commercial credit weakened, some banks stopped payments, and suddenly there was financial panic. That spring there had been another disastrous flood in Point St. Charles and Griffintown; in the summer the steamer *Montreal* exploded with five hundred Scottish emigrants on board; and then came a potato rot with a bad harvest almost everywhere that fall. The depression of 1857 brought the colonies down heavily to a low and almost stagnant level. Disillusioned and frustrated, people grumbled that there was no use looking forward to a national future. An exodus to the United States set in. Clandestine pressures for absorption into the United States were renewed. And in the taverns, where remedies are always on tap, the old talk of joining the States began to flow again.

The crash was real; and the talk of Annexation was real, too. Some have written that the plan of Annexation to the United States had died early in 1850. But it was merely submerged in shame. Annexation has been a persistent current in Canadian life. Though most of the time it has been an undercurrent, a crisis brings it to the surface, sometimes as a racial threat, at other times as an economic solution.

So in that critical year of 1857, with the colonies depressed and their value questioned, the future did not shine to the downcast with the promise it unfolded to the hopeful eye of D'Arcy McGee, just arriving in Montreal.

With the opening months of 1857, George Edward Clerk was still quietly working according to his lights to prevent, if possible, or at least to delay the start of McGee's newspaper in Montreal. Clerk was a fervent admirer of Bishop Ignace Bourget. The prelate, in turn, single-minded, saintly and overworked, was perhaps unduly inclined to consider new proposals from an ethnic point of view, and he placed great reliance on Clerk's interpretations of English-speaking Canada. McGee was known to the Bishop as a rebel, more inclined to be Irish than to be Catholic; and then, too, the Bishop had not forgotten his experiences with the religious immaturity of the rebel, Louis Joseph Papineau.

Clerk wrote candidly in his diary:

> January 2, 1857, Friday: Received a letter dated New York 29 *ultimo* from McGee. He evidently wishes for ecclesiastical sanction.
>
> February 4, Wednesday: Heard that circulars calling on subscribers for the McGee fund were being sent round.
>
> February 8: Called at the Bishopric with translation of Bishop Bourget's speech, and had a talk with Msgr. La Rocque about the McGee business of which he does not approve.
>
> February 22, 1857, Sunday: A letter from Rev. Mr. Ryan of Brantford wishing to know if the Bishops of the Province approved of the McGee scheme. Laid letter before Bishop Bourget who authorized me to reply.
>
> March 10: Had a visit and proposal from D. McGee, to which I gave an evasive answer.
>
> March 11: The *Commercial Advertiser* announces McGee's new paper as intended to trip up the *True Witness*.

Clerk found that most leaders in the Irish Catholic community in Montreal were in favour of McGee, which he interpreted as opposition to his *True Witness*. So he turned for sympathy to Bernard Devlin and Dr. Henry Howard, who were vacillating about McGee:

> March 13: Saw B. Devlin and Dr. Howard with whom I conversed on the McGee affair. The Irish clergy are favourable to it.
> March 30, Monday: Had a long talk with Dr. Howard. He has heard me accused of anti-Irish tendencies, which means that I am opposed to an exclusively Irish party.

McGee sold his interest in his newspaper the *American Celt*, paid off many of his debts with the aid of his Canadian friends, and moved to Montreal. Prudently enough, he came on alone, ahead of his wife and child, who remained behind for several months in Brooklyn. He immediately started to work in founding his third newspaper, to appear, as he had determined, three times a week in Montreal. The first issue, printed on a fine rag paper and containing four pages of seven columns each, with the editorials and principal news on the important second page, appeared on Monday, May 25, 1857.

There was something indomitable about its name. He called it *The New Era*, because Canada in its magnificence, he wrote, "has evidently arrived at such an era, with steam by land and sea, the sub-Atlantic telegraph, 'and looking to the West,' the probable annexation to Canada of a habitable region, larger than France and Austria combined." Foreseeing an "onerous future" when "the fair promises of the present" could be "fulfilled or marred," he pledged to do his best "within the free domain of his own conscience," and to make his politics "such as may best harmonize with the interests of a United Canada."

Brown Chamberlin's Montreal *Gazette*, having privately sized up McGee as "a political adventurer" (an epithet often hurled at McGee later on, and one which never ceased to rile him), carefully measured its public words of welcome to *The New Era*. With magisterial reserve the *Gazette* observed that it did "not like these special organs of particular races here." So in his third issue of *The New Era* McGee made his first of many gallant exchanges:

> As an abstract truth, we fully agree that a unification of population would be a great gain. But that result must be the work of time and times. Where there is diversity in the origin, time only can play the part of a solvent. Such a result cannot be hurried without being delayed. It ought not, on the other hand, be hindered.

We hope, 'ere long, the *Gazette* will be convinced by the evidence of the facts that the editor of *The New Era,* while cherishing a special affection and a particular gratitude to his original country and countrymen, is fully sensible of the duty of pursuing, above all, the best interests of his adopted country, Canada.

There then followed, in the next three months, a series of editorials and speeches by D'Arcy McGee which have become historic. They constitute the evidence that McGee was the first of all the Fathers of Confederation to advocate a Federal basis for a new nation. This he did in June, July and August of 1857, his first summer in Canada. It was the recurring topic of his editorials throughout the life of the newspaper. It began unnoticed in an article of June 27, called "Queries for Canadian Constituencies," with an acute analysis of some of the practical issues. This led the way to three important editorials which should be read together. They were written with verve on August 4, 6 and 8, 1857, within three months of his arrival in Canada, while most Montrealers were complaining of the heat and the hard times.

The first editorial stressed the need for union as distinct from uniformity. The second was on the role of the French language. And the third, the strongest and most original, was on Confederation.

What economic interests, McGee asked in the first editorial, could the several Provinces protect and control to greater advantage by forming a political unit? There were the fisheries and their fleets, reacting as a spur to shipbuilding, free access to the sea, more extended markets and busier reciprocal foreign commerce:

> Our railroads can never be considered complete till they abut on the Atlantic. Why should not the harbours of Saint John and Halifax have the preference of Canadian trade and travel, if they can compete with Portland?

Uniform currency was needed; so were a widespread banking and credit system, the establishment of courts of last resort and an organized postal system—"one is much more certain of his letters from San Francisco," he observed, "than from Saint John."

The solution had to be found in some measure of central control. Yet McGee was alive to the fears and the feuds that such centralizing proposals could generate. He urged his point in an apt phrase: What was needed was "legislative superintendence." Yet this could be static, and there was need for dynamism. "The new nation," he wrote, "that does not advance but gives way on the first trial, on any of its outposts, has no surety for the citadel itself."

The second editorial was devoted to the autonomous quality of Quebec, recognizing it as "the citadel of the language of Racine and Bossuet. It is their point of honour as well as their lever of power." McGee had already broached this topic in one of his first speeches in Montreal, when he was called upon to speak at the St. Jean Baptiste Society dinner in Guilbault's Gardens on June 17, 1857. Ten months later he was to amplify it in an editorial written on April 6, 1858, urging Parliament to adopt the proposals for Federation which Alexander Galt was about to introduce:

> We are in Canada two nations, and must mutually respect each other. Our political union must, to this end, be made more explicitly federative if we are to continue, even for the most general purposes, a united people.

When McGee recognized "two nations" in Canada, his description was just as controversial then as it would be now. Here McGee was speaking of a "nation" in its racial character as the French use it, rather than its legal sense which is more current in English. But the dispute over this phrase has never been eased through succeeding generations by overlooking its different implications in the two languages.

The third of his early editorials, published under the title of "Confederation" on August 8, 1857, was the most stirring. "The federation of feeling must precede the federation of fact," he wrote. That epigram not only exposed the fatal weakness of previous unions; it expressed his own abiding passion to arouse such a spirit, so that a new people could soon come together in the North.

It was remarkable that D'Arcy McGee, almost from his arrival, should have seen and said these things ahead of those who had long since been settled in the country; yet it was understandable. He had the advantage which a sudden, fresh view brings, and he was not cramped from childhood by local jealousies or parochial loyalties. To that, he brought a special talent to observe, discern and interpret, a buoyant spirit and an ardent, expansive desire to be patriotic.

It was his hope to avoid the dangers and to profit by the experiences of the American Federal system. "Canada," he urged, "should retain more of the social deposits of ancestral character." In politics he was a devoted student of Edmund Burke for theory, and of Daniel O'Connell for practise. These studies he sharpened by his own native intelligence and corrected as he matured through his own sharper experiences. Just as a physician will persevere and train his power of prognosis, McGee as a practitioner in politics reflected on what he saw, and developed vision.

Nor was he inclined to underestimate the difficulties:

They are many and mighty—interests of race and interests of religion, local rivalries and old obligations, considerations of finance, personal ambition, party predilections—all will have to be conciliated or overcome.

Yet he responded with imagination:

Look to the land next to Europe: Newfoundland. Again, away towards the sunset, lies the new Canada West, the field for another great Province. These are the facts, not dreams. Consult the map. There they stare you in the face, demanding the helping hand of wise and intrepid statesmen.

Through the heat of the summer, McGee worked steadily, though he was very lonely for his small family. Mary, his wife, could not travel then, so she was still living in Brooklyn with their young daughter Fasa. The deaths of their three other children had been deeply felt, and McGee would often recall the "fair ivory forehead" of one, the "blessed blue eyes" of another and "the cluster of chestnut hair" of his only son. "Men seek for treasure in the earth where I have buried mine," he wrote in his affliction, but when his wife was depressed he lifted her hope in a simple verse:

> Look up, my love, look up afar,
> And dry each bitter tear,
> Behold three white-robed innocents
> At heaven's high gate appear.
> For you and me and those we love
> They smilingly await.
> God grant we may be fit to join
> Those angels of the gate.

On a sunny Thursday, August 6, 1857, while D'Arcy McGee was attending a political picnic on the Back River at Montreal to commemorate the birthday of Daniel O'Connell, his wife in Brooklyn gave birth to their fifth child, Agnes, so fondly called Peggy.

A general election before the end of the year was in the air, and McGee's aim to enter political public life was clear. At that time, political parties were loose and complex, discipline was weak and party lines were perpetually fluctuating. Groups were formed as much around races, regions, religions and personalities, as they were on programs or political doctrines. The Clear Grits were a radical party. Their doctrine of Representation by Population was based on an irrefutable but very recent reality. It was tactlessly pushed, and George Brown, who emerged as their leader, was too often judged by his strongest words, which were chronically fierce. The result was that their methods supplied their opponents with their answer that Representation by Population was merely a means of having Upper Canada (largely English-speaking and Protestant) domineer Lower Canada (mainly French-speaking and Catholic). Outside of Upper Canada, the Clear Grits drew no support and, in fact, did not exist.

Sandfield MacDonald, a dour leader of the Old Reformers, held to his own solution of the Double Majority, which would require a majority of votes to be separately obtained from each of the Canadas before a law could be adopted. This was an unworkable scheme. But it had at least the merit of recognizing the reality and need of a Federal plan beneath the impractical fiction of Union. Meanwhile John A. MacDonald's way of getting a practical result was to try and woo his namesake Sandfield into his own political clan of Tories by offering him a post in his next Cabinet; but Sandfield sent back a dry answer: "No go."

The *Rouges* under Antoine Aimé Dorion were not very numerous. They appeared to their opponents as a strange mixture of extreme conservative nationalists who harboured coteries of anti-clericals and enough people who called themselves atheists to inspire general mistrust. Yet even they wanted Separate Schools, to protect, if not religion, then the French language. For all the *Rouges* were well aware that the Grit platform of Representation by Population was contrived "to swamp the French." On the other hand, the Clear Grits were outspoken Protestants irrevocably opposed to Catholic Separate Schools as a part of "Roman priestcraft." Yet somehow, the *Rouges* and the Clear Grits worked out together what was to each of them an uneasy and perhaps an unholy alliance.

There were also well-known and powerful Independents like Alexander Galt. And now on the sidelines, striving to come in, was a new Independent called Thomas D'Arcy McGee.

On such a slippery field, which was never free of mud, few could play the shifty game of politics as well as, and none better than, John A. MacDonald. Political theories were not much more than labels for

him. From 1854 on, the old Tories melted away through coalition, and
under his practical hand the new and ruling party emerged concerned
with projects like building railways rather than with doctrines and constitutions. Unashamedly borrowing programs, it began to take shape and
dominate under the bizarre name of Liberal-Conservatives. The French
Canadians within this fold called themselves *Bleus;* they could not be
said to be Conservatives, and George Etienne Cartier, originally a rebel
of 1837, and now rising as the leader of the *Bleus,* still styled himself
a Reformer. One way of explaining how the differences worked out in
practise was to state that a *Rouge* was anybody who was opposed to
Cartier. Heading the Government, John A. MacDonald and Cartier were
masters of the parliamentary process. Under the British system with no
pre-established date set for a general election, the Cabinet exercised a
strong weapon through its power to spring a surprise election. If public
opinion was running against them, MacDonald and Cartier could combine and realign votes to surmount a Parliamentary crisis, or if public
opinion was in their favour, they could suddenly provoke their own
crisis, force a dissolution of the House, and bring on an election at a
time to suit themselves.

The first political note McGee struck was a sturdy one of independence. In an editorial of September 15, 1857, on "The Coming Election"
he surveyed the parties. The Government of John A. MacDonald and
George Etienne Cartier was "one of expedients, a succession of make-
shifts," he wrote, "they draw the line after them as they go" and do
"not project it before them as the course they intend to take"; George
Brown's "Clear Grits have moulted their best feathers"; Sandfield Mac-
Donald's "Old Reformers show no sign of combined action"; and Dorion's *Rouges* do not grow; "like children dwarfed by strong liquors, they
are stunted by early indulgence in extreme theories."

The second note McGee struck echoed Lord Durham. It was one of
purgation, and it rankled. Orangeism for McGee was "a primary political
fact." In two vivid articles bristling with figures, names and examples,
followed by "An Open Letter to the People of Canada," he branded
Orangeism as "a threat to our liberties." His reasons for opposing it
sounded like the beat of their drums: "It is a secret society, a sectarian
secret society, and a political sectarian secret society. It makes a religious test of its politics and a political lever of its religion. And it revives
historic hatreds here that are dying in another land." He traced the history of the infection to the Ribbonists, with the Peep-O'-Day Boys and
the Protestant Boys, as the precursors of the Orange Lodges who finally

overawed the Government of Ireland from 1798 to 1828. They were banned in England. But in their pioneering passion in a new land (branching out from Brockville in 1830, and tieing in with an intense form of Toryism in Toronto and Kingston) they were now threatening Canada; they were organized with power, McGee maintained, and "obedient to their chiefs, rampant in the western, couchant in the eastern Province."

Furor followed. The Orange Grand Master wrote an uninhibited "Open Letter to *The New Era.*" The *Globe* called McGee "insolent" and "a fierce supporter of the Papacy" (although George Brown at the same time was privately describing Orangemen as a disruptive force of sectarian violence).

Then came the time for the hard-headed politicians to step in. They had to build up an election fund for McGee, and to start practising some of the dark arts of winning votes. On September 19, 1857, an announcement appeared in the press that a few prominent Irishmen had opened a McGee Testimonial Fund by depositing $950 with James Sadlier, the publisher, and the public was invited to contribute to the committee which would meet weekly from then on.

On October 9 McGee travelled to Ottawa, where he delivered a major address before St. Patrick's Association which was widely reported. It was aptly entitled "Canada and Her Destiny." He spoke candidly of his own past activities in Ireland, and of his present sentiments in his new land which "should have our first consideration." In those lights and shades, he pictured the two Canadas "as the true sphere of our duties, linked in unity, extending both east and west through future unions with other Provinces."

Back in Montreal, McGee was writing a leading political article three times a week: arguing against Ottawa as the capital; criticizing the Hudson Bay Company, and opposing "that levelling and despotic uniformity" which could frustrate "any future Federal Union where the autonomy of each Province should be safely secured."

Word came that an election was about to be announced. The signal was slightly premature, but a "jovial banquet" was held, in any event, at the Franklin House on Thursday evening, November 5. After messages were read from Toronto and Hamilton and one particularly from James G. Moylan of Guelph, a black morocco writing desk, containing a list of subscribers and $2000, was presented to McGee, as "they drank his health with three times three cheers and one cheer more."

McGee's days were crowded with activity. He met with Clerk, who after a long discussion apprehensively promised his support. On November 23 a large special meeting of St. Patrick's Society was called in Montreal; McGee then left for Toronto to deliver an introductory address before St. Patrick's Society on "Our Duties to Canada, the Land of our Adoption." The next day he was back in Montreal.

Finally the Government officially announced what everyone was anticipating: on November 29 *The New Era* carried it under a banner headline—"A General Election! Stand Together!"

A petition was rapidly circulated based on two plain points: "the Irish population constitutes one-third of the whole population of Montreal" and "it would be an injustice if we are not represented." It was signed by two thousand electors and published in *The New Era*.

At 8 P.M. on Tuesday, December 1, a great meeting was held in Bonaventure Hall on Haymarket Square. There was no doubt about its purpose. Dr. Henry Howard, the president of St. Patrick's Society, was in the chair. Its vice-president, Marcus Doherty, declared that the Irish according to the last Census were entitled to one of the three members for Montreal. Bernard Devlin then made the key-note speech. He moved and it was carried "as the unanimous sense of this meeting that Thomas D'Arcy McGee should be requested to allow himself to be put in nomination as our candidate for Montreal in the approaching contest." Knowing what they were about and with no time to be lost, James Sadlier, the publisher, proposed, with Henry Kavanagh seconding, that a committee be formed at once "to work the wards."

All this time, with impeccable political etiquette, D'Arcy McGee was kept outside Bonaventure Hall. He was now brought into the room. He accepted "with wit, humour and sagacity, and was most vociferously cheered." Then in a few serious and mellow words, McGee said something that was remembered:

> I cherish a high ideal of what the parliament of a young country like this ought to be and set the example of doing. I may be supposed to be a very excitable individual. But I have seen too much of the world to sacrifice the charities of life to any selfish or sectarian views.

Right from the start, even though the MacDonald-Cartier Government had designed it as a snap winter election, it was never a simple battle.

For one, Clerk, wielding the influence of the *True Witness*, was strongly against MacDonald and Cartier, but he was also unalterably opposed to the Clear Grits and their doctrine of Representation by Population. He had his reservations, too, about the irreligion of some of the *Rouges*. But he did feel that McGee should squarely oppose the MacDonald-Cartier Ministry, as this entry in his diary indicated:

1857, December 4: My anti-ministerial policy is now fully approved, and McGee will try and run the opposition ticket.

His friends are out campaigning, but the *Rouges* seem shy to join him as he is most unpopular with all the Protestant English.

The official nominating day was fixed for December 14 on Champs de Mars, and the polls would be open in Montreal on Monday and Tuesday, December 21 and 22. There were three members to be elected, one each from Montreal East, Montreal Centre and Montreal West. But the city was not then divided into electoral districts. All voted together; and the three Montreal candidates who polled the highest number of votes were to be elected to Parliament.

Immediately the names of six candidates unofficially came forward. George Etienne Cartier, John Rose, Q.C., and Henry Starnes were designated as the nominees of the MacDonald-Cartier Government. The other three candidates were Luther Holton, Antoine Aimé Dorion and D'Arcy McGee; but these three were not so easily classified.

Some of the lines of contest were already sharply drawn. Earlier that year John A. MacDonald was casting about to widen his Government as a coalition, and he had tried to persuade Dorion, the judicious leader of the *Rouges*, to accept a Cabinet post, which Dorion considered and then refused. So Cartier, as the emphatic and rather prodigious leader of the *Bleus*, was prominently set off against Dorion, the *Rouge*. *La Minerve* supported Cartier fully, and smaller journals like *L'Ordre* or *Le Pays* backed Dorion.

John Rose was a knowledgeable and influential lawyer who, as an intimate friend of John A. MacDonald, had just been appointed Solicitor General for Lower Canada. But his opponents, and even some of his colleagues in the Cabinet, suspected that he was chiefly an agent for the Hudson Bay Company. In many ways, Luther Holton could be contrasted with Rose. Holton was wealthy and was one of the incorporators of the Grand Trunk Railway, yet he held to advanced liberal ideas and controlled the support of the Montreal *Herald*.

Starnes as a banker had financial backing, but lacked popular appeal. As a close friend of Dr. Howard, the president of St. Patrick's Society, Starnes was busy, however, arranging to win over the Irish vote. Of all six candidates D'Arcy McGee had the most remarkable flair, the least

money and the most fervent following. Because he was new and his resources were intangible, McGee was feared as the unknown.

So the Government—the Ministerialists, as they were called—put the
proposition to McGee: "continue to campaign until the day before nominations," then "withdraw on the hustings in favour of Starnes"; later
on, in return, "a safe seat in the country will be found for you, and
you will be well rewarded." McGee rejected the deal with scorn. He
then proceeded to expose the matter publicly, and Starnes was taunted
until he finally released a confidential letter he had received about it
from Dr. Howard. This caused a sensation; and before the campaign
was over, most of the correspondence with its sordid bargaining had been
published. It had a sharp effect on McGee, as it immediately drove him
to make a working arrangement with Holton and Dorion, and the three
stood as "Liberal candidates."

Clerk noted the complexities in his diary:

1857, December 12: There seems to be quite a break up of the Montreal *Rouge* Party on account of McGee's coalition, which is very
unpopular with Holton's Protestant supporters, though the French
Canadians will perhaps vote with the Irish. The result, however, is
very doubtful, as the Ministerialists are very active canvassing the
latter, purse in hand.

The campaign became bitter. McGee had most of the press against
him. The *Gazette,* supporting the Government, called upon all loyal
Irishmen not to be "the abject tools of a mere adventurer." In smaller
papers like the *Pilot* and the *Transcript,* McGee was described as "a
stranger, a fomenter of strife" or "a disgrace to Montreal." Cartier's
organ, *La Minerve,* raked up his past in Ireland and printed columns
of his most extreme opinions as an Irish rebel of '48. Even the *Herald,*
which generally reflected Luther Holton's views, disassociated itself from
McGee. Meanwhile McGee's *The New Era* was more than busy putting
out extras every other morning.

Nominating day officially arrived on December 14, and McGee had an
outdoor rally that started on Champs de Mars and ended peacefully
enough five hours later on Haymarket Square.

It was the custom then to call for a show of hands from the supporters
of each candidate as his name was put in nomination, and this was often
interpreted as the first test of relative strength. Clerk was a close observer:

1857, December 14: At noon, nomination of candidates on Champ de Mars. All passed off quickly. Show of hands almost entirely for Dorion, Holton and McGee.

December 18: McGee's election very doubtful.

Some of the issues were fought out from six special points of view. So when the polls opened, even the prophets were prepared for surprises. The polls closed in the darkness of a Tuesday night, three days before Christmas, and the first results published in the newspapers were misleading. No one knew who had won; it was only clear that it was extremely close. Finally after the first figures were withdrawn and the revisions were made, the results were announced. They were recorded by Clerk in his diary, but with a slight error in the ranking:

December 22, Tuesday: Election proceeding quietly and concluding in the return of Dorion, McGee and Rose. I fear some of McGee's voters must have played Holton false.

The exact returns showed how close the election was, with less than 600 votes separating the highest from the lowest. Dorion led with 4565 votes, followed by Rose with 4463 and McGee with 4402. The defeated were Starnes with 4337, Holton with 4289 and Cartier with 3967.

As the last of the three defeated candidates, Cartier was humiliated. He was forced to find another seat, which he did in Verchères; but it was scarcely consoling. It was that election of 1857 which was the origin of a personal animosity between Cartier and McGee which smouldered for years. Nor were feelings permitted to quieten down when Cartier said the Irish electors of Montreal "could be bought for a barrel of flour apiece and some salt fish thrown in for the leaders"; or when McGee would hesitate and feign to forget as he referred to Cartier as "the honourable member from—ah—some country constituency."

Yet the MacDonald-Cartier Ministry did well in Lower Canada; out of the total sixty-five seats, the *Bleus* of Cartier appeared to have forty-nine elected as against nine *Rouges* for Dorion and seven Independents including McGee. But the Ministry was disappointed in Upper Canada. Of the sixty-five there, the most John A. MacDonald could claim for the Conservatives were twenty-eight, as opposed to thirty-three Grits and Reformers for Brown and Sandfield MacDonald, and four others. With instability as the probable future, the MacDonald-Cartier Government returned to office.

On his own first day of political victory McGee informally addressed his electors. "By mutual concessions and mutual forbearance," he urged, "let us keep the high ground we have gained." This statement was soon put to its test.

It was becoming plain that George Clerk was the antithesis of D'Arcy McGee. Clerk, with all his sincerity, was a doctrinaire. In an editorial published in the *True Witness* as "A Word to McGee," he placed the ground so high as to make it unattainable:

> Our main object in selecting you is that you exert yourself strenuously and unceasingly to procure justice for our brethren in Upper Canada; that from your seat in Parliament you insist in season and out of season, no matter what the consequences to any ministry or to any party, that the same measure of justice which in this section of the Province has been cheerfully and ungrudgingly dealt out to the Protestant minority be in like manner accorded to the Catholic minority of Upper Canada.
>
> Do this—and heart and soul we will support you.
>
> Fail in this, falter for one moment in your allegiance to the great and holy cause which we have chosen you to advocate, and you will find us as prompt to pull you down as we have been to raise you up.
>
> Your every action, your every vote upon matters connected with the School question and the general interests of the Church, will be closely watched, keenly scrutinized and impartially weighed. No excuses will be accepted, and no pardon or indulgence extended for the slightest deviation from the paths of rectitude.
>
> It depends entirely upon your conduct in Parliament whether we shall be your warmest friend or your bitterest and irreconcilable foes.

In practical politics it was far from simple. Of the sixty-five members elected in Upper Canada, only three were Catholics: Richard W. Scott from Ottawa, Sandfield MacDonald from Cornwall and his younger brother Donald A. MacDonald from Glengarry; and the latter two at this stage were indifferent to the need for Catholic Separate Schools.

In Lower Canada, too, even Clerk had to deal with his own problems of expediency. Early in February, with the help of Bernard Devlin, Clerk was preparing a petition on the School question, only to find that many French-speaking Catholics in Quebec City were adverse to any action "likely to disturb the Cabinet," and that English-speaking Catholics in Toronto received his proposals with indifference. Clerk then spent an evening with McGee revising his petition, but was discouraged when he received a letter on February 16 from the Vicar General in Quebec City "hinting at the impolicy of agitation on the School question." Confronted by this seeming opportunism and apathy, Clerk, with no further support from McGee, laid the whole matter before Bishop Bourget, who promised to consult the other ecclesiastical authorities. So little was expected to be done at the coming Session of Parliament.

McGee travelled to Toronto for the opening of Parliament on February 25, 1858, and put up at the Swords Hotel. "The city is gay and cold," he wrote, with "ice boats flying under their tall spit sails across the green ice of the bay."

Governor General Head had arrived under cavalry escort, and after a salute by nineteen guns started to read the Speech from the Throne. Everyone was apprehensive. Two months earlier John A. MacDonald's wife, a hopeless invalid for years, had died; yet as the House opened and he took his seat as Prime Minister he looked relaxed and appeared to carry his same professional, jaunty air. It hardly seemed credible that he had just written a private letter to his sister Margaret saying: "It will, I think, end in my retiring as soon as I can with honour. I find the work and annoyance too much for me." MacDonald expected that Session to be "a hard fight"; a scandal or a blunder could put him out, or a racial or religious issue could flare up and detach a bloc of French Canadians. He looked over the Independents to see what "loose fish" might rise to the bait. He expected the Opposition, particularly George Brown, to be truculent. Every member knew how wily John A. could be, but no one dreamt about the excess of cleverness that would be witnessed within five months.

Describing the new members, the Toronto *Globe* introduced McGee as "a doubtful personage" who "sometimes speaks the truth." McGee had just spoken in Griffintown on the historical friendships of Scotland, Ireland and France, and politicians read with a cynical eye what this Irish rebel had said:

We must train our temper to look outward in the New World with a just and patient eye on each other.

Sitting among the Opposition on the left of the Speaker, McGee made careful notes about every prominent member in the House. It was a young House: John A. MacDonald was forty-three, Cartier forty-four, Galt forty-one, Brown forty, Sandfield MacDonald forty-six, Dorion forty, Sicotte forty-six, and he himself was not yet thirty-three.

Burnt out at the age of sixty-three, his shoes removed for comfort, was the old rebel of 1837, William Lyon Mackenzie: "a small, slight figure, a large head, well covered with white flax-like hair, a restless blue eye . . . he has lost some of his teeth." This marred his enunciation, McGee observed; yet he admired how this distraught veteran could still stand up, and with the deadly measure of "his perfectly clear voice take the exact range of the room." But Mackenzie did not feel sure about young McGee and took the trouble to write to Dr. Edmund Bailey O'Callaghan, the Lower Canada rebel of '37 then living in New York, to ask if McGee was a dependable liberal or just a political adventurer. On the other hand, McGee was drawn to Mackenzie by the strong views he had recorded on the eve of the Rebellion about Orangeism:

> Orange Lodges in this Colony are a dangerous nuisance. Their main object is to oppose and oppress the Catholics.
>
> It has been clearly proved to the British Parliament that the Orange Lodges are linked together by secret signs and symbols of a nature as detrimental to the peace of society as they are inconsistent with the law of the land.
>
> How then comes it that the heads of the government here, trifling with the powers entrusted to them, are cherishing this public pest?

D'Arcy McGee did not obtain his own power to sway an audience by mere chance. He was constantly studying these talents and abilities in others, as his notes showed. John A. MacDonald, he observed, "had a halting delivery and repeated an awkward gesture with his left arm." Cartier was "quick and hot. So he runs a risk every time he rises." Sandfield MacDonald "leans painfully to one side. A clear speaker with a moderate, firm tone, but his manner is somewhat diffident, and he has a weak chest voice." Galt "has a comfortable manner, and an easy voice, silken in tone." Brown's "confirmed Scottish brogue makes him chary of his accent. He lingers on all the burrs and hisses. As Sheil said of O'Connell, Brown flings his ideas upon the world without a rag to cover them."

All the while McGee was waiting for his first opportunity to speak, and finally his opening came. It was about ten o'clock Wednesday night, March 3, when D'Arcy McGee rose to speak in reply to the address from the Throne. The members' seats on both sides were filled; but with its cynics, old hands and scoffers, and the lazy lounging in their chairs, it could not be described as a very receptive audience. More than a few had their guards up. What was this "advertised spell-binder," this "smiling little beggar," really going to say?

As it turned out, no one could have opened a maiden speech before

an impassive House in a more disarming manner than did D'Arcy Mc-
Gee. He was genial, relaxed and unemphatic. A spectator in the
crowded galleries remarked how "unassuming and collected" he seemed
to be, speaking "so quietly, in a low tone with few gestures," as though
he were with his own friends. The fine quality of his voice was unmistak-
able. His phrasing was poised, and what seemed to be facility concealed
all the hard work that showed only in the natural result. What was there
in his Irish diction? He sustained the vowels and lingered slightly on
the last syllables, toning down the harsh consonants of the English language. That very word "language," for example, was not spoken with
a flat Canadian *a*, nor was stress thrown on the hard mass of the double
consonants or the explosive sound at the end. He would make it flow
by opening the *a* and letting its jutting rushing sound fade away.

McGee opened with some banter, and the first tension eased. Much
was being made of the recent electoral defeat of the Tory Inspector General who at the height of his campaign had ceremoniously presented
Bibles to all the Orange Lodges in his county; and McGee made the dry
comment: "His defeat was a lesson in retributive justice. The electors
accepted the Gospel but rejected the missionary." There were a few more
sallies at the Government, and then a neat thrust. Their attempt, McGee
said, to relieve the economic distress of the depression by introducing
a new Insolvency Act was as comforting as an offer of more elegant
coffins to the sick.

With that, the burden of his speech rose imperceptibly, and his listeners found themselves on a higher plane. In the press gallery the *Globe*
reporter as he listened to him made a note: "—some perfect power of
impressing an audience—some magnetic power . . ."

The Government deserved praise, McGee said, for its necessary policy
introduced by Galt for the protection of industries in Canada and its
increase in the tariff. Even if it should happen to incur the disapproval
of the Imperial Ministry, it was a Canadian policy he commended, because it placed Canada's need first, to foster new employment at home.
This was certainly the stand of an Independent, because Brown and
the Clear Grits in Opposition were pledged to their platform of Free
Trade.

McGee then declared he had another clear statement of principle to
make. He was in favour of Catholic Separate Schools, a movement which
he knew he was as dedicated to advance as George Brown was determined to prevent. He would say no more at this stage, he assured

the House, other than to promise to return to the topic later on (which he did with care and a well-documented speech on June 25).

McGee then turned and faced John A. MacDonald across the House. "I next call attention to a serious imputation upon the Honourable Gentleman at the head of the Government." MacDonald cut in: "What is it?"

"It is this," McGee replied, picking up a document from his desk. It was a copy of a letter written by John A. MacDonald on January 18, 1858, addressing the Secretary of Orange Lodge No. 137 as "My dear Sir and Brother." "This is evidence," said McGee, "that the Prime Minister is a member of the Orangemen, and he extends his patronage to it."

"I acknowledge the fact" was MacDonald's immediate reply. McGee knew the value of timing. He let the effect of the rash answer sink in, with a pause.

When he resumed speaking, his sharpness was gone. He recognized a man's freedom to join his own societies, and he did not blame Prime Minister MacDonald for the unlawful acts of Orangemen:

> No doubt there was bigotry on both sides; but bigotry *dissociated* can never be as formidable as bigotry *associated!* It is the *system* in this case which gives longevity to the spirit.

Here McGee made his point:

> No man in the high station of a Prime Minister should use such a society for his own purposes when it has been the cause of so much heart burning, public disturbance and bloodshed.

Nothing more was said at the time. But as McGee moved on in his speech, those who knew John A. and his methods were ready to concede that, although MacDonald's attachment to the Orange Order was perfunctory enough to catch votes, and probably no more than that, his admission would do him harm as Prime Minister, particularly in Lower Canada.

After a brief caution that he feared the Queen's choice of Ottawa as the new capital of Canada would not be popular, particularly with the citizens of Toronto, Kingston, Montreal and Quebec, McGee registered his own view that this should have been a subject reserved for Canadians to decide upon for themselves.

McGee was now engaged in the main part of his speech. And it was apparent that from now on he would have to be reckoned with as one of the strong spokesmen for the Opposition.

He discussed the need for Canada to expand in the West with a clear vision. There was a rising desire among some British politicians, including William Ewart Gladstone, to get rid of the responsibility of governing and defending vast tracts of land in British North America, in the face of the growing strength of the United States. George Brown was now a Western expansionist. It had to be recognized that there was no more good arable land available in the Canadas, and there was a danger that the Americans on the march beyond St. Paul would encroach northward into the Red River area and the open West. MacDonald's Government had just gone on record, rather timidly, that there was a general feeling that the western boundary of Canada should extend to the Pacific, but later on the Government made the political error of referring to the Hudson Bay Company and identifying the West as "its"— the Company's—territory. McGee seized on this. "It is time," he asserted, "to bring such a servile attitude to an end"; the monopoly had to be broken, and these territories opened up fairly to Canadian enterprises.

He urged a bolder and more Canadian policy upon the Government, to hasten in bringing the Hudson Bay's control over the Western prairies under the rule of the responsible government of Canada:

> The timid, makeshift policy of the Government appeals to neither the heart nor the hope of the country. The new era calls for something more emphatic, hearty and manly. States have been made great by great souls. Politics were not the tricks of a trade, but the great science of affairs; the science which made small cities outgrow their walls and extend into the fields and pastures where cattle had once grazed.

There was a rumble of applause from both sides of the House as McGee sat down. Slight and rather tall, casual and outwardly very affable, Prime Minister John A. MacDonald then ambled across the floor and congratulated the new Member. McGee noted how "proficient in ready and dexterous expedients" MacDonald was. "Good humour is his most apparent characteristic," he added. Yet McGee never forgot the warm hand this friendly foe held out to him, as a new-comer near midnight that March 3.

The next day George Brown's *Globe* commented on McGee's maiden speech: "It was a very decided success. It is seldom that a popular orator makes so splendid a hit in first appearing before a Legislative Chamber. It was proof of his rare tact and talent. McGee undoubtedly is the most finished orator in the House." And even on the explosive school question, the *Globe* was moved, as it was so rarely, to be gentle: "That part of his address met with little sympathy . . . We liked his pluck, however, in standing up for his conscientious convictions."

The following Wednesday, March 10, a wild rumour swept through Montreal that D'Arcy McGee had been shot by an Orange fanatic in Toronto. Another rumour followed that he had not been hit but an attempt had been made on his life. Both were unfounded. They persisted, however, until they were denied the next day by McGee's own paper, *The New Era.*

Another week went by, as the clouds gathered. It was St. Patrick's Day in Toronto, 1858.

Unknown among thousands, a young Irishman clad in a short black coat, light corduroy trousers and a dark cloth cap was one of those marching that festal afternoon along Colborne Street in the annual St. Patrick's Day parade. He was twenty-two, the father of two children, and his name was Matthew Sheady. About three o'clock, as the bands played near King Street, an Orange mob surged out and attacked the parade. Stones, whips, knives and revolvers were used. A spade was seen. Suddenly a pitchfork was flourished in the air; then its double prongs were plunged into the back of young Sheady. He was taken to Miller's Drug Store on King Street. Later the coroner came. It was murder, openly committed. Yet all the while the crowd was growing wilder, and shouts were heard: "Pull McGee out of the House!"

D'Arcy McGee was the guest that evening at a dinner at O'Donohue's National Hotel on Colborne Street. Word that the dinner was proceeding spread through the crowd. With excited cries of "Get McGee!" and "Griffintown Papist!" four or five hundred men attacked the National Hotel, hurling bricks, smashing windows and sacking the ground floor. Finally, as a witness said, "there were more police around than rioters."

The dispersed crowd gathered again, to mill around Swords Hotel, McGee's residence in Toronto. But no damage was done.

Finally, about eleven o'clock, McGee managed to leave the National Hotel and took a carriage to go back to the House. He was spotted, and thirty or forty persons chased the carriage down the street, throwing stones. Someone got close enough to knock the driver from his seat. Fortunately McGee was near the House and escaped unhurt. A few days later another riot was feared as six thousand people attended the burial of Sheady. There was a show of indignation as the frail young widow appeared, but there was no disturbance.

Meanwhile the inquest had opened and was dragging on. What had happened in broad daylight had been seen by hundreds of witnesses. Everyone was talking about it outside, but no one before the coroner's jury. One man called before the coroner identified himself as "Robert

Watson, a Protestant who follows the water"; but he refused to testify and actually thumbed his nose at one of the jurymen. Watson was released with a reprimand, and the shabby inquest ended. No one was ever prosecuted and no one was even arrested for the murder of Matthew Sheady.

On March 22 the House recessed for Easter. McGee was returning as a Member of Parliament for the first time to Montreal, and excitement was still high about the murder of Sheady and the attack on McGee in Toronto. He arrived the next night at ten o'clock and was met at the Grand Trunk Depot by a huge crowd. Friends estimated it at ten thousand people, which probably was not too exaggerated. McGee was carried from the train shoulder-high to a sleigh drawn by a pair of greys. Then with Hardy's Brass Band playing, and Michael McShane and Thomas McCready on horseback as marshals, a long torchlight procession was formed which followed McGee along a route lit by lamps and coloured lanterns, to his home at 220 St. Antoine Street, with rockets bursting overhead and tar-barrels blazing in Richmond Square.

D'Arcy McGee had returned home in triumph—and he was tempted, as all men in triumph sorely are. He received the roars from the crowd, and indulged in the delirium of wild acclaim. Passions had been roused by the events in Toronto and were ready to flame in the excitement of the night. The horror they had felt could be fanned to hatred, and their defiance to revenge. A fiery word from McGee and the multitude would become a mob.

But the temptation was more insinuating than that. Triumphs, even with their classic dignity, had exalted Roman generals to the point of their undoing. But out there in that crowd of early Montreal and all around McGee were pioneers, and the rough spirit of the labourer, the carter, the canal worker, the longshoreman and the bridge builder. It was adulation, the overpowering form of flattery; and they were shouting for a speech.

That night as D'Arcy McGee stood on his balcony the course of his career turned. He was elected as a champion of a race, and had become its tribune. The next step could so easily lead to that triumph of ugliness—the demagogue.

He spoke at first with strong feeling, and some of his followers got out of hand. But within him a steadier flame was burning quietly; and he had seen Daniel O'Connell in such moments. He turned to his richest resource, his saving grace of humour, and soon enough it led to the wisest of all endings: "Well, it is getting late, and I think we had better go to bed."

D'Arcy McGee rose the next day above the battle. When he returned to Toronto after Easter, he urged self-denial and asked his fellow Irishmen in Toronto to set an example, in the spirit of St. Patrick, to abandon the daytime parade in the future and "give the morning to religion." His counsel was followed, and for the next three years the parade was voluntarily abandoned.

This support of the Irish Catholics for McGee as their leader was quite unanimous and remained practically intact during McGee's first year in Canada. But it was too good to last; and it had grown too fast to outdo the opposing Orangemen who were entrenched in Toronto and Kingston with their secret society claiming to have three men in the Cabinet, eighty thousand militants and their own method of getting their way.

Meanwhile the Fenians were beginning to conspire underground. Late in the autumn of 1857 an emissary from New York arrived in Dublin with a communication for James Stephens signed by John O'Mahony, Michael Doheny and others. He also carried a private letter from O'Mahony to Stephens, which was so secret that he "dare not whisper it to the very air." On January 1, 1858, Stephens replied:

> Bearer of this letter leaves by tonight's mail, and I undertake to organize in three months from the date of his return here, at least ten thousand men, of whom fifteen hundred shall have firearms and the remainder pikes. These men, moreover, shall be so organized as to be available, all of them, at any point in twenty-four hours notice at most.
>
> Now for the conditions. The first is money. You must furnish from eighty to a hundred pounds a month. Then I believe it essential that the centre of this organization should be perfectly unshackled— in other words, a provisional dictator.

Yet the Fenians were practically unknown in 1858. John O'Mahony, outwardly a hapless, poor scholar, had just published in New York his notable translation from the Gaelic of Geoffrey Keating's *History of Ireland*. He had nearly starved as he worked in a low attic on an imperfect Irish manuscript flawlessly written on vellum. His copious work brought him no money, and, in fact, it attracted an injunction against it in England. The mental strain thrown upon him led to a collapse, and he had to be placed for a while in an asylum. Those who saw O'Mahony when he came out said he was more intense than ever, stressing each word as he talked with a solemn movement of his head, his whole being absorbed with one idea—rebellion in Ireland.

But rebellion for McGee was like wrestling on the edge of a precipice, and he had rediscovered that the way of O'Connell was wise—the path of rugged peace. Like O'Connell, McGee, too, would soon hear it called "draggletailed appeasement." But he was accustomed to abuse, and it merely confirmed him in his path.

In his first year in Canada, McGee had climbed within sight of the summit. Strife and grief had left their marks, and he seemed older than thirty-three. But he had nerve when the north wind blew and the battle was on for the heights.

# PART TWO

# STRUGGLE

Man is born into trouble
as the sparks fly upward.

JOB V: 7

# 5

## THE DOUBLE SHUFFLE AND FIVE MEN

We should be liberal with the liberal, firm with the hostile,
not be outdone in courtesy by any, and be just to all.

TO THE CATHOLICS OF CANADA, JUNE 12, 1858
*Thomas D'Arcy McGee*

Politics, somewhat like logic, is neither a science nor an art,
but a dodge.

*John Morley*

In December 1857, D'Arcy McGee entered Canadian politics as an Independent. Four men were then emerging as prominent: John Alexander MacDonald, George Etienne Cartier, Alexander Tilloch Galt and George Brown. From that time on in the life of McGee, nothing lasting in political structures developed without these five men, and unforeseen patterns were cast by the shifting lines of battle among them.

From the start none of them were political friends of McGee, and MacDonald, Cartier and Brown were his marked political foes. Galt, as an Independent, could have been an ally, but he held himself aloof.

JOHN A.
MᴬᶜDONALD

The most fascinating man of all, because of his puzzling contradictions, was John A. MacDonald. He was a realist. He knew as well as anyone how weak the Union of the Canadas was. But he thought in terms of politics and not of constitutions. He was ready to do almost anything to keep the discredited experiment of Union from dissolving. He preferred to work on the betterment of a situation just as he found it, rather than discuss some new basic solution in regions where he felt politics did not reach. Very few politicians saw and knew more of human nature than John A. MacDonald, with his alert, rather watery eyes. To build and rebuild a Cabinet was his mastercraft. While he said it in jest, sometimes his actions seemed to recognize the usefulness of what he said that "the perfect political Cabinet would be twelve men, each of whom, if you liked, you could put in the penitentiary."

The opposition between MacDonald and McGee was plain and unthinking. MacDonald was a Tory and an Imperialist, and found it expedient to be an Orangeman. The tactics of MacDonald's group in trying to have McGee withdraw from his first election contest in 1857 had riled McGee; he had an instinctive reaction against Imperialists; and Orangemen drew his fire. So MacDonald and McGee were foes before they met, and when they first met in Parliament, it was head-on. Yet temperamentally they were drawn to each other.

Cartier, on the other hand, was temperamentally incompatible with McGee. Each was a natural target for the other's arrows. There were resemblances between them that might have been expected to make bonds between them. Cartier had been a Canadian rebel of 1837 and McGee was an Irish rebel of 1848. Both were nationalists and yet expansionists. But their first electoral battle in Montreal in 1857 was very bitter. Cartier was a key man in politics, and a prosperous lawyer with the Grand Trunk Railway as a powerful client. McGee was a new-comer; and when Cartier raked up McGee's past as an insolvent journalist it did not disturb him, but it did rankle when Cartier taunted him for his past as a rebel. Yet both Cartier and McGee faced the same political reality that each was pledged to his electors to support the controversial issue of Catholic Separate Schools in Upper Canada.

Cartier in 1858 was a different man from Cartier in 1837. He retained his fighting temperament and his invincible optimism. He was not brilliant, but he was firm and followed consistent paths. Not apparent in his fiery moods, there was a cautious, conservative side to him, where the line of tradition strongly marked his conduct. He was progressive and practical, avoiding needless chances. Reform, in his view, was a gradual not a speedy matter, and never abrupt or revolutionary. He was a builder and interested in wealth, and the best example of that was his success as the lawyer for the Grand Trunk. And such expansive projects as the Grand Trunk made him unsympathetic to the various forms of Laurentian provincialism which lure many French Canadians in politics. But anyone who appeared so intransigent, talkative and categorical as Cartier could not be other than foreign to the dour and intractable Methodists and Presbyterians who made up the hard core of the Clear Grits.

Cartier was indispensable in MacDonald's plans. As a *Bleu* of tireless energy, Cartier was working his way upward to control the majority of French Canadians in Lower Canada. MacDonald, manoeuvre as he would, could not count on more than an influential minority in Upper Canada, so he had to rely on Cartier and Lower Canada for power. On his side, Cartier knew he could attract no one on his own in Upper Canada, and MacDonald was the only man there with whom he could arrange to work.

Galt was a special case. He was an Independent, but he was moving further away from Liberals like Luther Holton and closer to the Tories. He viewed his role in politics as essentially the spokesman for the Protestants of Lower Canada, and though far less outspoken than Brown, he was, like Brown, ill disposed to Catholics. After Galt had in vain opposed the Rebellion Losses Bill in 1849, his reason for signing the Montreal Manifesto for Annexation to the United States was that he saw no other practical way of maintaining the ascendancy of the Anglo-Saxons and Protestants in Lower Canada over the French-Canadian Catholic majority. This position placed him apart from McGee.

Like Brown, Galt had interests which exerted a strong pull upon him to leave politics. In fact, Galt's interests in real estate developments such as the opening of the Eastern Townships for settlement by the British American Land Company, or promotions like his leading part in the Grand Trunk Railway or the first big speculative projects of joint stock companies in Canada, coupled with his skill in the financing of these large ventures, were primary, and more fascinating than his interests in politics, which tended to be secondary. Because of this, his colleagues found him politically fickle, which disturbed them in the critical moments, all the more so because of his great ability. He had a lucid, straightforward style, a keen power of analysis and, for a practical man, unusual imagination and foresight. But he was too much of a financier from Lower Canada to be trusted by the agrarian Clear Grits of Upper Canada. And Galt's world of finance was alien to McGee.

George Brown was the outspoken leader of the Grits, and the man who built the *Globe* into the largest newspaper in Canada by increasing its circulation of sixteen thousand to thirty-one thousand. The *Globe*'s language was always strong; "Galt," for example, "did not have the courage of a mouse"; and often it was more scurrilous than that. But that style did not bother Brown. With his enthusiastic, impatient and impulsive temperament, he lacked the imagination to put himself in another man's position and to study that other point of view.

For Brown to succeed, as he saw it, Cartier had to be put down, because Brown was determined "to swamp the French." As for Brown's attitude towards John A. MacDonald, ever since that wild day in Parliament of February 1856 when MacDonald lost his head and made an outrageous attack on Brown, calling him "a liar," "a perjurer" and "a hypocritical criminal," George Brown had refused even to speak to John A. MacDonald.

Brown was a fierce opponent of Catholic Separate Schools. So when McGee entered Canadian politics, Brown automatically labelled each early move by McGee as either "Popish priestcraft" or an "Irish plot." Yet the best of Brown was that he was open and genuine. He did not plan his moves and devise his schemes with the hard heart of a politician. He was too warm and too uncomplicated not to follow his deepest urges directly for all to see, and he would follow them when the time would come wherever they might lead him.

These with D'Arcy McGee are the five men who must be understood and followed in the years ahead. Abrupt turns, unpredictable alliances, personal ambitions, petty motives and selfless desires influenced each of them. Each one was a professional political warrior, faced with foes who in each temporary necessity seemed irreconcilable, until some driving force of politics, including the perennial need to win elections, acted on all of them in unexpected ways.

The precarious hold over the 1858 Session of Parliament exercised by the MacDonald-Cartier Government gave it a false air of dullness. Underneath the unexciting prospects of legislation were uncertainties and nervous tension. Almost every fourth man sitting in the House was faced with a petition contesting his election. Thirty-two of the 130 seats were under attack on charges of fraud and corruption, and in one district of Quebec the illegal practises had been so blatant that more votes had actually been cast than the total number of possible voters.

It was McGee's first Session in Parliament. Of all Sessions it proved to be the one to expose in the most dramatic fashion the fatal weaknesses in the Constitutional Act of Union of the Canadas.

All proposed remedies to the Constitution were being studiously avoided by the Government in its shaky position. Representation by Population was an inflammatory topic, and its mere mention shattered any attempt to discuss the relations between Upper and Lower Canada. Slogans took over, like "Four Frenchmen can't equal five Englishmen." Such assertions immediately provoked the alternative of Dissolution of the Union, which in its very conception was separatist and desperate. The device of the Double Majority, which was offered as a compromise, merely received lip-service.

The only other solution was Federation. This took two forms. There was the narrow, provincial one, with vague limited central powers and a residue of virtual autonomy for each of the two Provinces. This had actually been proposed by Antoine Aimé Dorion, the leader of the *Rouges,* in the 1856 Session, and was restricted to Lower and Upper Canada. On the other hand, there was the broad expansive plan of the Federation of all the British North American colonies.

D'Arcy McGee was steadily speaking and writing about the latter. But politicians considered the large plan of Federation of all the colonies as impractical and premature, an entertaining notion perhaps, but in no sense a political plan. In such circles McGee appeared as an enthusiast to some of them and to others as a visionary.

Even when Alexander Galt rose on July 5, 1858, to make his first remarkable proposals to the House for a Federal Union of Lower and Upper Canada, to be strengthened by including the Maritimes later, and to be widened by assuming the responsibility for the Hudson's Bay Territories, he failed to stir the apathetic House. Both John A. MacDonald and George Etienne Cartier sat in their seats and stared ahead in silence. Not even George Brown, as ardent as he was for Canada's annexation of the Northwest Territories, rose to speak to the resolution. Galt's resolution faced certain defeat, but it never came to a vote. Suddenly something occurred which affected the future course of Parliament and the future careers of its five main actors. It was the Double Shuffle.

Its first surprise was to see George Brown and D'Arcy McGee come together. In the early days of the Session, Brown with his majority of Clear Grits in Upper Canada was, typically enough, inclined to forget his utter weakness in Lower Canada. But as the Session advanced it was noted that Brown was becoming less violent in his anti-Catholic rhetoric and even somewhat less emphatic in his opposition to Catholic Separate Schools. One reason was that on May 26 McGee had indicated in the House that he saw some justice in Brown's platform for Representation by Population.

McGee expanded his views in a broadsheet issued from Toronto on June 12 to the Catholics of Canada:

As for that familiar bug-bear, I hope none of you are very much afraid of Mr. George Brown. He has endless energy for business, great earnestness, extensive political information and indomitable perseverance. But he must give convincing proofs of a different spirit from the spirit of the *Globe* during the last election.

I do not believe a Dissolution of the Union to be the real remedy. And I do not believe that numbers can be steadily ignored as the prime basis of representation.

A revision of our whole constitutional system cannot be far off. I am quite ready to admit that in any new arrangement the representation in the popular branch at all events must be proportioned to representation.

Abundant constitutional safeguards for the rights of Lower Canada —securing if need be under a Federal pact the autonomy of Lower Canada—can be found. My adhesion to such an arrangement would mainly depend on the condition of its being sanctioned by a majority of the people of Lower Canada.

Back in Montreal, Clerk of the *True Witness* took instant alarm, and he wrote a strong letter to McGee condemning any such a declaration. These concise entries in Clerk's diary revealed something of the rapid way the issue developed:

June 1, Tuesday: Received an angry note from McGee. He will give no explanation and may go his own road.

June 2: Heard from Sadlier about McGee who is very angry—the more fool he.

June 3: Had an interview with Bishop de Charbonnel of Toronto, who seemed to approve of *True Witness* policy.

June 12: McGee will have to pronounce himself explicitly on the question of Representation by Population. The *Globe* almost seems to claim him as an ally.

That same day McGee issued his broadsheet on Brown and reform of parliamentary representation, and it was followed by Clerk's open condemnation of McGee. In typical fashion, McGee on his return from Toronto called on Clerk to discuss their differences, face to face, but the meeting had little effect.

Meanwhile Brown was beginning to see ways of working with Dorion, and Dorion sensed that the hold of the MacDonald-Cartier Government over the House seemed to be slipping. On Wednesday night, July 28, it did slip.

Dorion's *Rouges* made a direct attack. Ottawa had been announced

as the Queen's choice for the capital of Canada; and placing it on this
royal level was designed to make the decision unquestionable. But it
was not well received. So the *Rouges* moved that Ottawa should not
be the capital of Canada. The citizens of Toronto, Kingston, Montreal
and Quebec were each convinced of the superior claim of their own
proud city to be the capital; and now they were inclined to submerge
their jealousies of each other, in their common disdain for that village
in the backwoods called Bytown and its claim as an upstart for such
an honour—and such a centre of patronage. The strategy succeeded. A
bloc of French-Canadian *Bleus* changed sides, and the Government
was defeated on the floor of the House by a vote of sixty-four to fifty.
Brown in triumph immediately moved for adjournment, only to see the
wayward *Bleus* return to their fold and defeat his motion to adjourn,
fifty to sixty-one.

It was now the turn of the master, John A. MacDonald, to make his
counter-move. What really went on in the inner circles no one will ever
know. Was some secret understanding reached or not? Anyhow, three
significant facts can be noted. First of all, the MacDonald-Cartier Government, having defeated Brown's motion to adjourn, was not itself
obliged to resign. But a second point was that MacDonald, Cartier and
their supporters still had nine pending election fraud cases hanging
over their heads. The third point everyone observed. When MacDonald,
Cartier and their Ministers announced their resignation early Thursday
morning, July 29, they did it with a show of banter and exultation.

In any event, Governor General Sir Edmund Head, much more of a
precise scholar than a firm Chief Executive, called in the impatient
George Brown to form a Government. Head and Brown disliked each
other, and their meeting was a stiff one. Brown asked for time in order
to consult with Dorion, which the Governor General cautiously granted.
Brown then went to work in a hasty, almost feverish fashion and hammered together the basis of a Cabinet around some amazing compromises, which were to have a lasting effect.

Friday was filled with discussions. On Saturday morning, Brown returned to Governor General Head and, to Head's surprise, declared that
he accepted the duty of forming a new Government. Head promptly
warned Brown that if he were to fail, a dissolution of Parliament could
not be guaranteed. Brown was irked by Head's didactic manner, but he
wasted neither time nor words and took his formal leave, bent on his
impetuous venture as the new Prime Minister.

On Monday, August 2, after one of the busiest week-ends of his life,

Brown was ready, with Dorion and their surprisingly strong Ministry, to be sworn in. Sandfield MacDonald, Oliver Mowat, Michael Hamilton Foley, James Morris and Skeffington Connor were joining Brown from Upper Canada; and Luther Holton (who had to find a seat), J. E. Thibaudeau, François Lemieux, Charles Laberge and Lewis T. Drummond were joining Dorion from Lower Canada. Apart from the good calibre of the men, one feature astounded everyone. George Brown, of all people, in selecting twelve men had included six Catholics—MacDonald, Dorion, Drummond, Thibaudeau, Lemieux and Laberge.

As the law then required, the proposed new Ministers had to vacate their seats immediately until they were returned in by-elections expressly confirming them as Ministers. Such by-elections were usually taken for granted.

While the new Ministers of this promising Liberal Government made up of Clear Grits, Reformers and *Rouges* were thus technically unseated, awaiting their by-elections, they were unable to speak or vote in the House; and this critically reduced the number of their supporters to a minority.

During such an interval it was customary to confine the business of the House to routine matters until the Ministers returned. But immediately, upon the first innocuous motion being made to issue the writ for Dorion's by-election, Hector Langevin, a protégé of Cartier, and John Beverley Robinson, a Tory rival of Brown, rose to amend the motion and turn it into a resolution of want of confidence in the untried Brown-Dorion Cabinet. It was an open breach of parliamentary courtesy, but it went through. So, after two short and empty days in office as Prime Minister, Brown was out.

Brown was outraged. This was abortion at birth. Tuesday morning, August 3, Brown stormed his way through a heavy rain to the residence of Governor General Head to ask, perhaps to demand, the dissolution of the House. Head, like a detached professor, said little, except to tell Brown to put his reasons in writing. But the next day Sir Edmund Head, in an elaborately reasoned document (whose real authorship has been debated ever since), rigidly refused to dissolve the House.

As the news spread in an excited and indignant House, D'Arcy McGee rose to defend Brown in the most scathing of all his fighting speeches. Through jeers and cries of "order!", McGee called it "back-stairs work," "a solemn farce," "cabal":

Canadians were not Sepoy slaves from the jungles of India who fawn, and fawn only to obtain an opportunity to stab. Canadians demand fair play, bonnie play.

Picking up the official documents which had just arrived, he noted the sardonic terms in which the Governor General as the Executive had refused to grant Brown the dissolution of the House. McGee was speaking for the defeated Ministers who could not speak for themselves, in biting words which flamed from a deep sense of wrong:

No one can fail to see through those documents an animus, a dexterous hand, a lawyer-like cunning and sagacity.

All my life I have been a student of style. And I can tell a professional form of expression from a non-professional. And I say a skilful technical hand has been at the framing of those documents. The country can trace the hand and the spirit that guided it, and will draw its own conclusions and act upon them.

The whole country prophesied that no matter what the House might advise, the Executive would not permit dissolution.

Suddenly McGee was interrupted by Ogle Gowan, the member from Leeds and the Orange Grand Master:

Every person of common sense knew that.

McGee saw his opening:

"Every person of common sense," that is, I suppose, every supporter of the MacDonald-Cartier Administration? Every person knew what would be the result?

Well, we are learning a new lesson, and have turned a new leaf in the history of responsible government.

Everyone, says the honorable gentleman, knew that the Executive of this country would not take a certain course, notwithstanding that his sworn advisers might constitutionally have advised him to take that course. Everyone knew that the Executive would not be bound by the advice of the men he had called to his council.

If that were true, I say it would be a mockery of all government.

Anywhere in Europe or America such a course of proceeding would dishonour any person who resorted to it, especially a gentleman in high station. Such a one would deserve to have his arms reversed, and the sword that dubbed him by the title he wears, broken before his face.

So, a Government was formed whose advice the supporters of the previous Government knew that His Excellency would not take?

If this be so, then the men His Excellency called in and invited to be his advisers were the men he mistrusted, while the men who had been discarded from his councils, the men who last Thursday went through the farce and the mockery of a resignation, were the men who still retained his confidence.

The honorable Member from Leeds spoke about common sense. But nothing is more adverse to common sense than its counterfeit, a low, mole-like cunning.

McGee then turned to the precedents of history, from the days of Magna Carta down to the Reform Bill, and made a stirring appeal:

When the rights of the people are assailed, we need bold speaking and outspoken candour, men who will see to it that the people will not be cheated of their rights.

A voice broke in:

And they won't be cheated now!

It was the aging William Lyon Mackenzie, drained of all his passions save that of anger, making one of his last interventions in Parliament, for he resigned his seat soon after, worn out by the degrading effects of politics.

McGee turned towards the old rebel of 1837:

I am glad to hear that response from the oldest living sentinel of public liberty in Canada.

McGee ended with an earnest plea. The Brown-Dorion Liberal Coalition, he contended, could have led to a truce in the religious and regional battles which have been waged so long and so fiercely in Canada. It could well have been a demonstration that the two Provinces could work effectively together:

As a lover of this country, and as one who has not abandoned the hope of seeing people of Canada working out their destiny with one heart and one will, I had hailed their appointment.

But, McGee added, it had been secretly strangled by "a devised scheme" and "a plot."

John A. MacDonald instantly rose in anger, taking it as a direct charge against his personal honour:

I say it is as false as hell!

And then MacDonald made his own counter charge against McGee:

He is carrying out in this country the disloyalty he had displayed in

Ireland. He plotted there to deprive Her Majesty of a Crown. He makes a dastardly attempt here to deprive her representative of his character.

The clamour became an uproar, as the Speaker's gavel hammered in vain to subdue the noise, the shouting and the angry insults. But finally through the pandemonium the House adjourned to let the tempers cool off outside.

Smooth protocol continued. On Thursday, August 5, Sir Edmund Head approached Alexander Galt to form a Government. As expected, Galt declined. On Friday, Head called MacDonald and Cartier back. But this time they came back with their names reversed, and accepted as the Cartier-MacDonald Government. Then they announced that Galt had joined them.

There was no other word but mummery to describe the ceremonials that followed. Each Minister punctiliously assumed a different portfolio from the one he held before. This was done in order to invoke the seventh clause of the recent Independence of Parliament Act, which provided that if a Minister should resign one office and within one month assume another office, he was not obliged to vacate his seat and submit to a by-election. So by stretching this special law to assume a grotesque shape, it was used to cover this wholesale shift and to avoid the legal requirement of by-elections.

At fifteen minutes before midnight of Friday, each of the Ministers of the Cartier-MacDonald Cabinet was, with the solemn formality of the words of office, sworn in by the Governor General faithfully to fulfil his duties. Then, at fifteen minutes after the same midnight, in order to bestow upon it the sham of two days in office, all again gathered before the compliant Governor General, and as each resigned he took a fresh oath of office reinstalling him in his original portfolio.

"So the old set is back," McGee mocked, "like the pupils in a country town, instructed by their dancing master. Grand right and left, turn corners and back to places."

That, briefly, was the notorious Double Shuffle. Some politicians thought it was "very clever" and ingenious. But morally, it was a trick. Demeaning as it was, however, it brought on through reaction some worthwhile developments.

George Brown, for example, had shown a new side to himself. He was apt to be rash and undiscerning, but he was not the intransigent, impossible person that some of his extravagant editorials in the *Globe* depicted him to be. There was evidence now that he was ready to collaborate. Indeed, Brown and Dorion had laid out a rough basis for collaboration. During that last week-end of July 1858, Dorion had conceded that Lower Canada could grant Representation by Population, provided Brown recognized that Lower Canada should obtain Constitutional protection for its language, religion and laws. This was one of the seeds of Confederation. Beyond that, Brown was even disposed to explore some solution for Catholic schooling in Upper Canada, and was willing to investigate a suggestion, which McGee had made on June 23, that a system might be devised by adapting some of the practises from Ireland's national schools.

Another plain result of the Double Shuffle was that D'Arcy McGee was now in a working alliance with George Brown. Shocked by that, George Clerk openly condemned McGee in his *True Witness*. Yet this break between Clerk and McGee had been coming for a few months. In June of 1858 McGee had written a private letter to James Sadlier in Montreal:

> As to Mr. Clerk, you may be assured it would give me the greatest pain to have to say one word in public against the *True Witness*. I believe poor Clerk, for whose sickness I am sincerely sorry, would, if left to himself, not choose to comment on details of policy on which he cannot have exact information.

The Parliamentary Session of 1858 was prorogued on August 16 with a notable announcement. The Cartier-MacDonald Cabinet declared that the Imperial Government and the Maritime Provinces would be asked to discuss the Federation of British North America with Canada. This was the result of a stipulation which Galt had made before entering the Cartier-MacDonald Cabinet: that his views on the need of a British North American Federation should be adopted. It seems clear enough that neither Cartier nor MacDonald in adhering to Galt's condition had any firm intention at the time to advance it in practical politics. But at least it led to Galt and Cartier going to London that September to discuss it with the Colonial Office. There the delegates were received with all the niceties, and their project was coated with official politeness. But the plan of Confederation had at least reached a new phase. From now on, it would appear and reappear as an item worthy of discussion on a practical agenda. McGee's earlier editorials on Confederation took on a new life, and some people read them for the first time.

The two main elements in Federation were actively pursued by McGee from that time forward. And they went hand in hand: Representation by Population, to let the majority speak as a majority; and Constitutional Guarantees, to safeguard the rights of minorities.

But the question that was agitating the minds of many people, shaping their motives and directing their opinions on Constitutional matters, came much closer to home for McGee. It was the highly contentious issue of Separate Schools.

# 6

## THE SCENT OF MORNING

Every important topic that can arise ought to be viewed by
the light and decided by the requirements of Canadian
nationality.

THE NEW ERA, JANUARY 19, 1858
*Thomas D'Arcy McGee*

But up there on the platform he looked small
And worn with study, exile, intrigue, jail,
Bewildered by the view inside the pale,
The years of hurt and work behind, the strong
Laws of authority, now his to flail
To right or left, defining right and wrong.
*Roy McFadden*

MacDonald and Cartier with their Double Shuffle had been too smart for the public and many citizens reacted. McGee was received as someone new and courageous. Suddenly he found himself in such demand as a speaker that Brown could write in a private letter from Toronto to Luther Holton in Montreal on September 17, 1858:

> McGee is immensely popular. He is received like a prince in every direction.

The people wanted to hear the champion of the Ministers who had been tricked in their absence, and McGee was now high in the ranks of the Liberals. That fall of 1858 there were flags flying, with bands and banquets for him throughout Upper Canada, in London, Hamilton, Toronto and Kingston. Naturally McGee indulged in this pleasant praise, and he did not always stay clear of excess. But generally he took it well, explaining it in his own manner:

> If in the past few months I have attracted some interest, it is partly accidental and partly due to the good sound abusing I received from those on the other side. Any prominence I now have I owe it as much to my enemies as my friends.

He began to hit harder, however, and he aimed his charges with temerity right at the top:

> The present Government is a government of corruption. Their faith is in corruption. Their hope is in corruption. Their creed is in corruption. They endeavour to corrupt every class in the country—every power in the country, the executive, the judicial and the popular power.
> And they draw into partnership a corrupt Governor General.

This national acclaim made McGee envisage his work on a larger scale. His quality of creative and passionate imagination, which moved others so deeply, had its weakness for him. It induced him to overreach; sometimes his wit was too biting, and his most withering attacks were unrestrained. Then the excitement led him on to overlook the limits of his own capacity, and to neglect his own private interests.

His rapid rise to prominence in his first Session of Parliament in 1858 left him with very little time for his own newspaper, *The New Era*. Michael Hickey, to whom he had entrusted the editorial duties early in 1858, had differed from McGee in supporting Ottawa as Canada's capital against McGee's preference for Montreal. Since it was not paying its way, McGee announced on May 1, 1858, that Parliamentary work compelled him "reluctantly to suspend publication of *The New Era* until further notice." As it turned out, though he retained the interests and the habits of a journalist and was soon to make other newspaper connections, that issue of May 1 was the last of *The New Era*.

McGee's aim was to conciliate the Catholics and Protestants of Upper Canada, and his own activities had brought him into an alliance with George Brown and the Clear Grits, who were anathema to the French and the Catholics. To reconcile his aim with his activities was far from easy, as McGee realized in explaining his dual role in Parliament:

First, an elected person is expected by his constituents to represent them as their own member on every question.

But he also has a duty to his co-religionist at large to represent them on certain great questions as fully as his own constituents.

Nor did his difficulty stop there, as he observed:

It does not help the cause when you know you have been industriously misrepresented beforehand as a fire-brand and an adventurer.

In Lower Canada, for every Irish Catholic there were five French Catholics. Viewing the situation from his seat in Parliament at Toronto, McGee felt he already had reliable friends in Montreal, and sensed the need to work closely with some similar group in Upper Canada. To further this, McGee met with a committee in June 1858 in order to found a new Catholic newspaper in Toronto. Alderman John O'Donohue and Thomas Devine were two of its leading members, and they arranged to buy up the subscription lists and the types of the *Catholic Citizen* a small newspaper which had been too inclined to use abuse for argument.

The new journal was started in Toronto as the *Canadian Freeman*. As chairman of the committee, McGee prepared its prospectus and induced James Moylan, who was then teaching in Guelph and known to McGee from their meetings in Washington and at the Buffalo Convention, to become its first editor. Some funds were raised, and Moylan brought Mallon in as a partner in the venture. Later, however, McGee helped Moylan to raise money to buy out Mallon's interests, and then when Hillyard Cameron as the Orange Grand Master sued the *Freeman* for libel, McGee helped in raising funds for the defence. "It was certainly our doing," wrote McGee to O'Donohue in November 1858, asking for further aid to the *Freeman,* "that they ever took it up."

This new venture distracted McGee's attention somewhat from his own constituency of Montreal, where there were two men working against him. The first man, Bernard Devlin, was a lawyer, an aspiring politician and ambitious. Though he had been one of McGee's prominent backers from the start, he was now drawing sections of McGee's support towards himself to strengthen his own personal political future. Devlin would have to be reckoned with in future electoral contests. On another level, and working against McGee with a different set of motives, was George Clerk of the *True Witness.* He was an intense person, guided by the inflexible passions of religion and logic. To do him justice, it must be recognized that he moved with consistency in his world of theory. "The question of questions," as he phrased it, "was the question of Catholic Separate Schools with its evil shadow of State Schoolism." All else in his politics seemed to flow from that basic proposition.

McGee, on the other hand, was equally intense, but he was a practitioner. He took his instructions from religion and experience, with the principles of one immersed in time, and the lessons of the other as lived out by men. What counted for McGee was to accomplish something and leave perfection for his dreams, as sustenance for inspiration. How to get on with men, to make allowance for their prejudices, to trim down their exaggerations and to overlook their passions as transitory, such was the method he followed in politics. The right of Catholic parents to send their children to Catholic schools was held just as firmly by McGee as by Clerk. But as to how it could be furthered through the shifts of practical politics, there they differed.

What Clerk was doing showed in his diary:

> 1858, September 14, Tuesday: Bernard Devlin seems to be strongly hostile to McGee. An open quarrel must come in time in which the *True Witness* will find itself involved.
>
> September 19: Had interview with Bishop Bourget about policy to be adopted in the School Question.
>
> September 28: Had an interview with Bishop Farrell of Hamilton and Bishop de Charbonnel of Toronto at Seminary. McGee called and

spent the evening, and I had a long talk with him on Catholic policy
and the Brown alliance. He spoke fair and may, I hope, act up to
his professions.

September 30: Had a long interview with the Bishops of Toronto
and Hamilton. Nothing done on the School question. *True Witness*
placed under the sole surveillance of Bishop Bourget of Montreal.
Its affairs, prospects and policy have been the subject of discussion.

This led to the central problem of politics, to Representation by Population and to George Brown. And all were involved by the next major
political event to occur. A group of Liberals, in which McGee was active,

GEORGE
BROWN

arranged to hold a banquet on November 4, 1858 in honour of George
Brown, right in the heart of Montreal. And that evening McGee introduced Brown with pleasant, casual tact and a refreshing touch of
candour:

Gentlemen: All of you have heard of Mr. George Brown as the
most active politician of the Upper Province.

He is by nation a Scotchman and by religion a Presbyterian. He
has long been settled in Canada, and was a zealous Reformer of
the Baldwin and Hincks School. He is a man, I should suppose, who

when struck is likely to strike back, who if hard names are called returns them in kind; which is no doubt an error in a statesman.

I observed him closely throughout the long Session of 1858, and Mr. Brown was the man best suited in all that House to be entrusted with the formation of a new Government. When Mr. Brown was called in, whom did he first send for? Mr. Dorion and Mr. Sandfield MacDonald, two men of the religion it was said he was impatient to oppress. Was that the act of a bigot? His eleven colleagues in his Cabinet were eleven guarantees that he would have given us a just, fair and liberal government.

Whatever the fault of Mr. Brown in Opposition, whatever his assaults upon us in past controversies, I do say that I believe when he was called to govern this country, he felt that a high place demanded a high disregard of old feuds and old feelings, and he rose like a statesman to the level of the occasion. It is a national misfortune that the Brown-Dorion Administration did not get a fair trial.

Clerk of the *True Witness* was shocked by McGee's participation in the organisation and the surprising success of Brown's banquet in Montreal; and he denounced McGee in almost the same extreme terms which he normally reserved for Brown:

> We look upon any man as the enemy of Catholic Lower Canada and therefore as our political enemy who gives, in appearance even, the slightest encouragement to the agitation of Representation by Population, or who does not condemn that measure as unjust in principle.
>
> To us of Lower Canada the question is one of life or death. This, in the interests of our religion as well as of Canadian nationality, is the vital question: Equality of Representation or Repeal of the Union. These are our last words.

Clerk meant exactly what he said. He set himself the task of persuading the Catholic hierarchy to bring about the retirement of McGee from public life. Hidden here was an unsuspected anomaly. While Clerk was working to detach the Catholic hierarchy from McGee, Tory journals were naïvely accusing McGee of some secret compact with the Catholic hierarchy of both Lower and Upper Canada to gain complete control of all the Catholic votes in Canada.

McGee was aware of what was going on, and he came to rely more and more on James Moylan in the *Canadian Freeman* of Toronto for an expression of his views. In a letter on November 8, four days after Brown's triumphant banquet in Montreal, McGee wrote to Moylan:

Nor do I think G. E. Clerk would be found a very congenial col-
laborator. Though by no means either small or vicious or selfish,
he is extremely self-willed and very impracticable.

Self-willed, Clerk certainly was; and certain, too, according to his own
lights, that McGee, in working with Brown and Dorion, was undermining
the position of the Catholics in Canada.

In 1859, Clerk's campaign against McGee reached its height, and a
glimpse of what was coming showed in Clerk's diary:

> 1859, February 10, Thursday: James Sadlier furious about an
> article in the *True Witness* on Brown-Dorion policy. Threatens all
> kinds of things, withdraws advertisements etc. Bosh!
>
> Mr. Gillies, *True Witness* publisher, had a stormy interview with
> Sadlier, who gives up our paper. I know my anti Brown policy will
> make me many enemies from the McGee clique.

Clerk brought his troubles to Bishop Bourget of Montreal, and the
Bishop responded by signing a letter in diplomatic, firm terms supporting Clerk. The Bishop then had this letter read from St. Patrick's
pulpit on Sunday, February 20, and its meaning was not lost on the politically allergic congregation:

> The *True Witness* enjoys the confidence of the Bishop of Montreal,
> who wishes to put down all rumours to the contrary. His Lordship
> hopes that private or party views may not endanger the future of
> all prospects of a Catholic journal in Montreal.

The letter had, within its own informed circle, a strong effect. And
Clerk noted one result within a few days:

> February 24, Thursday: To my surprise I had a visit at my office
> from McGee who evidently thinks it prudent to slacken hostilities
> for the present and to repudiate the extravagance of Sadlier.

When Clerk wrote "to slacken hostilities for the present," he was, as
he invariably showed himself to be, an accurate observer. For the combat was soon renewed. On March 11 the *True Witness* published an
abusive anonymous letter attacking McGee. This was followed by a similar second letter in April openly signed by Bernard Devlin and acknowl-
edging that he was the author of both. From then on, in every issue of
the *True Witness* and with mounting vigour, Clerk condemned both Mc-
Gee and Moylan of the *Canadian Freeman*.

McGee replied by "Four Letters to a Friend," which were published
in the *Canadian Freeman* through June and July, explaining his views

on the relations of the Irish Catholics with the French-Canadian Catholics, the Protestants and the political parties. Moylan, however, returned Clerk's fire directly, and their exchange became bitter. The climax came in August.

Clerk publicly stated that the *Canadian Freeman* was "about to be rejected by every Bishop in Canada." And this proved to be almost true. But on August 5, Moylan was able to show that he retained the support of the Bishop of Toronto. Four days later, McGee made a call on the auxiliary Bishop of Montreal in an effort to restore peace. But there was none to be had.

On August 11, 1859, Vicar General J. M. Bruyère of the diocese of Toronto released a letter to the press in Upper Canada. It was an obvious defence of McGee against the sustained attacks from the *True Witness*. Widely noted was this important part of the letter:

> I state what I know to be a fact when I say that the Catholics of Upper Canada have never appealed in vain to the Junior Member for Montreal for any service he could render them in his capacity of member of the Canadian Parliament. Mr. McGee employed his leisure moments in giving lectures for charitable purposes and on behalf of religious education.
>
> The people of Upper Canada keep in grateful remembrance the great and signal services they have received at the hands of this much maligned and much persecuted gentleman.
>
> I will add. To Mr. McGee we are indebted, in a great measure, for the spirit of forbearance and liberality which has succeeded the bigotry and fanaticism which, but a few years since, raged with fury in Upper Canada.
>
> Thanks to his skilful tactics the portion of the press formerly more hostile to us has assumed a more moderate and conciliatory tone.

This was published on Thursday in Toronto. In Montreal, two days later, on Saturday, August 13, the following "Declaration of His Lordship the Bishop of Montreal" was signed, and on the next day, Sunday, it was read from the pulpits of St. Patrick's, St. Ann's and St. Bridget's, the three Irish Catholic parishes in Montreal:

> The Episcopacy approves of the condemnation by the *True Witness* of those Committees by means of which certain politicians would impose on us Representation by Population in our present political and social condition.
>
> It is with the formal consent of the Bishops that the *True Witness* maintains unflinchingly the thesis of Separate Schools. It is with the

most ardent good wishes of the Episcopate that the *True Witness* so vigorously condemns the conduct of those politicians, whosoever they may be, who through imprudence or malice foment prejudices of race.

We think we have been explicit enough in these counsels to be understood by all of you. If our frank declaration should shock any one, we should be grieved.

On the following Friday the *True Witness* gave Bishop Bourget's "Declaration" special prominence and devoted its leading editorial to it. After drawing attention to the need which Bishop Bourget felt "to rectify matters for the second time within a few months," the editorial pointed out that the real questions in the minds of the Bishops were Catholic Separate Schools as opposed to State Schoolism, religious marriages and divorce, Representation by Population, Orangeism and secret societies.

When Clerk assumed the role of interpreting "the minds of the Bishops," he was accurate enough in attributing this list of general questions as "real" to them. But he went further, and became ambiguous. Without making it clear whether he was still referring to this list of general questions or to the particular letter of Bishop Bourget read from the Montreal pulpits the previous Sunday, Clerk added that "this has received the adhesion" of Bishop Baillargeon of Quebec, Bishop Prince of St. Hyacinthe, Bishop Guigues of Bytown, Bishop de Charbonnel of Toronto, Bishop Cooke of Three Rivers, Bishop Pinsoneault of Sandwich, Bishop Horan of Kingston, Bishop Farrell of Hamilton and Msgr. La Rocque, the Coadjutor of Montreal.

A public uproar followed. Politically, it turned strangely to McGee's advantage. Nearly all the newspapers of Upper Canada, and even McGee's pronounced enemies like the Tory *Colonist* and the *Leader,* joined forces with the *Globe,* and what the *True Witness* had officiously declared was condemned as unwarranted clerical interference in politics.

In private, the reactions were quick, sharp and strong. Some of the Bishops wanted to make it perfectly clear that the general issues they adhered to were entirely distinct from Bishop Bourget's specific letter which was unmistakably directed against McGee, and that they did not approve of such a letter. But most of the Bishops (including Bishops Farrell and Pinsoneault) did support Bishop Bourget.

D'Arcy McGee acted obliquely. He wrote a detailed commentary taking up Bishop Bourget's letter, point by point, and dealing with each in categorical terms. By a private letter of September 15 he forwarded it to his friend Alderman John O'Donohue in Toronto, asking him to see to it that it reached the hands of Bishop de Charbonnel of Toronto through his Vicar General, Father Bruyère. This resulted in a sympathetic exchange of letters between Bishop de Charbonnel and McGee. Then James Moylan of the *Canadian Freeman* arranged to tender a public banquet to McGee on September 30 in Toronto.

Father Bruyère responded favourably to D'Arcy McGee's commentary on Bishop Bourget's letter, and made several suggestions and proposed revisions, having in mind that these would form a basis for part of McGee's address at the approaching banquet. In fact, the dinner for McGee was well attended, and many supporting messages were read. Most notable of all, however, was a letter received and read from Bishop de Charbonnel of Toronto:

> I beg to thank the Committee for the kind invitation to the banquet in honour of Thomas D'Arcy McGee Esq. M.P.P., and to be excused for not attending it.
>
> Were my presence necessary to protest against certain misrepresentations about Mr. McGee, I would not hesitate to make an exception to my habit of not visiting a meeting of this kind. But his views, speeches and votes on education, voluntaryism and even Representation by Population are so well known to us that the reverend clergymen of Toronto will have the pleasure to state at the banquet that all acknowledge in Mr. McGee a true, practical friend of the principles and institutions of the Church.

Clerk's comment in his diary was subdued and objective:

> 1859, September 30, Friday: Report of McGee banquet at Toronto. A letter from Bishop de Charbonnel of Toronto published in the *Globe* gives an unqualified approval to McGee. The breach in the Hierarchy is hardening.

D'Arcy McGee kept very busy. In the eleven years he lived in Canada none of his days could be called uncrowded. But if there was any period when leisure brought its benefits, it was in those first four years up to the time of the outbreak of the American Civil War in 1861. In his private studies he was remarkably assiduous.

On November 3, 1858, he registered at McGill University as a student in the Faculty of Law. It was then located in a building at the northeast corner of Dorchester and Union streets, with John J. C. Abbott as its Dean; and the entry may still be read in William Cragg Bayne's register of new law students at McGill:

Thomas D'Arcy McGee;
Age 33; Carlingford, Ireland;
Montreal; Roman Catholic

McGee was fulfilling a dream long deferred. The dark-eyed boy who remembered every lesson from his mother and his hedge schoolmaster, and had worked his own way up from there by reading everything within his reach, was at last to become at the age of thirty-six a Bachelor of Civil Law. He was selected to give the valedictory address for the graduating class. But on that brilliant morning in May of 1861, as the students and their friends gathered under the elms of McGill, it had to be announced:

Parliamentary duties at Quebec City require Thomas D'Arcy McGee to receive his degree *in absentia*.

Constantly underlying his daily work was the lure of poetry and history. This was his refreshment, and it never failed to revive his buoyancy. In December 1858, McGee published his *Canadian Ballads and Occasional Verses*. As a book it gained some popularity, but he was seeking more than that. McGee, in writing of Columbus, Jacques Cartier, Cabot, Champlain and Marguerite Bourgeoys, was trying within his limits to strengthen a national spirit in Canada, somewhat in the way that in his earlier days and with more spontaneity, he, Davis, Duffy and Mangan had used their *Nation* to foster a genuine Irish pride through their ballads, old tales and historic legends.

Somehow McGee also found the time, working mostly in the Parliamentary Library with the encouragement of Librarian Alpheus Todd, to write his *Popular History of Ireland*. Finally in 1863, after many interruptions, McGee had his work published in two volumes by James Sadlier in Montreal, New York and Boston.

As stirring historical narrative, it was his best work. And his prose was never more moving than in its early pages, in that brief and beautiful passage, for example, when he followed "the new preacher, Patrick," up the hill of Tara, and witnessed the white fire burning through the grey mist as that ardent Christian upheld "the cause of all the souls who might inhabit this well wooded and watered isle at the western ends of the earth"; or, some ninety pages later, in the tragic ending of the battle of Clontarf when, towards sunset, as the men of Ireland lay dead upon their field of victory and the enemy were retreating to their ships, Brodar, the Viking, perceiving the lone tent of Brian unguarded, and the aged Irish king on his knees before a crucifix, rushed in, cut him down with a single blow and continued on his flight.

Scenes such as those followed one another, sombre or serene, until the close of the first volume with its dramatic setting from the perilous days of Queen Elizabeth when the last of the fierce Celtic chiefs was beheaded:

> High spiked upon the towers of the Castle, that proud head re-mained and rotted; the body, wrapped in a Kerns saffron shirt, was interred where he fell, a spot familiar to all the inhabitants of the Antrim glens as the grave of Shane O'Neil.

McGee's judgments on complex historic characters were keen and balanced, well illustrated by his stern portrait of the warring genius of Oliver Cromwell, or his estimates of Patrick Sarsfield with his sharp sword, or of Dean Swift with his sharper sword of satire which refreshed the free spirit of Ireland. Approaching his own times, as McGee com-mented on the Union of Great Britain and Ireland in 1801, his pen began to cut like a diamond:

> Had the Union, vile as were the means by which it was accomplished, proved to the real benefit of the country—had equal civil and reli-gious rights been freely and at once extended to the people of the lesser kingdom—there is no reason to doubt that the measure would have become popular in time. But the Union was never utilized for Ireland. It proved in reality what Samuel Johnson had predicted, when spoken of in his day: "Do not unite with us, sir," said the gruff old moralist to an Irish acquaintance. "It would be the union of the shark with his prey."

Near the end, McGee showed the feeling of an artist coming home, as he completed a short study of Irish eloquence, discussing the merits of Burke, Sheridan, Grattan, Flood, Curran, Sheil and Plunkett, with a final recognition of the master:

> Daniel O'Connell never had a model, and never had an imitator who rose above mimicry.

D'Arcy McGee's *Popular History of Ireland* was so well received that with the support of his Irish literary friends, the poets Samuel Ferguson and Denis Florence McCarthy, McGee was elected as a member of the Royal Irish Academy. As a popular history, it would stand the test of time. Twenty-five years after McGee's death it would still be in use as a text in the intermediate schools of Ireland. Today its eight hundred pages of close print in their deep green buckram covers lie in many libraries, unopened, waiting for some quiet reader seeking the fragrance of a day that is gone.

# 7

## UNCERTAIN HORIZON

I call it a northern nation. For such it must become, if all of us do our duty to the last.

*Thomas D'Arcy McGee*

Where there is no vision the people perish.

PROVERBS XXIX: 18

The year 1860 opened for D'Arcy McGee with an ugly incident which foreshadowed what would come with the close of summer. The Literary Club of Bradford in Upper Canada had invited McGee to lecture at its meeting in early January and had announced his subject as "The Historical Relations between Ireland and Scotland." It promised to be a rather scholarly evening, but it never took place.

When McGee arrived in Bradford he was met by the Orangemen of Simcoe County, known as "the Lambs" led by Thomas Ferguson, a member of Parliament. Armed with revolvers, they prevented McGee from speaking and eventually made him leave town.

The Toronto *Globe* in its issue of January 18 came to McGee's support and attacked the Orange Order. Then the criticism grew to such a point that the outrage by the Lambs in Bradford was condemned by the neighbouring Orange Lodge of Guelph. The incident seemed to close on that note. But the aggressive mood of those Orangemen of Simcoe County was merely a presage of the general crisis in September.

It was part of the political instability of those times that an arrangement had to be made to move the capital city periodically from one part of Canada to another. Since McGee's election in December 1857, Parliament had met in Toronto, where McGee had participated in the Sessions of 1858 and 1859. In 1860, according to plan, Parliament was shifted to Quebec City, where it would be convoked from then on every year until 1866, when Ottawa would be ready to receive it as the newly chosen capital of Canada. So Parliament opened on February 28, 1860, in Quebec City.

The Session had no sooner opened than George Brown made a blunder. The Speech from the Throne had been unexciting. There was a general atmosphere of torpor, and the Cartier-MacDonald Ministry appeared to be tired. Whatever energy it displayed was just enough to stay in office. John A. MacDonald seemed like a study of nerveless inactivity, playing out his time for the opportunity to divide and weaken the Opposition. Some spirit of renewal was needed. George Brown in the Opposition instinctively sensed this. But his impulse led him into the error of overlooking that the members of the Opposition were more apt to disagree than to agree among themselves. While John A. MacDonald had the restraint to wait and aggravate their differences, Brown could not wait to act.

Without consulting his colleagues in the Opposition, Brown made his move. He promptly gave notice that he would bring forward for debate his program of Constitutional Reform recently elaborated at the Toronto Reform Convention of December 1859. It was no secret that these Constitutional Resolutions were largely Brown's own work, which, because of the serious differences still prevailing among the Clear Grits, Brown had practically imposed on the Convention.

Earlier, in October 1859, the Opposition members from Lower Canada had met in Montreal. There a series of resolutions drawn up by D'Arcy McGee had been released as a platform for their Liberal Party, signed by Dorion, McGee, Lewis T. Drummond and L. A. Dessaules. They declared that a Federal Union of the two Canadas was "the true, statesmanlike solution." But what form that Federal Government would take had been purposely left vague in order to conceal their differences. Yet this much was said:

> The functions of such a Federal Government would be restricted to a few easily defined subjects of common or national concern, and supreme jurisdiction in all other matters would be left to the Provinces, with every guarantee for the integrity of their respective institutions.

Later on, D'Arcy McGee would change his view on where the residue of legislative power should reside, and he would take the firm stand that the undefined residue of power should be vested in a strong Federal Government. But in these years before the American Civil War, McGee shared the *Rouge* view of Dorion that each Province should control all powers except those specifically allocated elsewhere.

These two sets of Constitutional Resolutions from the Opposition, the first proposed from Montreal in October and the second from Toronto in December, were brave attempts to bring the Opposition closer together. But they revealed as many differences as they concealed.

Leading up to the Session of 1860, Brown had been working with a peculiar intensity. The strain began to tell. His nerves were frayed, and he became querulous and so imperious that most of his followers preferred to stay away from him, which merely fostered Brown's illusion that his dissenters had been put down. Under the strain Brown fell ill,

which made him miss the first week of the Session. His Resolutions were
accordingly delayed, and the delay was costly. All those in the Opposition
who disagreed with Brown and had not been consulted now had the
opportunity to grumble, and most of their criticism was so open that it
reached the ears of John A. MacDonald. In such a situation no one could
be more patient and say less than John A., particularly on a Constitutional question. On the other hand, Sandfield MacDonald, who was also
in the Opposition, became more difficult than ever. He awkwardly refused to co-operate with Brown, while the Old Reformers of Upper Canada openly expressed their resentment of Brown's domination.

To all this, Brown was insensitive. In the opinion of many Clear Grits,
all talk of Federation between Upper and Lower Canada was a sham.
They saw the choice under the Union of the two Canadas as nothing
else than Representation by Population within the Union, or Dissolution
of the Union pure and simple.

Brown, as he recovered his strength, tried to subdue the emphasis
on Representation by Population, because he had come to realize how
impossible it was as a practical political measure in Lower Canada. He
was advocating instead a form of Federal Union of the two Canadas,
which also indicated that the path was open for other suggestions of
broader scope. Here, however, many of his supporters could not follow
him.

Michael Foley was the first man among the Opposition to show his
exasperation; he openly disagreed with Brown and broke away from him.
Skeffington Connor then sided with Foley. "The Grits are broken as a
party," quietly noted John A. MacDonald.

Finally on April 30, two full months after the opening of the 1860
Session, Brown moved to dissolve the Union and to federate the two
Canadas. He added that while he was not opposed to a wider federation
with other British colonies in North America, he thought it was premature. What he now urged was that Upper Canada should control its
own local affairs and Lower Canada should do the same; and between
them a joint authority could be set up to look after what was common
to both of them, with its powers loosely described but strictly limited.

Brown delivered a massive address in Parliament which lasted more
than four hours. But it was ineffectual. Oliver Mowat, William Mc-
Dougall and then Dorion endorsed Brown's proposal in general terms,
but each one resorted to his own generalities in an attempt to conceal
his special differences with Brown. Sandfield MacDonald, on the other
hand, merely retreated to his tired theme of the Double Majority.

Through all this turgid talk, the Cabinet of George Etienne Cartier and John A. MacDonald sat there in silence, while the divisions among the Opposition widened with each speaker.

It was rapidly becoming a dangerous debate for the future of Canada. To mention Dissolution of the Union in any form was to open the way to Dissolution "pure and simple," and for the easy-going that was the downhill road to American Annexation "pure and simple." In that discouraging setting the turn came for D'Arcy McGee to address the House on Brown's premature resolution. He spoke on Wednesday, May 2, 1860, while workmen were still busy in the outmoded building trying to make it over into a workable House of Parliament for Quebec City.

Many of his speeches were for the most part impromptu. As a friend described his method, McGee would make a brief outline without any elaboration, "taking a few notes on his cuff or on some scattered pieces of paper. A short period of reflection sufficed for his most effective efforts."

From the outset McGee made it clear that the views he was about to offer were personal. This seemed to promise more disarray among the Opposition and more satisfaction for the Government. But it soon became apparent that McGee was well prepared and equal to the situation. He opened with a broad, quick survey of the Constitutional documents of the British North American colonies, and then just as quickly reduced the matter to this query:

> The real question is whether we ought to be here. What we are debating now is the tenure of our own existence.

In the preceding hundred years, McGee recalled, there had been no less than five different forms of government. The first change came in 1774 after fourteen years of a military executive. Then after a period of seventeen years as a crown colony, the next change came in 1791, with the creation of two Provinces. This lasted almost fifty years down to 1840. And the next change brought on the fifty regime, the Union of the two Provinces. McGee than made his point:

> We are a growing country and our history shows we outgrow our constitutions.
>
> It is this Act of Union, now in its twentieth year, which we, on this side of the House, propose to subject to the same test of experience, the test of fitness to our present circumstances, which the statesmen of 1840 employed towards the Constitution of 1791, and the statesmen of 1791 applied to the Constitution of 1774.

It was idle to pretend, McGee continued, that the Imperial Government would never permit a dissolution of the Act of Union of 1840. New Brunswick and Nova Scotia had formerly been united; Cape Breton had been separated and reannexed to Nova Scotia, as Labrador had been to Newfoundland; and Upper Canada had been one with Lower Canada until it was separated in 1791, to be reunited a half century later. McGee then dwelt on the rapid action in 1840 which followed Lord Durham's Report:

> The Act of Union was the work of two or three men done in a hurry in two short months.

It was conceived "in the Imperial spirit," and advantage was taken of the temporary agitation and reaction in Canada to force it, all imperfect as it was, into premature operation: "It did not deserve to be called our invaluable Constitution."

McGee presented the extremes, stripped to their essentials. Dissolution of the Union, he stated, "is altogether retrograde." On the other hand, "it is impossible to be in favour of the Union as it was in 1840, because it no longer exists":

> It has been frittered away, year by year, by Imperial legislation and by Provincial legislation, till it now hangs in tatters upon the expanding frame of this colony.

He went on to show that of its sixty-two sections no less than thirty had been repealed within the last ten years:

> But it is not altogether dead, though dreadfully mutilated. There is still a little life left; and the Administration of the day draws hope from it with desperate fidelity. It lies in its twelfth section which decrees an equality of representation independent of population.

McGee was speaking with frankness:

> That equality clause was introduced avowedly into the Act for the purpose of "swamping the French."
> But that purpose has been defeated. And I rejoice that it has been defeated. It was a deliberate conspiracy against the rights of one set of people, flagitious in the conception, and wholly indefensible in the enactment.

And then, with equal suddenness, he turned the question, and added:

> Why then should it be maintained and enforced now against another set?

In a colourful, vivid analysis McGee had described the original spirit of the Act of Union as an injustice against the French Canadians. But now, with the tables turned, he put the question:

Was the same unjust spirit to continue so that the smaller population of Lower Canada could dominate the future of the larger population of Upper Canada?

McGee had placed himself in the delicate position of balancing one passionate view against another, and now had to seek a way out. He adopted the direct method and spoke his own mind:

We are all free companions on this side of the House, and each of us has some peculiar view of his own which he will express, just as I have now risen to do.

McGee candidly added that he would have preferred to see Mr. Brown's Resolution proposed in a modified form. But on the whole, when it said that the Act of Union had failed to answer the designs of its projectors, he was obliged to concur and recognize the failure.

Yet the real question remained: What was the remedy for the future? McGee knew he was on dangerous ground where the Opposition had failed to find any firm footing in common. But since Brown had entered upon it, McGee felt there was no way out but to follow and make the best of it with his own views:

Are we of Lower Canada to rule our fellow subjects of Upper Canada on the pagan principle of *lex talionis?* Or rather on the Christian principle "of doing unto others as we would be done by"? I do not say that we should place ourselves or our institutions, differing so widely as we do from Upper Canadians, at their mercy. I mean nothing of the kind. I have never entertained any such idea.

But a remedy could be found by Upper Canada for her wrongs, McGee contended, with the very recognition of ample safeguards for the rights of Lower Canada:

Now my humble view, which I offer to the House, for what it is worth, is that the remedy is a bold application of the Federal principle. I am prepared to apply that remedy to our position with the sanction of the people of both sections of the Province, and not otherwise.

But the best and most desirable thing is the Federal Union of all the North American colonies.

Such a broad Federal Union, McGee said, was desirable commercially; but not as a mere commercial union, such as the German *Zollverein*, for without the superintendence of some central political power, it would not give sufficient security for the interests of all members of the confederacy. The need, McGee said, was plain and urgent:

> Such a Union is necessary for our system, unless we are to look forward to Annexation to the United States.

This for McGee was no time to be downhearted; the obstacles in the way towards Federal Union of British North America were far from insuperable:

> If Mr. Galt had put his resolutions to a vote in 1858, I should have felt it my duty to vote with him.

It was true, McGee admitted, that the New England States averaged thirty inhabitants to the square mile, whereas Canada averaged but seven, and New Brunswick and Nova Scotia, taken together, but eleven:

> At this moment each of these colonies is much more profitable to the United States than to Canada. We have reciprocity with strangers, but none with our fellow subjects.

The choice was clear. The alternative to Federal Union, McGee repeated, was Annexation to the United States:

> We have already advanced too far to halt in our march towards nationality. The law of our youth is growth, the law of our growth is progress.
> Nova Scotia is ripe for a general federation. New Brunswick is not actively adverse to it. The political interest below Quebec will be in its favour. And the commercial interest of England is well disposed towards it.
> The obstacles in our way are not greater than have been overcome by others. We have not a tithe of the difficulties to overcome which the fathers of the Swiss, Dutch and American Confederacies overcame.

D'Arcy McGee had spoken for barely half an hour. As usual, his attitude was quiet, and some observers said that except for a slight swaying and tension of his whole frame, he scarcely changed his stance throughout. Occasionally he would place his right finger on the other palm to mark a point, and then let both hands fall by his sides. How he imparted his enthusiasm to his audience was not easy to describe; much of the fascination came from his eyes and his voice, but mostly from a rare felicity of phrase.

He was now reaching the end, and he raised his hand as he stressed that the way through the difficulties was to show vitality. His conclusion was a vision of magnificence:

> I look to the future of my adopted country with hope though not without anxiety.
>
> I see in the not remote distance, one great nationality, bound, like the shield of Achilles, by the blue rim of ocean.
>
> I see it quartered into many communities, each disposing of its internal affairs, but all bound together by free institutions, free intercourse, free commerce.
>
> I see within the round of that shield, the peaks of the Western mountains and the crests of the Eastern waves.
>
> The winding Assinaboine, the five-fold lakes, the St. Lawrence, the Ottawa, the Saguenay, the St. John, the Basin of Minas, by all these flowing waters, in all the valleys they fertilize, in all the cities they visit in their courses, I see a generation of industrious, contented, moral men, free in name and in fact—men capable of maintaining, in peace and in war, a Constitution worthy of such a country.

Of all the speeches of D'Arcy McGee, it was his most skilful.

At the time, however, it had little effect. Attention was concentrated on Brown's mistake in insisting upon a debate when the topic could only reveal the divisions within the Opposition. So when the Session of 1860 was prorogued two weeks later, it was evident that the Opposition had lost ground. Later McGee's words would be recalled as one of the best visions of the new nation of the North. But to the hardened politicians and the sceptics of that day, McGee's eloquence merely seemed to contribute to Brown's discomfiture.

On a hot and very humid day in the middle of August 1860, Edward, the Prince of Wales, landed at Quebec City to begin the first royal tour of Canada. Within a month it would reach an unexpected and rabid climax.

Accompanying the twenty-year-old Prince, and directing every step, was the Colonial Secretary, the sagacious Duke of Newcastle. All was smooth and splendid until early in September, when the royal party approached Kingston, the Orange and Tory centre represented by John A. MacDonald.

Here the Orangemen, in their display of loyalism, had erected a special arch of welcome which was prominently bedecked with some rather belligerent insignia of the Orange Order. In Great Britain the Orange Order had been banned for a number of years as a disreputable secret society, but it was not an illegal body in Canada. As the royal steamer floated at anchor off the harbour of Kingston, the Duke heard of the Orange arch and sent word ashore that all Orange emblems must be removed from the civic decorations before the Prince of Wales would land. The Orange officials of Kingston indignantly refused to comply. So their arch remained, idly proclaiming their racial and religious exclusivism, while the Prince and the Duke sailed on to Toronto.

In Toronto the same unblushing game was played again, but with more subtlety. There the Orangemen tried to entice the Prince of Wales to leave St. James Cathedral by the main doors, where Orange emblems were hidden for a sudden display. But the Duke was not outmatched, and he diverted the Prince out through the vestry.

George Brown in the *Globe* roundly condemned the Orange Order for its offensive behaviour. But John A. MacDonald, counting up the Orange votes involved, did no credit to himself in a laborious and lame speech by siding with the Orangemen and condemning the Duke of Newcastle.

D'Arcy McGee was discreet. He suggested that a commission be formed to investigate the charges against the Orangemen. But beyond that he said little. Instead, he wrote to James Moylan in Toronto and wisely advised him to confine himself to moderate comment in the *Canadian Freeman*, and to avoid any exultant tone.

Orangemen went through a turmoil of embarrassment and anger. The publicity they received was bad and widespread, and they were deeply humiliated. In fact, it was a crisis for the Orange Order in Canada, and its claim to propriety was never the same again.

A few days after the visit of the Prince of Wales to Toronto, while passions were still excited, George Brown travelled over to the town of Galt to address a large political meeting of Reformers. While Brown was speaking, an Orange heckler broke in to catch him:

How can you explain having McGee as an ally—a Roman Catholic Irishman?

It was typical of Brown to reply with the fire that he instantly showed:

I would rather a thousand times act with McGee than the dough-faced Protestants that misrepresent Upper Canada.

When McGee heard of it he was prompt to write and thank Brown:

Its boldness was worthy of you and its kindness far more than I deserve.

A short while later, in a private letter of September 27, 1860, Brown confided in Luther Holton:

I hope I have done McGee justice. I intended to do it as handsomely as possible, for indeed he is a noble fellow and deserves a generous return for his many manly acts in favour of myself and friends.

# 8

## SHIFTING SANDS

"O Cormac, Grandson of Conn," said Carbery,
"I desire to know how I shall behave?"

"Not hard to tell," said Cormac.
"If you be too talkative, you will not be heeded,
If you be too silent, you will not be regarded,
If you be too hard, you will be broken,
If you be too feeble, you will be crushed."

THE INSTRUCTIONS OF KING CORMAC
*From the Irish, early ninth century*

The weary and the timid said no.
*Thomas D'Arcy McGee*

A trip to Quebec City in those years could be an adventure. The Grand Trunk train which left Toronto for Montreal and Quebec City for the opening of the Session on March 13, 1861 was crowded with members of Parliament. The engine burned wood and had to refuel with stocks of cordwood at every station. Though the funnel was bell-shaped and protected by screens, showers of sparks and cinders were puffed out with the smoke and floated through the woods or filtered back into the small cars jogging along behind on their light four-wheel trucks. Each car, coupled to another with link and pin, had its own set of hand brakes with a brakeman ready to cope with any emergency that could arise as the train reached its highest speed of twenty-five or even thirty miles an hour.

The chief officers of the railway were also on board and doing their utmost to impress their important political passengers with every illusion of efficiency and luxury. The reason was not hard to find. The Grand Trunk Railway was virtually bankrupt. With a total deficit of thirteen million dollars and its bonds selling at 50 per cent discount, it was currying the favour of the Government as its only hope.

At that time Cabinet Ministers were rather callously permitted to act as Directors of the Grand Trunk; political leaders like Alexander Galt or Luther Holton participated with profit in railway construction; and George Etienne Cartier earned large fees as the Grand Trunk solicitor. The interests of the Grand Trunk Railway were closely involved with the future Constitution of Canada, because it promised the expensive construction of the Intercolonial Railway to the Maritimes and future railroad expansion into the Far West.

D'Arcy McGee, in advocating the Federation of all the colonies, was attracting the attention of the executive officers of the Grand Trunk, who had not overlooked what McGee had written about the railway in the days of his *The New Era:*

Deducting for the many abuses, for all the weakening and corrupting intrigues which accompany the distribution of such large sums of money, the Directors of this great work are doing the business of the country and doing it well, though expensively;

and they were ready to go out of their way to win McGee's favour.

When the train arrived at Lévis, the passengers faced the peril of crossing the St. Lawrence River. That year "the ice had not taken" from Point Lévis to the north shore, so the ice bridge over to Quebec City had not even partially formed. The crossing had to be made amid the strong current and the ice floes in a heavy canoe which was specially built like a reinforced skiff. D'Arcy McGee was in the same canoe as Hope Mackenzie, a frail man, newly elected as a Clear Grit from Sarnia in Upper Canada. Together, through the moving masses of ice, they made a dangerous crossing under the skilled boatmen.

There was no sound but the crushing of the ice, the swish of the water and the thud of the heavy keel as they threaded their way through each opening as it appeared. Finally they reached a dismal shed on the wharf near Champlain market. They were completely drenched and Hope Mackenzie was exhausted. McGee had to hold him in his arms and help him ashore. Numb with cold in their wet clothes, they were quickly packed beneath thick buffalo robes, and their sleigh was driven through the narrow streets of Lower Town to climb up to their hotel.

For some weeks following, Mackenzie's health was so bad that McGee, who was staying with him at the Clarendon House, nursed him each day, before leaving for Parliament and again on his return. This kindness would not be forgotten by Hope nor by his brother Alexander Mackenzie, who followed him to Parliament two years later.

McGee himself was not too well during the first short part of that Session, which he described a week later in a letter from Quebec City to his friend John O'Donohue in Toronto:

Here I have been two thirds of my week in bed, from having ducked under two or three times in crossing the river, this day week. On reaching the Clarendon I was unpacked out of the ice, and have been since trying in vain to send a bad cough a-packing.

However it will be nothing by this day week, I hope and trust. Tomorrow, if my doctor will let me, I am going home.

The second part of the Session was livelier.

John A. MacDonald had the lesson of the Opposition's performance in 1860 before him, and he saw no political advantage in raising the Constitutional issue. Moreover, George Etienne Cartier, on whom he depended so heavily, had said earlier that he was ready to live with the Act of Union, just as it was, for another ten years. George Brown, who was financially harassed, had fallen seriously ill with pleurisy and was absent for the entire 1861 Session, which meant that his front of the Opposition at least was quiet. But the Constitutional issue could not be avoided.

The case for Representation by Population was growing stronger and stronger with each new estimate of the rapid growth of the population in Upper Canada. It seemed clear now from the first forecasts of the Census that the population of Upper Canada would exceed that of Lower Canada by at least a quarter of a million people. The question flared up on the floor of the House a week after the outbreak of Civil War in the United States, and in an offensive way.

On April 17, 1861, speaking from the Opposition benches as a Clear Grit, William McDougall was again stressing the injustice done to Upper Canada without Representation by Population; he was urging the abandonment of Equality of Representation and proposing Confederation as the remedy. Brusquely, he used an inflammable phrase:

Meanwhile Upper Canada is being oppressed by a foreign race.

Every French-Canadian member stiffened in his seat. But McDougall went on, and each phrase became more provocative, until he said:

The Anglo-Saxon race would not rest quiet. They would resort to some other plan.

Anglo-Saxons in Canada had relations of an intimate kind with people south of the border, and then would have no alternative but to look to Washington.

McDougall's impetuous final words were never forgotten. If ever a good case was spoiled by a bad phrase, that was it.

In fact, a reversal had occurred. The Act of Union, which was originally designed as an instrument to wipe out the populous French Canadians as a future majority voice, had become instead a fortress where the French Canadians as a minority sought protection. But it was becoming more difficult to defend each year as the siege increased. Really it was Cartier who had built the power of the *Bleus* within this fortress; and it was mainly because the *Rouges* under Dorion were suspected of submitting to the dominating members of English Protestants that the *Rouges* could never rally much strength.

The method followed by John A. MacDonald to stay in power as a

Government with George Etienne Cartier was simple and effective, if not inspiring. Cartier, in holding the French Canadians together, made up

GEORGE ETIENNE
CARTIER

the largest single bloc in the Conservative-*Bleu* Administration, and MacDonald felt that he had no choice but to yield and adapt himself to it. So he devoted most of his talents to working out coalitions, which meant compromises, intrigues and dodging contentious issues whenever they were too embarrassing, until the right time and tide arose to call an election and ride back to power.

But the outbreak of the American Civil War and the renewed clamour for Representation by Population were forcing John A. MacDonald to face Constitutional Reform as a practical political matter. And yet, at the risk of shaking considerable Conservative support in Upper Canada, MacDonald still appeased Cartier's following in Lower Canada, by repeating his formal stand that he was opposed to Representation by Population. Cartier, for his part, completely condemned Representation by Population both in principle and practise, and the excitement of an oration lasting five hours led him to say:

I care no more for your 250,000 Clear Grits in Upper Canada than so many cod-fish in Gaspé Bay.

In contrast, D'Arcy McGee had discussed the question of Representation by Population openly from the outset. It had earned him the stern opposition of Clerk in the *True Witness*, but McGee was heedless of its political consequences. As early as 1859, McGee had exposed the basis for his position:

> I understand the cry of Upper Canada.
>
> It was the great grievance of Ireland urged by O'Connell when I was a boy. The county of Cork in Ireland had 880,000 inhabitants and six members in the British House of Commons, yet the principality of Wales had some 900,000 inhabitants and was allotted twenty-nine members. Was this justice to Ireland in her Union with England?

McGee studied the Canadian question through the light of his own experience with the Irish question, and drew the parallel. The Act of Union of England and Ireland had been passed in 1800, as the Act of Union of Lower Canada and Upper Canada had been passed in 1840, the one to swamp the Irish, the other to swamp the French. The Irish, like the French, were largely Catholic; and since each faced a dominant Protestant power, the controversial political aspects of population and representation were vital to them for their survival.

Yet there was one remarkable difference. The Irish had practically abandoned their own Gaelic language, and Daniel O'Connell, although he knew no other tongue as a boy, was one of those who led the way, holding it was impractical to speak Gaelic and make a living. The French, on the other hand, as a minority in Canada and a much weaker minority in North America, never abandoned their French language.

McGee also recalled how O'Connell had opposed the Act of Union of Canada when it was passed in 1840 by the British House of Commons. O'Connell had objected that Upper Canadians, who were then outnumbered almost two to three by Lower Canadians, were unjustly being granted equal representation with Lower Canadians. But now that old basis of complaint had disappeared, and was being strongly reversed by the authoritative figures of the Census in 1861. Upper Canadians numbering 1,396,000 now contended that although they paid two thirds of the total taxes, they were being held down by 1,111,000 Lower Canadians to equal representation, with 65 members each in a House of 130 seats.

For McGee it was futile to argue against the facts and the figures, and he expressed it this way:

Property should have its weight. Intelligence should have its weight. But any man who, on this continent and in this age, did not believe that numbers should be the basis was as little to be reasoned with as a man who believed in the philosopher's stone.

The year 1861 was an election year, however, and what really counted was not how to win an argument, but what would win votes.

William McDougall had crassly called the French Canadians "a foreign race," and had added as a Clear Grit that the Anglo-Saxon race, in order to stay on top in Canada, should "look to Washington"; and George Brown's impulsive attempt to fabricate an appearance of unity in the Opposition around the vague political notions of "dual federation" and "joint authority" had failed dismally in the Session of 1860. So the prospects at the polls for MacDonald and Cartier began to look encouraging.

Then it was John A.'s turn to fumble. Two days after McDougall's mistake, MacDonald had just concluded what appeared to be a solid, forceful address, and it was received with applause. Oliver Mowat, who had once been a law student under John A. MacDonald, rose as the critic for the Opposition and charged that MacDonald had falsified the Clear Grits' views on Representation by Population. Whether or not MacDonald had previously been drinking was not recorded, but after a drinking bout he sometimes showed unexpected bursts of temper. In any event, something in Mowat's self-assured manner infuriated John A. MacDonald. The moment the Speaker left the chair, MacDonald strode across the floor directly at Mowat and shouted:

You damned pup, I'll slap your chops!

And the tall, loose-jointed and generally amiable John A. MacDonald, shaking with rage, had to be pulled away from the clever, rotund little Oliver Mowat, who was bristling with indignation behind his thick spectacles.

Since there had to be a general election that year and it was now called for July 1861, many observers felt that John A. MacDonald had lost his touch.

Oliver Mowat energetically sought his revenge. He decided to oppose John A. MacDonald in Kingston and, in fact, got off to an early start, throwing MacDonald back on the defensive in what promised to be a stiff battle.

In Toronto a change of lasting consequence occurred. As it turned out, the election contest of George Brown for the seat of East Toronto affected the political future, not only of Brown, but also, indirectly, of D'Arcy McGee. This effect would only show itself three years later when the course of Canadian politics would take a decisive turn in the Great Coalition. But to appreciate how surprising that turn would then appear, something should be said now about the characteristics of George Brown and D'Arcy McGee and the curious relation that developed between them in the election year of 1861.

Physically no two men could be more unlike than George Brown and D'Arcy McGee. Brown was tall, massive and solid in frame, and imperious, stern and intense in countenance. With his reddish hair, ruddy complexion, strong, blunt nose and prominent jaw, he was always well groomed, if not handsome, he was certainly impressive. D'Arcy McGee, in contrast, was ill-looking as a boy, and as a man ill-dressed. He was short and, what is more remarkable, entirely unconcerned about his lack of height, affecting none of those pert or aggressive stances which small men often adopt. His hair was black, kinky and unruly. He was quick in movement, and his expressions were alert and courteous. Indeed, Mc-Gee was cheerfully unkempt in his appearance and quite unaware of any charm about his homeliness. The eyes of each man were revealing. Brown had solemn, pale blue eyes which openly disclosed his emotions. McGee's eyes were keen and dark and usually merry, because that was his way to throw off sadness.

Both were partisan and combative; and of the two Brown was the more impetuous. Each fought openly and could be readily roused to down an opponent, but neither had that secret disposition to destroy a man. In a political sense neither was a good party man; both were tempted to play a lone hand; and of the two McGee showed more originality. Morally they were earnest men. Brown was the only one who could be called abstemious, though even he was learning, if not to relax, at least to enjoy a glass of wine. Brown became wealthy. McGee never knew what money was. Both were journalists, but McGee's newspapers were short-lived, while Brown with his *Globe* carried on what Goldwin Smith called "a long reign of literary terror."

Brown was an intense Protestant, drawing satisfaction from habits focussed on thrift, sobriety and self-reliance. McGee was an ardent Catholic, bearing scars of persecution and trying to keep free of the three Gaelic signs of a bad man: bitterness, hatred and cowardice.

Judging by what each one stood and spoke for, they should have remained as far apart as when they first met. But whatever the explanation, these two very different men were drawn to each other.

As Brown recovered from his bitterness following upon the Double Shuffle he became more aware how much politics was a game of schemes, and it trained him to see that if he was to adjust himself with any success from journalism to politics, he had to be less dogmatic in his views and less fierce in his expressions. Here, McGee influenced Brown.

From different backgrounds and experiences, Brown shared something of McGee's strong dislike for Orangemen. On November 4, 1859, for example, as Brown's Convention of the Reform Party in Toronto approached, McGee wrote to him from Montreal about the Orangemen. In it McGee renewed his pledge to suppress old animosities between Protestants and Catholics in Upper Canada, and then he cautioned Brown:

> Be sure to accept alliances proposed by Orangemen only if they come in as Reformers, but never as Orangemen.

McGee went on to suggest how the Convention should be confined to Constitutional questions. The advice was not lost on Brown, who, if anything, pushed his Constitutional views too exclusively. And Brown proved that he was politically capable, with the special help of McGee among the Irish Catholics, of defeating the Grand Master of the Orange Association of British North America, John Hillyard Cameron.

Many of his associates were reluctant to speak openly to Brown, particularly after his disappointing performance in the Parliamentary Session of 1860. Brown was weary and discouraged, and in periods of self-examination he would talk to his friends about his plans to retire from politics, but he would rarely receive in return replies that went beyond generalities. McGee, on the other hand, spoke to Brown with a candour that Brown respected. On October 1, 1860, for example, McGee wrote very frankly to Brown:

> Why cannot the *Globe* state its own strong case without using offensive epithets, such as "priestcraft," "popish," "Romish," or "Jesuitical"? They merely irritate and estrange many without any commensurate gain.

But the *Globe* had already pushed things too far. More and more Catholics in Toronto and Upper Canada, who normally would have been lifelong Liberals, were leaving the ranks of the Reform Party because they found the language of the *Globe* intolerable. They were turning to the Conservatives. In fact, for many Irish Catholics, who were instinctively repelled by Toryism as the party of Orangemen and Imperialists, it was a case of being driven into the arms of the Conservatives.

This change was mainly due to the question of Catholic Separate Schools and the influence of the Bishops, particularly Bishop John Lynch, who had recently succeeded Bishop de Charbonnel in Toronto. John A. MacDonald was privately promising Bishop Lynch future legislation for Catholic schools, while the Bishop was repelled by the abusive language of the *Globe,* which he interpreted as the hopeless stand of the Clear Grit Reformers on the matter. McGee described this as coinciding with "the *Bleu* influence from Bishop Bourget in Montreal," and noted in a letter to James Moylan how "Bishop Lynch believed Cartier's promises one hundred per cent."

Moylan, who up to now had always loyally reflected McGee's views in the *Canadian Freeman,* turned away under the influence of Bishop Lynch. As the election approached, and apparently without advising McGee, Moylan attacked Brown. This change was sudden and surprising. For McGee it lacked public justification, because Moylan, in order to accumulate all his reasons for the change, had reached back ten years into episodes that could well have been left buried. Coming at a crucial time when progress was being made, McGee interpreted Moylan's defection as thwarting all that they had worked for in their policy of Conciliation between Protestants and Catholics in Upper Canada. McGee reacted strongly, but did the cause no good by belittling Moylan.

Brown, who had always taken his rugged health and tremendous energy for granted, had driven himself into illness earlier that year and was undergoing experiences new for him: uncertainty and lassitude. His absence throughout the Session of 1861, because of his illness, left him languid and unready for the election called that summer. In fact, he had half made up his mind to retire when he rallied his spirit and announced in June that he would again stand as a candidate. But in doing so he made the mistake of publicly revealing faltering private feelings:

> Were I at liberty to follow my own inclination, most gladly would I now retire from parliamentary life, at least for a season.

Brown rallied, regained some of his fighting spirit and rose above his wavering moods, but his followers were dismayed. Brown went down to defeat by 191 votes. But more than that, his party lost its command of Upper Canada.

John A. MacDonald emerged from his own difficulties in Kingston, managed to defeat Oliver Mowat by a majority of 311 and found that for the first time he had gained a slight edge in Upper Canada. Thirty Conservatives were elected as against twenty-nine Liberals and Clear Grits, with six as Independents; so John A. MacDonald probably had a margin of one seat in Upper Canada.

In Lower Canada the results did nothing to remove the uncertainty. The Conservatives had managed to gain strength in Upper Canada by arranging to leave each of its candidates free to support Representation by Population, if he wished, while John A. MacDonald quietly kept to his formal stand in favour of Equality of Representation. But this ambiguity increased the fear of betrayal among the French Canadians and caused Cartier to lose strength in Lower Canada. His forty-eight *Bleus* were reduced by thirteen losses to thirty-five. On the other hand, his opponents rose from fifteen to twenty-six seats, and the remaining four were classed as Independents. But Dorion had personally gone down to defeat under Cartier in Montreal, and the *Rouges* as a party in Lower Canada remained relatively weak.

Opposition to McGee had been widely talked of and expected in Montreal West. But it was scattered. George Clerk was scandalized by McGee's link with George Brown, and men like Dr. Henry Howard took their stand with Clerk. But Clerk was blamed for fomenting Bishop Bourget's denunciation of McGee's policy, and commanded little political support. Bernard Devlin could find no safe issue to build upon against McGee, whose personal popularity in Montreal and national prominence appeared invincible. Nomination day arrived; no candidate came forward to contest the riding of Montreal West; so D'Arcy McGee was returned unanimously in 1861. McGee's meteoric rise to political success in Canada seemed to be assured.

But all told, it was a confusing result for the country. It offered no promises, and particularly no solution for the unworkable Constitution of Canada. Brown was defeated, and his drive for a remedy would be missed. Dorion, with a touch of dreary detachment, almost of resignation, conceded in his defeat that it was now the turn of men like Sandfield MacDonald and Louis Victor Sicotte to lead the Opposition. They called themselves moderates and were temperamentally ready to live from day to day by avoiding the Constitutional issue. It was up to them, Dorion reasoned, to try their hand and run the risk of having it exposed as empty.

Although D'Arcy McGee had been unanimously re-elected, he was disturbed by the way the sands were shifting. Sandfield MacDonald and Sicotte were not men of his liking. Moylan's withdrawal of his support in the *Canadian Freeman* made McGee feel that Moylan's newspaper could become another *True Witness*. With Cartier weaker, and John A. MacDonald stronger but disposed to temporize, McGee felt that, to achieve anything, he needed new associates and a sure footing.

# 9

## CRISIS AND RELAPSE

To build on hatred nothing; to be just,
Judging of men and nations as they are,
Too strong to share the councils of mistrust.
Peace has her victories, no less than war.
                        *Thomas D'Arcy McGee*

Two reasons why men fall short of justice:
deference to magnates; deference to the mob.
                        *St. Thomas Aquinas*

The most dangerous years for the future of Canada in that era were 1861 and 1862. Danger threatened almost everywhere, both outside and inside the country.

In those years particularly, Canada needs to be understood through the United States; for when the American Civil War broke out in April 1861, it was more than an alarm. D'Arcy McGee expressed the feeling graphically:

> That first shot fired at Fort Sumter was the signal gun of a new epoch for North America, which told the people of Canada more plainly than human speech can express it, to sleep no more except on their arms.

The year before, Lord Lyons, the disturbed British Minister to Washington, had reported privately:

> The Republicans have thrown over the head of their party, Mr. Seward, and chosen for their candidate a Mr. Lincoln, a man almost unknown, a rough westerner, of the lowest origin, and little education. They are very confident of electing him.

The historic topic of the Annexation of Canada to the United States had waned, only to return now with renewed power. On January 25, 1861, the same William Seward, now the incoming Secretary of State, thin, wrinkled and sallow, took the cigar out of his mouth and spoke to his Midwestern audience at St. Paul about the certainty of Annexation:

> I look upon Prince Rupert's Land and Canada, and see how an ingenious people are occupied with bridging rivers and making railroads and telegraphs to develop the great British provinces of the North, by the Great Lakes, the St. Lawrence and the shores of Hudson's Bay, and I am able to say: "It is very well; you are building excellent states to be hereafter admitted into the American Union."

Then the warhawks of the American press, led by the New York *Herald*, pressed it as part of the Manifest Destiny of the United States. The assertion was repeated so often and so casually that to those who were bemused by forecasts it almost seemed to be a foregone fact.

In the opening months of the American Civil War the economic and political balance of the continent was disrupted, and the Canadians stood by, nervous and somewhat fearful, awaiting a quick overpowering victory by the North. An economic depression set in abruptly, but it turned out to be as brief as the war itself was expected to be.

After the defeat of the North at the Battle of Bull Run in July 1861, the prospects of war lengthened, and the South, appearing as possible victors, gained the sympathies and interests of many in England and in British North America. When the North realized that it had to concentrate on production for a long war, artificial demands for Canadian products arose, particularly for food, horses and stocks of supplies. Excited economic activity brought on a perilous prosperity in Canada based on high prices and quick profits, while ship-owners increased their share in the carrying trade, and risked some lucrative blockade running.

Most aristocrats in England wanted to see the North defeated, if only to confirm their feeling that this undisciplined experiment in popular democracy by the United States was bound to find its own doom; and the merchants in cotton were led by their interests to support the South. Indeed, this preference for the South was also strongly held in the British North American colonies, where newspapers usually reflected the opinions of colonial aristocratic and mercantile circles. Tory manufacturers in Canada quietly hoped for the defeat of the North; and as time went on they became more outspoken; if the North was defeated, they calculated, its industrial strength would be undermined and its competition weakened; so they dressed up their own wishes in the uniforms of arguments. George Brown's *Globe* in supporting the North was a notable exception. Most ordinary persons in Canada had started with the simple view that since it was a war against slavery, there was no choice but to side with the North. But political circles were more cynical, and Lord John Russell, the British Foreign Secretary, saw one side as fighting "for empire, the other for power." It seemed that the doors of England, France and Canada were swinging strangely back and forth on the two old hinges of war: ideals and greed.

Among a dwindling minority, D'Arcy McGee held firmly to his support of the North. On July 17 McGee spoke at Ormstown near Châteauguay in Lower Canada:

I look for the preservation of peace between ourselves and the American people, and to the cultivation of a just and generous style of dealing with the national troubles of that people.

All this wretched small talk about the failure of the Republican experiment in the United States ought to be frowned down, whenever it appears, by the Canadian public. It is my hope and belief that the American system may emerge from its first great domestic trial, purified and disciplined for greater usefulness.

It is then, it seems to me, the duty of Canadian statesmen to show them in this day of adversity, that while preferring the system of Constitutional Monarchy for ourselves and our children, we can at the same time be just to the merits of the kindred system founded by their fathers. If we are freemen, so are they. The public calamities which befall one free people can never be matter for exultation by another.

The American system is the product of the highest political experience of modern times, working in the freest field.

Then, two months later, on September 26 in a gas-lit hall at the Agricultural Exhibition in London of Upper Canada, he delivered an impassioned address on Canada's interest in the American Civil War:

Are we to begin over again on this continent the great battle of first principles which in the Christian parts of the earth were thought to have been settled and established long ago?

He saw it as a struggle against "the monstrous doctrine of the innate diversity of the black against the hereditary mastery of the white"; and he concluded with fervour:

As between continental peace and chronic Civil War, as between natural right and oligarchical oppression, as between free intercourse and armed frontiers, as between Negro emancipation and a revival of the slave trade, as between the golden rule and the cotton crop of 1861, as between revealed unity and heartless heresy, as between the North and the South, I rest firmly in the belief that all who are most liberal, most intelligent and most magnanimous are for continental peace, for constitutional arbitrament, for universal if gradual emancipation, for free intercourse, for justice, mercy, civilization and the North.

But the danger that the war would spread increased, as anger was recklessly fanned into hatred by the newspapers in both the United States and England. And to make matters worse, the leaders were, on the one side, the New York *Herald* with the largest circulation of any newspaper in North America, and on the other side, the most influential of all newspapers, the London *Times*. In that charged atmosphere some incident was bound to flare up. And it did.

It was the famous *Trent* Affair, which threw everyone in Canada during the last two months of 1861 into an extreme state of nervous tension with people living from day to day expecting war to break out between the United States and England and the British North American colonies chosen as the natural battleground. The *Trent* Affair arose suddenly.

Captain Charles Wilkes, the grandson of the English agitator John Wilkes, had established a reputation in his own right as an explorer and scientist in the United States Navy. He was now in command of the American screw sloop *San Jacinto* with fifteen guns, blockading the South, and was cruising off Havana, studying international law in his spare time. Suddenly news came to him that the British royal mailship the *Trent* had left Havana, carrying two accredited envoys of the Southern Confederacy to England, Mason and Slidell. On his own initiative, he decided to act.

On November 8 he placed his ship across the Bahama Channel and called upon the *Trent* to heave to. But the *Trent* refused, until Wilkes placed a shell across her bow. Then he boarded her, removed Mason and Slidell and brought them as prisoners of war to Fort Warren in Boston.

Canada heard the startling news before England and anxiously awaited the stand which British naval pride would likely dictate. Meanwhile the American public and indiscreet members of the American Cabinet were acclaiming Wilkes as a hero. When the news reached England, the press became bellicose before the diplomats could speak. The English newspapers demanded the immediate release of Mason and Slidell, with an apology. To this, the New York *Herald* replied with defiance:

> In the event of England, in her folly, declaring war against the United States, the annexation of the British North American possessions, to which Mr. Seward looked forward in his speeches, will unavoidably follow.
>
> We could pour 150,000 troops into Canada in a week, and overrun the Province in three weeks more. In this invasion, we should be aided by a large portion of the inhabitants, two-thirds of whom are in favour of Annexation with the United States.

To the people of Toronto the Tory *Leader* wrote gloomily:

> There now remains scarcely a gleam of hope that peace will be preserved between England and the United States.

With popular feelings running towards the passions that start wars, the British Cabinet met under Lord Palmerston, who unfortunately gave way at first to bluster. Finally the British note was prepared. Toned down by the Prince Consort as one of the last acts before his death, it was delivered by Lord Lyons to Seward in Washington on December 19, and called, in correct, terse phrases, for the release of Mason and Slidell not later than December 26.

In the meantime the British War Office had dispatched fourteen thousand troops to Canada, and the first transports were racing for Rivière du Loup to reach its Grand Trunk railhead before the freeze-up of the St. Lawrence. One ship, the *Persia*, managed to reach Bic nearby, where six hundred soldiers were landed; but there was not time to unload their equipment, as the *Persia* had to leave quickly to escape the ice and return with the other ships to dock at Halifax and Saint John. From there the troops began a slow march behind large sleighs through the heavy snows, skirting the northern limits of Maine by the Madawaska Trail to reach Rivière du Loup.

A wave of military fervour swept across the British North American colonies, and troops of all descriptions, some more picturesque than effective, were mustered from Sarnia to Halifax. D'Arcy McGee's message to the Irish Catholics of Upper Canada was a good illustration of the height which this feeling had reached:

> The Irish throughout Canada will now have a glorious opportunity to show the world that they understand what genuine freedom is and that they know how to defend it.

It so happened that McGee had already been booked for some months to address the New England Society of Montreal at its annual Christmas meeting. He was now faced with a delicate decision, because the Society had been formed for the very purpose of promoting Canadian and American goodwill. McGee deliberated for three days. Finally he decided to withdraw because he felt such a gathering would be "out of season," and in an open letter to the Society he suggested that its members could perform a patriotic service by letting their fellow Americans know that the Irish would stand by Canada in the crisis, and it would be folly for anyone to presume that an American invasion would be welcomed as a liberating force.

Two days before Christmas a meeting was called in Montreal by McGee and others to recruit "the services of an Irish Battalion, or if need be of an Irish Regiment, for the defence of Montreal and the country." The meeting was well received by almost everyone. But not by George Clerk of the *True Witness,* even though he was outspoken in his sympathies for the South. Clerk confided to his diary:

> 1861, December 23: I hear great disgust expressed against McGee who is to preside tonight at the Irish meeting to organize an Irish Brigade. The man is trusted by nobody.

And in a later entry he added:

> It appears that many parties are offended at my freely expressed opinions of the Yankees, and the condition of Catholics in Yankee-land. They cannot be contested.

The Canadian Cabinet felt it was on the brink of war. Alexander Galt met Lincoln, and had "a long" and he carefully added, "a satisfactory private interview." He described Lincoln as "very tall, thin, with marked

ALEXANDER
TILLOCH
GALT

features and a fund of anecdotes. I liked him for his straight-forward, strong common sense." Returning from Washington, he felt assured of Lincoln' sincerity in his personal desire for peace, but he was doubtful about Lincoln's power to control his own Cabinet or the wave of jingoism. A curt retort to the British note was attributed to Seward, but there was no official confirmation, as everyone waited for the expiry of the ultimatum on December 26.

On Christmas Day, Lincoln called his indignant Cabinet together. It was the first big test for this "awkward backwoodsman" in international affairs. He listened to the different views of everyone at the meeting and kept his head. That Christmas he saw through the sadness of things and summed it up, it was said, very simply: "one war at a time."

Clerk recorded the event in his diary in this fashion:

> 1861, December 28: About dark, a telegram from Washington brought the good news that Mason and Slidell are to be given up.
> This will defer the war but it will not avert it.

The prisoners were released; there was no apology; but the incident was declared closed; and the war was, in fact, averted.

As 1862 opened, a feeling of relief eased its way throughout Canada. The *Trent* Affair had acted as a catalyst in bringing the British North American colonies together in the crisis. Now that it was over, there was a reaction. People turned to make the best of the good times brought on by the demands of the Civil War, and returned to their isolated ways and their apathy.

In the Northern United States there was rancour against England, and many talked of taking it out soon on the British colonies in North America. The Imperial War Office became acutely conscious of the military weakness of the threatened colonies, and saw the future union of the colonies as the soldiers' ideal solution. The slow trek of Imperial troops earlier that winter through the snows of the Madawaska Trail, and the humiliating necessity of being obliged a few months later to seek the permission of the United States to ship the military equipment of Imperial soldiers by rail across the State of Maine from Portland to Montreal, stressed the need for an Intercolonial Railway linking the winter seaports of Halifax and Saint John to the terminus of the Grand Trunk line at Rivière du Loup.

Canadian leaders had been startled by the weakness exposed in their isolated sections, and the spirit of a national feeling did not die. With its survival, however, there set in something else. It took hold as a conviction that if war did come to Canada it would come because of bad relations between the United States and England. Over this sphere of relationships Canadians felt that they had no control and if any incident should start a war, it would not be of Canada's making. With such an attitude, the sense of responsibility in Canada for its own defence remained slack.

Sympathy for the Southern cause grew stronger and more active, particularly in Montreal. But D'Arcy McGee's preference for the North, "so freely uttered in the doubtful and discouraging days of 1861," as he explained, remained during the succeeding years:

> Though they were never retracted, they were repeated less frequently and with several modifications. This was a natural consequence of the tone taken by the organs of Northern opinion, especially after the affair of the *Trent*.
>
> I hope that the hearty and friendly feeling of 1861 may be restored without any compromise of self-respect.

As the members were gathering in Quebec City for the opening of another Parliament on March 20, 1862, the atmosphere was still ominous.

Charles J. Brydges, freshly arrived from England as the new general manager of the Grand Trunk, made a point to be personally on board the special train which brought most of the members down from Toronto to Quebec City. Sir Edmund Hornby had been to Canada to push the interests of the Grand Trunk and had recorded his impressions of the venality of politicians:

> Twenty-five thousand pounds would have bought the lot, but I would rather somebody else had the job than myself. I confess I was annoyed at my ill-success and had half a mind to split the money among some dozen members who had been a little indiscreet in their proposals to me.

Nor did anyone have the illusion that the mission of the Grand Trunk officers was to purify politics.

McGee boarded the train with many other members at Point St. Charles in Montreal. It crossed the St. Lawrence River, through the hollow iron tube of Victoria Bridge almost two miles long, to follow the St. Lawrence and Atlantic line towards Portland as far as Richmond; there in that Eastern Township of promising mills, quarries and mines, the train turned northeast to travel ninety-six miles to Lévis; this was then the only railway route from Montreal to Quebec City. It was remarkable because, even counting the time it took for a few stops to shovel snow off the tracks, that trip from Toronto to Quebec City was done in record time of twenty-five and a half hours.

McGee felt the unease of the House as it opened in 1862. The power of the Clear Grits as an effective political force had been badly broken by the defeat of George Brown in the general elections of 1861; and the streak of Calvin's harsh logic in the most rigid of the Clear Grits seemed to McGee to be more uncompromising than ever. It would not yield to another approach. Without the leadership of George Brown, there appeared to be no access to that common ground where practical things could be achieved. Indeed, without Brown, D'Arcy McGee felt he was a stranger among the Clear Grits.

The Government of George Etienne Cartier and John A. MacDonald had survived the elections of 1861 by the expedient of officially abandoning, and in fact avoiding, any commitment to a plan of Federal Union of the Provinces. John A. MacDonald had left his Tory followers free in Upper Canada either to advocate Representation by Population, which many did, or to oppose it, which he did. His own views were now strengthening in another direction. The need for a stronger and closer central power was the obvious lesson which MacDonald took from the American Civil War. But publicly he remained silent. By resorting to pleasantries, he avoided the issue of the Constitution, and somehow he made it appear as if he were reflecting the vague wishes of the bulk of the people who were preoccupied with their own business. Through such a process he had contrived to win a majority for the Tories in Upper Canada. But here the political law of compensation had come into play. As it almost always happened, any gain made in Upper Canada was balanced by a corresponding loss in Lower Canada, and for the same reason.

Lower Canada feared the effects of Representation by Population only less than it did those of Centralization. The phenomenon of the Tories expressing contradictory points of view on the hustings, even when the opinion was qualified as personal and not the policy of the party, had been enough to weaken Cartier's following in Lower Canada. But Dorion, the leader of the *Rouges*, because of his suspect alliance with Brown, had not attracted those who fell away. They went instead to Louis Victor Sicotte, a former *Bleu* who had broken with Cartier and had persisted in opposing Ottawa as the capital. Sicotte gained voters by a combination of negative attitudes: he was known as an enemy of Brown; he was opposed to Representation by Population; and he offered no solution to the Constitutional problem other than a stiff promise to contest any attempt to change the present system of Equality of Representation. Sicotte had argued that Equal Representation was the sacred principle of the Union, and the Union was a compact. This was bad history, but as electioneering opium it had been powerful. So the cautious Sicotte was assessed by many as safer to follow than the ambitious Cartier.

Sandfield MacDonald, with his own pawky way of avoiding the difficulty, had kept to his unworkable expedient of the Double Majority. Under it, the fears of minorities were supposed to be allayed by the promise that no important Government Bill would be passed without obtaining two separate majorities, one from Lower and the other from Upper Canada. He let himself be carried away to this extreme statement in 1862:

> Lower Canadians are determined to resist the demand for Representation by Population. I feel assured that an oppressed people will rather appeal to arms—or join the Americans tomorrow—in preference to yielding.

In reality the last thing the French Canadians would dream of doing would be to join the Americans, but it was another curious twist in the use of Annexation as a threat, in any emergency.

Though they were far apart on most matters, George Clerk of the *True Witness*, who was adamantly opposed to Representation by Population, was one of the few who had supported Sandfield MacDonald's scheme of the Double Majority. But Clerk later withdrew his support to promote his own solution of Dissolution of the Union. That drastic demand to dissolve the Union seemed to be spreading, although those who spoke openly for it were not numerous. Clerk, even while he was advocating the scheme of a Double Majority, was well aware that, hidden within it, were the seeds of separatism. But just as he favoured the separatist stand of the South in the American Civil War, Clerk seemed resigned to separatism in Canada.

For D'Arcy McGee, all this was obsolete contriving, like trying to walk into the future backwards. He warned of the danger that a "compact phalanx" could be formed on each side to tear the country apart by "a war of races." His aim was to explore the problem in the open and to seek a solution which the future "in all its fullness" was bound to bring. The extremists could never be satisfied, he argued, but an expansive solution could attract the moderates on all sides:

> All I have heard or read of statecraft goes to show that when a question has become one of political reality, it can no longer be met by a flat negative, but only with an alternative.

The Act of Union as the Constitution for Canada was out of date, and with the passing of each year was producing more dangerous distortions. It was the dead hand of the past, McGee maintained, attempting to confine the future within rigid limits; and a reform of the Constitution was urgent, if only to respond to the shape of present reality.

He recognized that Representation by Population, as a single measure, could not serve as a total solution. It needed to be fitted in to a larger and more balanced plan. So in March of 1862, McGee made a proposal based on three points. There would be Representation by Population in the more powerful Lower House; the Upper House would be retained as a safeguard, based on Equality of Representation; and both Houses would then operate within the framework of a Constitution which would protect Lower Canada "with guarantees for the fullest religious and civil freedom":

> The power of final interpretation in cases of doubt arising under the Constitution would reside in a Bench of judges composed of an equal number from Upper and Lower Canada.

McGee had made amends with James Moylan, and the *Canadian Freeman* once again supported McGee's stand. But the *True Witness* condemned McGee for these proposals. In Clerk's eyes, they were a betrayal of the trust which McGee owed to Lower Canada. They also made McGee very suspect in the whispered views of French Canadians. Earlier, Dorion had said he was ready to work out a solution on such general grounds, but he was now withdrawing, with the experience that such opinions had badly weakened his support from French Canadians.

There was a great gap to bridge. To the English-speaking Protestants of Upper Canada, the French Catholics could appear under many aspects, as picturesque or pathetic, as romantic, devout or backward, as traditional or as frightened defenders of the past—but they always appeared as strangers. Likewise in the eyes of the French Catholics of Lower Canada, the Methodists, Baptists and Orangemen of Upper Canada could appear as progressive or stiff-necked, as self-reliant, bigoted or heretical, as modern or as mere specialists in minor virtues—but equally always as aliens.

With their weakness shifted from Upper to Lower Canada, the Cartier-MacDonald Government had survived the elections of 1861, but it showed little leadership. John A. MacDonald was drinking heavily, and his Cabinet's feeble policy drifted into loose administration and extravagance. As the Session advanced and each vote was called, its slim majority in the House was whittled away. There were signs the Government was going to pieces. In May of 1862, under the weight of its own Militia Bill, it finally crumbled.

John A. MacDonald as the Minister of Militia never gave a worse performance in Parliament than his weak and rambling presentation of the Militia Bill. His desultory speech seemed to promise little else than a likely deficit of over five million dollars, military conscription and even more dubious patronage. When his strange speech was finished he disappeared on a drinking bout for a week. Then on May 20, when the Bill came up for its second reading, for some puzzling reason which no one explained, neither John A. MacDonald, Cartier, Galt nor indeed any member whatsoever rose to speak. So with a suddenness that astounded everyone, the vote was called. Fifteen members did not vote. Fifteen *Bleus* broke from Cartier, to his chagrin, and followed Sicotte to oppose the Bill. It did receive a small majority of seven from Upper Canada. But when the full count was taken the Militia Bill was defeated, sixty-one to fifty-four.

McGee admitted it was difficult for him to make up his own mind; but he finally cast his vote against the Militia Bill on the grounds of its excessive costs and vagueness, and the Cabinet's indifference to corruption. So the Government of John A. MacDonald and George Etienne Cartier, which under various combinations had held office continuously, except for the few days of the Double Shuffle, through the two elections of 1857 and 1861, finally went down to defeat. It was defeated as McGee stated, not "by the Militia Bill, but on the Militia Bill."

Perhaps MacDonald and Cartier in their shrewdness, with defeat looming up as inevitable, thought it was best to seem to fall as victims of disloyalty on such an issue as the Militia Bill in 1862, just as they had chosen to go down in 1858 as loyal to the Queen's choice of Ottawa as the capital. It appeared to have the makings of a popular ending, since they saw that in any event the curtain was coming down. But that would be surmise. There was a plain cause apparent. The Government fell from decay.

# IO

## A PERSISTENT POLITICIAN

"O Cormac, Grandson of Conn," said Carbery,
"What were your habits when you were a lad?"

"Not hard to tell," said Cormac.

"I was a listener in the woods,
I was a gazer at the stars,
I was blind where secrets were concerned,
I was silent in a wilderness,
I was talkative among many,
I was mild in the mead-hall,
I was stern in battle."

THE INSTRUCTIONS OF KING CORMAC,
*From the Irish, early ninth century*

Nothing is so hard that it does
not yield to that which is harder.
*St. Bernard of Clairvaux*

In this political welter of reactions and frustrations, with loose and multiple groupings clustering around persons rather than platforms, Lord Monck, the new Governor General, called upon Sandfield MacDonald to form a Government; and the latter, an astute politician with mediocre ideas, looking for an unadventurous ally, turned to another man of mediocrity, Louis Victor Sicotte; and together they accepted.

D'Arcy McGee was approached to join the Cabinet as Minister of Agriculture, Statistics and Immigration. Word of his proposed nomination spread so favourably through Upper Canada that it provoked an intense reaction in Lower Canada. McGee's ambition to develop a strong department controlling both Immigration and the Census was not well received among the French Canadians, and Cartier heatedly criticized the choice of McGee as "a barrister at the head of Immigration who can hardly speak a word of French." The result was that Sandfield MacDonald and Sicotte were afraid to appoint him. So instead, on May 24, 1862, McGee entered the Cabinet as President of the Council, with an assurance that Immigration would later be transferred to him. This promise was kept dangling before him for so long that it began to grow stale. But on June 9 McGee wrote with renewed hope from Quebec City to the Sadliers in New York:

> The radicals are a poor pack. Their spite is not a whit smaller than their politics. I *am* to have charge of immigration matters after all.

The Ministry for Immigration was allotted temporarily to François Evanturel, a lawyer from Quebec City, while rumours of shifts in the Cabinet continued. George Clerk noted in his diary that he had heard that McGee would become Provincial Secretary. But Sandfield MacDonald asked Dorion to accept this post, and although he was ranked under the inferior Sicotte, Dorion agreed to serve. A month later Clerk made a further entry which indicated a strong trend of opinion:

> July 10: By the Irish papers, it is evident that an angry feeling is growing upon the question of making McGee Immigration Minister in the place of François Evanturel. This may lead to something im-

portant and disagreeable as the jealousy against the French Canadian is increasing.

Immigration was watched with vigilance and suspicion. French-speaking Canadians, being born in Canada but with an injured feeling of being treated as outsiders, held very opposite views to those of English-speaking Canadians, who were mostly immigrants themselves. Sandfield MacDonald, who was born in St. Raphaël near Cornwall in Upper Canada, was a notable exception to this rule. More typical of English-speaking political leaders were John A. MacDonald, George Brown, Alexander Galt and D'Arcy McGee, all of whom were immigrants. Yet there was a difference among immigrants. John A. MacDonald, Brown and especially Galt came to Canada with the protection of their parents, whereas McGee migrated alone as a boy and knew the lonely feelings of an immigrant much more intimately than the others. The fact, too, that he came to Canada much later than the others made McGee very conscious that he was an immigrant. Most of his friends were in the same position. Nor was McGee one to hide his origins, and he remained constantly interested in the problems of immigrants.

McGee had acted since 1860 as the chairman of a special standing committee on Immigration in the House. Through his efforts, a stronger policy and improved practises had brought about better campaigns for immigrants overseas, and larger facilities, wiser supervision and more attractive receptions for them as they arrived at the port of Quebec. "In a sense, all men are immigrants," he had said. And now and then, in the early summer days when the Session was on in Quebec City, McGee would go down to the wharf and wait in the warm sun for the mast-head of an immigrant ship to appear, or walk up Little Champlain Street to Breakneck Steps or down the narrow *Sous le Cap*, where the poorer Irish lived, with the sparkling crystals in the black slate of Cape Diamond high above them.

How many immigrants were coming in to Canada and where they were settling, what language would they speak and what was their religion: all were part of a very sensitive question. The total immigration to Canada had more than doubled from 1860 to 1862, rising from ten thousand to twenty-two thousand a year. McGee considered that twenty-two thousand persons could be absorbed each year, as they represented a ratio of less than one immigrant to every hundred of the settled population.

French Canadians were profoundly disturbed when they saw these

immigrants to Canada streaming right through Quebec. The numbers from France were not worth counting. The majority were English-speaking, and to them French Canadians appeared like a closed society. So the bulk were travelling through Lower Canada to settle in Upper Canada. As this was plainly increasing the disparity between their populations, it intensified the demand for proportionate representation. And with it, the Census and its methods became a contentious political issue.

Sandfield MacDonald let time drift by and make the decision for him. The Ministry of Immigration did not go to McGee. It remained with Evanturel, and the rising annual number of immigrants dropped during his year in office by more than 12 per cent.

McGee was ill at ease in the Sandfield MacDonald-Sicotte Ministry. The change for McGee from the role of private member to Cabinet Minister was difficult enough. He had made his political reputation for his outspoken and independent views. Now he found himself enclosed in an atmosphere of reticence and compromise, meeting under Sandfield MacDonald, who, in the unkind words of an opponent, thought of little else than how "to shuffle out of his responsibilities."

Like their predecessor in office, the new Cabinet of Sandfield Mac-Donald and Sicotte had no policy for Constitutional reform. But it was worse than that. Where members of the previous Government had at least urged their reforms privately, in this Cabinet a neutral view prevailed that reforms need not be discussed privately, because things were quite all right just as they were. Immigration, population and Western expansion, as topics, became taboo. Yet these were the very staples of McGee's political imagination; and he was hurt when Sandfield Mac-Donald referred to the immigrants as hordes who had just been "whitewashed" at Grosse Isle. Not only McGee was distressed by the backward mentality of the Cabinet. Lord Monck privately described them as "a wretched lot of parish politicians."

To add to his difficulties, Sandfield MacDonald was barely in office when he found himself the target of heavy criticism from British Imperial spokesmen. He scarcely merited this attack because it was due to the complicated causes of the defeat of the Militia Bill in the dying days of the Government of Cartier and John A. MacDonald. Nonetheless, strong feelings of resentment were expressed in England by Lord Palmerston and others; and both Sandfield MacDonald and Sicotte were looked upon as "unpatriotic colonials" who were usurping authority and trying to build on the ruins of the rejected Militia Bill. On June 6 the London *Times* preached this cold doctrine to Canada:

> Great Britain cannot protect Canada without any aid on her part. It is not in our power to send forth from this little island a military force sufficient to defend the frontier of Canada against the numerous armies which have learned arms and discipline in the great school of the present Civil War.
>
> Opinion in England is perfectly decided that in the connection between the mother country and the colony, the advantage is infinitely more on the side of the child than of the parent. Should the colony wish to put an end to it, we would never draw the sword to defend it; and if Canada will not fight to protect its independence from foreign invasion, neither will England.

If they are to be defended at all, they must make up their minds to bear the greater part of the burden of their own defence. This will be the case if they separate from us. This will be the case if they remain by us.

Such a scolding was badly received in Canada. John Charles Dent, a Canadian journalist who spent much of his time in England, observed that Canada received it like an "unmerited slap in the face"; and it brought about "a change in sentiment of a radically different stripe" from the loyalty which animated Canadians during the *Trent* Affair.

McGee was a leader in this development of a stronger Canadian public opinion, which was taken up later on by men like William Foster and Goldwin Smith in the Canada First movement. At the Reform Demonstration at Welland that September, McGee struck a popular Canadian chord in criticizing the old unquestioning Imperial sentiment:

If we are to be an independent people, which I do not apprehend to be an immediate probability, let us be an independent people with a seaboard, as well as an inland country.

If we are to be an Imperial people, which I think is at present our position, then let us be an Imperial people and not an Imperial puppet.

But the excitement which such exchanges engendered faded away. Wartime prosperity fostered a false sense of security in Canada. The months beginning early in the summer of 1862 and stretching late into the following summer turned out to be the quietest of all periods in the relations between the British North American colonies and the United States. This appeasing calm disarmed almost everyone, and lasted almost two years.

It was during this quiet period that D'Arcy McGee's interest turned towards the Maritimes. One practical channel for that interest was the project of the Intercolonial Railway.

When Parliament was prorogued in June 1862, McGee spent the month of July with his family at Cacouna, near Rivière du Loup and the waters of the humpbacked whale. His health was not good, and he was suffering from bilious attacks. But it gave him the opportunity to hear at first hand all about the risks that were run in trying to land the troops at the eastern end of the Grand Trunk line the previous winter; of their forced march through the snows of the old Madawaska Trail made by the Micmac Indians, and of the sole telegraph line from Canada to the Maritimes running directly along the Maine border, exposed to easy attack and manned, in fact, by American technicians. That summer McGee made up his mind on the vital and urgent need of the Intercolonial Railway to link Rivière du Loup overland with Saint John and Halifax.

In September, McGee became the chairman of the Intercolonial Conference held at Quebec City. It brought the governors of New Brunswick and Nova Scotia with their advisers to meet the Canadian delegates; and together they studied the proposals of the Colonial Secretary, the Duke of Newcastle, on three connected matters: the Intercolonial Railway, the increase of trade between the Maritimes and Canada and a Union of the British North American colonies.

The Conference was made up of fourteen members. There were eight from Canada, three from New Brunswick, led by the precise apothecary Leonard Tilley, and three from Nova Scotia under that ardent warrior Joseph Howe. Sandfield MacDonald and Sicotte were among the Canadian delegates; and as it turned out later, though it was not too apparent then, the Canadian delegates were reluctant participants, fearful of any further financial liabilities; that is to say, all the Canadians except McGee. He led the Conference forward as its enthusiastic chairman on a theme of expanding patriotism. After a week of difficulties, surmounted in a fashion either by compromise or by resort to generalities, McGee drafted a memorandum which was signed in a revised form by all the delegates. The main point, which remained unsettled, was the extent of the Imperial financial guarantee of the Intercolonial Railway as a necessary measure of military defence. The further need for Imperial contributions in opening up the Northwest was also broached, but not more than that; enough, however, to reveal that most of the Canadian delegates were more interested in linking up with the West than with the East.

Notwithstanding its hesitations, the memorandum was an important document in its expression of "an anxious desire to bind the Provinces more closely together." Proceeding from that to the practical problem of paying for the Intercolonial Railway, it recorded their willingness to assume the liability "under the Imperial guarantee," and the proportions were set at five twelfths for Canada and seven twelfths equally divided between Nova Scotia and New Brunswick.

Here the general agreement stopped. But a subsidiary memorandum went further. It provided for the appointment of a joint commission to construct and manage the road, for a survey to determine the line as soon as the enabling laws were passed, and for a delegation to be sent to England to arrange for the loan. This second document was signed by McGee, Howe and Tilley.

Little progress was made on the matter of reciprocal trade, and it was postponed. On the whole, McGee was pleased with the results of the Conference. But his sense of accomplishment did not last long. A strong reaction was quick to come; and it came from two separate quarters.

When the signed agreements were read at a full session of the Canadian Cabinet, Dorion, the Provincial Secretary and head of the *Rouges*, declared that he was completely opposed to the construction of the Intercolonial Railway. He immediately resigned from the Cabinet, which stirred up a storm in the newspapers.

Then to back up the *Rouges*, which they rarely did in those days, the Clear Grits spoke out. With George Brown absent on an extended holiday in the British Isles, they recorded their opposition through the *Globe* and supported Dorion.

In fact, those who were pushing the project of the Intercolonial Railway were prompted by differing motives. The Imperial authorities wanted it for military reasons. Politicians in Nova Scotia and New Brunswick saw it as a good way to win elections. Many merchants expected it to improve trade. Railway contractors saw it as a lush, lucrative growth of renewed patronage. For McGee, who was oddly detached from economic interests, yet probably used by those interests, it was a move towards building a nation, another link in communications that one day would extend into the Far West.

Because they had promised to do so, although they were badly shaken by Dorion's resignation, Sicotte as Attorney General and Howland as Minister of Finance left, in any event, for England as the delegates from Canada. But they had serious misgivings and lacked enthusiasm. The opposition of the *Rouges* and the Clear Grits to the Intercolonial Railway threatened their precarious majority. The newspapers were crying for retrenchment, and the public was fearful of new taxes. In contrast, Howe for Nova Scotia, who never lacked self-confidence, and Tilley for New Brunswick, who naïvely assumed that political agreements would not be broken, were anticipating a success.

In England, Gladstone was more exacting than expected, and he stipulated that a sinking fund must be set up in Canada to assure repayment of any Imperial loan through safe British bonds. Sicotte and Howland saw this as their opportunity to withdraw, and they left England rather brusquely without adequate explanation. The Maritime delegates were caught off guard. They waited uneasily. When no message came from the Canadian Cabinet other than an obscure evasion, they began to interpret the Canadian withdrawal from Gladstone's plan as a breach of contract.

What promised in September 1862 to unite Canada with the Maritimes by solid military and commercial bonds was now within three short months dissolving in a spirit of mistrust and anger. McGee realized that to regain what had been lost would take more than plodding patience.

Here the narrative must be suspended to go back a few years and consider the growth of another important issue.

One of the great contentions of that era, which if misunderstood can distort a proper view of political developments, came from the sustained efforts of the Catholics to establish adequate Separate Schools for their own children in Upper Canada. McGee played a persistent role in this organized movement from his first election in 1857, and it can be related with less intricacy if a strong trait in McGee is made clear.

His early training and his temperament had been somewhat blighted by his own wayward experiences and some bitter deceptions on "the grim shores of those who forget the fear of God." But they led him, by an independent path that could hardly be called devout, to become a religious man. His early career was so romantic and irreverent and his conduct, carefree if not careless, lacked so much of that decorum which popularly cloaks the pious that they tended to obscure his solid qualities from most people. But his friends saw beneath his modesty and through his failings, and knew where his roots were; and his intimate letters and verses showed him as a man with too much humour to be blinded by any conceit that he need not pray. Experiences of death and sorrows worse than death had revealed to him the religious sustenance of life.

So when it came to education, McGee held a simple, traditional view. Religion, he had found, was the strongest of the schools, the proper discipline for the wildest impulses and the only light to pierce self-deception. He had a firm belief that towards his children a parent is a steward of God's mysteries.

Two other points should be noted in order to clarify the Parliamentary history of Separate School Bills.

Those days for Christians were far from ecumenical. It was popular for Protestants and Catholics to regard one another with anything from faint contempt to open enmity. Blame for this can be apportioned among all. In Upper Canada, however, where the Protestants were in the ascendancy, the Catholics, being poorer, less well instructed and inadequately represented, carried a heavier burden of disdain and oppression. Catholic parents were opposed to placing their children under Protestant teachers, even when their motive went no deeper than the natural one of protecting them from insinuations and derision.

Nor were these aggressive religious attacks confined to Catholics and Protestants in the struggles over the schools. The most notable example was the bitter battle for the control of education which was waged by Egerton Ryerson, the Methodist minister and vigilant Superintendent for Education of Upper Canada, against John Strachan, the Anglican Bishop and the skilful, pertinacious Chancellor of the University of Trinity College in Toronto. Ryerson was determined to establish a homogeneous system of education, and he was most active in opposing any extension of Separate elementary or secondary schools in Upper Canada. When he faced the mounting opposition of the Catholics, he felt justified by remaining faithful to his own ideals. But he was oblivious that his lights, in the eyes of others, were Methodist lights.

The second point to be mentioned was that the Catholic Bishops of Canada were constantly working for Separate Schools; and this led them into politics, where they exercised a quiet but never a negligible force. Far from what is usually imagined, however, the Bishops were not united among themselves and frequently followed conflicting political paths. Bishop Lynch, who had succeeded Bishop de Charbonnel in Toronto, moved over to act with the majority of the Bishops in looking to the Conservative Party under John A. MacDonald and Cartier for Catholic Schools. But both these politicians were promising to obtain results for the Bishops, and in exchange were hoping, under this benevolent patronage, to gain more Catholic votes. This was weakening McGee's political strength. And the *Globe* made matters worse by its rhetoric about "the slaves of Rome," pushing voters into a false dilemma of either opposing Catholic Separate Schools or opposing Representation by Population. No one, argued the *Globe*, could be in favour of both. Such an attitude, as will be seen, gradually widened the gap between McGee and the Clear Grits.

Though the history of Catholic Separate Schools goes back further, it can be briefly recounted starting from 1860.

It was in March of that year when Richard William Scott from Ottawa introduced his first Bill to extend the Catholic Separate Schools. It was scarcely published as Bill 69, when it was quickly killed. The following year he presented it again as Bill 11, and this time it was received, politely read, and allowed to languish and die. Scott persisted. In April of 1862 he presented it early, as Bill 2.

D'Arcy McGee had staunchly supported each Bill. In 1862 he made a special effort and surpassed himself. Speaking then as a private member in the Opposition, under the strong cross-fire of the Clear Grits, it was said that "he fairly whipped into line more than one half of the Opposition members from Upper Canada." Luther Holton in a confidential letter of May 5 to George Brown could not conceal his admiration for McGee's speech. But he was more than impressed; he was "a good deal exercised" about the members who were swayed to vote with McGee. Yet he added:

> I do not blame any of our friends for voting as they did, and I shall not be sorry to see the question settled.
>
> McGee is looking remarkably well this Session and is rapidly taking a high position. For his own sake, as well as ours, I hope he is not going to throw himself away.

What Holton was referring to, and what continued to disturb him as well as Brown, was a forthright statement made by McGee, which some Clear Grits interpreted as a threat. At that time, which was before the Cartier-MacDonald Government fell, McGee had stated that he had always acted with the Opposition since he first entered Parliament, because he felt that there was greater liberality among them than with the Government:

> But I must say, if this debate shall satisfy me, that the religious liberties of the Roman Catholic minority of the people of Upper Canada are more safe in the hands of what has been called the Conservative Party than they are in the hands of the Reform Party in the House, however painful it may be to me personally, I shall not, for any party or earthly consideration, hesitate to make my choice in favour of the party which guarantees religious rights.
>
> I shall make my mind up as to which side has the greater liberality, by the toleration they exhibit on this question.

But the *Globe*'s answer was immediate, uncompromising and impolitic:

> McGee has always been an advocate of Separate Schools and seems to think he will find more sympathy from the Conservative Ministerial Party than from the Opposition.
>
> Doubtless he is right. We cannot hold out the slightest hope that there will be any change of views on the subject.

The *True Witness*, on the other hand, which had practically dropped McGee from its columns, momentarily turned and praised McGee highly for his speech on Separate Schools.

In early May of 1862 it looked as though Scott's Bill would, at long last, ride through on the wave of support stirred up by McGee. But it was suddenly referred to a committee by John A. MacDonald, and with a shrug of the shoulders from Sandfield MacDonald, off it went to the political graveyard. "Bishop Lynch has been humbugged by John A. MacDonald," the *Globe* exulted.

But, as already mentioned, more than that happened. In the third week of May 1862 the Government of Cartier and John A. MacDonald collapsed; and Sandfield MacDonald, ineffectual as a Catholic, formed a new Government with Sicotte based on the promise that important laws would require a Double Majority. This appeared to kill all hope for the hapless Catholic Separate School Bill.

Three attempts and three failures would be enough to discourage most people. But not Richard Scott. That summer he continued to work. With a revised and less objectionable form to his Bill, he succeeded in bringing Egerton Ryerson, Upper Canada's Superintendent of Instruction, together with Vicar General C. E. Cazeau from Quebec and Vicar General Angus MacDonnell of Kingston, to study it. At this momentous meeting, which began by promising little, they reached an agreement on the provisions for a new Bill. Later on, when the question was re-opened, a dispute was to break out on whether their agreement was final or not; but it became known that a working arrangement had in fact been reached by the influential Methodist minister and the French Catholic and Scottish Catholic priests. This was sufficient to subdue most of the opposition to it, except of course the indomitable *Globe*.

Early next Session, on February 27, 1863, under the new Ministry of Sandfield MacDonald and Sicotte, Scott presented the Bill for the fourth time, as Bill 3, entitled "An Act to restore to Roman Catholics in Upper Canada certain rights in respect to Separate Schools." McGee was now a member of the Cabinet and President of the Council, and was stronger and more determined than ever to see it through. Here, McGee and Sandfield MacDonald rubbed each other the wrong way. And Sandfield's neutral views about the development of religious schools prompted McGee to describe him privately as "the blank leaf between the Old and the New Testament, belonging to neither one nor the other."

Within a week a motion was abruptly presented to give the Separate

School Bill a six months' hoist. This time, however, the motion was defeated, and the Bill received its second reading. Then Thomas Ferguson asked Sandfield MacDonald if he intended to apply the principle of the Double Majority to the Bill. There was an embarrassing silence, and Ferguson could not obtain a reply from the canny Premier from Cornwall.

On March 12, long awaited and well prepared, McGee rose to speak in support of the Bill. Approaching a subject on which the Members could quickly choke up with anger, he let the solvent of a little laughter enter first, and then expressed his views with an air of disarming serenity.

The end of education, in McGee's view, was to nurture in the child all those human longings for excellence, to let innocence mature as a rare adventure and "to replenish the world's ideals"; let the girls be led through the gracious arts to intuitive wisdom, and let the boys be trained by sturdy habits and the steady sciences to a calm, complete and accurate view of life. If such an objective was handed over to be pursued by the State, McGee maintained, it would be determined at the level of the indifferent kind of State it happened to be. And would the State not find it convenient for its interests to use education, as John Stuart Mill had feared, as "a mere contrivance for moulding people to be exactly like one another"?

The common school system, with the single mould controlled by the State, had come, McGee contended, as a project of Frederick the Great from Prussia, through Revolutionary France. When the discipline of Puritanism lost its sternness, this vaporous Deism entered the educational system of North America:

> The school is now serving some politicians in the United States as a crushing mill to manufacture natives out of Germans and Hibernians.

He then made two plain points. Catholic Separate Schools were sought to satisfy the conscience of a large number of citizens. It was a matter for their conscience, and it could not be answered by others substituting their conscience for the conscience of these citizens:

> This is not a got-up debate. The question before this House has its origin in the deepest and most enduring elements of our nature.

Answering the cry that this was "a priests' Bill," he made it clear that it was and would always be "a parents' Bill":

There must be in every father's heart a latent or active sense of responsibility for the spirit and the genius of his child as well as for his flesh and blood.

The danger is in these new realms, so bare of all traditions, that materialism may spread, that the sceptre of the fireside may be broken and the moral magistracy of the parent be overthrown.

The Catholic Separate School is a practical method of uniting the three great social forces of the parent, the pastor and the State, in one of the noblest and most durable works of reform within our compass.

Reaching the end, McGee appealed to the justice of his cause. A reporter noted that he was now motionless, and his words seemed to move across the House like a light wind over a field of wheat, as he spoke of "the mysterious relation of parent and child, which inspires the hearts of all but the very stolid or the very depraved, with a double anxiety" for the future of their children, both here and hereafter, hoping that finally they will "see splendour and have glory break upon them."

The following day, on its third reading, a vote was called. In Upper Canada twenty-four members including John A. MacDonald voted in favour of it, and surprisingly most of them were Orangemen; but twenty-seven voted against it, made up mainly of Clear Grits. In Lower Canada, however, with religion bringing the French and the Irish Catholics together, only one vote was clearly recorded against it. But a sizable group of twenty-six members, almost equally divided between the two Provinces, abstained from voting. So the simple majority in favour of the Catholic Separate School Bill was seventy-four to thirty.

As Prime Minister, Sandfield MacDonald was inwardly disturbed about the way his policy of a Double Majority had been challenged, but he gave no sign of his anxiety. He voted for the Bill, merely making an offhand remark that he considered it was a private Member's Bill and not a Government Bill, and did not need any Double Majority. So the Bill was adopted. But the fiction of the Double Majority had been exposed. For it was a clear example of a law affecting one Province, where it had the support of a minority, enacted by a majority from the other Province. George Clerk, who by now had abandoned the idea of a Double Majority, recognized in the *True Witness* that the Bill would never have passed if the principle in force had been Representation by Population and not Equality of Representation as between the two Provinces.

Richard Scott's Bill for Catholic Separate Schools in Upper Canada received Royal assent as law on May 5, 1863. It was done by dogged persistence, and for Scott and McGee, as will be seen, it was done in the nick of time.

# II

## BREAK-UP

I was wounded in the house of my friends.
ZACHARIAS XIII: 6

There is a mysterious medley of good and evil in our hearts.
*Thomas D'Arcy McGee*

The political weakness which spread through Canada in 1861 and 1862 had practically become an infirmity by 1863 when the parties could not escape from their deadlock. Changes of Government had occurred, and each one faced the same stalemate, its fate hanging upon the transfer of a few fickle votes. Whether the leaders were calculating or callous, they were trapped in by the unworkable Constitution.

Here George Brown with his fortitude, brash and turbulent as it could be, had been badly missed. When Brown was defeated in the general elections of July 1861, Parliament, which only functioned when groups were drawn tightly together by strong persons, had lost one of its magnetic centres.

Brown was defeated and sick, a bachelor, worn out and weary of it all at the age of forty-three. So he decided to travel through England and Ireland and then go on to his native Scotland for a good, long rest. He asked D'Arcy McGee what he should do in Ireland, and McGee's reply of August 5, 1862, was written with the wistful air of an exile. He enclosed a letter of introduction to Timothy Sullivan, one of the two brothers who had recently taken over the *Nation* from his old friend Charles Gavan Duffy:

> In that fair city of Dublin, he will give you his version of Irish affairs which you ought to hear before making up your Irish judgments.

The more McGee matured, the higher he ranked Daniel O'Connell; so he told Brown:

> Be sure to go to Glasnevin Cemetery and visit the grave of Daniel O'Connell. I had the honour to know O'Connell slightly in his latter days, and the misfortune to differ from that illustrious man.

For the ailing Brown, who had slumped too early into the feeling that his public life was finished, there was a lesson in the achievements of O'Connell, who, with a full life behind him, replete with foes, successes, reversals and thankless friends, had entered the Imperial Parliament for the first time at the age of fifty-four to begin a second career of seventeen momentous years.

But the unexpected happened. George Brown met Anne Nelson of the prosperous publishing family in Edinburgh, married her and returned to Canada a changed man. Although his wife did not encourage him, Brown decided to re-enter Parliament. Winning a by-election, he took his seat in the House in the spring of 1863, too late to speak against the Catholic School Bill which had just been passed.

John A. MacDonald sat in Opposition, as Brown described him, like a green-eyed "grimalkin," transfigured, "at the door of the pantry watching for mice to come in or out." And Sandfield MacDonald and Louis Victor Sicotte hardly dared to make a serious move. They had managed to survive for a year, by one expedient or another, as a casual form of government. Thrown together by the failures of their predecessors, and strangely sustained from without by the very excess of the attacks made on them by the extreme Clear Grits and the radical *Rouges*, Sandfield MacDonald and Sicotte had little to hold their Cabinet together from within. They saw their policy as one of status quo, and did not see the changes all around them.

Difficulties made Sandfield MacDonald secretive and irritable. Now and then he would indulge in some reckless talk, followed each time by

SANDFIELD
MACDONALD

a period of complete inaction, which the truckling politicians around him used to their advantage without disturbing him. He would quarrel with Sicotte, then with Foley and finally with McGee; not without provocation, however, for there was something in the jab of a journalist that "Sicotte, Foley and McGee are his drinking majority."

One night in early May 1863, when McGee was expected to be on hand to answer an attack by John A. MacDonald, McGee failed to appear in the House. Someone whispered to Sandfield MacDonald that McGee had had "too convivial a dinner." That was certainly an understatement, but it was enough for Sandfield MacDonald.

Instances of incapacity caused by drink were far from lacking in that House, where many members like John A. MacDonald, Alexander Galt, Michael Foley and D'Arcy McGee repeatedly drank with gusto, if not to disgust. Politicians were hardened to that. But this incident precipitated a political and therefore a stronger feeling. McGee had persisted in supporting the Intercolonial Railway, which had cost Sandfield Mac-Donald the loss of Dorion; McGee wanted to promote more immigration to Canada, which merely aggravated Sandfield MacDonald's sensitivity to Representation by Population; McGee insisted on pushing through the Catholic School Bill, which made a mockery of Sandfield MacDonald's safeguard of the Double Majority; and now McGee was placing the Government's slight majority in peril by an irresponsible absence from the House. All this was repeatedly upsetting Sandfield MacDonald's ingenious balance of moderate neutrality.

Three days after the Catholic School Bill became law, the Sandfield MacDonald-Sicotte Ministry faced its final test; long feared and up to now averted, a vote was forced on a motion of want of confidence; and on May 8, 1863, after less than a year in office, the Government of Sandfield MacDonald and Sicotte went down to defeat, sixty-four to fifty-nine.

A series of secret meetings in the Russell House of Quebec immediately followed. Sandfield MacDonald called in Dorion and Holton, who were outside the Cabinet, and with them he worked out a scheme for a new Government. Dorion stipulated that he would only re-enter the Cabinet if the Intercolonial Railway was abandoned. Sandfield MacDonald accepted this condition, and in so doing they concurred in the ouster of McGee. Luther Holton, although he had nominated McGee in every one of his elections, also agreed that McGee should be dropped, and he accepted the post of Minister of Finance.

Brown was consulted, too, and Sandfield MacDonald, Dorion and Holton secretly met with him and Oliver Mowat. Brown, with a peculiar unyielding caution, stated that, personally, he would not enter the new Cabinet. Nevertheless, he took the lead in the discussions, promised his support, shared in the plan of throwing aside the Intercolonial Railway and agreed that Dorion should be left entirely free to select the Lower Canada half of the Cabinet, which meant that McGee would be excluded. Brown was holding himself apart from McGee, but he was not the only one. It was simply the cruel side of what has always been called "good politics," to have nothing to do with a politician about to be thrown to the wolves.

All the while McGee, who was also living at Russell House, was meeting Dorion and Holton socially every day, but was completely shut out from what was going on. He sensed what was coming, however, and his refuge was the tavern. There in his favourite corner, this small man in his loose suit, with his full large mouth like that of an actor, his black curly hair and deep complexion (which explained his nickname "Darky"), would sit and entertain his cronies by the hour. His talk was glorious. He would recall "the stormy gusts of other days," those days of '48 and "the trouble in earnest," or quote at length from Mangan— "Far away from my friends on the chill hills of Galway"—or chant his own ballad "The Haunted Castle of Donegal." If someone interrupted with an oath, D'Arcy had his soft answer ready: "It's a comfort to be cursed by you, my bucko." Then with a flourish he would order drinks for the house to this tune:

> I drank till quite mellow
> Then like a brave fellow
> Began for to bellow
> And shouted for more.
> But my host held his stick up
> Which soon cured my hiccup
> As no cash could I pick up
> To pay off the score.

Finally, when his brilliant talk became blurred, his erstwhile friends would disappear one by one, and the small dark man in the rumpled, spotted suit would slump over in his dim corner and fall asleep. The next morning he would be "craw-sick." That week, too, his health suffered, and ulceration broke out badly on one foot.

A week later the House was dissolved, with Sandfield MacDonald publicly denying the rumour that his Cabinet was being reconstituted. The truth was the new Cabinet had already been made up: Dorion would come in as Attorney General and the leader for Lower Canada; Sicotte, when asked to serve under Dorion, had refused; Foley and Evanturel would be replaced; and D'Arcy McGee, without the courtesy of a consultation, would be discarded.

More than that was happening. John A. MacDonald had hoped that the Governor General would not grant a dissolution of the House, but would turn to him to form the new Government. But the new Governor General was the practical Lord Monck and not the haughty theorist Sir Edmund Head, and the days of the Double Shuffle were dead. When Sandfield MacDonald asked for a dissolution, Monck agreed. This meant another general election.

McGee privately heard the final news that he had been dropped on the day the House was dissolved. The next day, Saturday, May 16, he wrote a long letter from Montreal to his friend John O'Donohue in Toronto, marking it "Confidential":

After a year's self-denial in office, where I had the name without the reality of power, I find myself personally relieved, by quitting a false position, into which I had fallen from want of accurate knowledge of some of my confreres, and from which there was no escape but resignation.

But the way in which the thing was brought about and the situation which has followed, are equally extraordinary. If you have seen Foley on his way home, he has probably given you a brief of the whole transaction. Even so, I shall repeat, in substance, the story.

Sandfield, elated beyond bounds at what he called his "Upper Canada Majority," on the 6th of May, treated his own section of the Cabinet with a high hand, and ours with the most offensive disrespect: We, the Lower Canadians, he said, were in a minority. We had not the confidence of our section. He had of his. He was Premier. He was not bound to give us, from Sicotte down, any explanations of his out-of-doors negotiations. If he wanted us, he would keep us. If not, not.

I being one of those in our section, and Foley in his, who resisted and resented this dour dogmatism, were specially sacrificed—to make an example. And the detail of the mode in which this was done was still more offensive than the spirit, if that were possible.

What gave me additional offence was this. My old colleagues, Dorion and Holton, were parties to this sort of outer Cabinet arrangement, which existed in Quebec from Thursday to Thursday, and was often held under the same roof where I was, without ever once letting me know their position or agency in the intrigue.

Just at the last moment, eve yesterday, they called on me as I was packing up, with a view to soothe my wounded sense of fairness and fellowship. But I told them frankly that "we were quits."

So here I am, "an independent candidate."

I had almost forgotten to add that "any office" I might name was hinted at; but I instantly clapped the extinguisher on such an overture in such circumstances.

Writing "under great difficulty, with my bad leg propped up on another chair," McGee granted O'Donohue permission to tell what had happened to their friends. With that, he turned to the future:

What then is my position? I answer: I am in the hands of my friends.

Etiquette will not permit, nor will self-respect, that I should publicly arraign my ox colleagues. But I shall conceal the facts from no one. Then let the electors act.

On May 23, a week after the dissolution, Sandfield MacDonald publicly released the news of his revamped Cabinet and introduced Joseph Thibaudeau as McGee's successor: "He is a man of wealth and influence whom we have known all our lives, *un enfant du sol*." And MacDonald could not resist twisting the knife in McGee by adding: "He is no mere adventurer."

John A. MacDonald saw his chance, not to pounce, but to entice. He wrote to Moylan of the *Canadian Freeman* in Toronto urging him to support Conservative candidates, and dropped a hint that one of them could conceivably be his "friend McGee."

In his opening statement to his electors, McGee did not hide his anger:

I do not intend to hoist Mr. Sandfield MacDonald's and Mr. Dorion's colours, and drag the flag of my own honour in the dust.

But he made it clear that if he had to choose between voting for the old Conservative Coalition and the present Administration, "no vote of mine as an Independent Member will be instrumental in bringing back the old Coalition."

In ample, direct statements, showing that he had not lost sight of his large objectives, McGee declared that his policy remained broad and national, based on a monarchical rather than a democratic principle, and favouring "conciliation of our different creeds and classes." He would continue, he pledged, to work for internal reform, new settlements, increased population, the Intercolonial Railway, the expansion of the West and "our new northern nationality." Later, when he heard Sandfield Mac-Donald and Dorion openly state that they had abandoned plans for the Intercolonial Railway and Western expansion, he called them "shameful," the parents of "a pooh-pooh policy."

As nomination day for the general elections approached, it seemed that D'Arcy McGee might again be returned unopposed. But Sandfield MacDonald interpreted McGee's independence as hostile, and he succeeded in bringing out John Young to run against McGee in Montreal West. John Young was an experienced and very wealthy citizen, best known for his development of the Port of Montreal, and appeared to be far too formidable an opponent for McGee to defeat on his own. Cartier saw it that way, too, and he wrote to John A. MacDonald urging him to arrange to support McGee, quoting Galt that "McGee must be won over to get the Irish vote."

There was a familiar echo of McGee's first election of December 1857 in the air. Then, the three Montreal seats had been contested by Cartier, Rose and Starnes as against Dorion, Holton and an Independent newcomer, D'Arcy McGee. Now, six years later, the Opposition candidates were Cartier and Rose with a vacancy significantly left open for McGee as against Dorion, Holton and Young for the Government. Yet again McGee chose to run officially as an Independent.

John A. MacDonald and John Rose brought private support to McGee. How much was never clear. McGee in his own heart felt rather pushed out by Sandfield MacDonald than drawn towards John A. MacDonald; although McGee did not abandon his Independent stand, there was speculation as to how long he could retain it.

When the votes were counted, D'Arcy McGee had defeated John Young. More than that, Cartier and Rose had defeated Dorion and Holton, forcing the latter two to seek safe seats elsewhere. The Toronto *Globe*, which had belatedly disapproved of Sandfield MacDonald dropping McGee from the Cabinet, was perhaps right when it attributed the defeat of Dorion and Holton to the extraordinary strength of McGee in Montreal.

In Ottawa, however, Richard Scott felt the "serpent's sting of political ingratitude." To the surprise of many, notwithstanding his success with the Catholic Separate School Act, a bloc of Catholics withdrew their support, and he was defeated. But Scott went down with at least the consolation that his Bill had been enacted at the eleventh hour while he was still a member, before Brown's return, and while McGee was still a Cabinet Minister before the Government of Sandfield MacDonald and Sicotte fell.

McGee, elected again as an Independent, was prompt to rise above any feeling of isolation which an ousted Cabinet Minister with a brooding temperament might have entertained. He was buoyant in his misfortune. But he was weary of the tame unrealities of the Government and the Opposition's timid speeches on the Constitution, and he decided to conduct a personal campaign for the neglected cause of Confederation.

On July 1, 1863, there appeared the first of four open letters which he wrote to the Montreal *Gazette*. Their clarity and simplicity attracted attention. So he rewrote them as an article which was published in August by the *British North American Magazine* and widely quoted. The tenour of McGee's plea was this:

> Upper Canada says to Lower Canada, unmistakably, that the present state of things between us cannot continue much longer.
>
> Great Britain says the same thing to the North American colonies. And the American Government echoes, with the voice of its cannons, that the former condition of this Continent is finished.

McGee offered his solution in a series of propositions:

> Unless we are resigned to drift, we must assert our own distinct principle of government, and rally our population around it.
>
> Our principle, distinct from the American, is founded on an equal union of authority and liberty under the form of a constitutional monarchy.
>
> The whole of British North America, from the Atlantic to the Pacific, should form one nation; and our safety lies in the growth of the national sentiment that we are a people amongst the great peoples of the world.

In the heat of July, McGee left Montreal and, with aid from the Grand Trunk Railway, toured the Maritime Provinces. There he advanced his views, which he was careful to say "are personal to myself," on the need of the Intercolonial Railway and the advantages of a union of Canada with the Maritimes. Large audiences in Halifax and Saint John received him with an enthusiasm that ranked his eloquence above that of their own Joseph Howe, as he expanded his views:

> Our greatest obstacle is ignorance of each other's true resources and condition. It is not the distance. It is not the cost. It is not dis-

pute about routes or modes of construction. It is intercolonial ignorance which primarily stands in the way of the Intercolonial Railway.

Our country needs a population sufficient in numbers, in spirit and
in capacity to become its own master. And this population needs, as
all civilized men need, religious and civil liberty, unity, authority,
free intercourse, commerce, security and the law.

Of more practical benefit than his speeches were the renewed opportunities McGee had to discuss his objectives with Joseph Howe, Charles
Tupper and Leonard Tilley. By this time McGee was recognized in the
Maritimes as the most popular Canadian public figure. D'Arcy McGee
arrived home in August, buoyed up with the success of his Maritime
tour, and ready for the early opening of the Session on August 13.

Sandfield MacDonald was precariously back in power; Dorion was
seeking a safe seat after his defeat; and Sandfield had at most an unworkable majority of one or perhaps two seats. In Upper Canada he
was counting on forty-one Reformers against twenty-four Tories. In Lower
Canada he could control a bare twenty-four or twenty-five against forty.
The obvious prospect was another stalemate. And it looked as though
McGee's independent vote and influence in such an evenly divided House
could probably represent the balance of power.

As the Session opened, what nervous tension Sandfield MacDonald may
have felt was hidden by an air of careless unconcern. He had no support
to spare. Yet he had recklessly cast aside Sicotte, Foley and McGee, in-
curring their personal animosity at the risk of his political future. But
there was no foretelling. McGee's mind still hovered in suspense, probably more inclined to support the Reformers as the lesser of two evils,
yet hoping that some third group could emerge as more compatible with
his views.

The Session was barely under way when a crucial point came up contesting the right of a Government supporter, Rankin, to take his seat
for the riding of Essex. The normal rule was to refer such a question
to the Privileges and Election Committee. But the Government moved
that the House should forthwith declare Rankin elected. This was
vigorously opposed as contrary to precedent. Brown, however, supported
the motion; it was the efficient thing to do, he argued, and he referred
to the usages of the House as cobwebs to be brushed aside.

D'Arcy McGee took sharp issue with Brown:

We are here not that we may be above the law, but we are here in this high place that we may set a conspicuous example of obedience to the law.

He deplored this levity towards the customs and traditions of Parliament. Allegiance to the interests of a political party was one thing, McGee went on, but "our first duty" was loyalty to the law. Speaking then on the relations of a member to his Government, McGee added:

I have always acted in good faith and loyalty to my party.

And Sandfield MacDonald suddenly cut in: "At home and abroad?" Something snapped inside McGee. The House sensed it, as McGee stiffened slightly, then turned his back on Sandfield MacDonald and faced the Chair:

Yes, Mr. Speaker, at home and abroad. Although there may have been imprudence and many errors in the early career of one who was an editor at seventeen, and although there have been many things that my own judgment at this day does not approve, at all events throughout the whole long road, the honourable member will find no act of duplicity, no instance in which I ever betrayed a friend or intrigued against an associate.

McGee's words were burning like an avenging fire:

I have not been fair to men's faces and false behind their backs.
I have not condoled with sinister sympathy with the friends of a public man whom I desired to injure while at the same time I placed in the hands of his enemies weapons of attack, forged by malice, and poisoned by slanderous personalities.
I resume my appeal to the honourable gentlemen of the Reform Party. Perhaps it is the last I can, with propriety, make.
Will you, for a Premier who obtained his position by accident and retained it with duplicity, will you set aside the salutary enactments which prescribe the proper tribunal to decide the facts relating to this election?

Not a person on the floor or in the galleries stirred. Sandfield MacDonald did not move. He flushed and then grew pale; it was noticed that his hands twitched and he bared his teeth in the semblance of a smile. But he did not reply.

The days that followed were sad ones for D'Arcy McGee. He did not appear in the House. He was tired to death of the fret and the rancour and the emptiness of politics. Too much passion had been stirred and too much of his energy drained away for something serious not to set in. It came on as in 1849, when his *New York Nation* was collapsing under him and he was worn out and embittered. To forget his troubles, he began to disintegrate with them. D'Arcy McGee was drinking heavily.

And there were very few by his side to help him. One was Michael Hamilton Foley, a fellow Irishman representing North Waterloo, who had been dropped as Postmaster General from the Cabinet with McGee. As a Protestant with remarkable talent as a speaker and a journalist, Foley could have led the Opposition when Brown was defeated in 1861, but Foley's weakness for alcohol was worse than McGee's. So his assistance fell pitifully short of his good intentions. However, Thomas Devine, McGee's steady friend, was on hand. In 1856 when Devine was in Toronto, he was one of the earliest supporters of the move to bring D'Arcy McGee to Montreal, and now as the Assistant Commissioner of Crown Lands he had moved with the Parliament from Toronto to Quebec City. But on this occasion "true-hearted Thomas" (as McGee called him) could do very little for poor McGee. Because so much had been hidden from him by Sandfield MacDonald, D'Arcy McGee had been breeding suspicions, and suddenly he found the political soil very sour. It was a dangerous period of bitterness for him, when pride, revenge and other weeds of passion could grow with choking swiftness. It had gone far beyond the excesses of social drinking. What at first had been his escape and means of forgetting had become his necessity. So as a last resort Thomas Devine asked McGee's wife to come down from Montreal.

It was not the first time that Mary Teresa McGee had been so summoned. But this time it was more urgent and deeply rooted, as a private letter she wrote in those distraught days showed. It was written on a Thursday afternoon, August 20, from Mount Carmel, a short street near the Terrace on the Cape in Quebec City, where Mrs. McGee had joined her husband. She was writing with a heavy heart, in her swift, sloping hand to Thomas Devine, when she was interrupted half-way through:

Dear Mr. Devine:

As my visit to Quebec has not been productive of any good result, and as my staying here is not the least check to Mr. McGee's unfortunate propensity, I have come to the conclusion to return today (if weather permits).

He has just come in, and from his appearance, it is just a repetition of yesterday, so that I have given up all hope.

I have this moment received your note. If I knew what was the result of his conference with Mr. Foley, it would determine me whether I should go up to Montreal or not. Perhaps as you advise, it is better to remain to-day. I wish very much to see you, if convenient. Will you call after your office hours. Thanking you for the kind interest you have always taken,

> Believe me, dear Mr. Devine,
> Your sincere and obliged,
> Mary Teresa McGee

That week it seemed that D'Arcy McGee's meteoric career had burnt itself out. He continued drinking until a filmy haze obscured his vision and he dropped senseless to the ground. Awakening from his stupour, he was feverish, exhausted and deathly sick, with ringing ears, a violent headache and a throbbing heart. As if alcohol could cure what it had caused, McGee tried to deaden the pain and the poison of the morning after with more drink. And each desperate cycle of drunkenness and sickness spun him further away from recovery.

Despite her impulses Mary decided to stay with her husband in that bleak, high-ceilinged room on Mount Carmel. Where others saw a foul and foolish drunkard, she could still see the man of her memories, the ardent youth addressing a Temperance meeting, or the poet of Young Ireland who had written to her:

> My Irish wife has clear blue eyes
> My heaven by day, my stars by night,
> For she to me is dearer

> Than castles strong, or lands or life.
> An outlaw—so I'm near her
> To love to death my Irish wife.

She gained the grace to persevere, and gradually she enforced abstinence upon him. The next week D'Arcy rallied.

The most deadly error is the illusion every man has about himself. Mc-Gee had felt he was strong enough to be able to indulge in his weakness at will, and without lasting harm. He had to be prostrated by it to realize how wrong he was, and he expressed it as a prayer:

> Grant us, O God, the soil, the sun and the seasons,
> Avert despair the worst of moral treasons.

With remorse, but with no sullen envy or tinge of the morbid, he struggled; and with the great and quiet help of his wife, he came back through humiliation to himself. When he returned to the House, he was ready to fight it out in the clear. And soon enough he was engaged in a vigorous though vain plea for some statement of Government policy on the Constitution, something to foster, as he said, "at least a morale" which could lead to Federation. But a political shock was coming.

A few days later Sicotte proposed a motion of want of confidence in the Government of Sandfield MacDonald and Dorion. It was strongly supported and, in fact, almost succeeded, but was finally defeated by a slim three votes. Then like a thunderbolt an announcement came on September 5. The same Sicotte who had led the attack, and who, the day before, had urged both McGee and Foley to repel every form of advance or inducement from the Government, had accepted an appointment as a judge of the Superior Court from that very Government.

With Sicotte out of the way, Sandfield MacDonald felt less close to the precipice. The days began to drone on, and little was accomplished. McGee, if not formally allied with the Opposition, was virtually lost to the Government. This became plain on Tuesday afternoon, October 2, when McGee rose and openly charged the Government with bad faith in breaking the 1862 agreement with the Maritimes to construct the Intercolonial Railway.

Luther Holton replied for the Government in biting language. It was most unfortunate that McGee had ever been a member of the Government, Holton said; the Government could not undertake to defend any acts to which McGee had been a party; and moreover, McGee by his conduct had denied himself the right to receive any courtesy other than the bare minimum exacted by the etiquette of the House.

LUTHER
HOLTON

Talk went on, as one speaker followed another. Alexander Mackenzie, who had joined his brother Hope as another Clear Grit, spoke bluntly against the Intercolonial Railway, as a costly project which was utterly useless to Upper Canada; and then George Brown expressed a similar view. About midnight Lucius Seth Huntington of Shefford, the Solicitor General for Lower Canada, began an ill-prepared speech in support of Holton, which turned into a drawling lecture to McGee "for deserting his friends and joining his enemies."

It was one o'clock in the morning when McGee had his chance to reply:

> Mr. Huntington had referred to the hard things I have spoken respecting Mr. George Etienne Cartier and Mr. John A. MacDonald. But these were said in open warfare.
>
> They have said hard things of me. I have struck back as hard in return. But Mr. Cartier has never acted with me in political alliance. He has never been in my confidence. He has been an open enemy.
>
> The best friends I have ever made were made on the field of battle. And I hope I shall make him my friend in the same frank and outspoken manner in which I have made him my enemy.

McGee reminded both Holton and Dorion that even in the last election, although he had been told of their intrigue, he had refused to canvass against either of them, because they had once been his friends:

> But I see now that when a man has drawn his sword in politics in

Canada, it is better that he should throw away the scabbard altogether.

With that said, D'Arcy McGee irrevocably crossed the floor.

Brown had drawn apart from McGee during the issue of Catholic Separate Schools and had warily kept away during those critical days and
nights when McGee was wild with drink. And now that McGee had
broken with Sandfield MacDonald and Dorion and had joined, of all
Brown's enemies, "that most appalling John A. MacDonald," little or no
communication might well have been expected from then on between
Brown and McGee. But this did not happen. McGee kept in touch with
Brown. And from that rather fractious friendship something grew that
went far to shape the future of Canada.

In October 1863, in the dying days of that barren Session, Brown consulted McGee about a plan to set up a committee in the House to study
the Constitution. Its express purpose would be to propose changes and
find some way out of the impasse which was blocking every road. McGee,
although he was now politically aligned against him, promised Brown
that because he was "not fighting for himself, but for the cause he has
at heart" he would support the plan on a nonpartisan basis.

The motion to set up this Constitutional committee was proposed on
October 12, 1863. There was, of course, no chance to deal with it in
that Session, but it was introduced then to let it serve as a notice of
intention for the next Session. With that as unfinished business, the House
adjourned three days later. In that season of decay a seed had fallen
by the wayside where no one knew if the soil was good.

# PART THREE

# SACRIFICE

And we've a short space only
to be triumphant and brave.
*John M. Synge*

# 12

## FOES AS FRIENDS

An open foe is better than a false friend.
*Thomas D'Arcy McGee*

Human nature is a thing that even men can understand.
*G. K. Chesterton*

D'Arcy McGee was never blindly attached to a political party. His career can be better followed through his political projects rather than through his parties. Tracing his transition from the ranks of the Reformers in 1858 to those of the Conservatives in 1863 shows a gradual process, marked clearly enough even in its early stages.

Writing to his friend John O'Donohue of Toronto in the autumn of 1860, McGee sensed this movement himself:

> There is no such thing as taking a single step in politics. Each step must be one of a series, forward or backward.

At that time Moylan in the *Canadian Freeman* was drawing apart from McGee, and working to align the Irish Catholics of Upper Canada with the views of Bishop Lynch of Toronto. This shifting of preferences, McGee confessed to O'Donohue, could well "buff us out of the Reform Party."

In 1861, when Brown was defeated, McGee was repelled by the Clear Grits without Brown and saw little choice but to link up with Sandfield MacDonald. What bothered McGee, however, was the way that both Sandfield MacDonald and Sicotte had closed their minds against any expanding immigration or any change in the Constitution. This, McGee felt, was far from a liberal mentality.

Clerk foresaw McGee's development, when he wrote in his diary in March of 1862:

> McGee will join the Ministerialists, Cartier and MacDonald—but gradually.

Indeed, McGee himself had mentioned that his loyalty to the Catholic Separate School Bill was above his allegiance to any party. It was plain to those who knew both of them that McGee could not continue to get along with Sandfield MacDonald. So when the open break came in 1863, it was really the story of the last straw. But McGee's enemies did not let it appear that way. They accused McGee of being "a turncoat": politically because he "quit the Liberals to join the Conservatives," and racially because he "abandoned the Irish to become a British loyalist."

When the Session closed in mid-October 1863, McGee, having lost his salary as a Cabinet Minister, had to supplement his income to support his family. So he turned again to the lecture platform and made a tour through Upper Canada, appearing in Peterborough, Whitby, Port Hope and Toronto that November. Lecturing in the evenings, McGee kept active in the daytime working in the local political circles preparing the ground for the next general election, which he felt could not be far away.

A dinner was being organized in Toronto to honour the Conservative Opposition, and McGee was asked to speak on "Immigration and Settlement of the Country." McGee could not attend, however, and he expressed his apologies in a letter from Montreal on December 16, which also indicated his distaste for the name "Conservative." The immigration policy of that "poor-souled politician" Sandfield MacDonald was "suicidal," McGee wrote; active settlement of the country was needed to attain "our great object of the union of all British America and the paramount project of northwestern extension." No doubt, many who were taking part in the dinner would "differ as to the past government of the country," as they would about the "precise meaning to be attached in these days" to the terms Conservative Party and Reform Party. Then McGee disclosed what was on his mind. What he was "looking forward to now," and it could only arise from the Opposition, was "a Constitutional Party in Canada." George Brown saw the importance of McGee's letter, and he published it in the *Globe* on Christmas Day.

Usually shrewd, Sandfield MacDonald could at times be surprisingly rash. When the Session ended in 1863, he still had to complete his Cabinet by appointing a new Solicitor General for Upper Canada. Brown wanted him to select a Clear Grit who could be returned without a contest. But, instead, Sandfield MacDonald picked Albert Norton Richards, a loyal supporter of his own, from his own neighbourhood in Brockville. Richards was an able lawyer from an influential family, but his appointment meant that he had to reopen his riding of South Leeds in a by-election; and, despite the strength of the Richards family, it was not a safe seat. Nor was the choice too popular. Indeed, Brown thought it was a "very wrong" appointment.

D'Arcy McGee was prompt to point out that Sandfield MacDonald and Dorion had not carried "any test vote in the last Session by a majority of more than two or three," and had in fact "in the first ten days endured two tie votes." He expected this single by-election to be crucial, and he was soon in the riding of South Leeds, busy with the spade-work.

Michael Foley, who had been dropped by Sandfield MacDonald, wrote to John A. MacDonald, saying that he had joined the Sons of Temperance and would soon declare himself as an outright Conservative. Since this promised to be one more vote to count on in the House, John A. Mac-Donald decided to wage "war to the knife" in South Leeds. Brown Chamberlain of the Montreal *Gazette* sent money from Lower Canada; and, to counter the financial backing which Richards was feared to be receiving from the Bank of Montreal, the Grand Trunk Railway made a substantial contribution to John A. MacDonald's fund.

McGee's first report to John A. MacDonald came from Brockville, the chief town in Leeds. It was written hurriedly on Wednesday, December 30, 1863, just before he returned home for the holiday. On Friday, New Year's morning, the coming battle in Leeds was still on his mind, and he sent a telegram to John A. asking for "a hint" as to who would be his candidate to oppose Richards. McGee returned to Brockville on Monday, but there was no word yet from John A. MacDonald. "Everything depends on the candidate," McGee wrote that night in a further report. He found some of the Catholic clergy "deeply committed" to Richards:

> But I have their pledge to remain neutral—unless some very objectionable man was named on your side.

A possible candidate, mentioned to McGee, was James O'Reilly, an active lawyer from Kingston and a friend of John A. MacDonald; McGee added that O'Reilly was influential in Westport and Gananoque but he had run into some "very savage" feeling against O'Reilly in Brockville.

Finally, on Friday, January 8, John A. MacDonald replied from Kingston to McGee, but the name of his candidate was not divulged. McGee could not understand this delay, and he answered promptly from Ottawa the next day, ending his uneasy letter, just as he was about to leave for Montreal, with a message that would stir any political warrior:

> Is there anything else I can do or endeavour? All your political friends say, if you "go into it, it is all right."

Earlier that same night in Ottawa, D'Arcy McGee had written a more relaxed letter to his old friends the Sadliers, in New York:

> My winter leisure has so far been spent mostly in Upper Canada in the service of myself and the Opposition. I think I am putting a new national basis under this party—at least I hope so.
>
> You can hardly imagine the interest I now take in this country, and all that belongs to it. But it does not and never can supply the

field for mental labour and affectionate inspiration which Ireland would have been. However, God disposes.

At last, when John A. MacDonald sensed the time was ripe, he publicly announced that his candidate to oppose Richards in South Leeds would be David Ford Jones, who was also from a family prominent in the founding of Brockville. Yet Jones himself had been ready since New Year's Day, when he was privately urging John A. MacDonald to help him on the hustings and to bring D'Arcy McGee with him and range through the riding in the tracks of his opponent. And that was the plan followed.

The county of Leeds stretches for thirty miles along the north shore of the St. Lawrence River, where it is known as the Lake of the Thousand Islands, from Cananoque to Brockville, rising from the river in a succession of ridges. The river road was marked by a number of large homes set back on their stately terraces with an elegance that was then rare in Upper Canada. The northern boundary of the county was reached by travelling up through the heartland for thirty miles to Rideau Lake, the summit of the watershed, where the Rideau River flows off as the eastern outlet to the Ottawa, and the western outlet empties into Lake Ontario through the Cataraqui. It was in this country, in January of 1864, that D'Arcy McGee came to know John A. MacDonald intimately.

This was a new experience of Canada for McGee as he realized how much he had in common with John A. MacDonald, including a taste for old ballads. McGee recalled "The Man from the North Countrie," the simplest and probably the best of his own ballads:

> He came from the North and his words were few,
> But his voice was kind and his heart was true,
> And I know by his eyes no guile had he,
> So I married the man from the North Countrie.

That winter the countryside was white and silent. As the cold runners of their sleigh made a crunching sound in the dry snow, he noted that the bare woods in the low sun appeared as a dusky mauve and silver. One tall pine laden with snow seemed to McGee to be sailing with its canvas spread, across a lake of marble. Later he put his impressions into verse:

> Fast fell the snow and soft as sleep,
> The hillocks looked like frozen sheep.

Travelling together from one village to another, around frozen lakes and through the quiet hills, MacDonald and McGee made a droll pair— one tall, the other small, each on the homely side, and neither missing a chance to exchange a story with a passer-by, to amuse a group or to stir an assembly. As Sandford Fleming recalled, when McGee walked in and on the stage, wrapped in his oversize fur coat, he could be mistaken for the driver, until he started to speak. Out in the bracing air all day, and in overheated halls in the evening, there was time at night beside a blazing fire for a few stiff drinks. Here the local talk always seemed to turn towards the summer, as McGee was inundated with tales about their wild fowl, and their abundance of black bass, pike, *doré* and the mighty *maskinongé*, which the biggest story stretched to fifty pounds and eight feet long. As someone stirred the logs, McGee would "take an air of the fire," content for a spell with his easy accomplishments:

> To smoke his *dudeen*
> And drink his *cruiskeen*,

until he was reminded that his throat was "as dry as a blacksmith's pipe." Then he and the willing John A. would lead the group in the old Irish air, "I think it no treason to drink when I'm dry," which finished in the tender meditation:

> A drunken man is a terrible curse,
> But a drunken woman is twice as worse.

Politically, they were so successful together that the *Globe* became apprehensive. "Two outsiders," it called them, a "pretended" Orangeman and a "pretended" Roman Catholic. Friends boiled in politics, it was said, were tasteless. But something else was happening here. Two arrays of political talent, strongly opposed to each other for six years, were being annealed together by the temper and the rising heat of the combat.

The vote came at the end of January, and Richards, who had won his previous election by a margin of 135, was defeated by seventy-five votes. The *Globe* grumbled; and George Brown wrote to Luther Holton: "Here is a pretty mess." It was a victory for Jones. But more than that, it was a signal victory for a new political combination which many felt could become almost invincible.

About two weeks after the by-election in Leeds, the Session opened in Quebec City. No one expected the Government to last very long. The Montreal *Gazette* calculated that with Foley supporting John A. MacDonald, it could result in a tie vote. But James O'Halloran, the member from Missisquoi in the Eastern Townships, had, in Cartier's words, "deserted his party and his friends" and gone over to Sandfield MacDonald. Perhaps others would follow O'Halloran, the *Gazette* commented, "for the sake of their own snug things."

The Session was scarcely more than a week old when O'Halloran and McGee clashed in an ugly incident. George Clerk entered it in his diary in his own fashion:

> 1864, February 26, Friday: McGee and O'Halloran have been copiously blackguarding one another in the House of Assembly. "The pot and the kettle."
> McGee's violent speech much spoken of. He is getting desperate at being out of office, and will commit himself this Session.

What happened was this. Late Wednesday night O'Halloran, described by the *Gazette* as "a radical democrat," rose in a rather drowsy House to explain his position. He alluded to some transactions of the former

Government of Cartier and John A. MacDonald as corrupt. With that said, he then opened an attack on D'Arcy McGee for coming out as "the father of the Constitutional Party." There were only two parties in Canada, O'Halloran said, no matter what labels were used, the Reform Party and the Old Tory Party, and the Tory party was the child of the Family Compact and corruption:

> McGee is a gentleman who has changed completely around. Once a defamer of the Constitution, now he is a self-constituted father of the Constitutional Party. It is well known that Mr. McGee has spent the best part of his days in endeavouring to destroy the Constitution.

To support his attack, O'Halloran went back fifteen years and read from an inflammatory article written by McGee on March 31, 1849, in the hectic days of his *New York Nation.*

McGee was on his feet the moment O'Halloran sat down, and began his reply with remarkable composure:

> When I wrote that article in the *New York Nation,* I was a new-comer, and had a very imperfect knowledge of the country in which I resided, much less of Canada. Since then, I have gone through fifteen years with my eyes and ears open. I would now advise any young friend who intended to edit a paper not to express his senti-ments so freely where he knew so little.
>
> Since those youthful days, I have changed my opinion. But there is a baseness to which a change of political opinion cannot be com-pared. It is found in the man who changes or pretends to change his religious views for the sake of his own advancement.

Here McGee seemed to lose control, and suddenly he flashed with anger:

> In a public room in a public hotel, before four witnesses, whom I now cite—the honourable members from Frontenac, Beauharnois and Carleton and the Solicitor General for Lower Canada—this very honourable member from Missisquoi, who attacks me, stated that he would hang every priest in Canada.

The charge caused a sensation. Then in the excitement that followed, William Ferguson, the member for Frontenac, was heard to say that he corroborated McGee, and W. F. Powell of Carleton rose to state that he understood O'Halloran to have said "it would be better if a priest or two were hanged" or that "we would never have peace until all priests were hanged."

McGee then turned on O'Halloran with scorn:

> He talks of corruption. How naturally that word flows from his lips like filth to the grating of a gutter.

That turbulent sitting of the House did not adjourn until three o'clock in the morning. The next day George Brown wrote to his wife:

> There was an awful scene of abuse in the House last night. McGee, O'Halloran, Ferguson and others pitching into each other like fury. Fortunately I stayed home to nurse my leg, playing a couple of games of chess. The debates so far have not had one hour of practical common sense in them. There ought to be a shake-up, and I hope there will be.

A week later George Brown wrote to his wife and enclosed a photograph of D'Arcy McGee:

> I think you will say he never looked so well in his life. It was a great thing in him to give it to me. But I believe he does not think me quite as bad as the rest of the Ministerial party—but rather as a redeeming point.

The debates improved in the days that followed. McGee's hopes for the Intercolonial Railway were renewed when the Government announced it would at least make a survey of the proposed line at its own expense, and appointed Sandford Fleming to carry it out. McGee was speaking on the railway project on March 10 when he announced that he had just received good news in a letter from Halifax:

> Laying aside all partisan and personal considerations, the leading spirits of the Maritime Provinces have simultaneously proposed to reunite Nova Scotia, New Brunswick and the Island of Prince Edward into one great maritime community, with one tariff, one treasury and one legislature.

Then on March 14 George Brown proposed, with the support of D'Arcy McGee from the other side of the House, that the House should set up a nonpartisan committee of nineteen members to study the reform of the Constitution. It was similar to his motion in the previous Session, and was based impartially on the memorandum of Galt, Cartier and Rose of October 1858, which had recognized, even then, that there was an urgent need of "a remedy for a state of things that is yearly becoming worse."

In the discussion that followed, John A. MacDonald poked fun at

Brown and went so far as to say that the Federal system was a failure in the United States. "We should have a Legislative Union, in fact, in principle, and in practice," he added; but Cartier quickly interjected: "That is not my policy." In any event, that night John A. MacDonald, Cartier and then Galt spoke against Brown's motion. Disappointed but not yet discouraged, Brown let it drop without a vote, determined to bring it up later in the Session.

Three days later something minor occurred in Montreal which had a foreboding aspect for McGee. That year the *Gazette* in describing Montreal's activities on St. Patrick's Day included a disturbing report. The parade was a success, the *Gazette* stated, and St. Patrick's concert that evening had an audience of two thousand, but there was also another gathering; the Hibernian Society, a new group in Montreal, met at the Exchange Hotel; a hundred were present at this meeting, and the *Gazette* went on to say that

> the tone of the speeches was disloyal and seditious. One speaker
> said he hoped the day was fast approaching when all Irishmen would
> be a Fenian Brotherhood, and Britain as a nation would cease to
> exist.

In a sharp editorial the *Gazette* added that "the Catholic Church of the Northern States has condemned the Fenian Brotherhood, and the Bishops have issued pastoral letters against it."

D'Arcy McGee was in Quebec City right in the midst of a Cabinet crisis. But on March 21 he wrote an open letter in strong terms, which filled a full column of the *Gazette*. "Of the 30,000 Irish in Montreal," it was a pity, McGee wrote, that "even 100" could gather for such a purpose.

McGee mentioned that he was well aware that "emissaries from the Fenians in the United States have been working in Montreal for the past two years." Then he disclosed that the letter condemning the Fenians published by the Montreal *Herald* two years before over the name *Civis Canadiensis* had, in fact, been written by him. Taking the broad view that he had long been opposed to all secret societies, McGee felt the Fenians must be condemned on that ground alone; and McGee pointed out that just a few days earlier he had opposed a Bill in the House incorporating an Orange Society because it was secret.

The Head Centre of the Fenians, McGee went on, was John O'Mahony:

> a gentleman of good standing and excellent education, a graduate,
> if I am well informed, of Trinity College. Arriving in the United

States, he became incurably insane on the subject of spiritualism, and while in that state nearly took the life of his friend and entertainer, Mr. John Mitchel. Subsequently he passed several months in a mad-house near Flatbush, Long Island.

McGee declared that it was a test of membership in St. Patrick's Society of Montreal that no one could belong to a secret society, and that last September Bishop Bourget's letter against such secret associations had been read from St. Patrick's pulpit by Father Patrick Dowd. Direct action was needed, McGee said:

Secret societies are like what the farmers in Ireland used to say of scotch grass. The only way to destroy it is to cut it out by the roots and burn it into powder.

Then he added this postscript:

I see the disease has broken out violently in Toronto. Those who are responsible for that community should act at once and decidedly.

In such a position, where other men might merely say a quiet word, McGee was bold and fearless. But such is the course of things that bold attacks on secret societies make secret, cunning enemies. Unknown at the time, John O'Mahony was then in Montreal.

Through most of that month of March the Government of Sandfield MacDonald and Dorion tottered but somehow did not fall. A rumour

ANTOINE
AIME
DORION

spread that Dorion was about to be appointed to the Bench, which proved to be groundless but did Dorion political harm. Then on March 21 (the same day that D'Arcy McGee wrote his open letter on the Fenians), when it was apparent that the Government was about to fall from its own inertia, Sandfield MacDonald spoke with admirable self-command and announced the resignation of his Government.

It was a trying period, and Mary McGee this time cautiously remained in Quebec City at the side of her husband. The two children were at home in Montreal with their grandmother; and the younger, seven-year-old Agnes (or Peggy, as her father called her) kept three of the letters she received from her mother. The first was written on March 10 from Quebec City:

> My dearest Agnes:
> I am looking forward with great pleasure for Friday when I hope to receive the letter which you promised to write, in which I hope to hear that you have been quite well and have been good and obedient to grandmother, and taken great care of her, and that you looked after the house, Puppy and Tiny, nursing all the pussies, and not forgetting the cock and hens.
> I hope also to hear that you have said your lesson to your grandmother daily, and that you are making great progress in your reading and writing and prayers.
> Your Papa and I often think and speak of our poor Beauty, and hope to find you in good health and spirits when we meet at Easter. Papa joins me in love and twenty kisses. God bless and keep you.
> Your affectionate Mamma

The next day was Friday, but no letter came, so Agnes received a reminder:

> My dear Agnes:
> I have been expecting a letter from you ever since we left home, and it has not yet arrived.
> Fasa told me in her letter that Ellen was kind enough to make you a Patrick's cross which you have to wear, also a bread pudding which you intended eating—which I hope you did, and enjoyed. I suppose Tiny assisted you. Tell him that his mother, Topsy, has two wee little pups, all black like her.

A third letter followed, dated "Holy Saturday" March 26:

> My dear little Agnes:
> How I wish I could be with you tomorrow. But I hope to see you next week.

I will be thinking of you all day tomorrow, and I am sure you will think of your Papa and Mamma and wish they were with you.

Your grandmother tells me you say your lesson every day, and that you and Puppy and Tiny then play on the gallery. The little dogs here are not so playful as Tiny, and they seldom go out of doors.

Your Papa and I send you a great deal of love, and twenty kisses. God bless my Agnes and protect and guide her, is the wish of her affectionate,

Mamma

The reason why D'Arcy McGee had to remain in Quebec City over Easter arose from the succession of attempts and failures of others to form a new Government. This time McGee was in the midst of the negotiations. Adding to the difficulties, however, John A. MacDonald was again talking of retiring. What this meant to his friends was well expressed in a letter to him of March 25 from James O'Reilly of Kingston:

If you take the helm all is well; if not, disaster is certain to follow. Surely all our conquests, our fights, our triumphs are not to end this way. John A. not the U.C. leader! Bosh. The Government won't stand.

Finally, on March 30, the venerable Etienne Taché was persuaded to come out of retirement, and he headed a Ministry, with John A. MacDonald really in control. Cartier was Attorney General, Galt was Minister of Finance and Foley was Postmaster General. Then as Minister of Agriculture and Immigration, and fulfilling his cherished ambition, was D'Arcy McGee.

McGee's enthusiasm for the position was already on the record: to fill "the still unsettled parts of Upper Canada between Lake Huron and the Ottawa," to settle the Eastern Townships, which, "instead of a quarter million, are capable of sustaining three to four million souls," and to settle the St. Maurice Valley as well:

The summer traveller who hears steam blown off at night at Three Rivers seldom dreams that he has just passed a great river which drains a country larger than all Scotland, and as capable as Scotland of bearing its three million of inhabitants.

The next day the House adjourned to permit the new Ministers to stand for their by-elections. McGee was returned by acclamation. But Foley, bitterly attacked by the Clear Grits as a deserter, went down to defeat in his by-election, which turned out to be as crucial as the defeat of Richards in Leeds.

D'Arcy McGee and his wife and two children were excited, for they were moving from St. Antoine to a new home on St. Catherine Street. When he was appointed to the Cabinet, his supporters decided to honour and help him, and very few men had more generous friends than D'Arcy McGee. They formed a committee, including Lawrence Devaney, Walter MacFarlane, William O'Brien, William Molson, Thomas McKenna, James Donnelly and Leo Shannon; they collected gifts ranging from the widow's mite to the contractor's calculated contribution; and that spring they presented a new house to the very grateful McGee family.

It was a handsome home, built of Montreal cut limestone, with brick stables behind, in the new Montmorency Terrace on the Redpath farm on the south side of St. Catherine Street, two doors east of Drummond. Its front windows were distinguished by two stone lintels quarried at *Saint Marc la Carrière*, and carved with twenty-six shamrocks. In this spacious three-storey house, with a new furnace in the basement, a large range with all the fittings in the kitchen, the latest in bronze gaseliers, deep full curtains in the dining and drawing rooms, and well carpeted throughout, with oilcloth in the lower and upper halls, and even a special clothes-press in the nursery, D'Arcy McGee would spend his best hours, beside the fireplace among his family or upstairs in his well-stocked library.

The title deeds were presented to him on April 26, 1864, at a public gathering. It was as open and healthy a way as there could be to make such a magnificent political donation. McGee recognized the great debt he owed to all his friends as he responded:

It is a gift not to be repaid by words, but by faithful and loyal service.

Generous though they were, the sums donated did not quite cover the full price, and McGee assumed the balance of $2500 as a first mortgage at 7 per cent interest. In time McGee would find this burden heavy. True, he was not a good manager, but his household expenses always seemed to mount beyond control. Mary McGee's mother, Mrs. Caffrey, lived with them until she died in the summer of 1866. So did his younger half-brother, John, who was studying as a surveyor. And there was a standing welcome for poorer relatives and friends arriving from Ireland, as they passed through the city or perhaps overstayed their welcome, naturally assuming that a public man of his prominence had to be prosperous. Not far away in New York City his young brother, James, had a growing family, and D'Arcy helped them. James McGee had worked with D'Arcy on the *American Celt* and had continued to write, publishing a few books; but the financial returns were small, and "Jimmy" had enlisted in the Irish Brigade under Thomas Francis Meagher in the American Civil War.

The family ties were strong and deep. Though D'Arcy was away for long periods, when he was at home, he did his best to make up for his absence. Mary, his wife ("Molly" in his letters) was the true centre, "a guide, a lamp, a star," he wrote, the steady and devoted mother. Fasa, her father observed, was "growing very studious, a good musician and a great letter-writer," and Peggy "though not strong," was "well, and lively as ever." But his lasting regret was that he was away from home too often.

No theme recurred more frequently in his verse than that of absence. Whether it was from his family or his native land, it impelled him to write. And the first pangs of exile inspired his best poem, "The Celts":

> Long, long ago, beyond the misty space
>     Of twice a thousand years,
> In Erin old there dwelt a mighty race,
>     Taller than Roman spears;
> Like oaks and towers they had a giant grace,
>     Were fleet as deers,
> With wind and waves they made their 'biding place,
>     These western shepherd seers.
>
> The Druid's altar and the Druid's creed
>     We scarce can trace.
> There is not left an undisputed deed
>     Of all your race,
> Save your majestic song, which hath their speed,
>     And strength and grace;
> In that sole song, they live and love, and bleed—
>     It bears them on through space.

The evening before the deeds to his home were given to him, McGee following Pierre Chauveau talking in French, was the principal speaker at Montreal's tercentenary celebration of Shakespeare's birth. Here he had the good sense to rely on his own insights. He spoke of the paradox in Shakespeare as the genius who could be content to work with a misprinted copy of "Hamlet," and the poet who remained shrewd: "joyous in society, an occasional hard drinker and yet contemplative, even to sadness, in his solitude." The Shakespeare who enraptured him was the man "looking straight out into all space," speaking calmly to other men "of the mysteries of life and death, of duty and destiny, of liberty and law and of remorse and blessed peace." McGee closed his remarks in his own fashion:

> But if Shakespeare were present in person this evening, he would take far more pleasure to mingle among so many fair ladies than to talk dull didactics here on this platform.

In his new home D'Arcy McGee was a warm and cheerful host. As he greeted his guests and shook their hands with evident pleasure, his homely features would melt away with his smile, and he would join every group to make their small talk crackle with his fun:

> What do you think of the weather we're having? As they say in Galway:
> "If you can see the Arrans, it's a sign of rain. And if you can't see them, it's raining."
> And have you heard the Irish boy's epitaph to his cow?
> > When she lived she lived in clover,
> > And when she died she died all over.

When he was at home he was in his library almost every evening. There he worked steadily, his coat carelessly tossed across a stack of books and his notes scribbled in his rapid hand scattered everywhere over his desk and on the chairs. And invariably before they went to bed, Fasa and Peggy would come in to see him.

D'Arcy McGee slipped with ease into the airy, brilliant world of his children. They would follow him gladly through his comical talk into whimsical lands and on to the realm of marvels. He only had to whistle an old air he had heard as a boy and it brought back numberless stories to recount. Fasa and Peggy would listen to their favourite tales of "The Brewery of Egg Shells" where the story goes that the mother was husho-ing the babe in the cradle when she was startled to hear the infant sud-denly speak to her with the voice of a very old man; or "The Saga of King Olaf of Norway and His Dog" about the faithful Irish wolf hound, Vig, who died for his master in their last brave battle; or "Bewitched Butter" when, in times gone by, an elegant but bitter red cow was moan-ing in the grey haze of a summer twilight only to be freed from an evil spell by a hag of great age and a thousand wrinkles. And in "The Soul Cages" they heard tell of the peculiar doings of Jack Daugherty, the fisherman, in his wild situation among the seals and the sea gulls where he lived all alone (but for his wife).

Eerie stories did not deter them, even if the dog howled outside. Most ghosts assumed many shapes and meant no harm, but if anyone ever saw a butterfly near a corpse, that was the end. There was the frightful "Bull-aworrus," the spectral bull with fire blazing from his eye-sockets who guarded buried treasure galore through the night. And there also was "The Headless Ghost" who in the course of time was descended from the Irish giant who swam the channel with his head in his teeth.

Most uproarious of all was the tale of "The Mischievous Goblin" who appeared at odd times in the form of a buck goat. His great ambition was to get some unfortunate galoot on his back, and then, *no ho* to flying, race furiously through the bogs, marshes and wild woods, around the crags, under the cliffs, over the rocks and amid the briars, until the wretch of a rider on his back was nearly dead with terror. Then, *Whist!* He would pitch him into a swamp. But this goblin was not malignant. He did not kill people.

D'Arcy McGee knew all the Irish fairies, those who called out "Glic! Glic!" and "Hwee! Hwee!" and those who cried in a hollow tone "A weel! A weel!" as they clapped their hands together. Their chief and capricious occupations, old men said, were feasting, fighting and making music and love. Dancing, too—as one little woman near the village of Ballisodare could testify, for she had lived among them on the *Plain a Baun,* wherever that was, and when she escaped, she came home with no toes—she had danced them off. She was the one who knew the imp who could dance on a trembling rain drop. Sad to say, nearly all those tricky little fellows would give their weight in gold for *pottheen.* But, apart from their powerful thirst for mountain dew, whether it brought success or bad cess, the solitary *leprechaun* hammered away on his single shoe; the *banshee* went forth riding and wailing on her headless horse; and the *pooka* was always abroad—indeed, one *pooka,* very old and very odd in shape, used to stand and yawn in a Sligo street on dark nights, till lately.

In that large and shadowy room his daughters heard him in silent wonder as he told them of *Eman,* the wayward student, who sighed to see the Irish isle of *Hy Brasil* "as beautiful as the morning's smile." Fishermen told *Eman* they had often seen its ruined chapel beneath them as they sailed over the clear green sea on a sunny afternoon; and every seventh year the hidden isle emerged from the depths of the ocean, far to the west of Arran. But the race of men were shut out. So too were age and death and tears and loud laughter. *Hy Brasil* was only for the little sea people, a few spans high. Their bonfires could be seen on its dim sands only "at midsummer midnight from a moonbright bay." This was his ballad of the tragic "Voyage of *Eman Oge,* in the western ocean's water where the sinking sun is lost."

He talked to his children, too, of the Far West and the Far North of Canada; about the wapiti, the buffalo and the beaver, *le loup-garou,* the *voyageur* and the trapper. "Who teaches the doe and the fawn to run in the track the moose has made? Who whispers in every breeze that stirs the birch canoe? Who hangs the reindeer moss on the trees for the food of the caribou?" He was telling Fasa and Peggy of "The Arctic Indian's Faith":

> That Spirit we worship who walks unseen
> Through our land of ice and snow,
> We know not His face, we know not His place,
> But His presence and power we know.

The House reassembled on May 3, and in its first test the Government of Etienne Taché and John A. MacDonald was lucky enough to obtain a slight majority of two votes, it was that close. Brown promptly revived his motion to set up a committee to study the reform of the Constitution, and D'Arcy McGee gave a stirring speech in support of it. "I have always advocated such a step," McGee maintained, recalling his very first Session in 1858 when he had seconded a motion to study the plan of uniting all the British North American Provinces.

Brown's motion, which McGee supported as nonpartisan, met with formidable opposition, however, and finally on May 20 it was put to a vote. John A. MacDonald, Cartier, Galt, Sandfield MacDonald, Dorion and Holton all voted against it. But, to the surprise of both Brown and McGee, their motion was carried fifty-nine to forty-eight. McGee was one of the most ardent and assiduous members of this Constitutional committee. On June 14, an oppressively hot day in Quebec City, the committee released its report. Notwithstanding the refusal of both John A. and Sandfield MacDonald to sign it, the majority of the committee declared that it favoured "changes in the direction of a federative system, applied either to Canada or to the whole of the British North American Provinces."

It made little difference then, it seemed, because late that night, on Dorion's motion of want of confidence, the Taché-MacDonald Government was defeated by two votes, to bring it down. What could happen now? Another general election would be a farce. Within two years there had already been two elections and four Governments. With the impasse facing everyone, an astounding chain of events was rapidly set in motion.

Brown saw more than a coincidence between his committee's report on a new Federal era and the collapse of another Government in the worn-out framework of Union. He remarked to some friends of the defeated Taché-MacDonald Government that now was the time to settle forever the Constitutional difficulties between Upper and Lower Canada. Then he added: "I am ready to co-operate." The message was quickly relayed to John A. MacDonald.

Most things, it seemed, came down to a single question of practical politics for John A. MacDonald: how to get an absolute working majority. But Brown, who had not even spoken to him in eight years, represented a personal and emotional problem that was practically intolerable. Yet there was nothing to lose. John A. was audacious and swallowed his pride.

The next day was Thursday, June 16. The heat was almost unbearable in Quebec City, ninety degrees in the shade, and nothing was expected to happen. About three o'clock as the members were languorously taking their seats for another dull afternoon in the House, John A. MacDonald walked over to the centre of the floor and, in an awkward attempt to be casual, spoke to Brown:

"Have you any objection to meet Galt and myself for a discussion?"
"Certainly not," Brown replied.

A definite appointment was made for one o'clock the next day. So on Friday afternoon the three men met in Brown's drab bedroom in the St. Louis Hotel. It was a stiff meeting, Brown intense and rigid, Galt stout and very warm, and John A. a little weary but of the three the least ill-at-ease.

Brown stated at once that he was ready to take extraordinary steps because of the extreme urgency. MacDonald and Galt accepted "that footing" and asked Brown to join them in a Coalition Cabinet. Brown instantly reacted. He was repelled, he said, by the thought, and "the public mind would be shocked." Brown's personal refusal to enter the Cabinet was not discussed further, and the talk turned to general terms, seeking some solution on a broad working basis.

Eventually these alternatives seemed to be satisfactory. They would adopt the Federal principle, either for all British North American colonies or for Canada alone, with a provision to admit the Maritime Provinces and Northwest Territory later on. But they could not agree on which alternative should be presented first. So they adjourned, agreeing to report on their progress to Parliament.

The next day, Saturday, Cartier joined them. This was helpful. Eight years of frozen anger between Brown and MacDonald could not melt; and Brown and Galt were jealous and watchful of each other. Despite all the harsh words Brown had used about Cartier, he seemed to have a liking for this tenacious, inventive leader of French Canada. Brown spoke of Cartier as he could not speak of MacDonald, and probably not of Galt, as "fair, frank and manly." Together the four men drew up a memorandum; then Brown went off to discuss it with his friends. One he saw, whom he trusted for an independent view, was D'Arcy McGee.

Later that day, at six o'clock, Brown met MacDonald, Galt and Cartier again. Finally, after carefully resorting to vagueness (which revealed MacDonald's elastic touch), they were at least able to concur in this rather roundabout proposal:

> The Government are prepared to pledge themselves to bring in a measure next session for the purpose of removing existing difficulties by introducing the Federal principle into Canada, coupled with such provisions as will permit the Maritime Provinces and the Northwest Territory to be incorporated into the same system of government.

On Sunday they returned to discuss the make-up of the Cabinet. Brown still refused to enter it personally; and then there was a dispute about the number of Ministers Brown could obtain for his own group in the Coalition. For three days it seemed to be the stumbling-block.

On Tuesday, June 22, McGee had a long, earnest talk with Brown, urging him to join the Cabinet himself. Lord Monck, the Governor General, urged the same thing. Later that day McGee wrote a letter to Brown which, as Brown confided to his wife, had a strong influence on him. It was pointed and practical:

> My dear Brown:
> I wish to impress most strongly on you, in sequence to the conversation of today, that the prospect of the settlement of the Constitutional question now before us, may be most materially affected, either furthered or closed, by your acceptance or refusal of office.
> How can you hope to secure the settlement without your own personal participation in the preliminary and advance stages of the negotiations?

The negotiation must go on, during recess and session, hail, rain or shine. But you, unless a Minister, cannot be on the spot, cannot enter the Council Chamber, cannot, in short, speak, think or act for yourself, unless you are a member of the Government.

I can only add to what I might make a long letter of reasons, that, should you conclude to join this Government with the view of settling our great and increasing constitutional difficulties, I can assure you, you will find in me, if not a very able, certainly a very willing coadjutor.

Believe me, very truly yours,
Thos. D'Arcy McGee

George Brown made up his mind to join the Cabinet. When the news was announced, it was received in different quarters with loud rejoicing and great consternation.

*La Minerve,* which supported Cartier, expressed it with a shock of unbelief:

What? Impossible! Brown, the enemy of Lower Canada, supporting a Ministry of Taché and Cartier! Come. Come. It is a ruse on his part at the very least. He wishes to compromise the leaders of our party with the ultimate hope of extracting fatal concessions from them later on.

The *Rouges* under Dorion moved to take advantage of the dismay and regain some of their lost strength. They took a stand as the true defenders of the French-Canadian nationality while their journal, *Le Pays,* branded the Coalition as "an immoral and infamous agreement which would sell out the French Canadians," a web of "notorious cowardice and blackest treason."

With two out of three persons in Lower Canada being French-Canadian, the Montreal *Gazette* was perplexed and did not show its hand:

The more extreme Ministerialists are afraid that one cannot touch pitch and not be defiled; that one cannot have any political intercourse with Mr. George Brown and not make some lamentable sacrifice of principle.

Even Brown's own *Globe* seemed to be caught off guard. Two months earlier when there were rumours that Sandfield MacDonald was trying to save his Government by a Coalition with Cartier, the *Globe* had written that if that were true, then Sandfield MacDonald "would be the basest traitor to be found on British soil." Yet George Brown had just done what Sandfield MacDonald had failed to do.

Then *La Minerve* rallied. "Let us trust our leaders in taking up their heavy duties. They are tried patriots" were its second thoughts. "Let us give them our solid support." Whereupon the *Gazette* remarked that in any event it would advocate "a strongly centralized federation," and advised its readers to suspend judgment and "rely on our representative men in the Coalition."

Frances Monck, the sister-in-law of Governor Monck, reflected some of the excitement of those days in her diary with this curious entry:

> Some of us went to the House of Commons at Quebec. M. Cartier was introduced to me! That most quaint-looking McGee was also introduced—he looks like a wild Indian.

With so many disconcerted, D'Arcy McGee made a keen remark:

> In the House, George Brown has been the strongest man within his own section, but outside of it, the weakest.

Yet that was looking backwards, and McGee was now concerned with the immediate future:

> Brown has a large, loose vigour, with a manliness which it is impossible not to respect whatever one may think of his policy.

On June 27 McGee left the excitement of Quebec City, to travel into Galt's territory, where he delivered an address at the annual Convocation of the University of Bishop's College at Lennoxville:

> Patriotism will increase in Canada as its history is read; and our history is rewarding because it forms an inseparable part in the annals of the best ages of both France and England.

Three days later, as the sun was going down beyond the ramparts of Quebec City, the new Cabinet was announced. With reason, it has been called the Great Coalition. Under the aegis of Etienne Taché, it included John A. MacDonald as Attorney General for Upper Canada, Cartier as Attorney General for Lower Canada, Galt as Minister of Finance and Brown as President of the Council—bringing with him from his group Oliver Mowat as Postmaster General and William McDougall as Provincial Secretary. And D'Arcy McGee returned to his portfolio as Minister of Agriculture and Immigration.

After eight years of bitter differences, experiments, crises, splintering, failures, frustrations and deadlock, the Coalition was created in a spirit of exaltation. It pledged itself to seek, by sending representatives to the Maritimes and to England, to secure those interests which are beyond the control of our own legislation to such a measure as may enable all British North America to be united under a general legislature based upon the Federal principle.

Many were elated, with some rising almost to rapture; others were suspicious and nursed a sense of betrayal; current feelings were, indeed, as contrary as they were intense. And the unspoken questions remained: Could the Coalition last? Would it endure beyond the crisis and the temporary cause which created it?

It could not be forgotten that the Coalition Cabinet called on many old foes to work together. In it were five very different men, and it would be difficult to sum up all their differences. Perhaps their varied approaches to politics can be indicated. If it be true to say that Brown went at politics as an industry, for Galt it was a business, for Cartier a profession, for MacDonald a craft and for D'Arcy McGee it was a passion.

As the House prorogued on June 30 McGee paid this tribute to two of his colleagues:

Brown has given the greatest exhibition of moral courage I ever knew. Next to him the man who has taken the greatest risk to his political future is Cartier. But Cartier is shrewd and far-seeing.

These qualities, and other unexpected ones, would be required of each of the five former foes in their pledge to work together.

# 13

## DOWN EAST

Of D'Arcy McGee I would speak tenderly, because, whatever be his errors, he is a man of genius—an elegant writer, an eloquent speaker, and a pleasant fellow over a bottle of wine.

*Joseph Howe*

Reasons for Confederation are as thick as blackberries.
*Thomas D'Arcy McGee*

Very few men then, and few at any time, could command a following in both Upper and Lower Canada. A politician came to take it as a warning that his popularity was waning in his own Province when he saw it increasing in the other. To these offsetting ups and downs, D'Arcy McGee was an exception. From the start of his career in Canada, McGee had been able to exercise a marked influence in both Provinces. Added to this balanced support in the Canadas, he had won some renown in the Maritimes through his visits there almost every year. This gave him a unique position in the Coalition Government.

John A. MacDonald felt that the Coalition Cabinet had at last overcome this fatal sectional weakness by combining two singular powers. It had Cartier's majority in Lower Canada and Brown's in Upper Canada. Together, instead of the chronic unworkable margin of two or three votes, they could now bring an over-all majority of fifty votes—a promise of political omnipotence. It was this reality of practical politics, much more than any theory, which led John A. MacDonald to talk effectively about Federal Union. The Coalition Government lacked homogeneity, certainly. But there was no organized strength in the Opposition. And none threatened, as long as Cartier and Brown, so discordant and divergent in the past, had a common will to work together.

Ever since July 2, 1863, when, as the proud Vermonters claimed, the army of the North pivoted around them to drive the South to defeat in the Battle of Gettysburg, officials in the British North American colonies feared that the North would soon win the Civil War. Outside of a few newspapers like Brown's *Globe* in Toronto, Holton's *Herald* and Dorion's *Le Pays* in Montreal, and in New Brunswick the Saint John *Morning Freeman* of Timothy Warren Anglin (a former Irish Rebel of '48, like McGee), most of the newspapers in the Canadas and the Maritimes openly hoped to see the South win. Gettysburg made them very doubtful, and the concern about the military weaknesses of British North America became worries once again.

A faint resemblance of the dread felt during the *Trent* crisis reappeared. In fact, British Imperial authorities had just received their own secret military report that Upper Canada was really indefensible, and that troops and fortifications would have to be concentrated in Montreal and Quebec.

In the last month of the Session of 1864, reports kept arriving in Quebec City that delegates of the Maritime Provinces would soon meet to discuss their own Union. But the reports were strangely vague, and no one knew where or when. So on June 30, the very day the Coalition Cabinet was sworn in, Governor General Monck, with a sense of some urgency, wrote "to ascertain whether the proposed Union may not be made to embrace the whole of the British North American Provinces," and to ask, too, about the place and date of the meeting and if Canadians would be welcome. Several weeks then passed. But there was no reply.

This desire to form a Maritime Union—or Reunion, as Dr. Charles Tupper of Nova Scotia called it—derived, despite parochial jealousies, from a common sense of loyalty and plain reasons of geography. But the impulse also came from two negative forces. Besides a beneficent fear of the United States, there were feelings of anger against Canada caused by the Canadian announcement in September of 1863 that the Intercolonial Railway agreement had been abandoned. The cry went up that Sandfield MacDonald's Government was "bankrupt in truth" and Dorion was openly branded by the Saint John *Telegraph* as "a liar." Others, in sadder tones, spoke of the Maritimes turning away from Canada "as from a stranger."

In a contrasting light, Maritimers continued to recognize McGee as a friend for his unchanging support of the Intercolonial Railway. When he broke with Sandfield MacDonald, McGee became "something of a provincial hero in New Brunswick." McGee's popularity in the Maritimes was important in what followed, because most of the other members of Canada's Coalition Cabinet were personally unknown in the Maritimes. When McGee first entered the Cabinet, he met with so much Canadian indifference about the Maritimes that no one seemed disturbed when, in response to his request, not a single map of the Maritimes could be found in the Government offices in Quebec City. What interest there was in the Maritimes too often appeared in English Upper Canada with the complacent air of a big brother, or in French Lower Canada as a bitter memory of the dispersion of the Acadians. In McGee's view, Intercolonial Union needed an Intercolonial Railway, and to build both, the task was, as he expressed it, "to tunnel through ignorance."

But a change occurred in March of 1864. McGee's speech in the House urging diplomacy in the railway project was coupled in the Maritimes with the good news about Sandford Fleming, the well-known engineer.

At the sole cost of the Canadian Government, he had already left Rivière du Loup and was about to set off from Rimouski on snowshoes to survey the line of the Intercolonial Railway through ninety miles of wilderness to the Restigouche.

Earlier that winter McGee and Fleming had been talking about the Canadian lack of knowledge of the Maritimes, and both men had agreed that to advance a Union of British America, a representative group of Canadians should make a personal tour of the Maritimes. Fleming did not forget the conversation. In April 1864 he suggested to Premier Charles Tupper that Nova Scotia might sponsor such a visit. Tupper did not respond favourably, but a group of businessmen in Saint John did, and in turn they interested some friends in Halifax. The result was that in June the Boards of Trade of Saint John and Halifax invited the Canadian Parliament to send a group of its members to visit the Maritimes that summer. But the invitation was received during the Cabinet crisis in Canada. It was hastily considered and declined, much to the annoyance of the Maritimers.

In July, however, McGee and Sandford Fleming, with the aid of James Ferrier, a director of the Grand Trunk and a member of the Upper House, managed to have the invitation renewed, and this time it was accepted. They then proceeded to organize a representative group of Canadians for the excursion. Almost at the same time, by good luck, the Canadian Government received its reply that the Conference on Maritime Union would open on September 1 at Charlottetown, and that Canadians were free to participate in it, but unofficially.

Arrangements were quickly made for the tour to leave Montreal early in August and return in three weeks. Some thirty-two members of Parliament accepted, and with eighteen more from the Upper House, some businessmen and twenty-three journalists, they made up a party of one hundred. It was a noteworthy group with most of the important newspapers represented, including Toronto's *Globe* and *Leader*, Hamilton's *Spectator*, Kingston's *British American*, Montreal's *Gazette* and *La Minerve* and Quebec's *Canadien*, *Journal* and *Mercury*. McGee headed the party as the only member of the Cabinet to go. The rest of the Cabinet remained in Quebec City in order to prepare their proposals for the Charlottetown Conference.

The Grand Trunk furnished free transportation to the whole excursion over their line to Portland, Maine. Indeed, the route they had to travel, by rail down to the busy naval base of Portland and then up the coast of Maine by ship to the Maritimes, and the necessity of submitting to customs' examinations at each Provincial border carried their own lessons on the military and commercial need of the Intercolonial Railway, and of Federal Union. And these lessons were heightened by a renewal of the rumours that some impatient Maritimers had cast aside all hope of the Intercolonial Railway and were then making plans to build a new "European and North American railroad" with American capital, as soon as the Civil War was over, southward to Portland.

On Thursday, August 4, the good-will excursion got off to a bad start. After a long, hot and sleepless journey in crowded day coaches from Montreal, the hundred weary travellers arrived the next day in Portland. It was pouring rain. From five o'clock Friday evening, there they were, during a long desolate hour of low tide, standing, drenched, on the grey open dock waiting among the fish barrels for their ship, which had not yet arrived. Some of the party turned back and went home. Finally their pert steamer, the *New England*, appeared.

But she had only seventy-five berths, her captain explained all too plainly. Any other place to sleep? No, except on her board deck. "Well, that's all we were promised," McGee murmured, "free passage and board." Extra mattresses were finally found, however, and that night the deck was "paved with sleeping carcasses." Happily, the next day was bright and sunny.

Saint John and New Brunswick were very much astir over the visit, and the arrival of the Canadians was "the chief topic of conversation at street corners." Friday, as the *New England* sailed through the islands and along the rough, rocky coast covered with pines, spruce and hemlock, the dreariness of the day before had been forgotten. They arrived at Saint John about eight o'clock in the evening and were amazed to see ten thousand people on Reed's Point waiting to greet them: "Too long estranged," the Saint John *Telegraph* wrote, "and too long unknown." The official welcome was carefully reserved, however, to Premier Tilley's proper words addressed to McGee: "I am glad to see you."

Saturday was a very pleasant, misty blue day. Handbills were distributed inviting everyone in town to meet the Canadians at a Court House reception, and that evening a lavish dinner at Stubbs Hotel lasted until all the wine was gone. Sunday, as it was so wisely appointed long ago, was a day of rest.

On Monday, August 8, the Canadians sailed up the quiet Saint John River country on the *Anna Augusta*. It was another soft summer day. The banks were a gentle green and the water a deep violet, reflecting

SAMUEL
LEONARD
TILLEY

the fleecy clouds overhead. Towards evening they crossed the still, deep stretch approaching Fredericton singing "*A la claire fontaine.*"

That night in the trim Provincial Building of Fredericton there was another lavish dinner. The toasts were friendly and the speeches good. Even Tilley, who began cautiously by trying to limit his remarks to a customs union, was moved to express a hope in a future "populous and prosperous British North America," and finished off his speech emotionally by joining hands with a Maritimer and a Canadian on either side. D'Arcy McGee showed his enthusiasm as he spoke on the prospects of Union:

> Your destiny and ours are as inseparable as the waters which flow into *La Baie de Chaleur*, rising though they do, on the one side, from the heights of Canada, and on the other, from the Highlands of New Brunswick.

There was another reception the next day as they left Fredericton.

At daybreak, Wednesday, the Canadians boarded an ancient ferry called the *Emperor*. Chugging across the strong tidewaters of the Bay of Fundy, they felt very much in the mood for the old paddle song led by the French Canadians "*En roulant ma boule.*" At Windsor, Nova Scotia, they were met by those two rugged political rivals Charles Tupper and Joseph Howe. A special train carried them across the narrow peninsula to Halifax, where, late that night, the travellers went to bed "tired, very tired."

Thursday, August 11, in Halifax was another day of sunshine. They joined in a dance called the "bonnet hop" on board the eighty-one-gun flagship HMS *Duncan,* and then sailed around the Northwest Arm with the Halifax Yacht Club. It was a glorious day at sea with a stiff breeze and the bunting flying all the way to Bedford Basin. There they had a picnic. In "a manly and exhilarating game of leapfrog, Bluenoses sprang over Canadians with shrieks of delight, Canadians bounded over New Brunswickers and tripped over Nova Scotians, while editors mingled in the fray, seeking the bubble of reputation."

Meanwhile long tables were set up on the grass, laden with "Hodge-Podge and Chowder." The chowder was "cod, herring, salmon, sole and haddock, boiled and boiled," said one squeamish soul, "to the point of suspicion." The hodge-podge was mutton and vegetables "boiled up together to become a palatable mixture, with a flavour of ashes." There was music, and they "laughed like parrots at the bagpipes," as the frisky old mayor of Fredericton danced the Highland fling.

On came the speakers. Joseph Howe and D'Arcy McGee vied with each other, and enjoyed it. As Howe said, he always felt in good form when he "could take off his coat and dance with his friends"; and that evening as he warmed up in his own headlong, prolix style, his vocabulary was never saltier. McGee responded with "a merry speech—one of his best." Harcourt, the correspondent of the Toronto *Globe,* rendered his decision in these terms:

> I intend by no means to detract from the fame of Joseph Howe when I say that Nova Scotians acquainted with him and who heard D'Arcy McGee acknowledge McGee to be the better orator of the two.

It was an "overpowering day for constitutions, especially my own," McGee acknowledged late that night as they sailed back to Halifax under a full moon.

The climax was reached on Saturday night, August 13, at a great public dinner given for all the Canadians in the vast Drill Shed on Spring Garden Road in Halifax. McGee pleaded for the cause of Confederation with such passion that Joseph Howe was carried out of himself in response. It was on this occasion that Howe made this exuberant pronouncement in favour of Confederation, which he would retract a few years later as "wild words":

> I am not one of those who thank God that I am a Nova Scotian merely, for I am a Canadian as well. I have looked across the broad continent, and studied the mode by which it could be united, the mode by which it could be made strong and vigorous while the old

flag still floats over the soil. I am delighted to see such a scene as this, which gives promise that that which was the dream of my boyhood will be realized before I die.

And why should Union not be brought about? Is it because we wish to live and die in our own insignificance? The day is rapidly approaching when the Provinces will be united, with one flag above their heads, one thought in all our bosoms, with one Sovereign and one Constitution.

The Canadians left the Maritimes a few days later. While they were sailing back to Portland, an alarm was issued that a Confederate gunboat, the *Tallahassee*, which had been ranging up and down the coast destroying Northern shipping, was in pursuit. Fortunately nothing happened. McGee hurried back home and then on to Quebec City to report enthusiastically to the Cabinet.

A remarkable change had occurred in the Maritime newspapers. Where they were cool before, they were now quite won over to the idea of a Federal Union with Canada. There were some exceptions. One was that vigorous man with side-burns, Timothy Anglin of Saint John. In his *Morning Freeman* he suspected that the hidden purpose of the visitors was to spread political propaganda for a Canadian scheme, and he declared himself opposed to Confederation.

But the Saint John *Morning News,* Tilley's newspaper, from then on urged Confederation with Canada rather than Maritime Union. Tupper enthusiastically declared that he was ready to give this greater plan of British North American Union his warm support. And his newspaper, the Halifax *British Colonist,* describing the Canadians as former "strangers" and now "friends," expressed the hope with a convert's zeal that it could aid in advancing

> that grand scheme which all the more intelligent politicians of our common country have at heart—a complete political consolidation of these British North American colonies.

With all that, it could not truly be said that Canadians were now popular in the Maritimes. But at least some Canadians were not unpopular.

Six months before, Maritimers looked upon Canadians as a people who had rebelled in 1837, had burnt down their Parliament, thrown rotten eggs at the Governor General, asked for Annexation to the United States, fought over schools and religion, changed their capital city every few years, been corrupted by the Grand Trunk and broken their word on the Intercolonial Railway; not only were they a people who had failed to govern themselves and had fought to exhaustion, but they were now expecting to be pulled out of their deadlock by placing some fancy, expensive legal harness around the neck of the Maritimers.

The mission of good will which McGee led through the Maritimes that August had at least dispelled some suspicions and dispersed many prejudices. Many Maritimers were ready to reconsider Canadians as trustworthy, and some of their political leaders were stirred as they looked inland to the western horizon.

McGee returned to controversy in Canada. George Clerk of the *True Witness* had closed his mind completely against Confederation, and he spoke of McGee's excursion to the Maritimes with disdain. "The Big Intercolonial Drink," as he called it in his diary on August 24, "is much criticized in town . . . disgraceful affair."

Even among the newspapers which supported Confederation a sharp debate had broken out as to what it meant. For *La Minerve,* federation was a league of independent states, with each one *maître chez-lui.* But the *Globe* saw the plan in the opposite light; Canada must reverse the American Constitution and establish sovereign power in the central government, making the local governments its creatures. The Montreal *Gazette* then came out strongly for unity and centralization, and around those two words a heated disagreement developed between the *Gazette* and *La Minerve.*

It was clearer than ever that if the plan for Confederation was to meet with any success, it had to depend on the determination of Brown, Cartier, Galt, McGee and MacDonald to work together. In fact, they did make headway. As the opening date of the Charlottetown Conference approached, MacDonald let it be known that the basic Federal plan was in a form which all members of the Coalition Cabinet accepted, and could best be described as "qualified centralization."

Then on August 28, the day before they sailed for Charlottetown, an unexpected crisis arose in the Coalition Cabinet at Quebec. The Cabinet had been summoned to meet at noon, and George Brown told what happened in a letter to his wife:

> Shortly after that we were all assembled but John A. We waited for him till one—till half past one—till two—and then Galt sent off to his house specially for him. Answer—will be here immediately.
>
> Waited till half past two—no appearance. Waited till three, and shortly after, John A. entered, bearing symptoms of having been on a spree. He was half-drunk.

Lunch is always on the side table, and he soon applied himself to it. And before we had well entered on the important business before us he was quite drunk with potations of ale.

Yet the meeting went on, and it was very troublesome. After a debate of two and a half hours on their plans for Charlottetown, MacDonald in a fierce mood shocked Brown by trying to push through claims for extras of over a half million dollars on the construction of the new Parliament Buildings in Ottawa, which had already exceeded their original estimate by 70 per cent. When it was postponed, as Brown described it:

John A. burst out furiously, declaring that his friends had deserted him, and he would not hold office another day. He will not think of it when he is sober.

To say the truth, were our visit to the Maritime Provinces and to England over, I would not care how soon a rupture came. The Constitutional question would then be beyond all chance of failure—and I would be quit of company that is far from agreeable.

Eight members of the Coalition Cabinet went to the Charlottetown Conference as the Canadian delegates. The first five were John A. MacDonald, Cartier, Brown, Galt and McGee. With them were Alexander Campbell, MacDonald's former legal partner; Hector Langevin, who had studied law under Cartier and was the younger brother of the Bishop of Rimouski, and William McDougall, who had been brought into the Cabinet by Brown.

Very well documented on what they planned to say, but quite uneasy about their "unofficial" role as self-invited guests, they sailed out of Quebec City on the *Queen Victoria* at sunset on Monday, August 29. Within two hours they were beyond the Isle of Orleans, passing a group of low islands. This was the country of wild fowl, sandpipers, ring plovers, ducks, curlew and teal. Soon the snow geese would be coming, winging their way from the Far North in their rapid, noisy wedges towards these flats. One of the islands was Grosse Isle, stretching long and low for three dismal miles with its sad air, which brought McGee's own lines back to mind:

Why are the women crying
Far to the west away?

There in the ship fever plague of 1847 over ten thousand Irish immigrants were buried in unmarked, shallow trenches, row upon dreary row, in a depression of six acres at the western end of the island.

D'Arcy McGee was on deck that evening under a star-lit sky. Someone forward was whistling quietly to himself, and that was the only sound, save the steady splash of water off the bow. Twenty-two years before, when he had sailed past Grosse Isle for the first time, McGee recalled how pleasant it then seemed. His first sea voyage was then almost over, and he was standing with his sister Dorcas in the weather bow near the jib on the old brig *Leo*, listening to his older brother Lawrence talk about Canada. They were moving slowly up the river on the rising tide, and he was watching the low islands slip by on the starboard, and eagerly awaiting his first sight of Quebec Citadel.

All this was on his mind that evening in late August 1864, as he watched a greyish green glow wavering over the black hills of the receding north shore. The weather signal from Father Point promised it would be clear and sunny for Tuesday, Wednesday and Thursday; and so it was. On Tuesday they appreciated the bold scenery of the St. Lawrence. The names along its south shore were a legend of adventure: Rivière du Loup, Trois Pistoles, L'Islet au Massacre, Le Bic. . . . Early on Wednesday they had coasted around the land's end of Canada, the peninsula which the Micmacs had called *Gaspay*. Rank after rank of steep sea cliffs in ancient formations of dark shale and limestone, showing their upturned edges to the sea and dipping inland, created an illusion that somehow the world had tipped to the north.

Veering south, they gave wide berth to the reefs of Cap des Rosiers. At that time, the fabulous boulder the Ship Head—which sailors called The Old Woman—was still standing in deep water, and on that calm day it loomed out like a phantom ship under full sail. A few years later the Ship Head toppled over into the sea. But then it marked the spot, known to D'Arcy McGee, where the *Carrick* was wrecked in a sudden snowstorm late in May of 1847, and nearly all its 181 Irish immigrants from County Sligo were drowned.

After Cap des Rosiers was skirted, the *Queen Victoria* made her only stop of the voyage, in Gaspé Bay, where dollar fish, star-fish and arrays of strange shells were seen in profusion. Then Percé was sighted, and Bonaventure Island appeared, completely covered, as if by a cloud, with snowy gannets, black cormorants and silvery gulls. Beyond were the vast dark waters of the whale, the seal and the dolphin. "It was Jacques Cartier's undiscovered sea," McGee wrote. "The region was hard, iron-bound and cold."

When dawn broke on Thursday they had just sighted the West Point of Prince Edward Island. The ship was heading southeast through a rolling sea, and now and then her bow would dip to send up a film of spray over the rising sun. It was September 1, the opening day of the Charlottetown Conference, and they would be late. The sunny, spacious days at sea were over. Yet they had served to open their minds and prepare them to present their views on the future of the northern half of the continent.

Most of Thursday morning was spent in the Northumberland Strait, close to the south shore of Prince Edward Island. It was level and pleasant country. The green grass looked bright on the red soil, the farmhouses were tidy and white, and along the water's edge were strands of sandy loam or banks of stiff red clay. By noon they had sailed through Hillsborough Bay and were carefully entering the harbour of Charlottetown.

They could see Charlottetown clearly, a buff-coloured town of seven thousand, "all rectangles and red earth," on a slight elevation between two small rivers. Under the hot noon sun, no one was stirring. A drowsy horse was hitched to a post on the dock. Then they saw some gulls circling over a small oyster boat. In it was William Henry Pope, the Secretary of the Island, perspiring slightly under his stovepipe hat and long red beard, rowing out to meet them.

While the whole town's attention was focussed on the travelling circus of Slaymaker and "the great trick rider" Nichols, the Charlottetown Conference had nonchalantly opened its first private session without the Canadians. There were fourteen delegates present, some of them reluctantly, to discuss the proposal of Maritime Union.

The most enthusiastic Maritime delegation came from Nova Scotia. There were five representatives from both political parties, led by their forceful and rather dashing forty-three-year-old Premier, Charles Tupper. Notably absent was Joseph Howe. "He was the first man I invited to attend," Tupper explained later. "Mr. Howe, however, wrote declining the invitation on the ground that he was then a Fisheries Officer in the employ of the Imperial Government, but he wished us success." Later on, Howe would have a different and much more caustic explanation than just that. Still vigorous at the age of sixty, though somewhat disillusioned, Howe was then sailing on the corvette *Lily* off the coast of Labrador.

A similar nonpartisan delegation of five was there from New Brunswick, led by their Premier, Leonard Tilley. Slight in stature, with a careful half-smile and a clear forehead, Tilley was not so favourable to the proposal of Maritime Union as Tupper was. Newfoundland, which had received a late and rather indifferent invitation, was not represented. John

Hamilton Gray, tall and gaunt with the air of an old soldier, was the host as Premier of Prince Edward Island. One of his five delegates was ill, and the rest, except Pope, were rather half-hearted about the Conference.

When word came that the Canadians had arrived in the harbour, the Maritimers decided, with a promptness that revealed their loss of interest in a Maritime Union, to postpone their own business and hear the Canadians at once on the larger plan of Confederation. So the rest of the afternoon was given over, as Brown described it, "to the shake elbow and the how-d'ye do and the fine weather." There was also another excuse to celebrate, for the tallest and almost the oldest man there, Edward Palmer, the Island's Attorney General, was fifty-five years old that day. Except for D'Arcy McGee, who needed few introductions, the Canadian delegates were strangers to the Maritimers. McGee, then thirty-nine, was almost the youngest man there. He was certainly the shortest. With a tangled lock of hair falling over his forehead, and his sloping shoulders badly supporting his black cut-away broadcloth coat, he moved about the white and gold Council Chamber with a word for everyone, as bright and sparkling as the wine.

The next morning, Friday, at ten o'clock all the delegates returned to the Colonial Building. It was the pride of the Island, a Georgian structure built twenty years earlier from massive stones quarried in Nova Scotia and carried across the strait in schooners, to be broken by prisoners in chains from the town jail. It was located on Queen Square with its old cannons and new gas lamps, beside the low Round Market, and under the spire of St. Dunstan's Cathedral. In the Council Chamber of the Colonial Building, the twenty-three delegates and several secretaries managed to crowd their arm-chairs around a long mahogany table built on castors to accommodate sixteen persons.

It was decided that the procedure would be informal, in order to encourage free conversation and to avoid "buncombe speeches." Accounts of what took place are very scanty and somewhat inconsistent. All the sessions were private; in fact, the Island newspapers complained that they were "so secret as to suggest a conspiracy."

George Etienne Cartier, who at fifty was the oldest of the Canadians, opened the case for Confederation. His intense, vigorous style of pleading, with his penetrating voice, made a strong impression. Indeed, his very presence as an enthusiastic French Canadian was an unspoken personal guarantee that the plan of Confederation had to respect at least some local autonomy. Cartier's opening presentation was skilful, and served as good tactics to allay Maritime suspicions of any overpowering Canadian plan of merger.

John A. MacDonald followed Cartier on the same theme, but his manner was much more relaxed and off-hand. Here in an easy atmosphere he was at his best, making full use of his special talent to make friends as he talked. He spoke of precedents in Federal systems and the weakness of the American structure at its centre. The Maritime delegates listened and, aside from asking some questions, spoke very little. But they noted that Cartier stressed the freedom of the Provincial units where MacDonald placed an emphasis on the central federating power. At three o'clock they adjourned to Pope's home and hospitality on Mount Edward Road overlooking the Bay, where they enjoyed wine and lobsters until the full moon was high in the sky.

The next morning, Saturday, September 3, Alexander Galt spoke as the Canadian Minister of Finance. Large and arresting in appearance, with a strong grasp of figures and an imaginative sense of presentation, he gave a commanding performance. The Federal Government, he said, would be ready to assume all Provincial debts, grant proportionate subsidies and allot sources of direct revenue to the local governments. The Maritimers were accustomed to listening to their men of finance, such as Tilley, speak in accurate, undistinguished prose. But Galt, inheriting a gift of style from his father the novelist, had a contagious way of presenting a large financial project.

The Conference adjourned at three o'clock. All the delegates were rowed out in small boats to a lunch (as it was modestly called) given by the Canadians on board the *Queen Victoria*, floating at anchor in the harbour. Endless supplies of "every delicacy" were served in "princely style." Especially enjoyed were the Malpeque oysters from the North Shore, which, everyone readily agreed, as the champagne continued to flow, were "unexcelled, neither too large like Saddle Rocks nor too small like Blue Points." Those two old opponents Cartier and Brown were each easily moved to make a "radiant speech," and "every man," it was recorded, "was as sober and as serious as D'Arcy McGee's wit would allow him to be." Even Leonard Tilley, a strict teetotaller, did not feel out of place (although later George Brown had a bilious attack from too much "dissipation"). That memorable afternoon Confederation was celebrated like a wedding. And late that evening, as all the delegates made their way to the shore for another lavish meal (this time recognized as a dinner) any resolution would have passed unanimously, as long as it was convivial—which, in spirit, was the hope of Confed-eration.

On Sunday, after Mass, McGee had the opportunity to develop his friendship with Edward Whelan, the editor of the *Examiner* and one of Prince Edward Island's few enthusiasts for Confederation. Whelan was a Mayo man, one year older than McGee, and had arrived in Charlotte-town at the age of eighteen after working as a printer's devil for Joseph Howe. It was easy for McGee to feel at home among the strong settle-ments of Irish Catholics, who made up thirty-five thousand of the Island's population of eighty thousand at that time. Two features in their lives on their "green wood farms" strangely resembled what they had left behind in Ireland. They had joined in the century-old struggle against the sixty-seven absentee proprietors of Prince Edward Island, and they were cultivating the potato. But the rent payable to the absentee pro-prietors of Prince Edward Island was really negligible in contrast to that exacted by the absentee landlords of Ireland. As for the potato, its blight and famine had driven them from Ireland, but on Prince Edward Island it was full-sized with a healthy purple hue.

The Charlottetown Conference resumed at ten o'clock, Monday morn-ing. George Brown spoke at length on Representation by Population in the Lower Federal House, and then on the thorny question of equal regional appointments to the Upper House, on the assumption that a Mari-time region would be formed to have twenty members, balanced by the two regions of Lower and Upper Canada, each also with twenty mem-bers. Then, on the vital matter of the division of powers between the Federal and local governments, he maintained that the American Fed-eral principle of State sovereignty had to be reversed, so that the residue of power would be vested in a strengthened central Federal Government.

Here there emerged some evidence of a startling character. It was not an official report, but it was contemporaneous. Edward Whelan, who had special sources of information, reported in his *Examiner* on September 5 that the central government of the British North American Provinces would be vested with "the power to enforce uniformity of education."

There is in fact no certain way of knowing what division of powers Brown proposed to the Conference that Monday. But if Whelan was accurate, such a proposition would have been consistent with Brown's own strong views. There was a variety of speculation in other journals, however, as to what was said. The inadequate evidence indicates that Brown's proposed list of powers was detailed in some areas, but purposely left vague on the crucial points.

If such a proposal had been insisted upon to enforce uniformity of education, it would have wrecked all chances for Confederation. The Canadian Coalition Cabinet must have sensed this, because three weeks later it released a semi-official statement through the Montreal *Gazette* and *Le Courier du Canada* which stated that no final decisions had been taken at Charlottetown, adding vaguely that "safeguards for the educational interests of minorities appeared to be desirable."

The general plan for Confederation had been set out. So on Tuesday a number of delegates spoke. John A. MacDonald quietly emerged as the acknowledged leader of the discussions as they became more open. He repeatedly returned to the American Civil War as the object lesson of the potential separatism to be avoided in granting sovereignty to each component state. He would have preferred a Legislative Union, but he realized that there had to be a concession made to the Federal system. The French Canadians, and indeed the Maritimers, particularly the delegates of Prince Edward Island, would hear of nothing else. As Brown put it: "We had either to take a Federal Union or drop the negotiations."

What strength the central government would have was left as an open question, it seems, beyond a clear recognition that whatever powers were not specifically allotted to the local governments were to remain vested in the central government. In fact, the prevalent understanding of the Canadian proposal was that the local governments were to be restricted to almost municipal functions. On that note, at the end of the fourth day of the Charlottetown Conference, Canada closed its case.

The Maritimers then met alone on Wednesday, September 7. Prince Edward Island took a firm stand that it was opposed to Maritime Union. So they deferred their own debate, and agreed to explore further the idea of Confederation with Canada. George Brown summed it up in a hopeful letter to his wife, without too much concern for the important "if" which he had to add:

> They were unanimous in regarding federation of all the Provinces as highly desirable, if the terms of Union could be made satisfactory.

With a feeling of achievement, the Conference was then adjourned to resume on the following Monday, September 12, at Halifax. But the intervening time was not lost. They proceeded to put into practise what Howe had recommended in high good humour at a dinner in Montreal three years before: "Oh, if you fellows would now and then dine and drink with us fellows." Luncheons, receptions, excursions and dinners followed. And on Thursday night there was a grand ball in the Colonial building. The celebrations did not cease until eight o'clock on Friday morning, when the *Queen Victoria* finally pulled up anchor and sailed for Nova Scotia, with twenty-three very sleepy delegates all counted and safe on board.

Most of the delegates disembarked at Pictou to proceed to Halifax overland, but John A. MacDonald, D'Arcy McGee and Hector Langevin, no doubt wisely, remained with the *Queen Victoria* to sail through the Gut of Canso and down to Halifax. There on Monday, September 12, the historic decision was reached: an official Conference, with all participating and including Newfoundland, would be held on the Confederation of British North America on October 10 in Quebec City.

That Monday night, during a heavy thunder-storm, at a great dinner in the Halifax Hotel, the coming Quebec Conference was enthusiastically announced to the public. MacDonald, Tupper, Cartier, Brown, Tilley, Galt and others—all spoke. In truth, there were ten addresses that night, and Brown was so enthused that he talked for an hour and a quarter. Finally it was McGee's turn. Called upon to propose a toast to immigration, he was wise enough to be brief. It was folly to fear a pauper immigration, McGee said:

Bless me! Something like half this continent has been made by paupers.

Then they moved on to Saint John, New Brunswick, where another great dinner was held in Stubbs Hotel on Wednesday, September 14. This time, because MacDonald missed his train at Shediac, the roster of speakers was slightly less formidable, but effective enough as Cartier, Brown, Galt, McDougall and McGee spoke for Canada.

The cause of most of the surprising Maritime enthusiasm for Confederation must be attributed to D'Arcy McGee. It was largely his creation. But what did it mean? Behind the glowing words at the banquets, there was still the unknown and perhaps unmoved reserve of the Maritimers. Newfoundland had not yet been consulted; Prince Edward Island had not yet really spoken; and the city of Halifax was not the Province of Nova Scotia. And the Canadians were cautioned not to overlook this.

That last Wednesday at the dinner at Stubbs Hotel in Saint John, two different incidents occurred which made some wonder what reactions would follow. At one point the enthusiasm ran so high that George Etienne Cartier stood up and in his shrill voice, more at ease with words than a tune, sang "God Save the Queen" in English, and then, amid thunderous applause, he sang it in French. But when a toast to "Colonial

Union" was proposed and the whole assembly rose, one man stiffly refused to stand. He was the outspoken Irish Catholic editor of the Saint
John *Morning Freeman,* whose son would become the Chief Justice of
the Supreme Court of Canada, the former rebel schoolmaster in the days
of '48, Timothy Anglin.

# 14

## THE POLITICAL LABORATORY OF QUEBEC

Analyse our aggregate population.

We have more Saxons than Alfred
had when he founded the English
realm. We have more Celts than
Brian had when he put his heel on
the neck of Odin. We have more
Normans than William had when he
marshalled his invading host along
the strand of Falaise.

We have the laws of St. Edward
and St. Louis; Magna Carta and
the Roman Code. We speak the
speeches of Shakespeare and Bossuet.
We copy the constitution which Burke
and Somers and Sidney and Thomas
More lived or died to secure or save.

In the name of the future generations
who shall inhabit all the vast regions
we now call ours, I invoke the fortunate
genius of a united British America, so
that, hand in hand, we and our descendants
may advance steadily to the accomplishment
of a common destiny.

*Thomas D'Arcy McGee*

Three weeks later in Quebec, it was snowing.

The lazy heat of summer had lingered through September, and October brought the golden mood of fall until it seemed that the delegates would be welcomed to the Quebec Conference by those rare days of Indian summer. But all of a sudden on Saturday, October 8, a gale blew in from the north and it started to snow. Sunday was a sight of strange beauty, with the white snow falling over the russets and the warm crimsons of the foliage. But then, just as suddenly, the snow turned to heavy rain, which did not let up. Bad weather set in, and the Quebec Conference opened at eleven o'clock Monday morning, October 10, 1864, in rain, slush and mud.

The Conference was held in the Legislature, a plain building with no pretensions. Built in a hurry to serve as a future post office as soon as Parliament would be moved to Ottawa, it was a structure of whitish grey brick with a central block three stories high and two lower wings. Its roof had a slight slope to it with three awkward skylights, which were drumming relentlessly that week under the rain.

But the site was superb. The Legislature was perched on a ledge hewn out of the great precipice of Quebec, on the ruins of the old Château St. Louis, flanked on one side by Laval University, and buttressed on the other by the Grand Battery, with its hundred guns, and Mountain Hill, which ran as steep as a timber slide down to Lower Town.

D'Arcy McGee was seated, looking unusually small and quiet, among the thirty-three delegates at a long table covered with deep red felt in the reading room of the Legislative Council on the second floor. The room was narrow, but McGee did not notice it, for facing him were high, round-arched windows commanding a wide view over the battlements and the steeply pitched roofs below. Under the dark, low, wet sky the river looked like a heavy sheet of luminous metal. Several rafts of timber, acres wide, their surfaces spotted with small triangular huts, were lying at anchor off Point Lévis. In the distance, dimly seen as a whitish wisp, were Montmorency Falls. And to the right was the Isle of Orleans, its muted colours soaked in rain.

Seated on McGee's left were Alexander Campbell and his inseparable

partner, John A. MacDonald, comfortably chatting together. To Mac-
Donald's left, in the centre of the table, was Sir Etienne Taché, the re-
spected and benign chairman, sixty-nine, the oldest man there, and with
his best years behind him, for he only lived another nine months. On
Taché's left was Cartier, his eyebrows bristling for a battle; and then
Galt, with his large hands resting prominently on the table.

Facing Taché on the other side was George Brown, sitting severely
upright with a withdrawn air. Oliver Mowat, like a bright, bespectacled
owl, was on his right, and next to him, courteous and even-tempered,
came James Cockburn. On Brown's left and close to him for consultation
was William McDougall. Next was Hector Langevin, who at thirty-eight
was one year younger than McGee; and then Jean Charles Chapais, a
rarity because he was clean-shaven.

This constituted the entire Coalition Cabinet of twelve members from
Canada, occupying the centre of both sides of the table in a solid block.
The delegates from Nova Scotia and New Brunswick were at one end,
and those from Prince Edward Island and Newfoundland at the other.

The latter, attentively sitting to the left of Galt, were a new delegation of two, Frederic Carter and Ambrose Shea, both from St. John's,
Newfoundland. Across from McGee, slightly to his right, was Premier
Charles Tupper of Nova Scotia. Tupper was accompanied by Jonathan
McCully, relaxed with his coat opened and gazing towards the ceiling;
bald and bearded George Archibald; William Alexander Henry, with
a competent air and a large powerful frame, and Robert Barry Dickey,
fifty-three years old and one of the few men present with grey hair.

To McGee's right, mostly on his own side of the table, was the delegation from New Brunswick which had been increased from the five at
Charlottetown to seven members. Premier Leonard Tilley occupied that
end of the table, with his papers precisely arranged in front of him.
Grouped around him were Edward Chandler, William Henry Steeves,
John Mercer Johnson, Charles Fisher, Peter Mitchell, who had to leave
the Conference a few days before it closed, and John Hamilton Gray,
who bore the identical name of another delegate seated at the other
end: John Hamilton Gray, the Premier of Prince Edward Island.

The delegation from Prince Edward Island had also been increased
to seven. One of the two new members was Edward Whelan, whom
McGee was glad to see, for among the reluctant Islanders Whelan had
become an ardent supporter of Confederation. Thomas Haviland, with
his large forehead and steady gaze, was the other new-comer. Edward
Palmer was there, slightly stooped but still looking very tall, his heavily

lined features and long thin nose relieved under his bushy eyebrows by his light eyes. Then there was George Coles, not so healthy as he would have liked to be, looking wind-blown and rather blustery. Beside him was William Henry Pope, who had welcomed everyone so attentively at Charlottetown; he was the same age as McGee, and was known to be, with Whelan, very well disposed towards Confederation. Finally there was Andrew Archibald MacDonald, busy making notes.

The Canadian delegation had the discipline and cohesion of a complete Cabinet, with no members of the Opposition present to obstruct its work. But all the other delegations lacked this unity, for each of them included representatives of the party in power and the party in opposition. This difference would soon show itself.

Twenty-four of the thirty-three delegates were native born, notably the Maritimers and the French Canadians—the whole delegation of five from Nova Scotia, the two from Newfoundland, six of the seven from Prince Edward Island, five of the seven from New Brunswick, as well as the four French Canadians and two from Upper Canada, Mowat and McDougall. Of the remaining nine, there were four born in England, Galt, Campbell, Cockburn and Johnson; two in Scotland, MacDonald and Brown; two in Ireland, McGee and Whelan, and one in Bermuda, Gray of New Brunswick.

In religion the Canadian delegation was rather evenly divided, with seven Protestants and five Catholics. The other delegations were predominantly Protestant, eighteen being Protestants and three Catholics. There were two doctors, Taché and Tupper, seven businessmen; three journalists, Brown, Whelan and Shea; and the rest were lawyers, though some of these were also journalists, like McGee and McCully. The average age of the delegates, disguised by all varieties of whiskers, was under forty-eight; four were in their late thirties; and the youngest, Andrew Archibald MacDonald, at thirty-five, displayed the bushiest beard of all.

These were the thirty-three men who are now enthroned so remotely under the venerable title of the Fathers of Confederation. When William Notman took their photographs, they had to pose in frozen attitudes for a full minute and a half while his lens was exposed. Then a generation later, when Robert Harris composed his statuesque painting of the Fathers of Confederation, he sketched directly from these solemn likenesses. So nourished, popular imagination over the century has thus enshrined the Fathers of Confederation, behind uniform inkpots and blotters and backed by uniform series of statues, all in their uniform Victorian attire, looking so grave and pensive as to seem almost godlike.

But they were far from that. Otherwise the railroad promoters, the contractors and the other lobbyists would not have been waiting outside.

The procedure adopted for the Quebec Conference, like that of Charlottetown, was private and informal to make discussion easier. But this time, unlike Charlottetown where there were no resolutions, they decided to work as a committee of the whole, beginning with a resolution, followed by a discussion and decided by a vote.

It did not take long for this more precise procedure to reveal that what had appeared as agreement at Charlottetown was nothing firmer than a vague concurrence of views. Everyone kept saying that there had to be a Union, but no one was openly resolved on what form the Union should take.

Was it to be a Legislative Union, a proposition which John A. Mac-Donald was reluctantly relinquishing, and which Jonathan McCully of Nova Scotia was aggressively advancing again? The Montreal *Gazette* still hoped for a "strong Central power, from which all authority in the state is derived, and in the name of which all functions of government are exercised." Or was it to be a Federal Union, on which Cartier insisted, supported by Langevin, Chapais and Taché, with surprising backing from Robert Dickey of Nova Scotia? But *La Minerve* reported rather disconsolately on October 13 that "general opinion is in favour of a Legislative Union that recognizes the rights of Lower Canada." The test between the two would be, of course, the measure of local autonomy to be allowed. Some maintained, George Brown passionately, and George Archibald of Nova Scotia dispassionately, that local governments should be reduced to the scale of town councils. Then, with a suddenness that startled everyone, the other extreme was proposed by Edward Chandler of New Brunswick, that each Province should be sovereign and endowed with all the residual powers of government. Here D'Arcy McGee kept to a middle course: "Institute the legislative body in each Province first," he said, "then assign its powers."

The Quebec Conference had scarcely started when a local tragedy cast a shadow over everyone, and particularly McGee. On the second day, Tuesday, about six o'clock in the evening, as McGee was leaving the Legislative Building where the Governor General had just entertained fourteen hundred guests, he heard a sudden crack nearby, followed by a heavy crash like a thunder-clap. A huge mass of rock had sheered away from the height of the Citadel to fall three hundred feet into Little Champlain Street below, completely destroying three homes and entombing everyone inside. McGee and others rushed down Mountain Hill and Breakneck Steps to the scene. All night, rescuers worked to reach the victims, trapped beneath the rock and debris. McGee knew the homes well, for he had often passed them on his favourite walk through the old, narrow streets of Lower Town. They were typical Canadian neighbours, of Irish, English and French origin. An Irish immigrant, Justin McCann, lived with his family in one house, and a stevedore, John Hayden, lived with his family in the second. Both families were buried inside. But in the third—where a carpenter, Robert Leseur, lived —although it was damaged worst of all, no one was home at the time. Finally after frantic work, some injured victims were reached and rescued; but four were found dead, Janet McCann, John Hayden, his wife and his daughter Mary.

The next day was Wednesday and McGee was back at the Conference table. It quickly became apparent, however, when the delegates resumed their work that as soon as they got beyond the generalities of Charlottetown, it was no longer easy going. By the end of the first week sharp differences had broken out, and there were times when it seemed that the Conference was near collapse. Both Tupper and Tilley were impeded by strong dissenters working within their own delegations. They recognized that the principle of Representation by Population would be used to determine the number of members for each Province in the Lower House. This was taken as settled at Charlottetown and, at this stage, no one appeared to challenge it. But the Maritimers, with their relatively small populations, feared being outnumbered. So they decided to press very hard for larger representation in the Upper House.

Edward Whelan explained what had happened:

> The admission of Newfoundland into the Conference perplexes the arrangement, as the agreement was at Charlottetown to give equality of representation to the Maritime Provinces of Nova Scotia, New Brunswick and Prince Edward Island with Upper and Lower Canada.

But John A. MacDonald adhered to his stand that the four Maritime Provinces, now taken together, should not have any larger number of representatives than that originally proposed for the three. Some threatening words were used, and as Friday's very controversial session closed, Whelan wrote that matters certainly did "not look very promising."

By Monday, October 17, the weather had cleared somewhat and so, too, had the sombre air of the Conference. Over the week-end the Canadians had decided to concede. A motion from Tupper was accepted as the basis, and the Upper House was constituted with seventy-six Senators, allotting twenty-four to Upper Canada, twenty-four to Lower Canada, ten to Nova Scotia, ten to New Brunswick and four to Prince Edward Island, with an extra four to Newfoundland. This was adopted, but not smoothly, for it was only done after another wrangling debate, with Prince Edward Island still dissenting.

Then on Tuesday, George Brown led the way to establish the Lower House on his cherished principle of Representation by Population. Taking the number of sixty-five seats for Lower Canada as the fixed pivot, eighty-two seats were allotted to Upper Canada, nineteen to Nova Scotia, fifteen to New Brunswick, eight to Newfoundland and five to Prince Edward Island to make up a House of Commons, as it would now be known, of 194 members. The arithmetic was accurate, and the principle had been accepted at Charlottetown, so a unanimous vote was expected. But Prince Edward Island again dissented. "Perfectly absurd," Brown growled. And with that, tempers flared. Later the softer tones of persuasion were tried. But the Islanders muttered it was just "the glory argument." From then on, the delegates from Prince Edward Island, except for Whelan and probably Pope, did not relent in their opposition.

A second interruption of a different nature suddenly occurred on Thursday, October 20, when a report raced around that a crisis had arisen with the United States. Little was known for certain, but early that morning Governor General Monck had apparently received an urgent message. He then held hurried conferences with some members of the Canadian Cabinet. It involved a military raid, and the message had come, it was said, from the Governor of Vermont. But the Conference heard nothing officially. Later on, everyone would hear much more of the happenings at St. Albans in Vermont. By this time Montreal was greatly excited. But in Quebec the Conference continued on, absorbed with its own troubles.

Saturday and Monday were two heavy, long, nervous days of argument. Then, when the elaborate affair of the division of legislative powers came up, what had been taken as settled in principle at Charlottetown once again was ignored. Tupper, who probably spoke more often though never longer than any other delegate, grew impatient:

> Those who were at Charlottetown will remember that it was fully specified there that all the powers not given to local Government should be reserved to the federal Government. It was a fundamental principle laid down by Canada and the basis of our deliberations.

The Quebec Conference was now two weeks old. Yet on that bleak Monday failure seemed to hang over the long table like a dull, black cloud. It looked as if the division of powers could never be accepted. Two small words were causing most of the trouble: "central" and "local." The moment either word was used to describe a government, it started a heated argument. Finally Tilley had the common sense to suggest that the word "local" should be dropped; and later when the words "Federal" and "Provincial" were imperceptibly adopted, progress was made.

Oliver Mowat moved that each Provincial Legislature should be granted competence in sixteen fields. But most of that Monday was wasted, as one drastic amendment after another was made in sweeping general terms, then debated loosely before being finally defeated. With this fruitless day behind them, the delegates then decided to consider each power singly in its turn. And with little difficulty the field of Agriculture was accepted as a Provincial matter because it was recognized as concurrent with a Federal power in the same area.

Tuesday's work seemed forbidding when the morning session opened at ten o'clock. The first point on the agenda was the second of the sixteen powers allotted to the Provinces, stated in one word: Education. No other topic threatened to provoke such an electrical storm of debate. What happened was the unexpected.

D'Arcy McGee, speaking with an ease of manner, immediately moved an amendment. He proposed that this proviso be added to the Provincial power over Education:

> . . . saving the rights and privileges which the Protestant or Catholic minority in both Canadas may possess as to their denominational schools at the time when the Constitutional Act goes into operation.

The bearded young Catholic Scot from Prince Edward Island, Andrew Archibald MacDonald, sitting at the far end of the table to McGee's left, seconded the amendment. Whatever the debate was which followed was not recorded. But it seems it was surprisingly short and even cordial, for the amendment was found to be fitting. The meagre official record simply says that McGee's amendment on Education was "agreed to," and no more. Nor was there any mention that the French Canadians intervened in the debate.

A. A. MacDonald wrote in his own notes, which were published years later, that in the morning session McGee's amendment was "unanimously adopted." But in 1866 Brown would assert, against this evidence, that he had opposed McGee's amendment. Nor is it known if Galt spoke, but later events would indicate that he must have been unhappy about its wording.

By all accounts, that Tuesday was a remarkable morning. And it marked a turning point in the Conference, for from then on, discussions proceeded apace.

The touchy question of Finance, which on the previous Saturday had become so acrimonious that it had to be referred to a committee, then came back before the delegates. The Federal Government, it was decided, must possess capital assets and taxing powers sufficient to support its future vast undertakings from ocean to ocean. In return, the Provinces, as a supplement to their power to levy direct taxes, would be compensated by Galt's ingenious devices of annual subsidies and debt allowances, calculated according to their populations.

Prince Edward Island was disappointed; and George Coles, its Opposition leader, expressed particular dissatisfaction. He claimed that at the Charlottetown Conference the Island had been promised a grant of a million dollars to buy out its absentee proprietors, and now this promise, he said, was being broken. But Brown was unbending: the Island had already received more than enough. So under the firm direction of Galt, with Tilley now in agreement and wasting no words, everyone accepted the terms of the proposed financial settlement—except Prince Edward Island.

To speed up the work, the delegates were now sitting until midnight. Looking to the east and to the west, they agreed on the project, so strongly backed by McGee, to construct the Intercolonial Railway, and to provide for the admission of the Northwest Territories, British Columbia and Vancouver Island. There remained the arduous task of revising and recasting all their conclusions.

At last, on Thursday, October 27, a consensus of final agreement was reached, and the delegates left Quebec for Montreal, while the first proofs of their Resolutions were being run off the press.

These Seventy-two Resolutions of the Quebec Conference became historic. They were, as they had to be, an intricate complex of balances and compromises, enthusiastically pulled together into a peculiar and perhaps incongruous unity. That enthusiasm was spreading. But not everywhere.

In the Maritimes, Charles Tupper, a man of extraordinary endurance, exercised the most influence in favour of Confederation. Jonathan Mc-Cully and William Henry supported him. But serious opposition was slowly building up in Nova Scotia, and Tupper, too exuberant to be downhearted, was astute enough to be wary. As for New Brunswick, Leonard Tilley was less sanguine in private than in public, but he did declare to Brown: "We must fight it through, and No Surrender is our motto." Ambrose Shea of Newfoundland confessed to Galt how refreshing it was to have such a plan instead of the "wretched broils of our colonial life." Edward Whelan admitted that Pope and he would have the odds against them in Prince Edward Island, but he hoped that "ultimately, even here, the cause will be triumphant."

In Canada, MacDonald, Brown, Cartier, Galt and McGee, as former opponents, now shared the leading ground in common. But each one had reached it with his own approach and different interests. What appeared as agreement on the unbroken surface hid some secret reserves of conflicting private interpretations.

George Brown revealed what he really felt in a hurried note written to his wife just as he was leaving Quebec:

> All right!!! Constitution adopted—a most creditable document—a complete reform of all abuses and injustices we have complained of! Is it not wonderful? French-Canadianism entirely extinguished.

For George Etienne Cartier, on the other hand, it was a practical success. He had aligned the defence of French national rights with the Maritimes' desire for local self-government. It was a new and untried alliance. But he felt that they had forged out enough Provincial sovereignty to let a French majority dominate its own Provincial Legislature in Lower Canada; and moreover they were now protected against Annexation by the United States.

Alexander Galt saw it as the fulfillment of his early vision—at least in the East. Six years before, on July 5, 1858, when he had first joined John A. MacDonald and Cartier, he had made his remarkable proposals on the need to expand in both the East and the West:

> Such a thing had never occurred to any people as to have the offer of half a continent. Half a continent is ours if we do not keep on quarrelling about petty matters and lose sight of what interests us most. The door should be opened to the young men of Canada to go into that country. Otherwise the Americans would go there first.

For his part, John A. MacDonald had every reason to be content—and to be tired, too, as he was. He had worked harder than anyone. Fifty of the Seventy-two Resolutions, as McGee later revealed, had been drafted by MacDonald. Some complained about their lack of logic and simplicity. But those who did had perhaps confined their experience to a blackboard and knew little of what the draftsman has to suffer to meet the demands and the notions of thirty-three articulate men at such a meeting, especially when twenty-one of them were lawyers. In reality, the Resolutions were an achievement of patience and inventive phrasing. In their cumbrous clarity, they represented MacDonald's success in managing men and their phrases. In MacDonald's mind, which had a strong cast of loyalty, Confederation was now the only way out of a deadlock in Canada. He saw the link with the Maritimes as leading to the founding of a broader British Kingdom, and, although the unity of monarchy was loosened, it was not broken by the concessions to federal and republican ideas. And behind it all, unvoiced, it represented a new military union to rely on, against the gathering American threats.

For D'Arcy McGee the Quebec Resolutions were the promise of a new nation. His first editorials on Confederation, written in his *New Era* in the summer of 1857, would later on appear with an aura of prophecy. But he never saw himself under a halo. Now that the work was done, he wanted to relax.

The mayor of Montreal had decreed that October 28, Friday, would be a holiday to welcome all the delegates arriving from the Quebec Conference. The citizens were in a gala mood. But the weather was abominable. It started to rain Thursday night, and the wind rose until a gale almost made the streets impassable. The steeplechase, the parade and the fireworks had to be cancelled. But the banquet and the ball went on.

A thousand guests, undaunted, using every carriage, calèche and cab available, made their way through the driving wind and rain to dart as fast as elegance would allow under the rattling canopy on Craig Street, and there enter the brilliant arcade of St. Lawrence Hall. At the head of the wide stairway was the radiant owner, Henry Hogan, with his side whiskers, curled moustache, pince-nez and rosy cheeks, welcoming every guest by name.

The banquet, a triumph of *canards noirs, dindes farcies* and champagne, was followed by the grand ball, grand indeed, for the champagne was still flowing. Thorbahn's Quadrille Band "discoursed sweet music" in the glittering ballroom. But the floor was so crowded, as the couples whirled about, that the excited *Gazette* reporter could not overlook that "many a flounce had to be retired for repairs." Wherever there was hilarity there was D'Arcy McGee. By his side, rightfully and glowing, was his wife, Mary, in a gown of striped silk taffeta gathered high at the waist and flaring out over countless crinolines. And if the exhilarated observer from the *Gazette* is to be given credit, "they chased the glowing hours with flying feet."

The next afternoon at two o'clock everyone was back at St. Lawrence Hall for *déjeuner*, which, it must be believed, lasted almost six hours. Sir Fenwick Williams, the resplendent Commander-in-Chief of the British forces in Canada, headed a host of speakers. But McGee was not listed on the program among them.

During an interval the audience called for McGee. Later, when Tupper was concluding his address, the cry started again: "McGee! McGee!" Tupper recognized it and asked for a few remarks from "the gentleman whose great ability and eloquence has made Colonial Union a household word from one end of these Provinces to the other."

D'Arcy McGee came forward. The men gave him a vigorous round of applause and the ladies waved their handkerchiefs in the air as he stood there, his sensitive fingers resting lightly on the table and his dusky features lit up by a smile.

It was a simple speech, and perfectly genial. It is hard now to say how he took such a hold on his audience that day. The newspapers said he was "very witty," "in marvellous form" and "at his best." But the subtle and the silent things that move men and make them laugh can never be recounted.

He started by saying he had come that afternoon in a reverent spirit to listen and not to talk, so he would be brief:

We are becoming better friends. Religious bigotry is at a discount. We cut each other's throats no longer for the love of God.

Then he alluded to the work of the Conference and its surprising length. By that time fairly accurate summaries of its main conclusions had been published. But why the Conference had lasted, not a few days as expected, but three weeks was still a guarded secret. The delegates had not gone into the Conference, McGee assured them, to invent any new system of government:

Sorry we were so long in that political laboratory of Quebec. But we went in with a view to promote the common prosperity, to secure the common safety and to establish the common liberties of all British North America.

This seemed to stir him and he went on to speak with unusual fervour. The *Gazette* had four shorthand writers there, but not one of them could capture the magic that was moving through the room. Somehow, in a few minutes, D'Arcy McGee awakened the spirit of his listeners to see a noble destiny ahead. As he finished, everyone got to their feet and cheered.

# 15

## A DERRINGER PISTOL

This American Civil War is a true continental crisis. It is a
Canadian crisis as well as a republican crisis. And we can no
more escape from its consequences than we can throw up a
Chinese wall of exclusion.

*Thomas D'Arcy McGee*

And if sad the music is
It is sad with mysteries.
*Alice Meynell*

Shots split the air; one man fell, mortally wounded, outside the drug-store, as twenty-one raiders, their morocco satchels stuffed with green-backs and silver, jumped on their stolen horses and rode off bareback at a furious pace towards Canada, shooting in all directions.

It was October 19, 1864. Up to three o'clock it was a dull Wednesday afternoon in St. Albans, a Vermont village of three hundred houses, eight-een miles south of the Canadian border. Then, as the clock was striking the hour, a well-drilled band of young men, some with full whiskers, emerged quickly from separate hotels. They were dressed in curious civilian garb, some wearing small wool hats with narrow brims or fur caps, and bluish-black coats of ample size with Navy Colt revolvers in leather holsters. They divided into four teams. One went to a nearby livery stable and seized its best horses. The other three entered the St. Albans Bank, the First National Bank and the Franklin County Bank just as they were closing on Main Street.

"What's the program?" gasped the teller of St. Albans Bank, when a large revolver was pointed at him, three feet from his chest. Two quick questions let him know:

"Where is your gold?"

"We have none."

"Have you any silver?"

"Yes, we have."

The safe was opened and three bags of silver removed.

"Are you Jeff Davis' boys?" the teller asked.

"We're Confederate soldiers. And we've come north to rob and plunder, like the North did under Sheridan in the Shenandoah." Then they swore the teller and the other employees to secrecy with a strange oath of al-legiance to the Southern Confederacy, locked them up and left.

Within minutes the four teams with their booty met on the village square; they threw some bottles of Greek fire into some frame wooden houses, herded the frightened citizens together, threatened to blow their brains out and fired a few shots at random, ironically killing the only Copperhead in the village. And then they made off for Canada with $208,000.

On the hill overlooking the village the wife of John Gregory Smith, the Governor of Vermont, saw what was happening, barricaded her house and picked up a rifle. Nearby a young captain on leave from the Northern Army summoned up a posse of forty men, and with the Governor's wife spurring them on with cries of "Kill them! Kill them!" they set off in hot pursuit. The posse was gaining. So the raiders set fire to a barn to throw the pursuers off, but to no avail. Then luck intervened. Near Swanton was a covered bridge, and a hay waggon was lumbering through it. The raiders set the hay ablaze and left the bridge burning and the posse cut off behind them, as they scattered and disappeared into Canada.

Governor Smith was told in Montpelier that Vermont was being invaded from Canada, and he dispatched three telegrams, one to Secretary of State Seward, another to General Dix of the Northern Army and a third to Governor General Monck in Quebec City, which was the message that interrupted the Quebec Conference. Meanwhile the Vermont posse crossed the Canadian border and started a hunt for the raiders throughout the Eastern Townships in Lower Canada.

That same night a few raiders, their pockets bulging with money, were picked up at Elder's Tavern in Stanbridge, twenty-five miles north of St. Albans. Close by, a couple were found sleeping on pillows stuffed with greenbacks. A few more, spattered with mud, were discovered asleep in the hay in a Dunham barn, their revolvers by their sides; another, completely fatigued, was arrested with a map of Canada on him in the railroad station at Farnham; and finally another, who had offered to sell his horse for twenty-five American dollars at Hall's Hotel in Waterloo, was captured in a railroad car. A total of $19,000 was recovered that night. But most of the raiders with most of the money were still at large. Those who were taken as prisoners in the Eastern Townships asked that a telegram be sent to Clement C. Clay, a Senator from Alabama who was accredited to Canada as the Southern Confederate agent in Montreal, to inform him that they had been caught.

General Dix received his telegram from Governor Smith of Vermont while he was at a dinner party. One of the guests was Lord Lyons, the British Minister to Washington, who was then on his way back from the opening of the Quebec Conference in Quebec City. Acting at once, the General issued an order to his troops to pursue the enemy "into Canada if necessary and destroy them." Lord Lyons was very disturbed. When Secretary of State Seward was informed, he at once saw the danger of igniting a war with England. So he asked that any person captured be extradited from Canada, and he took the text of the order issued by General Dix to President Lincoln.

In Quebec City, Governor General Monck was interrupted at breakfast by Governor Smith's telegram. Monck hastily conferred with members of the Cabinet who were preparing for the morning session of the Conference. The son-in-law of Sir Etienne Taché, the chairman of the Quebec Conference, Judge Charles J. Coursol, was promptly instructed in Montreal to arrest any raider found within Canada. Within four days fourteen of the twenty-one raiders were in custody, and $84,000 of the $208,000 recovered.

The news of the St. Albans raid spread through the United States while the presidential elections were in the air. A strange series of events had been started. In the minds of many Canadians they filled what proved to be the last six months of the Civil War, and seemed to be linked in some mysterious way with Montreal. This chain of events led on (whether wholly through chance or not, it cannot be said) to reach an end in the assassination of Abraham Lincoln. And in McGee's life they served as a tragic foreshadowing.

In that same month of October 1864, living at St. Lawrence Hall in Montreal was a pale, overly handsome young man of twenty-six, with hair dark as night, strongly marked eyebrows and intense eyes too closely set. Like so many strangers then at St. Lawrence Hall (which boasted of the only bar in Canada to serve mint juleps), he appeared to be idle. He passed his time playing billiards, drinking brandy and talking politics. His name was John Wilkes Booth.

One night in the billiard room he held up his cue and proudly displayed a large seal ring on his little finger; then, with his dramatic way of pushing his head forward for emphasis, he was heard to say:

Abe's contract is near up. And whether re-elected or not, he will get his goose cooked.

Booth went almost unnoticed then, but six months later when he was charged with eight others for conspiracy to murder Abraham Lincoln, investigations revealed that five of those eight were then active around Montreal.

The youngest was John H. Surratt, twenty-one, tall and spare, with receding hair, a silky moustache and moody eyes. He was a Confederate spy, running messages hidden in the heels of his boots or inside metal buttons or under the planks of his buggy, between Richmond, Virginia, and Montreal. His mother, Mary Surratt, was one of those executed for the assassination. The other four in Montreal were leaders of what was called the Southern Confederacy's "Canadian Cabinet," a rebel group with headquarters in St. Lawrence Hall. They were Senator Clement C. Clay; George N. Sanders, a former American Consul in London; William W. Cleary, a lawyer from Richmond, who spoke of meeting Booth in Montreal, and Jacob Thompson, one of the wealthiest men in the South. When Booth was in Montreal he consulted with Thompson, who was reputed to have a Montreal bank account of over $300,000. Working closely with Thompson was Senator Clay, whom the St. Albans raiders had wired as soon as they were arrested. Earlier in June, Clay had been told of the proposed raid, and in September he advanced $2000 to the raiders before they left Canada on their foray into Vermont.

Most of the missing St. Albans money, it seemed, was turned over in Montreal to Senator Clay; and he sent Sanders with $6000 to engage the services of three outstanding Montreal lawyers to defend the raiders. Leading for the defence was John J. Abbott, who had first gained prominence as one of the signers of the Annexation Manifesto of 1849, and was the Dean of McGill's Law Faculty while McGee studied there, and a member with McGee in the Cabinet of Sandfield MacDonald and Sicotte.

All the prisoners came from Kentucky, except two who came from Texas and one from Georgia. Six charges were laid against them: murder, attempted murder, robbery, assault, attempted arson and horse stealing. The United States Government engaged Bernard Devlin as special counsel, and he immediately asked that the raiders be extradited to stand trial in Vermont for each of these crimes. Proceedings opened towards the end of October in St. John of Lower Canada, and were moved to Montreal. The courtroom was crowded every day, and a strong sympathy for the Southern raiders was evident. The case moved slowly under Judge Coursol. But the raiders were living in solid comfort in the jailer's own home, playing chess, reading all the newspapers and enjoying wine with their meals.

On November 9, D'Arcy McGee with Cartier and McDougall met in the Montreal office of the American Consul, David Thurston, to make plans to prevent any further raids from Canada. They told the Consul that they hoped the trial before Judge Coursol would result in favour of the United States, and Cartier promised his full support as Attorney General.

The defence of the raiders was that a legitimate act of war had been committed which was neither planned nor performed in Canada, and no crime in the civic sense was involved that was subject to extradition.

Both Sanders and Cleary testified on behalf of the raiders. To buttress their plea, the defence then obtained a delay of thirty days on November 15 to let them obtain proof from Southern Army headquarters that the raid was part of a Southern military plan.

When trial was resumed on December 13, Abbott for the defence immediately challenged the jurisdiction of Judge Coursol. His argument, elaborate and highly technical, was based on treaty arrangements which required, so Abbott asserted, that the warrant to be valid should have been signed by Governor General Monck himself, which of course had not been done.

With an alacrity which left observers wondering, Judge Coursol immediately accepted this argument and rendered judgment off the bench, declaring that he lacked jurisdiction. Then without binding the prisoners over for appeal or any hearing on other charges, he freed them at once. The raiders disappeared into the cheering crowds. Meanwhile Montreal Police Chief Lamothe handed over the official court receipt to an agent of Jacob Thompson who rushed to the Bank of Ontario nearby where, although the bank had closed a half hour before, the impounded $84,000 was handed out to him through the back door.

The reaction was swift and angry. The next day, General Dix issued a second order from New York:

> Rebel marauders who were guilty of murder and robbery at St. Albans have been discharged from arrest. Other enterprises are actually in preparation in Canada.
>
> All military commanders are instructed to cross the boundary into Canada and pursue the rebels wherever they take refuge.

The Chicago *Tribune* called on the North to take Canada by the throat and throttle her. When *The New York Times* wrote with deliberation that this may "lead to a war with England," it seemed so to John A. Mac-Donald, who blamed it on Judge Coursol as "that wretched prig of a police magistrate."

Most Canadians were slow to realize what was happening. But some, including D'Arcy McGee, suddenly saw what, up to then, had seemed impossible: that by their own act, without any intervention of British Imperial power, they could bring on a war with the United States. And they also realized that the Southern Confederacy, faced with impending defeat, was attempting to stave it off by provoking a war between the North and Canada. Was it too late to avert it? To make amends, the Canadian Government offered a reward for the recapture of the raiders, and promised to reimburse $50,000 to the banks in St. Albans. In the meantime Police Chief Lamothe was busy with part of the booty buying a whaling ship for some of the raiders to escape to Newfoundland.

Then on December 17, Abraham Lincoln intervened and revoked the order of General Dix, who had authorized military movements into Canada as neutral territory. Tension lessened. Five of the raiders were recaptured near Quebec City, and Cartier ordered a new investigation and trial in 1865.

Canadians awakened with a new realism. Police Chief Lamothe was later seen in different colours when he advocated Annexation to the United States. And John A. MacDonald set up a Secret Police force to patrol the American border under Gilbert McMicken. But fears were far from abated. Some claimed they knew that McMicken had been an unpaid agent for the Southern Confederacy. And others said they heard that General Dix was seen at a Fenian meeting where plans were discussed for the invasion of Canada. From this point on, the strength which Confederation could bring by uniting the British American colonies began to emerge as a military need.

Throughout 1864 most public men in Canada and the Maritimes contemplated their common future in the shadows cast by the events of the American Civil War. When the Seventy-two Quebec Resolutions were published on November 8, 1864, they received wide coverage in the newspapers. The amount of comment which followed was extraordinary. The public, which had been fretting about the outcome of the Civil War, were relieved to be stirred up about domestic affairs by the numerous editorials, letters, speeches and debates on the proposals for Confederation. These comments were exciting but not too enlightening. In the heat of this debate most of the journalists wrote loosely about the political idea of federation or confederation; and the word "Federal" was used as a slogan without any exact meaning. Even Galt lapsed into this confusion by asserting that "the federal principle" had been recognized in the Act of Union of 1840.

Strict political doctrine or legal theory was never the concern of the delegates at the Charlottetown or Quebec Conferences. They were looking for a practical solution that would work. In that respect they were entirely unlike the men who wrote the Constitutions of the French or American republics, for the British North Americans were in no way absorbed or enamoured by any new ideology about the citizen and the State. But they, like everybody, were very conscious of the Constitution of the United States and the threat to tear it asunder by the seceding Southern States. At the Charlottetown and Quebec Conferences, delegates repeatedly compared their proposals with the American Federal system. But one basis for such a comparison was lacking; and it was Clerk of the *True Witness* who put his finger on it.

When the Federal Government was set up by the United States, the states had their own autonomous and sovereign character to share among themselves. In contrast, none of the British North American colonies even desired such independence or autonomy in 1864. Each was a dependent colony. Legally this meant that if the matter was not of Imperial concern (and the distinguishing line was scarcely clearer than that), then the colony exercised its own ministerial responsibility. But no one questioned the fact that sovereignty still plainly resided in the Imperial Government.

Nonetheless, comparisons were continually made between what the United States had done and what the colonies were aiming to do. Overlooked in these comparisons was the vital point that the former had its own sovereignty, and the latter did not. So the misleading process continued; similar abstractions were made from superficial analogies which were drawn from different realities. Clerk saw this error clearly, but he pushed his arguments to the other extreme.

Clerk argued that a federal distribution of powers in British North America was impossible. Canadians, in Clerk's view, were governed by the Imperial Parliament, except where local matters had been assigned to the Provincial Government in Quebec City; since these two governments between them occupied the whole field, Confederation was an impossible proposal to insert a third government between these two. "There is no need to fuse down and recast all our political institutions" Clerk wrote, "the most that is required is a commercial league or a *Zollverein*—a common tariff and a common system of currency."

On this subject Clerk was in constant touch with Bishop Bourget of Montreal and was really advancing a special French-Canadian point of view; and in that view was the seed of separatism. Clerk maintained that the Imperial Government was already fully exercising all the functions which were designed for the proposed new Federal Government; and in answer to *Le Courier du Canada* he wrote:

> The day will come when we will eventually cease to be British Provinces. Would not *Le Courier du Canada* then rather have Lower Canada a sovereign independent state?

On the other hand, John A. MacDonald, Brown and Galt were very pragmatic in their approach to such matters. They saw the proposed new central government as an extension of the Government they headed, and they were not too disturbed to call it "Federal" as a concession to sectional resistance. Where Clerk saw a Federal Government as the insertion of something new, they saw it as the enlargement of the old government; what would be new in their view would be the creation of local governments in each Province.

But statements on the nature of Confederation by John A. MacDonald could not support exact analysis. At times he spoke of it as a "treaty" or a "pact"; at other times as a "Legislative Union"; and on other occasions as a "Federal system." Too often these were merely useful terms designed to suit the audience he was addressing.

D'Arcy McGee did, however, go further. He carefully prepared a small book on the subject in which he analysed the various forms of federation as they had appeared from the earliest days of history. It was published that year under the title *Federal Governments Past and Present* and had the merit of delving beneath appearances to assess the common elements and essential differences in all those governments which in history had been called federations. But the pith of Confederation as a solution for the British North American colonies was empirical, a synthetic tissue of necessary compromises. And working strongly to bring it about, as McGee would soon state more plainly than others, was the impact of the war in the United States and the fears that it fostered in the Canadas and the Maritimes.

The leaders left the Quebec Conference determined and confident that Confederation could be achieved in 1865. MacDonald, Cartier, Brown, Galt and McGee were of one mind that there was no time to lose. Tupper was as positive and confident as ever; so, in his milder way, was Tilley. And even the delegates from Newfoundland and Prince Edward Island had not cast aside their early optimism.

McGee fell ill in November 1864, and he was unable to attend a dinner held in Sherbrooke on November 23 to honour Galt. It was at that dinner that Galt assured the Protestants of Lower Canada that the Government intended to sponsor a measure, before Confederation took place, which would grant them further protection on their school system and establish a separate department for Protestant education in Lower Canada.

Galt's statement, coupled with a renewed campaign by the Toronto *Globe* against the Catholic Separate Schools in Upper Canada, caused

Moylan to write in the Toronto *Canadian Freeman* on December 29 that the Protestant demands for further guarantees of the Protestant school system in Lower Canada should stir Catholics in Upper Canada to demand the same rights. It was known that Moylan was speaking for Bishop Lynch of Toronto; and Bishop Lynch's views had weight with John A. MacDonald. Just two weeks before, on December 13, Bishop Lynch had privately written to MacDonald to assure him that Clerk of the *True Witness* was not the spokesman of the hierarchy in politics and that, although the Bishops had not pronounced on the plan of Confederation, he himself was favourable to it. Yet it was a matter of some conjecture how the Bishops viewed Confederation.

Cartier and Langevin, backed by Taché and Chapais, felt they had sufficient support for Confederation from the French-Canadian hierarchy in Lower Canada, notwithstanding Bishop Bourget and his group who spoke against it through the *True Witness*. In Upper Canada, where there was some division of opinion, Bishop Lynch of Toronto supported Confederation and made his views known through the *Canadian Freeman*. But the most energetic and influential supporter of Confederation among the Catholic hierarchy was McGee's friend Archbishop Thomas Connolly of Halifax. He did not speak through others; he spoke for himself.

Meanwhile George Brown had gone to England and was puzzled by the views he encountered in London. The London *Times* had written at the close of the Quebec Conference:

> Our colonies are rather too fond of us and embrace us, if anything, too closely.

And in December, Brown wrote back to John A. MacDonald:

> I am much concerned to observe that there is a manifest desire in almost every quarter that, ere long, the British American colonies should shift for themselves, and in some quarters evident regret that we did not declare at once for independence.

Yet Edward Cardwell, who had recently succeeded Newcastle as Colonial Secretary and was remarkable for his lack of enthusiasm on most matters, had come to see Confederation as urgent, writing thus:

> The time is short. Those who have undertaken this great measure desire to bring it forward during the ensuing session for the decision of the Imperial Parliament.

On December 22, in Compton of the Eastern Townships, McGee de-livered an address on Confederation which was thoughtful and appealing. He explained how they had proceeded at the Quebec Conference in-versely to the course pursued in the United States; first there was a clear recognition of the sovereignty of the Crown; then, beneath the sovereign powers of the Imperial Parliament, the general government was made supreme, and the local governments, derivative; whereas the Americans had done the reverse:

> We build on old foundations, though the result is popularly called the new Constitution.
> There will be no reason for anyone to say what the French book-seller replied, when he was asked for a copy of the French Constitu-tion, that he did not deal in periodical publications.

"Under the mild sway of a Sovereign, whose reign is coincident with re-sponsible government in these colonies, we are called upon," McGee said, "to consider what further constitutional safeguards are needed"; the Fed-eral form of government was at once a partnership and a compromise, "peculiarly adapted to conciliate differences of language and origin":

> The Federal field is fertile. There will be both liberty and unity. For unity without liberty is like rain upon granite. And liberty without unity is like rain in the desert.

But another undercurrent was flowing again from the Fenians and the United States, which deeply affected D'Arcy McGee.

It started early in November 1864 from a report in Toronto that the Orangemen were planning a demonstration against the Catholics on Guy Fawkes Day with the intention of burning the Pope and Daniel O'Connell in effigy. But a menacing reversal occurred. Guy Fawkes Day was a Saturday, and throughout November 5, groups of men, some of them masked and others armed, mysteriously appeared here and there in To-ronto. Surprisingly, the strangers seemed to be roaming about under some form of discipline. Their purpose was to prevent the Orangemen from assembling, and it succeeded. Yet through the night and into the early hours of Sunday morning the masked men were still to be seen. Suddenly a number of shots were heard from one end of the city, followed im-mediately, like an echo, by a similar volley from the other end. Then there was an unnatural calm.

The newspapers said they were Fenians; and the *Globe* wrote it up sensationally: Beware of a Fenian massacre of Protestants on November

16, the *Globe* warned. In the villages of Orangeville, Listowel and Morpeth of Upper Canada there was almost a panic. The police received anonymous letters: "four boxes of pistols had been seen"; "the priests are drilling Fenians nightly"; "Catholic Churches have become arsenals," and so on. A few magistrates authorized searches around Toronto, which were carried out provocatively, and some Catholic graveyards were indecently disturbed. In the county of Bruce, several nervous officers started to arm one class of citizens against another. Finally the Toronto *Globe,* on the authority of its Montreal correspondent, asserted that there were fifteen hundred Fenians organizing for sedition in Montreal.

The annual meeting of St. Patrick's Society was to be held on January 11, 1865, in Montreal. So D'Arcy McGee returned from a Cabinet meeting in Quebec City to address it. He spoke first on the needs of the Catholic University of Ireland, expressing deep regret that Lord Palmerston had refused to grant it a Parliamentary Charter. This was his main topic. Then, as he concluded, he made a firm statement on the exaggerated reports about Fenians in Montreal, and added that Fenians were "seditious, secret and pagan," originating in New York. But as to the wild rumour that there were fifteen hundred Fenians in Montreal, McGee denied it absolutely in the name of the Irish Catholics of Montreal:

> I say there could not be fifteen such scamps associated and meeting together, not to say fifteen hundred, without your knowledge and mine; and I repeat absolutely that there is no such body amongst us.

McGee recognized that some "emissaries from the United States have been among us," but if there were Fenians in Canada, "they are as wholly insignificant in numbers as in every other respect," and he urged all Irishmen in Canada to purge their ranks "of this political leprosy." The speech had an immediate effect. McGee began to receive a series of threatening letters; and from that time on, this anonymous stream of abuse never stopped.

Vast drifts of snow were whirling around the Citadel of Quebec as a new Session of the Canadian Parliament opened on January 19, 1865. Monck privately hoped that it would be "the last Canadian Parliament that will ever assemble. I trust next year we shall have the Parliament of the Union." And this air of expectancy was everywhere, as the Speech from the Throne spoke of a "new nationality."

The plan was that Canada, because it was assured of a large majority vote, would take the lead in adopting the Resolutions of the Quebec Conference; then the Maritimes would follow. So the second week of February was set aside for the great debate on Confederation, and the Canadian Coalition Cabinet decided to make its case with its five strongest speakers.

On Monday, February 6, John A. MacDonald introduced the Seventy-two Resolutions. He had been ill, and his voice was weak as he carefully analysed the whole complex plan. He spoke for over two hours. What he said was not new to those who had heard him at the Charlottetown and Quebec Conferences. It was adequate, detailed and effective, but it was not stirring. Indeed, Brown in a letter to his wife went further than that: "It was a very poor speech for such an occasion," he wrote.

Cartier followed on Tuesday with a speech half as long, but with twice the fire. He accepted the "new nationality," not as an attempt to merge races, but as a higher concept which could help to put an end to the disintegrating effects from the exaggeration of the differences. Turning to Lower Canada, Cartier made a special point by contrasting three main opponents of Confederation in Montreal. "George Clerk of the *True Witness* was saying that if Confederation were adopted, the French-Canadian Catholics were doomed"; while Clerk's inveterate Protestant opponent and "brother in violence," as Cartier called him, John Dougall of the *Witness*, was maintaining that the people in peril were English-speaking Protestants. Adding to that paradox were the extreme young men of the *Institut Canadien* who, as Socialists, Secularists and Annexationists, were arguing against Confederation by taking religion under their suspect protection. Since each party was prophesying that it would produce the most widely different results, it would be hard to find, Cartier concluded, a stronger argument than this for the wise balance of Confederation.

As Cartier finished, there was still time for another speaker. Brown, who was to follow, was not ready, so he asked Galt to take his turn, which Galt obligingly did, moving through the intricacies of the financial structure of Confederation with ease and distinction. Galt left no doubt about his skill and his power to lead the English-speaking Protestants of Lower Canada.

Brown spoke the following night. It was a tremendous effort lasting four and a half hours, delivered with deep personal emotion and rugged vigour. In it he referred to the Catholic Separate School Act of 1863:

> I was not in Quebec at the time, but if I had been there I would have voted against that Bill, because it extended the facilities for estab-

lishing Separate schools. It had however this good feature that it was
accepted by the Roman Catholic authorities, and carried through
Parliament as a final compromise on the question in Upper Canada.

Brown then declared that when McGee made his amendment on Education at the Quebec Conference "to bind that compact of 1863 and declare it to be a final settlement," it was a "proposition that was not rashly
to be rejected." Brown recognized it as one of the concessions he had to
make, and he accepted it "as a necessary condition to the scheme of
Union."

Late that night at the hotel Brown wrote to his wife to describe his
speech in one hurried sentence: "I suspect it was pretty successful"; and
McGee gladly took a rest from the preparation of his own speech, to
trudge through the snow to the post office and mail the letter for the
exhausted Brown.

There were heavy snowdrifts throughout Thursday, February 9, but
that night at eight o'clock the House was crowded as D'Arcy McGee rose
in his place on the front bench to close the case for the Government on
Confederation. In the press gallery a reporter turned to his neighbour
and said: "When McGee starts to speak, I am tempted to throw down my
pencil and just listen."

McGee opened with some light touches, and the reporters noted that
the House was laughing for the first time that week. Dorion had previously unearthed one of the early copies of McGee's *New Era* to show that
the phrase "a new nationality," which was used in the Speech from the
Throne, had been first devised by McGee when he was a Liberal in 1857,
and not by any Tory. It was true, though McGee pleasantly discounted
the honour:

> But I will own when I saw my bantling held up in the delicate
> and fostering hands of Mr. Dorion, there was some tingling of paren-
> tal pride.
>
> I do not think it ought to be made a cause for belittling the im-
> portance of the subject that eight years ago I used the identical
> phrase employed in the Speech from the Throne. The idea itself is
> a good one, and it may have floated through the minds of many men.

McGee then introduced his main theme:

> We are compelled to make a great change. And this change is being
> shaped by three influences, with warnings coming from without and
> from within.

The first warning, McGee said, came from England, which had given notice that the old order of relations with colonies had ceased and that a new order must take its place:

> We may grumble or not at the necessity of preparation which England imposes upon us; but, whether we like it or not, we have at all events been told that we have entered upon a new era in our military relations to the rest of the Empire.

The other warning from without, McGee noted, was the American warning. There were notices to abrogate the Reciprocity Treaty, to impose a vexatious passport system, to arm the Great Lakes and to construct a canal for war vessels around Niagara Falls. There also was the enormous expansion of American military power from an army of ten thousand in 1861 which increased within two years to an army of six hundred thousand. But the most frightful aspect lay in the change which was taking place in the spirit of the American people themselves:

> They coveted Florida, and seized it; they coveted Louisiana, and purchased it; they coveted Texas, and stole it; and then they picked a quarrel with Mexico, and got California.

McGee, who was more conscious than others of this danger, because of the threatening letters he was receiving from the American Fenians, quoted from a strong speech by Archbishop Connolly of Halifax to support his view:

> A cavalry raid or a visit from our Fenian friends on horseback, through the plains of Canada or the fertile fields of New Brunswick and Nova Scotia, may cost more in a single week than Confederation would for the next fifty years.

The acquisition of Canada, McGee contended, was the first ambition of the American Confederacy, and had never ceased to be so even when "her troops were a handful and her navy scarce a squadron. Is it likely to be stopped now?"

The third warning came from within. It was the voice, McGee stated, "of our own experience in the Government of these Provinces," as five tremulous Governments have risen within four years, with each one depending for its life on the success of a search for some absent Member whenever a sudden vote was called. In such a precarious state the House was fast losing its hold on the country, and the administrative departments were being disorganized by such frequent changes. Hard work, great abilities and self-sacrifice brought about an extraordinary armistice in party warfare at the Quebec Conference; McGee declared:

> The Treaty was concluded and signed by us all. And there it lies for your ratification.
>
> Question it you may, reject it you may, or accept it you may, but alter it you may not. It is beyond your power or our power to alter it. For one party to alter a treaty is to destroy it.

To McGee, the Resolutions of Quebec were not perfection, but "an approximation to the right," or what an ancient called "the possible best." The crowded House was listening in silence to his sombre warnings as the wind whistled mournfully outside. Then McGee turned to consider the Maritimes. Here his words seemed to take on a warmth, like the soft light from the gas lamps overhead, as he spoke of "the congenial peoples in our proposed Union."

He recalled how all the territories of the separate colonies had once been united as New France; Newfoundland still had its "French shore"; in the heart of Evangeline's Acadia the waves till echoed "the roll of Longfellow's noble hexameters"; and from the Miramichi to the Metapedia, "the forts and the farms, the churches and the festivals were still held by the tenacious Norman and Breton race."

The population of the Maritimes, McGee remarked, was almost universally a native population of three or more generations; in New Brunswick the immigrant population was about 12 per cent; in Nova Scotia, about 8, and in the two islands, even less:

> We admit of no disparity between natives and immigrants in this country. But it is to be considered that where men are born in the presence of the graves of their fathers, the influence is great in enhancing their attachment to that soil.

Referring to Brown's remark which indicated discontent with Catholic Separate Schools, McGee observed that, for his own part, he had accepted the Catholic Separate School Act of 1863 as a finality with this reservation:

> I will be no party to the reopening of the question. But I say this. If there are to be any special guarantees or grants extended to the Protestant minority of Lower Canada, I think the Catholic minority ought to be placed in precisely the same position—neither better nor worse.

McGee was nearing the end. He had spoken for almost two hours, and if, as he admitted, he was slightly fatigued, it was not noticed as his final words were heard with full attention:

The small colonies which your ancestors could hardly see on the map have grown into great communities. A great danger has arisen in our near neighbourhood. Over our homes a cloud hangs, dark and heavy. We do not know when it may burst. With our own strength we are not able to combat against the storm. But what we can do, we will do cheerfully and loyally.

We want time to grow. We want more land tilled, more men established through our wastes and wildernesses.

We of the British North American Provinces want to be joined together, that, if danger comes, we can support each other in the day of trial.

It was the best speech of that historic Session. The stern warnings given by McGee with all the fire and power that were his, had stirred the minds of many as they left the House to struggle homeward through the blinding snow, while the storm raged over the darkened heights of the Citadel.

As the Session of Quebec City continued, news began to come in that opposition to Confederation was hardening in Prince Edward Island and Newfoundland. In Nova Scotia, Joseph Howe was regaining strength by his ridicule of Confederation as "Botheration." And in New Brunswick, considered as the key Province, Tilley, within a week of his return from the Quebec Conference, was in trouble; and it grew more intense as 1865 opened. Finally, against his better judgment, Tilley was persuaded to dissolve the Legislature on January 30 and submit the plan of Confederation to the people in a general election. "An obvious absurdity" was John A. MacDonald's acid observation on Tilley's move.

Albert Smith, known for his hot temper and strong jaw as the "Smasher Bully Boy," led the attack against Tilley. The Saint John *Globe,* the chief "Smasher" newspaper, turned against Tilley. So did the *Telegraph,* which deplored the haste:

If Confederation comes, it will be a six months conception and a sickly child.

Timothy Anglin in his *Morning Freeman* attacked the very basis of the authority of the Quebec Conference, and argued that an Imperial Statute embodying the Quebec Resolutions for Confederaton would undo the achievement of responsible government. Anglin's influence was so strong that most Irish Catholics in New Brunswick began to fear that a Union with Protestant Upper Canada would be as bad as Ireland's Union with England. A similar dread took hold of the French Catholics along the North Shore. The climax came when the vigorous young Bishop of Saint John, John Sweeny, was persuaded to issue a letter calling on the people to oppose Confederation.

Tilley conducted a spirited campaign, but he was no match for the "Smashers." To reject Confederation, now that the real dangers had been revealed by the St. Albans raid, said Tilley, "would be a direct invitation to American aggression." The election was a sad rout for Confederation. Every delegate to the Quebec Conference lost his seat, including Leonard Tilley; "a British North American calamity" was the comment of the Halifax *British Colonist*.

The bad news of Tilley's defeat came over the wires on Saturday, March 4, 1865, to the Members of Parliament in Quebec. Over the week-end a rumour developed that the Coalition Cabinet was breaking up. But on Monday, John A. MacDonald faced the House and made a firm statement. He recognized that it was a serious check upon the project of Confederation, but the Government did not intend to alter its course. It was but "an additional reason for prompt and vigorous action; the debate on the Quebec Resolutions must end with all convenient speed," and the question of their adoption must be put to the House.

When Dr. Thomas Parker of Wellington North stated that the four Maritime Provinces were in effect repudiating Confederation, D'Arcy McGee replied directly: Dr. Parker was wrong about three of the four Maritime Provinces; and in respect to the recent defeat in New Brunswick, McGee drew upon the knowledge he had gained from ten different visits there, and his answer was realistic:

> It was a fair stand-up fight of Yankee interests on the one side and British interests on the other; and those who are here ungenerously and unwisely rejoicing over the defeat of Hon. Mr. Tilley are in reality rejoicing in the triumph of Yankee interests.

Then the last day of the prolonged debate on Confederation came. Dorion, Holton, Dunkin and Sandfield MacDonald had tried in vain to oppose the adoption of the Resolutions and Sandfield MacDonald had one card left to play. In an impatient House he moved an amendment that the entire control of Education in Upper Canada be vested in that Province, and that McGee's safeguard to protect minority rights be deleted.

The tactic was to entice Brown away from the solidarity of the Cabinet, but it failed, and the amendment was soundly defeated by a vote of ninety-five to eight.

Finally the main question was put at the end of a night-long sitting. With the windows rattling under the force of a raging blizzard, the vote was taken in a weary House at half past four in the morning of March 11. The Seventy-two Resolutions of the Quebec Conference were adopted without change, by a vote of ninety-one to thirty-three. Those who opposed included some *Rouges* like Dorion, Reformers like Sandfield MacDonald, a few Clear Grits, Luther Holton from Montreal and Christopher Dunkin from Brome; but the main opponents were nineteen French Canadians, who feared that they would lose their identity in Confederation.

Meanwhile a new trial of the five recaptured St. Albans raiders had been proceeding before Judge James Smith of the Superior Court in Montreal since January 1865. The question of fact was simple: were they robbers or soldiers? But the questions of law seemed endless.

No one for the defence could get through to Southern headquarters in Virginia to obtain any documentary proof that the raid was part of an authorized military plan, so John Houghton, a lawyer from Montreal, went to Washington, D.C., on behalf of the prisoners to seek a pass to proceed to Richmond. On January 31 Houghton finally obtained an interview with President Lincoln. Wearied by those long four years of Civil War, Lincoln had been receiving an increasing number of threatening letters, and Houghton found him looking extremely tired as he listened to the request. Lincoln's reply was brief, and his exact words were entered in the legal record in Montreal:

They are rebels, who have been cutting and slashing around. I do not see it as any part of my business to help them.

Two months later, on March 29, 1865, the famous trial in Montreal came to an end; and Judge Smith spoke for three and a half hours in rendering judgment. He held that what the five raiders had done was not one of the offences listed in the Ashburton Treaty and so could not be extradited to Vermont:

I have no jurisdiction over them. The prisoners are discharged.

This elaborate judgment, which in fact confirmed the summary decision of Judge Coursol, was greeted with loud cheering in the old Court

House of Montreal. Officers were unable to suppress it. And the cheers were taken up and repeated by the crowds in the lobbies and outside on Notre Dame Street. This popular sentiment in Canada was largely a frightened reaction against the great military power of the Northern States, and by this time almost anything that went against the North was instinctively welcomed by most of the inhabitants of Montreal.

But this time the police were ready. The prisoners were kept in custody, and remanded to a later date to be tried on a further charge. On April 5 Cartier decided to proceed against the raiders for breach of the neutrality laws of Canada, and to have them tried elsewhere. So on the same day, a special train removed them to Toronto. From then on, the public began to lose interest as the Civil War approached its end, and eventually, some six months later, with little publicity, the raiders were discharged in Toronto.

George Clerk, who had been following the trial closely, turned his attention to the last events of the Civil War, and on April 10, 1865, he wrote briefly in his diary: "News that Lee has capitulated with entire army on 8th instant. End of war may be looked for now any day", and sighed in Latin: "Eheu." Three days later in Montreal, McGee completed his latest book, a collection of *Speeches and Addresses* which he had made on "a new nationality" in Canada and the influence of the Civil War on Canada's development towards Confederation.

The next day, April 14, was Good Friday, and at the end of that day's entry in his diary, Clerk added an ironic note: "No news from the United States." But the next morning Clerk, McGee and indeed everyone in Canada and elsewhere heard the dreadful news.

At half past ten Good Friday evening at Ford's Theatre in Washington, John Wilkes Booth entered the President's box and shot Abraham Lincoln at close range through the back of the head. As Lincoln slumped forward in his rocking chair, a hole the size of a lead pencil could be seen behind the right ear where the lead ball had entered. The President was carried across the street to the home of William Peterson, a tailor. There in a sparsely furnished room with a low ceiling, on a poster bed that was too short for him, Lincoln lay unconscious throughout the night, his chest heaving deeply. The next morning while a cold rain was falling outside, at twenty-two minutes past seven, someone in the darkened room noticed that "a look of unspeakable peace came over his worn features," and they folded his huge hands together.

There were very mixed reactions in Canada on the murder of Lincoln. Two of the St. Albans raiders were overheard in the bar of the Queens

Hotel in Toronto praising the assassin, Booth. Bernard Devlin wired Governor General Monck that some of the conspirators (on what evidence it was not known) were then on their way to Quebec. Later it was discovered that John Surratt had written a letter from Montreal to his mother in Washington, postmarked St. Lawrence Hall, April 12; and a few days later, to avoid arrest as one of the suspected conspirators, he was hiding in disguise in the presbytery of St. Liboire in Lower Canada until he escaped to Europe.

Two comments in Montreal on the death of Lincoln were in sharp contrast. In an editorial in the *True Witness* George Clerk described Lincoln as "a man remarkable chiefly for his great mediocrity." But D'Arcy McGee was deeply moved by the assassination, and the full meaning of what he said in his eloquent tribute to Lincoln would be revealed three years later, almost to the very day:

A pistol cannot kill the reputation of a virtuous and worthy citizen.

On the floor of the presidential box in Ford's Theatre, the fatal weapon had been found. It was a six-inch, single-shot brass pistol, and on its ornate handle was the name of its make: Derringer.

# 16

## SECRECY AND SPIES

Liberty is a serious game, to be played out, as the Greek told the Persian, with knives and hatchets, and not with drawled epigrams and soft petitions.

THE LONDON TIMES

Many battles have been won
Along with the boys in blue,
And we'll go and capture Canada,
For we've nothing else to do.

FENIAN MARCHING SONG

Under a heavy air of calm, the enemies of D'Arcy McGee were gathering together. McGee realized that his policy of peaceful resistance to any outrages of Orangemen would come to be interpreted by many Irishmen as draggletailed appeasement. And so it was. He also knew that his primary devotion to Canada, which carried an inherent loyalty to the Crown, would be misconstrued as an abandonment of Ireland's cause against England. And so it was also. But there was no way out.

It had early been taken for granted by Orangemen and Protestant Tories, on the one side, that McGee, despite his denials, was at heart disloyal to the Queen. This assumption waned with experience, but it never really died. As Confederation approached, Lord Monck could still be expected to doubt (at least in Luther Holton's mind) whether McGee was fit to be a member of the Privy Council. Yet, on the other side, that very profession of loyalty by McGee was taken as subservience to a hostile sovereign by many Irish Catholics in democratic America.

Both these views were rancorous; and they stemmed in part from the same noxious soil, which must be recognized in order to follow the last years of D'Arcy McGee. The trouble lay in the bad and twisted tradition of the secret society. Their members could be fierce or brash or brave or proud, and on any of these counts they could fascinate many. But in McGee's view as a citizen, they were instruments of a secret society, committed to conspiracy, and he was unalterably opposed to them on this clear ground.

Ireland had suffered deeply from secret societies. There had been the Orange Peep-O'-Day Boys, and their rivals, the Rapparees; the Heart of Steel Boys in Antrim and the Terry Alts in Clare; the Black Feet and the White Boys; the Ribbonmen and the Attacots of Old. One side was as dangerous as the other; and D'Arcy McGee expressed it in one sentence in his *History of Ireland:*

> Right Boys and Defenders, and a dozen other denominations descended from the same evil genius, whoever he was, that first introduced the system of signs and passwords and midnight meetings among the peasantry of Ireland.

This evil had been imported into Canada, and at its core were the texts of two secret oaths in McGee's possession. The first was the secret Orange Oath, which in essence was this:

> I solemnly swear to bear true allegiance to Her Majesty Queen Victoria so long as she shall maintain the Protestant religion and the laws of this country.
>
> I swear that I am not nor ever will be a Roman Catholic or Papist, nor am I married to nor will I ever marry a Roman Catholic or Papist, nor educate my children nor suffer them to be educated in the Roman Catholic faith, if in my power to prevent it.
>
> So help me God and keep me steadfast in this my Orangeman's obligation.

The second was this secret Fenian Oath:

> I do solemnly swear allegiance to the Irish Republic, now virtually established;
>
> That I will take up arms at a moment's notice to defend its integrity and independence;
>
> That I will yield implicit obedience to the commands of my superior officers;
>
> And finally I take this oath in the spirit of a true soldier of liberty.
>
> So help me God.

Following the assassination of Abraham Lincoln and the close of the Civil War, events moved rapidly in the American Republic. Canada was indiscriminately blamed together with England for the support which had been supplied to the South, and relations with the United States were scarcely worse than they had been at any time since the War of 1812. In this fetid air the Fenians began to grow. They were the bitter fruit of the Irish famine, but in the United States they were fostered by something more.

For thousands of Irishmen in the United States, the wounds left by the famine and the forced clearances in Ireland became ulcerous, as a general spirit of vengeance against England spread through the Northern United States. The four devastating years of the Civil War had trained large numbers of exiled Irishmen in the trade of warfare, and many had contracted a fever for firearms. Those without work and those with no training in a trade other than soldiering were ready recruits at the end of the war for the ranks of the Fenians.

There was also the political setting, which favoured their growth. When talk first began to spread among the Fenians about the notion of invading Canada, this was recognized as a novel and violent form for the older idea of Annexation of Canada; and it was promoted, if only indirectly, by attitudes within both American political parties. There were radical leaders within the Republicans who encouraged these Fenian plans in order to embarrass the Administration of President Andrew Johnson; and among ambitious Democrats it was a tactic obviously practised to flatter the military vanity of the Fenians in order to capture the increasing Irish vote. Astute diplomatic calculations were also being made. American claims had been lodged against England for outfitting privateers like the *Alabama* to help the South during the Civil War. To press the settlement of these heavy claims, any warlike threats from American Fenians could be quietly exploited, and Canada could be considered as the hostage, or perhaps the battleground.

On the other hand, in the British North American Provinces, the Civil War had left a legacy of vague fears. The older slogan of the Manifest Destiny of the United States to expand both northward and westward was now being described by an excited New York *Tribune* as the "Dazzling Destiny". There were, of course, a few big talkers with their "blood and iron policy." And there were also those who pushed their interests forward to look like the inevitable:

> There is no need to shake the tree. Canada will fall like a ripe fruit into the American garden.

These American views fitted in with a rather widespread feeling, particularly in Montreal, Toronto, and Saint John, New Brunswick, that Annexation could well be the panacea for commercial and financial ills. But the important aspect was that these opinions, in their turn, nurtured the fear that the "Little England" group in the United Kingdom would use these attitudes as further arguments to persuade the British Imperial military power to withdraw from North America and leave the Provinces exposed to envelopment. There was also the abiding fear of absorption into the American Republic by the simple force of economic gravity.

So it was not simply a military concern when reports kept coming in that the Fenians, in the North and even in the South, were enrolling recruits in their secret army in unexpected numbers. It gave a sinister aspect to the familiar political threat of Annexation. Since it had a strong effect on the movement for Confederation throughout British North America, the influence of the Fenians must be appreciated, even if their secret doings cannot be fully probed.

The irreligious spirit which pervaded the revolutionary movements of 1848 in Europe, such as the disillusioning attack of Young Italy and the Carbonari on Pope Pius IX, came out vehemently in the *Communist Manifesto* of Marx and Engels in 1848. As D'Arcy McGee knew from his own personal experience, Young Ireland was somewhat tainted with it. James Stephens and John O'Mahony, two of the insurgents of 1848, had taken lessons in conspiracy from a volcanic group of revolutionists in Paris; and Stephens had gone further and fought at the barricades in the Red resistance to Louis Napoleon's *coup d'Etat* in 1851. But years of oppression and direct experience with the wickedness of men did not usually attract the Irish towards any idolatry of human nature.

Archbishop Paul Cullen of Dublin, though himself the son of an Irish rebel of '98, had lived through the worst of the revolution in Rome, and was prompt to condemn the Fenians under Stephens in Ireland as a secret, subversive society. "Cullen has Carbonari on the brain," the Fenians fired back. But the Irish Bishops followed their Archbishop. So, too, did a number of American Bishops when they came to grips with O'Mahony's Fenians in the United States; there the Bishops of Chicago, Philadelphia and St. Louis took the lead in condemning the Fenians, although some American Bishops thought it would be prudent to delay any pronouncement.

D'Arcy McGee had no doubts on the matter, and he spoke his mind in a letter to James Moylan in Toronto:

> Fenianism is an irreligious revolutionary Society, in which patriotism takes the garb of indifferentism or hostility to religion.
>
> It is not honest men gone astray we have to deal with, but dogmatic, anti-clerical demagogues, a new sect, in fact, who aim at changing the heart and mind of Ireland. This sect is altogether novel in Irish history, and is not to be put down by half apologetic pleadings of *good intentions*.

Accurate facts about the Fenians in Canada are very difficult to establish. Spies as sources of information are notoriously unreliable, and papers of a secret society are often deliberately fabricated to mislead or to frighten. It seems clear, however, that the first active Fenian in Canada was Edward O'Meagher Condon, who came from New York in 1859 and set up a small Circle in Toronto. Condon left Canada soon after that, and little is known of his subsequent activities until he was sentenced to death in Manchester as a Fenian in 1867 (which was later commuted to penal servitude for life because he was an American citizen). But this lone Fenian Circle in Toronto never had more than sixty members. From it, in some indistinct manner, Michael Murphy, a thriving cooper, emerged as the Centre.

A few delegates from both Upper and Lower Canada attended the first National Fenian Convention at Chicago in November 1863. Two Canadian delegates were also present at the second Convention in Cincinnati in January 1865. But they were part of a nameless underground. The front for the Fenians in Toronto was probably the Hibernian Society (which should not be confused with the Ancient Order of Hibernians); it had started as a society of Irish Catholic immigrants to protect themselves from the dominant Orangemen at the time of the unpunished murder of Matthew Sheady in 1858. At least that is what an informer Patrick Nolan, writing under the alias of "E. C. Burton" in 1865, told Gilbert McMicken, the head of Canada's Secret Service:

> The Government thinks that the Hibernian Society is all Fenian. It is a mistake. There are not half of them Fenians. They have two oaths, and there is half of them will not take the second oath.

Nolan illustrated the sort of difficulty his undercover agents were encountering:

> Captain Prince had a lot of men out in plain clothes some time ago watching for the Fenians. One of them thought he had a lodge full one night on Nelson Street, but it turned out to be an Orange Lodge. I think the Captain got tired of them telling lies.

Early in 1865, John A. MacDonald expressed his belief that Fenians in Canada "were contemptible in numbers." In fact, the secret proceedings of the Fenians in Cincinnati at the time did not claim more than two Canadian Circles, one in Toronto and the other in Montreal. Estimates made by informers, checked with those from the Secret Police, together with the calculations based on the amount of dues claimed as received, would indicate that in 1865 there were about 600 to 800 Fenians in Upper Canada, and 500 to 600 in Lower Canada; of the latter, there were probably 200 in Quebec City, and 350 in Montreal. Starting with Murphy's trade as a cooper, the occupations of the members were mostly tailors, shoemakers, cab drivers, gardeners, waiters, blacksmiths, brick layers or labourers.

In the spring of 1865, D'Arcy McGee was sent by the Canadian Government as Minister of Agriculture and Immigration at the head of a delegation to the International Exhibition in Dublin. Accompanying him as one of the delegates was his friend the engineer, Thomas Devine.

So McGee went back to visit his boyhood town of Wexford on the southeastern tip of Ireland. It was still the ancient sea-washed town that he had left when he was sixteen. From the great sweep of its harbour it rose in its soft lights and edgeless shadows on a series of shelves linked by steep lanes and narrow winding streets, with their neat rows of attached homes set right out on the sidewalk, and distinguished by their doors of different colours. Wexford's embattled history, which had enraptured McGee's youthful imagination, stretched far back to the terror of the Viking raids. Oliver Cromwell's butchery and the rebels' pikes, scythes and dreadful ferocity of '98 were all part of its scar tissue.

McGee recalled how twenty-three years before, he was sitting on a tattered tarpaulin in the stern of the *Leo* while she spread her sails for the North Atlantic, and as Wexford faded in the distance over "the still and silent sea" he wrote his farewell as a boy "to the friend of my early days, my happiest hours, the rocky wilds and sunny meadows and the wondrous tales." Now he was returning at the age of forty. "With riper years come care and sorrow's sense," he had written then as an emigrant boy, with more meaning than he knew. His boyish haunts were still there: the Bull Ring with its high grim cross in the centre of the town; the crumbling walls, the massive strongholds, caves, castles and keeps; a waterfall flashing out of a deep green glen; an ancient abbey and a holy well where birds nestled; the entangled beauty of the River Slaney; long sweeps of yellow sand along the shore; and off-shore, the reef-girt islands.

On a Sunday afternoon, May 14, McGee walked over to the West Gate Tower. Nearby were the ruins of Selskar Abbey in pale rose sandstone, and in its shade among the ferns, he knelt at the grave of his mother— "too pure," he had written as a boy, "for the tenants of this earth."

McGee had been invited to address the Wexford Young Men's Society the next day. He decided to speak on "Twenty Years' Experience of Irish Life in America" and prepared his text with care, because he had made up his mind to speak "frankly, fully and fearlessly." If that last word sounded unnecessary, those who had seen the anonymous letters he had been receiving realized what it meant.

By eight o'clock Monday evening the voices and laughter of his old schoolfellows could be heard as they emptied their pipes and crowded into the assembly room. The mayor of Wexford was "unavoidably absent," so Rev. Mr. Lambert presided. McGee began with a wistful greeting to his friends in "this good old town," where but one of his family "remains to bid me welcome. The rest lie quietly in the shadows of

Selskar churchyard." He then made another reference to the past, which was received with silence:

> I was one of the Young Ireland fugitives of 1848. I am not at all ashamed of Young Ireland, Why should I be?
>
> Politically, we were a pack of fools. But we were honest in our folly. And no man need blush at forty for the follies of one and twenty, unless indeed he still persevered in them, having no longer the fair excuse to plead of youth and inexperience.

It was an inept beginning, and McGee sensed the uneasy feeling, which he tried to relieve:

> But I feel I must avoid such reflections for fear of getting into a scrape. I know that this is a land of philippics, and that the immense vituperative resources of the language are nowhere better understood.

Then he opened his main topic, to present the true position of Irishmen in North America, for "there are as many Irish now in America as in Ireland." And he proceeded directly to the facts, as he saw them in a cold, hard light:

> The six New England States, still strongly tinctured with Puritanism, proud of their prosperity and highly trained in mere school learning, hate the Irish Catholic emigrant for his creed, despise him for his poverty and underrate him for his want of book learning.
>
> In great cities like New York and Philadelphia, the Irish have been used and abused by native-born and Irish-born demagogues. They have come roughly into competition with native labour. They have jostled native respectability at the polls. They formerly arrayed themselves insanely and most cruelly against the Negro, while right and justice were plainly on the side of the slave.
>
> It is for these and for other reasons that the Irish of this generation, their numbers and industry considered, are socially and politically the weakest community in the Republic—weaker than the Negroes themselves in the free States.

The catalogue he listed of things against the Irish was depressing: "illiteracy and squalor of the famine emigration," "herding together in great cities," "running up debts with storemen in idle periods," "squandering wages when flush with cash" and, finally, "overbearing insolence of our own demagogues." And his picture of the demagogue was unforgettable:

He is not seldom a dealer, by wholesale or retail, in spirituous liquors. Sometimes a lawyer. Sometimes an editor.

He is always ready with his money subscriptions to the church, but seldom goes to church. He lies up Sunday after the toils of the week, reading a sporting journal or a police gazette.

He has a ready, rowdy sort of rhetoric, and is never at a loss when called on to propose or second a resolution.

He is particularly savage of England, and grows quite pathetic, unprepared as he is, at the mere mention of the old land. A fair share of mother wit, a sufficient stock of spending money, and a vast deal of brass complete the equipment of this very active, very important and much-courted individual.

McGee then turned his attention from this "dealer in the manufacture and sale of his countrymen's votes" to present the other and better side of the picture. But in the retelling of what he said at Wexford, the complimentary side was overlooked, and the first unbalanced part prevailed. He did, however, make it clear that evening that there were many celebrated Irishmen who were recognized as worthy leaders in the United States. And his listing of them was not narrow. Besides mentioning friends like Mrs. James Sadlier as an author, and old colleagues of Young Ireland like Thomas Francis Meagher, who had risen to become a brigadier general in the Civil War, and Richard O'Gorman, who was then prominent in the New York Bar, he paid a magnanimous tribute to his old opponent Archbishop Hughes and even to his vitriolic adversary John Mitchel. It was no fault of the Irish, McGee added, that they had been scattered across a continent; and this, despite their great efforts, had broken the family ties of multitudes, but "I have met as well-ordered Irish families in the United States as there are in Ireland." This cruel pulverizing of so many destitute families was introducing a new reading of the old Commandment: "Parents, obey your children, that your days may be long in the land."

He mentioned with a twinge of pain the efforts made in 1855 at the Buffalo Convention to settle the Irish "with some system" on the open lands of the United States and Canada.

But, though I still believe it was a good plan, it failed for want of support. And the next year I voluntarily transferred my household goods to the valley of the St. Lawrence.

Here he paused; and then decided to say something more.

The names he had been called at the time of his move to Canada,

McGee had not been able to forget; and he repeated them slowly to his Wexford audience: "traitor"—"renegade"—"apostate." Here he stopped:

> Forgive me, Sir, I did not intend this. But having now mentioned my removal to Canada, you will expect me to say something of the position of our countrymen in that and the adjoining Provinces.

This led him to describe the vast expanse of his new land covering "one third of the continent"; its rapid growth with "an increase of nearly 400 per cent in one generation to a population of four millions," and the maturing of its citizens:

> If they have shaken off any painful servility of manner, they have not yet mistaken impertinence for independence.

Turning to the Maritime Provinces, McGee selected four men for impartial praise (although his personal feelings for the last man to be mentioned were far from warm): Ambrose Shea of Newfoundland, Archbishop Connolly of Nova Scotia, Edward Whelan of Prince Edward Island and Timothy Anglin of New Brunswick.

Changing the subject, he stated that he had a few plain things to say about the attempts of American Fenians to undermine Canada.

> I have never myself seen a specimen of the genus Fenian in Canada; but I hear there are, and I dare say there may be, some odd ones among our half million, since Solomon says that "the number of fools is infinite." But their number is at most insignificant.

He warned his Irish audience, however, not to make the mistake of construing anti-English feelings among the Americans to be pro-Irish sentiments, nor to be misled by deliberate Fenian exaggerations of their strength in the United States, nor to be fooled by "any surface slang as an expression of settled national sentiment of the American people, which is not one whit more pro-Irish than it is pro-Japanese." It was not palatable, but nonetheless what McGee was saying about those times was true.

> Some of these Fenian emissaries seem to think that as I was a Young Irelander some twenty years ago, I ought to have some lenity for them.
>
> Why, Young Ireland, as I am free to say, was politically a folly, but the men were honest and manly. Men like Thomas Davis and Charles Gavan Duffy and others still living would have scorned to range themselves with these Punch and Judy Jacobins.

It was the speech of a realist; and McGee concluded it with some frank words for the Minister of Immigration in Canada:

I am not here to advise any man to emigrate. You seem to have a mania for emigration upon you in Ireland, and I certainly feel it no part of my duty to pander to that mania.

On the contrary I would say to every man and woman who can live at home, stay at home. If wages in North America are much higher, life is far shorter. The average life of the Irish labouring man in the great cities does not exceed ten years from the date of his arrival.

"Canada," McGee added, "is a hard country for the soft-handed. But we can easily provide for the accession of fifty-thousand adults a year, provided they are willing and able to work their way. It is a climate cold in winter, but beautifully clear and most wholesome." And he brought his unusual address to an end with a note of concern: "Whatever may betide, I hope I shall not discredit the good people of the town of Wexford."

For nearly an hour following his talk the people of Wexford gathered around McGee, questioning him on many points. A reporter of the Dublin *Evening Mail* wrote that they "assured him of their thorough concurrence in his views." If, indeed, this was so, and not just the politeness of Wexford, it certainly was not true elsewhere.

D'Arcy McGee's speech in Wexford was both brave and rash. No one in his home town could properly have expected him to return and speak to them as the poetic stripling they had once known, unchanged. In Canada, McGee had lived as a politician, continually confronting the realities of life, and had come to know men as they are, and not as paper-thin abstractions which hide between book covers. But the strains under which he had been living, and the threats which haunted him and hovered over his family, led him to misjudge the passions which such a speech would rouse.

Stephens' Fenian newspaper in Dublin, *The Irish People*, denounced him at once as "a hireling and a hypocrite," as a "philosophic poltroon" speaking at a "hole and corner meeting":

This wretched man has come to Ireland with government gold in his pocket to preach loyalty to the Irish people, while he was in touch with "goulahs" who were ready to sell him their secret minutes and members' rolls.

Such comments from the Fenians were of course expected. But others were not. One of McGee's most trusted friends, Charles Gavan Duffy, whom Dublin was welcoming back from Australia as Premier of Victoria and a delegate to its International Exhibition, found McGee's remarks on Young Ireland needlessly harsh; "I prefer McGee's folly at twenty to his philosophy at forty," he remarked.

Whatever balance there was in McGee's strong views was almost completely lost in the reported versions when the London *Times* led off with full column of patronizing comment:

> The poor and excitable natives of the neighbouring country have lived in an atmosphere of falsehood and deception fostered by adulation.
> No fact reaches them in its true and original form; everything is distorted and perverted to meet their hopes, their fears and their prejudices.

McGee's picture of the Irish in America, the *Times* commended as eminently graphic and interesting, and then added:

> We have been surprised to find that notwithstanding a Government administered with great mildness and impartiality in all its branches, Ireland has continued to grow in discontent instead of becoming more reconciled to the British connection.

The best comment came from the Dublin *Nation*, the old journal of Gavan Duffy and McGee, now edited by Timothy and Alexander Sullivan, which recognized that the lecture showed "the marked ability, the originality and the vigour of thought that have raised Mr. McGee to a high position," but "Irish nationalists will surely be startled by the boldness and severity of his judgments."

> His references to the "folly" of '48, however, are but harsh expressions of what nearly every one of his colleagues in that movement, less hurtfully but not less frankly, confesses.

Turning to the grim picture which McGee drew of Irish life in the United States, the *Nation* was relieved to note:

> Though he is evidently indisposed to flatter them in any degree, he did not endorse the revolting descriptions of our countrymen in the Northern States drawn by General Thomas Francis Meagher in his memorable letter of last year which designated them as "a degraded herd," "beneath respect and beneath contempt."

The *Nation* was not prepared to say with McGee that Irishmen would be better off in Canada than in the United States, but it did concur in this:

> The masses of our countrymen in the States are largely used in American politics, and have notably been heartlessly and thanklessly used in the last War.

It then concluded:

> While we dissent from some of Mr. McGee's judgments, his lecture has an attraction of great power. In these days when mere rhetoric, rhodomontade, buncombe and clap-trap have flooded popular platforms, it is absolutely refreshing—though it were only for the effect of a cold bath—to note the moral courage of Mr. McGee in speaking wholesome, though unpalatable truths to the people.
> The sickening effects of so much confectionary oratory need a few draughts of bitters as a salutary tonic.

But "bitters" were not as popular in North America. The most outspoken parts of McGee's speech in Wexford were quoted widely throughout the United States and Canada. And what chiefly circulated was an infuriating mixture of the imperialistic lullaby of the London *Times* and the tireless abuse of the Fenian *Irish People*. It made many enemies for McGee and dismayed many of his friends. In Toronto *The Irish Canadian,* which covertly supported Fenians and was openly hostile to McGee, saw his future from then on as "a gradual decay" and "a darkened existence."

It did darken his life to some extent, though McGee would not admit it. From then on he was a marked man. Unknown people would follow him at night, and after each mention of McGee's name, *The Irish Canadian* began to print: "tramp, tramp, tramp." McGee seemed to push most of these incidents aside, but something was left to haunt the back of his mind.

Two months after his return McGee had some second thoughts in Montreal about his speech in Wexford. In a letter of July 24, 1865, to a friend in Upper Canada, he admitted that his speech had been deliberate.

> It will be said I was too hard on the Irish demagogues in the Atlantic Cities. Perhaps I erred on the side of severity.

But, he explained, it was only someone who "has laboured for a decade to create a clean and upright spirit" among the Irish immigrants, and someone who knows what those demagogues did, who should judge on the matter. Regretting that some of his censure had been taken by "public-spirited families" as directed against them in the United States, he acknowledged that his praise for them and their accomplishments had been too skimpy in Wexford. McGee's moderating letter was published, but it received comparatively little attention in the glaring light of controversy which was focussed on the Wexford speech itself.

No politician could have shown more raw courage and done himself more needless harm than McGee did by that one speech in Wexford. He had bruised the romantic sentiments of maturing Irish rebels, who were reuniting to meet Duffy and McGee in Dublin; he had fanned the hatred of the American political bosses, with whom it was pointless to pick a quarrel; and he had also chosen a clumsy way of attacking the underground movement of the Fenians, by openly provoking them to conspire in secret for revenge.

Privately, the Wexford speech could be explained as a recoil of his strong emotions from the personal attacks he had suffered and the injuries done to his pride of achievement. But in his public life it was a tidal turn.

Within the occult inner circles of the Fenians deep and disturbing changes were occurring.

James Stephens, the bearded "Hawk" under the alias of "James Daly," had toured through the United States in 1864 raising money for "the men in the gap" and pledging that they would "strike for freedom" in Ireland in 1865. It was a bold promise, impossible to fulfil. As each month passed in 1865 and there was no news of action in Ireland, a break began to appear among the Fenians in the United States. This split, as it was called, was largely fomented by a big, glib man called "Red Jim" McDermott, who was also called "St. Sylvester" because of an undeserved cross of that Order which he wore on his chest. There were good reasons to mistrust McDermott, but John O'Mahony, his practical judgement impaired by his recent mental breakdown, insisted that Red Jim, though "morally a bad man," was "politically necessary." In truth, in Red Jim's heart there was the "bad drop"; for, as it was later revealed, he was as informer, a reckless "stag."

In Ireland the Fenians received a devastating blow. On Friday night, September 15, just as the issue of *The Irish People* had been printed for delivery on the next day, the police broke into the Fenian newspaper plant in Dublin and seized its press, books, records, subscription lists and all the confidential correspondence. With one stroke the Irish headquarters of the Fenians had been smashed. But James Stephens escaped. Two months later at Fairfield House in Sandymount near Dublin, a mild "Mr. Herbert", who seemed to spend most of his time in his greenhouse arranging his geraniums and japonicas, was arrested. The news spread like fire: the Hawk had been caught.

On November 15 James Stephens stood in the dock for his preliminary inquiry. He was of medium height and strong build, seedily attired, with long hair and flowing beard, and his small penetrating eyes under a massive forehead were dry and hard with scorn. Asked by the court if he had anything to say, he folded his arms and answered:

Yes. Take it down. I have employed no lawyer in this case, because in making a defence of any kind I should be recognizing British law in Ireland.

I defy any punishment and despise any punishment.

Ten days later, during a blinding storm just before dawn, Stephens escaped over the high wall of Richmond Prison. He hid in a widow's home in a small place called Summer Hill, issuing new passwords to his secret followers cleverly devised as "quarrelling words," until finally his chance came one night to flee north through Malahide towards Balbriggan. There, in a cove, a lugger was waiting for him, and as soon as Stephens boarded her, she was underway.

This strange man with his masterful arrogance, who could boast indifferently of his skill with the rifle or the fiddle, saw the Irish coast disappear in the night, as someone on a lonely flute played "The Bold Fenian Men." Stephens had made up his mind. He was going back to Paris to build a new conspiracy.

Meanwhile the split was widening in the ranks of the Fenians in America. As it became apparent that, notwithstanding Stephens' promises, there would be no insurrection in Ireland in 1865, an impetuous new Fenian wing arose in the United States. It was directed by workaday men who were also out of patience with the febrile schemes of O'Mahony as Head Centre.

The organizer was William R. Roberts, a successful dry-goods merchant from New York who was much more energetic than vain men usually are, and could cast a glow of excitement over his proposed ventures. Working with Roberts was a capable military leader, Thomas W. Sweeny, who had lost his right arm in the Mexican War, had fought through the Indian Wars and had also gained distinction in the Civil War. Impatient young Irishmen were ready to follow this soldier they called "The Armless Sleeve." Roberts and Sweeny were to be the "men of action," where O'Mahony had been a "drag chain."

But their plan of action was a poorly guarded secret. And although it seemed like a roundabout way of getting at England, it was simple enough and close to home: Canada should be invaded, its territory seized and occupied, and then handed over to establish the St. Lawrence River as the northern boundary of the United States. O'Mahony opposed the plan. But it had already been broached to Secretary of State Seward and to President Johnson. Both of them listened to it and said very little. They did remark, however, and with dangerous ambiguity, that governments often acknowledge accomplished facts.

The military reports made to London during October of 1865 by General Sir John Michel, who was in command of the armed forces in British North America, showed how well informed he was of the plan of Roberts and Sweeny. The Fenians were aiming at a vulnerable area, Michel explained, planning "to cross at Niagara and Detroit" and then spread to that "most vital, attackable position in Canada, Montreal." The purpose of the Fenians, if accomplished, was accurately foreseen by Michel:

> Under the idea that they might be partially successful, the Fenians would then receive belligerent rights from the United States, and thus embroil her with England.

Word went out that the third National Convention of the Fenians was called for Monday, October 16, 1865, at Fenian Hall in Philadelphia, where Roberts and Sweeny were resolved to revise their Constitution and curb the authority of O'Mahony. D'Arcy McGee heard of it and on the same day wired John A. MacDonald to get a report:

> Someone should be sent to Philadelphia immediately.

MacDonald and McGee learned that six hundred delegates were there, one from each Circle, and no proxies were permitted. Michael Murphy, the Toronto Centre, was present as one of the delegates. As expected, it was a stormy convention, and Murphy sided with O'Mahony. But Roberts and Sweeny won out by establishing the real power in a new Senate which they controlled and which soon shackled O'Mahony's authority.

Acting for the new Senate, Roberts, Sweeny and a third man rented Moffat Mansion, near Union Square in New York City, as the new Fenian headquarters. The third man was Bernard Doran Killian, who ten years before had worked as assistant editor with D'Arcy McGee on his *American Celt* in New York City. Killian had ability and initiative. In the interval he had become a lawyer, and had been active in St. Louis and New York, but his flaw was still impetuosity. How much money the Fenians raised was never known. Their propaganda spoke of collecting a dollar a head from four million Irish in America, and they did collect substantial sums mostly through small donations. For Moffat Mansion, they paid $18,000 rent in advance for eighteen months, and posted $6000 cash as security against damages. Then from its top window they put out the green Fenian flag of the Harp and the Sunburst.

D'Arcy McGee was well informed of what was happening, and on November 2, he wrote another letter to John A. MacDonald:

> A constant agency at New York, filled with the very best men we can get, with an understood system of cypher, is now becoming essential.
>
> The enemy have their headquarters permanently there, and there ought to be no easier place in the world for a good secret agent to do his work in than New York.

It is the sordid fortune of spies to work in a field without honour, where the same man will often sell secrets to both sides. Such men, called "goulahs" by the Irish, were never busier; and it was obvious that each side was receiving detailed reports on the other. An incident that occurred in Montreal was typical of what was continually happening.

Late in November 1865, on a raw, moonless night, the waterfront of Montreal was deserted. The last of the fall fleet had departed for the Atlantic, and the only sounds came from the current around St. Helen's Island and the bare elms bending with the wind. A hooded figure slipped through the shadows of the dense grey stone buildings facing the river, and stopped for a moment at the corner of St. Sulpice Street. He was then in front of a structure of a different style. Steps led up through pillars to a wooden gallery, stripped bare for winter, and above was a plain sign, "Old Countryman's Inn." Here was the centre of the Fenian *junta* in Montreal. The unknown person went up to the inn door as the steps squeaked under him and he slipped a letter through the crack at the threshold. Then he disappeared.

The letter was written by a husband in New York to be delivered to his wife in Montreal through the keeper of the inn. But it never reached her. It was intercepted and turned over to the police. With a score of other yellowed documents (including a torn envelope addressed to James

Stephens) this letter, somewhat cracked in the creases, has been preserved. It was a message, dated November 11, 1865, written in a jagged
scrawl:

> Tell Frank I am an out and out Fenian. Advise him to draw all his
> money out of the Bank and hide it, for that one of these fine days
> we intend crossing over to Canada and taking the contents of every
> Bank in the Province. The traitor McGee will come in for a *roasting*.

The paths taken by the men of Young Ireland after 1849 were indeed
crossing in puzzling ways. John O'Mahony had written in an early state
of despondency that Thomas Francis Meagher, John Blake Dillon, William Smith O'Brien and Richard O'Gorman—all those who could be
called Constitutional Nationalists—would have nothing to do with Feni-

anism. O'Mahony said the same thing about John Mitchel; but in this he was wrong. John Mitchel was, as always, unpredictably different.

That clever and most contrarious character had moved from New York to Tennessee just before the Civil War, when his enmity towards D'Arcy McGee was most intense. Pursuing his career as a journalist in the South, Mitchel shocked all who idolized him as an apostle of freedom when he callously wrote:

> We deny that it is a crime or a wrong or even a peccadillo to hold slaves, to buy slaves, to sell slaves, to keep slaves to their work by flogging or other needful coercion.

In the early organizing of Fenianism, when James Stephens was travelling in America, he paid a visit to Mitchel in Tennessee; and Mitchel gave this account of it:

> A gentleman appeared at our door who announced himself as James Stephens. I had never seen him before and knew him only as having turned out with Smith O'Brien in 1848 with his pike in good repair.
> Glad to see an Irishman of such antecedents at Knoxville.
> For two days he remained with us, telling me romantic tales of his armed, sworn, organized forces in Ireland. All he wanted was that I should publicly call on my fellow countrymen in America for money, and more money, and no end of money to be remitted to him for revolutionary purposes.

Mitchel declined to act, but gave Stephens fifty dollars.

Time passed. The Civil War was fought. Mitchel edited the Richmond *Enquirer* and actively supported the South. He lost his two sons, one at Fort Sumter, the other at Gettysburg, both Confederate soldiers; and he himself was captured and imprisoned in Fort Monroe.

Right after the Fenian headquarters were raided and destroyed in Dublin, on September 15, 1865, Stephens wrote from his hideaway to O'Mahony in New York, saying that to reorganize the rebellion in Ireland, "while the enemy were still in the dark," a special agent should be sent to Paris at once to serve as a trusted intermediary, with $25,000; then he added:

> Should John Mitchel be available (and an effort should be made to have him so), he is the man.

Bernard Doran Killian saw both President Johnson and Seward and, after a brief delay, managed to obtain Mitchel's release from prison. Mitchel agreed to act, and left for Paris with $60,000. His instructions dated November 10 from O'Mahony were precise:

> To pay out the money only to the order of James Stephens;
>
> To obtain receipts always in the handwriting of Stephens;
>
> To work, if Stephens be arrested, only through his accredited agents;
>
> To weave through the diplomatic circles of Europe with *carte blanche*;
>
> To regard any Fenian raid into Canada as a mere diversion, designed to drag the United States into war with England;
>
> To bear in mind the first grand requisite to success: that a revolutionary organization in Ireland is absolutely essential to her liberation.

The crisis among the Fenians in America came to a head in December of 1865. O'Mahony was issuing Fenian bonds over his own signature in denominations of ten to five hundred dollars repayable "six months after the independence of the Irish nation" by the Treasury of the Irish Republic. Roberts, questioning his right to do this without the authority of the new Fenian Senate, speedily called an emergency meeting on December 2 in New York and deposed O'Mahony. But not before O'Mahony had risen at the meeting and read from a letter he had just received from James Stephens, citing this extract about the revolting Fenian Senate: "Lash them from you like so many dogs." The split became irreparable.

Most of the Fenians in Canada sided with John O'Mahony as against the more extreme wing under Roberts and Sweeny. Some of the unrest felt in Montreal appeared from an entry made by George Clerk in his diary:

> 1866, January: There was some public showing of ill will against McGee at the St. Patrick's Society concert, but it was easily suppressed.

On February 12, 1866, the Toronto group of Fenians condemned the scheme of Roberts to invade Canada, and no Canadian delegates attended the fourth National Fenian Congress held a week later at Pittsburgh, because it was organized by Roberts and Sweeny and excluded O'Mahony.

John A. MacDonald received a full report of these Fenian proceedings from his secret agent Patrick Nolan, who wrote:

I sleep in one room with three Senators and two Congressmen every night.

Their full determination is to organize immediately and make a strike for Canada. If they can arrest the Governor General and D'Arcy McGee and other Government officers they will do it.

At the same time, Bishop John Lynch of Toronto was making his own careful inquiries about the Fenians, and he wrote privately on February 1, 1866, to Archbishop Connolly of Halifax. To deplore the existence of Fenians was not enough, he commented, without also doing something to remove the cause; the Fenians were a festering of an old wound; daily he was meeting impoverished immigrants who held a deep hatred in their hearts against those who had tried to exterminate them and to give their place in Ireland to cattle:

Those people and their children swell up the ranks of Fenians. All acquainted with the sacred ministry know the difficulties to induce these poor people to forgive their landlords.

Yet the Irish Catholics who were settled in Canada, Bishop Lynch wrote, did not want Annexation, and the United States did not offer them better lands or greater commercial advantages. In the meantime, he pointed out, the borders of Canada had to be guarded against the Fenians at the cost of more than a million dollars a year; it would be much better to devote some of that money towards a real cure, and to urge a settlement of the grievances in Ireland.

In England a sense of alarm began to spread as "the number of Americans wearing square-toed shoes and felt hats became noticeable in Dublin." Almost every visiting Irish American was assumed to be a revolutionary Fenian, and the number of arrests on suspicion increased. Then on February 17, 1866, the British Government took a drastic step, and permitted arbitrary imprisonment by suspending the *Habeas Corpus* Act. In Parliament, Lord John Russell explained its necessity with this argument:

Towards the end of the American War the Irish residents in America formed themselves into a vast conspiracy. They collected at one meeting subscriptions of a million dollars. Sometimes an invasion of Ireland and at other times an invasion of Canada were threatened.

That night the American Consul in Dublin reported to Seward in Washington that 150 persons had been arrested during the day in Dublin, including many American citizens under this "arbitrary and extreme proceeding." This news stirred Irishmen in the United States to a high pitch of excitement; and the Fenians promptly exploited it by convoking a mass meeting of one hundred thousand Irish Americans at Jones Wood to hear the Fenian orators.

In Canada as St. Patrick's Day approached, the wildest of rumours were rampant, which George Clerk reflected in his diary:

1866, March 9: Great excitement about Fenians. Rumours of all kinds. Prescott is to be attacked. Know not what to believe. Toronto in a strange state: rumour (incredible) that Bishop is about to leave diocese. Everything denotes a row of some kind. Banks here said to have sent specie to Quebec.

In Toronto there was almost a sense of panic as a fearful clash with Orangemen was anticipated. D'Arcy McGee wrote to George Brown:

I have taken the liberty, *entre nous,* though he is no great friend of mine, to suggest to Bishop Lynch that he ought not allow a St. Patrick's procession to be held this year.

Bishop Lynch responded. A few days before March 17 he published a letter through the Toronto clergy exhorting the Irish to be loyal, and asking the Hibernians not to parade to church on St. Patrick's Day. Privately, he also wrote to John A. MacDonald asking him to arrange for the prohibition of the St. Patrick's Day parade, as well as the Orange parade on July 12. But John A. MacDonald saw no political profit in adding that. Finally, Lord Monck wrote to George Brown stating his decision that he could not prohibit the St. Patrick's parade because "the meeting is not in itself illegal."

In the meantime Michael Murphy of the Toronto Hibernian Society had privately given an assurance to Gilbert McMicken, who was acting for John A. MacDonald, that no offence would be offered by the Hibernians in their parade, and that they would "undertake to police themselves." In fact, St. Patrick's Day passed off quietly in Toronto. A meeting was addressed by Murphy and others, and the Montreal *Gazette* reported that there was "nothing treasonable or seditious in their utterances." Murphy made a special point of stating that he had no quarrel with Canada, and then, as though to stress his opposition to Roberts and Sweeny, he proposed three cheers for James Stephens and John O'Mahony.

On that very same day in New York, however, O'Mahony convoked his own private central council in concealment, and decided to attack Campobello Island in Passamaquoddy Bay, New Brunswick. The date was set "in black secrecy" for April 17.

Such are human secrets.

At the top secret council of the Fenians in Paris, right beside James Stephens and John Mitchel, and acting as one of their most trusted agents, was John Joseph Corydon. He was high in the confidence of the Fenian conspirators, and also deep in the pay of the English secret service. By this time, too, in the rival part of the divided Fenians, Roberts and Sweeny had selected Colonel John O'Neill, who had a good military record under General Sherman, to lead the Fenian invasion of Canada through the Niagara Peninsula. Working intimately with O'Neill, through all his military planning, was his friend and comrade Major Henri Le Caron, a dashing Frenchman. In truth, Le Caron was Thomas Miller Beach, a professional spy born in Colchester, England. But this remained unknown until Le Caron's book, *Twenty-Five Years in the Secret Service*, created a sensation in the nineties. Then he admitted that he had been in the pay of both the English and the Canadian Governments, and had drawn as much as $10,000 in two years.

These were but two of the hundreds of spies who riddled the ranks of the Fenians. But one series of reports which came to John A. MacDonald from Alexander McLeod in Buffalo during March of 1866 was particularly alarming. McLeod was writing at first hand:

> I am in the headquarters of the Fenian organization. The owner of the premises is an auctioneer. He is an ignorant little Irishman, pretty well off. The auction room is being fitted out for a drill room. They can drill 200 men in it at a time.
>
> The auction room is full of Irishmen, a number of officers of the U.S. Volunteers are there just now. Their talk is not *sotto voce*, for I can almost hear them, although my door is shut and they near 50 feet from it.

McLeod proceeded to give elaborate details:

> There are now about 1000 stand of muskets here—and revolvers. At least 10 men are busy lowering cases of arms into the cellar. Ammunition, military accoutrement and wagons are now ready in the city for an invading force of 5000 men. I don't think the time to advance is fixed yet. Some say in about a week, others not until May. They will have a navy then.
>
> The general attack is to be made simultaneously on a line of 1500 miles by at least 100,000 men in arms.

Then McLeod inserted this warning:

My employer's son, a lad of 18 and a Fenian, came into the office from the auction and said one thousand dollars is offered in gold to anyone that will bring in D'Arcy McGee's head.

# 17

## CLOSING THE GAP

McGee's resistance to a Fenian invasion of Canada, a country where Irishmen were generously received and fairly treated, was not an offence but a merit.

There was not a member of the Young Ireland Party from Davis to Meagher who would not have done the same thing.

*Charles Gavan Duffy*

Give the hand of fellowship to those not of our faith, and be at peace with them.

FROM THE SERMON AT ST. PATRICK'S
CHURCH, MONTREAL, MARCH 17, 1866

Even for those who were unaware of spies and their murky plots or of the desperate weakness of the military defences, particularly in the Niagara Peninsula, the tranquil air in Canada through the summer of 1865 seemed strained. Most people were not very worried about the political difficulties, as bad as they were. But everyone agreed that the prospects of Confederation, so promising at the opening of the year, were now gloomy.

The defeat of Tilley in the elections of New Brunswick, which held the key position to Confederation, was taken by many as fatal to the movement. But the Canadian politicians did not see it that way. They were more concerned about the United States. The Civil War had come to an end leaving over a million men still under arms in the field. Hundreds of thousands were being disbanded by the Union Army, and for six dollars any soldier could bring his gun and equipment with him.

After his speech at Wexford and the International Exhibition at Dublin, D'Arcy McGee crossed over to London. There he joined MacDonald, Cartier, Galt and Brown in their negotiations with the British Government for Confederation based on the Quebec Resolutions. They also discussed the military defence of Canada based on Galt's financial proposals, which had staggered Gladstone with his strict economical views of colonies.

On May 31, 1865, the five Canadians went to Epsom Downs for Derby Day; MacDonald backed the favourite "Gladiateur" and won; and while the coach took five hours to travel the crowded road of sixteen miles back to London, George Brown played like a boy with a bag of peas and a pea-shooter. But that was the last time Brown was in a good mood with his colleagues of the Coalition Cabinet.

McGee also attended a banquet for Irishmen in London, which he enjoyed with Gavan Duffy, Dillon and his friends of Young Ireland. They had failed to meet in Dublin because of the feeling which McGee's speech in Wexford had stirred up. But Duffy later recalled the pleasure of that evening in seeing the faces of his old colleagues of the Dublin *Nation*, and particularly in meeting McGee:

One of my closest associates in trial and danger, who in whatever else he had changed, had at least remained steadfast in his kindness to me.

Then McGee paid a brief visit to Oxford when John A. MacDonald received an honorary degree, and was deeply impressed by the traditions and the university, as he revealed in a lecture on Oxford the following January in Toronto:

The highest lesson which Oxford teaches is this. It is possible to combine stability with freedom. Not perfect stability with perfect freedom—neither of which can we hope to see united in earthly institutions or constitutions—but so much of each as shall be preservative of both; so much as may occupy the young man's heart and satisfy the old man's judgment.

Away from his family for almost three months, McGee arrived back in Montreal in the first week of July 1865 to face his friends who were very perturbed by his controversial Wexford speech, and to prepare for an important Cabinet meeting in Quebec City on July 12. McGee knew by this time that the British Cabinet had decided to support every necessary step to carry through Confederation, and Colonial Secretary Cardwell had promised to intervene in the Maritimes. But more than time or patient diplomacy was needed to cope with such formidable opponents of Confederation as the unpredictable Albert Smith and his government of New Brunswick or Joseph Howe, who was making large audiences laugh with derision at the very word.

The five Canadian Ministers reporting on their mission to London were able to reassure the Cabinet on the likelihood of the eventual passage of Confederation, but on military matters they brought small comfort: the Imperial Government had renewed its pledge of military assistance to Canada in general terms, but any plan of building up an effective militia and defence of Canada had been postponed. Looking anxiously to the United States, the Cabinet had to consider the Fenians. "I am watching them very closely. The movement must not be despised either in America or in Ireland," MacDonald wrote to Monck. But there was bigger work to do than to watch.

Sir Etienne Taché died on July 30, 1865. As Prime Minister and head of the Coalition Cabinet, he had been effective and unobtrusive. The Ministers had learned to rely on his spontaneous sense of diplomacy; and his lack of personal desire for power had become a centre of trust and balance in a Cabinet which had precious little of these qualities to spare.

On August 3, the day after Taché's funeral, Brown laid down his own exacting terms about continuing in the Coalition. The main condition was that John A. MacDonald could not succeed Taché as Prime Minister. Earlier that day Monck had already asked MacDonald to become Prime Minister. A crisis opened. While different alternatives were tried, other sensitive balances were upset. Eventually the problem of selecting a new Prime Minister seemed to be solved by introducing Sir Narcisse Belleau, an elderly *Bleu*, to replace Taché. Admittedly, Belleau was a figurehead; he was venerable like Taché, but too neutral and nominal. Behind this screen John A. MacDonald was straining for more power, and Brown sensed it. Brown's old and deep dislike for MacDonald, which he had tried to suppress, returned with renewed intensity.

In fact, bad feeling had been growing over the past several months. Earlier in March, Brown had opened a rift with his colleagues by threatening to resign twice within six hours. This difficult behaviour was partly tactics, and the tactics were working; but Brown overdid them.

Facing this badly divided Cabinet (which could hardly claim the name of a Coalition now) was the work to be done in the Maritimes. So D'Arcy McGee again turned his attention eastward to bolster the cause of Confederation there. The visiting delegation of Canadians which McGee led to the Maritimes in August of 1864 had been so successful that it was decided to invite the Maritimers for a return visit to Canada in September 1865. Some 240 invitations were sent out, and McGee took charge once more. But he found it difficult to stir up enough enthusiasm and to raise enough money to match the hospitality which the Canadians had received the year before. When Dorion and Holton ridiculed McGee's plan in the Montreal *Herald* and Dougall's *Witness*, McGee sent a letter to Galt, followed by two telegrams, urgently asking for financial support. McGee raised $1800 through eighteen friends and finally on September 23 Galt subscribed $5000, which was matched by a similar contribution from Nova Scotia. In the end, however, only fifty-four delegates came, twenty-three from Nova Scotia, twenty-eight from New Brunswick and three from Prince Edward Island.

They were well received at the Western Fair in London of Upper Canada, but in Montreal, McGee had trouble holding his committee together; their welcome, despite McGee's enthusiasm, lacked warmth. By comparison, this return visit was dull and lacked creative spirit. Naturally McGee was disappointed.

For more than half his time now, McGee was away from home and

travelling; and that fall was particularly gruelling. All this official enter-
taining provided too many excuses to drink, and McGee's health suffered.
Towards the end of October he admitted in a letter to his half-brother
John, who was then living at the McGee home in Montreal:

I think I have finally shaken off a derangement of my system which
I have courted a year past.

Signs were more frequent that fatigue was beginning to prey upon the
mind of D'Arcy McGee, and he confessed in another letter:

My health is poor, and I am utterly drained of money.

When McGee was crippled by his bad leg, it was usually accompanied
by a heavy drinking bout. Nor was this a mere coincidence. McGee was
suffering from serious trouble with the circulation of blood in his legs,
a kind of thrombotic condition due to contraction of the arteries, generally called Buerger's disease. Alcohol, as a depressant, could cause the
encircling nerve fibres to relax, permitting the arteries to expand with
a better flow of blood; and an ounce of whisky three times a day is pre-
scribed as a relief from the disease. So when McGee took refuge in drink,
he was easing the pain of his ailment. But McGee could not stop at an
ounce. The tightening pain in his foot and the increase in his drinking
were each connected with a common cause of tension.

Inwardly McGee was very concerned about the way criticism had increased in the months following his speech in Wexford. Some of his
friends, he sensed, felt that he had shown bad judgement; and a hostile
trend, centred around Bernard Devlin, developed among the Irish in
Montreal to question McGee's leadership. To offset this, in November
1865, a dinner was held in McGee's honour. John A. MacDonald was
there and in good form. Unmentioned, but with the Wexford speech obviously in his mind, MacDonald asked the audience:

Now, gentlemen, what do you think of D'Arcy McGee?

The question evoked the cheers MacDonald was seeking, and he
brought in his own verdict:

I really think you will say: Not guilty, but he must not do it again.

Alexander Galt was more explicit in his remarks. He referred directly to
the Fenians as demagogues in the United States who were threatening
to assault Canada, while McGee was left in his lonely and thankless
stand against them.

McGee was reassured by this expression of needed support, and set off on a trip to Newfoundland to continue his efforts to win over the Maritimes to Confederation. This meant that he was absent from the Cabinet meetings in a period of crisis, but McGee's visit to Newfoundland was important in itself.

For a politician, McGee could be very candid, and he gave a good example of that intrepid quality in his address on Thursday, December 7, 1865, at the Town Hall in St. John's, Newfoundland. As Cabinet solidarity continued to degenerate after the death of Taché, the intricate balance between its English- and French-speaking Ministers and the Protestant and Catholic representatives had been greatly upset. So when McGee spoke on "The Whole of British North America," he conceded from the outset that it would be "a country difficult to govern." He then dealt openly with the two main sources of division:

> I have never concealed from myself nor from others the fact that the bilingual line which divides us socially is one of the difficulties. But it is by no means a serious danger, unless it were to be aggravated by a sense of injustice, inflicted either by the local French majority on the English minority or by the English majority on the French minority.
>
> So long as we respect in Canada the rights of minorities, told either by tongue or creed, we are safe. For so long it will be possible for us to be united. But when we cease to respect those rights, we will be in the full tide towards that madness which the ancients considered the gods sent to those whom they wished to destroy.

On the great line of division drawn by religion, he spoke with directness:

> I notice that the men who do less to edify, who do less to justify the superiority of their own religion, are usually more exacting and aggressive. I never knew a sincere Christian who was anxious to thrust down the throats of others his own religious belief.
>
> If there be superiority on one side—as I believe there is—let the professor of that faith show it by his deeds and not by his theories.

It was the most objective of his many speeches on Confederation and he concluded with an ardent plea "to make one third of this vast continent a sublime outline of the future." But Newfoundlanders would not see it that way for generations.

There was also pressing work to be done in the United States. The Reciprocity Treaty, which had governed trade with the United States to Canada's advantage for ten years, had been due to expire at the end of

1864, subject to a notice of one further year. After some delay this notice of termination had been served by the United States. Some of the spirit behind this notice came out in a speech by John Potter, the American Consul in Montreal, when he openly stated that Reciprocity should be brought to an end as a means of driving the British colonies to seek Annexation on their own with the United States.

Strong efforts were made to have the Treaty renewed, or at least replaced by some partial substitute. Brown and Galt were each working on it, but they disagreed on the methods to be followed. Both men were uncomfortably alike in their shortcomings; each was too touchy and too impulsive to work well with the other. Within the Cabinet, Galt was gaining precedence over Brown on many small points, and this irked Brown. When Galt won the upper hand on this larger question of Reciprocity, jealousy deepened between the two men, which flared up in a series of further disputes within the Coalition Cabinet.

In November of 1865, when Galt went on a mission to Washington and started negotiations to replace the expiring Reciprocity Treaty with a plan of reciprocal legislation, Brown complained that he had not been previously consulted. It resulted in a sharp break between the two men. McGee was then in Newfoundland, and perhaps he could have exercised an influence over Brown if he had been there to act as a mediator; but Brown was very fixed in his course. On December 19 George Brown handed in his resignation from the Coalition Cabinet, and after some half-hearted efforts to have him change his mind, it was accepted on December 22 to close out the disappointing year of 1865.

Brown was not impressive in his resignation. He always maintained that he acted on principle; but others saw it as clouded by several lesser motives. His wife and family, his personal wealth and the lure of his powerful newspaper were all urging him to withdraw from the emotional entanglements and imperious demands of politics. Yet Brown would have been big enough to resist the attractions of a quieter life and follow the call of public duty, if that were all there was to it. At the heart of it, and not without reasons to explain it, there was a brooding feeling of enmity for MacDonald and jealousy for Galt.

The issue of Reciprocity was not so firmly marked out that Brown could stand on it as a clear matter of principle. Indeed, as it turned out, the differences of tactics followed by Galt, as against those proposed by Brown, mattered very little because the Reciprocity Treaty came to an absolute end, and nothing replaced it. With the Coalition Cabinet seriously shaken, the cause of Confederation at its low point in the Maritimes and trade relations between Canada and the United States disrupted, the outlook for 1866 was dismal.

The support which the Fenians were getting in the United States worried McGee. The New York *Herald* and several newspapers in Chicago and the Midwest were quick to see that Fenian designs upon Canada coincided with their own ambitions for American continental expansion. And the Fenians, exploited by these publicists, were equally alert in using this publicity for their own purposes. McGee was their target. And they would not let the Americans forget those parts of his speech in Wexford in which he had exaggerated the conditions of the Irish to the detriment of the United States.

Almost a year after his visit to Wexford, McGee sent an open letter on March 3, 1866, to the editors of the Irish press on "The Irish Position in British and in Republican North America." A few weeks later it was published as a booklet, supported by his valuable notes on the history of the Irish settlements in the Maritimes and Canada. This time he made sure that his views were stated more fully than in the unbalanced excerpts which most newspapers had published from his Wexford speech. His controversial sense was more acute as he formulated his charges: while the Fenians manufactured "imaginary republics for other lands from Moffatt's pillbox" (referring to O'Mahony's headquarters originally built by the rich pill manufacturer Moffatt), those same Fenians would heartlessly avoid the dismal lanes in the fourth and sixth wards of New York, which they "passed daily on their walks," where, without help, their countrymen were "perishing by the hundreds, body and soul":

> There in those damp hideous places, crowded sometimes with as many as six hundred under one roof, is an Ireland enslaved. There is the glorious, redeeming work to be done for her in America.

There was a widespread ignorance in the United States about conditions in Canada. As McGee pointed out, many Fenians did not realize, as plans were made for them "to dash against this peaceful Province, which has done them no harm," that they were being used as pawns of the American Know-Nothings who would rejoice to see another "war kill off the Irish." McGee maintained that the Fenians had no foothold in Canada, except in Toronto:

> In Toronto one extreme is made auxiliary to the other. Orangeism has been made the pretext of Fenianism. And Fenianism is doing its best to justify and magnify Orangeism.

He closed his open letter with this message as the Minister of Immigration:

> I do not circulate these views in order to stimulate emigration from Ireland. But if among those who must emigrate somewhere, there are some thousands left, who are neither dreamers nor dupes, and joyfully obey good laws, then let them try Canada.
>
> Soon, with the blessing of God, British America will be one country, with one system of administration and one wide field of enterprise and settlement.
>
> Four hundred thousand of your countrymen—nearly two millions of your co-religionists out of our total of four millions—are here to guarantee you a fair field and no disfavour. Come and join with us in building up for our common descendants a free, an unaggressive and a prosperous nation of the north.

It would be a mistake to consider that these Fenian plans of invasion were as wild or impossible as they may now appear to be from our remote view, which is so detached from the American temper of those times.

Almost one third of the population of British North America was of Irish descent in 1865. In New Brunswick more than one third was Irish. This proportion was not as high in Nova Scotia, but it was substantial. In Prince Edward Island some counts estimated the Irish as making up almost half of the population. And in Newfoundland, where the oldest of the Irish settlements could be traced back to 1660 at Ferryland, a good half were Irish. In the three cities of Canada—Montreal, Toronto and Quebec—the Irish were not merely numerous but very conscious of their numbers and organizations. And it must not be overlooked that many Irish were settled along the border of the United States.

All this was fact. But it also led to a grave miscalculation by many Americans. It was imagined, because of their heritage and their sentiments, that the Irish and the French in Canada would be ready to overthrow British rule and cast in their lot with an invading force of a revolutionary colour. But as they had developed in the New World, the British institutions were largely free of the old class system and its repressions. Nor did the French, who were deeply rooted in the land and not strong in the cities, in any way constitute a proletariat. In Canada the Irish also had a more rural character than in the United States, where they were essentially urban. In the Northern American states the underground force of the Annexationist movement was now coupled with the anti-British feeling which was open and widespread after the Civil War; and Americans tended to project their own feelings into Canada and mistake the reflections of their own emotions for Canadian realities.

Americans in the Northern states were indignant that Canada had failed to curb a handful of Southern conspirators in the St. Albans raid, and their anger was sustained by the exasperating outcome of their trials in Canada. In a similar way, Canadians and Maritimers were incensed that the American Government could be so complacent in tolerating the inflammatory mass meetings of Fenians, while influential American newspapers quietly assisted the Fenian agitators and their threats of armed invasions. As long as this hostility lasted and appeared to grow, it prompted Gladstone and his group in England to calculate whether the cost of maintaining British colonies in America was not becoming too high a price to pay for what it brought in return. Within Canada, too, particularly in certain closed financial circles, Confederation had been questioned as worth nothing more than the value of the new territory extending to the Atlantic to be obtained as against the excessively high cost of building the Intercolonial Railway. And within the Maritime Provinces, particularly in their strongest sectional cliques, Confederation had been summarily assessed as entailing the loss of their own identities. These closed and influential circles remained curiously untouched by every appeal for Confederation made within Canada and the Maritimes, but they were effectively moved when outside influences from both Great Britain and the United States were recognized as threats to their separate existences. Indeed, these outside influences combined in a strange way towards the making of Confederation; and of all these the most unpredictable was that of the Fenians.

To appreciate how the Fenians affected the relations between the Maritimes and Canada, each area should be considered in its turn. And it so happened that the first move made by the Fenians was against New Brunswick.

Of all the members of Albert Smith's Cabinet in New Brunswick, the Minister most outspoken in opposing Confederation was Timothy Anglin; and he was able to widen his influence as the editor of the Saint John *Morning Freeman*. Moreover, Bishop John Sweeny of Saint John had also spoken publicly against Confederation, so most Irish Catholics of New Brunswick were inclined to distrust it. To offset this, John A. MacDonald wrote to Bishop Edward Horan of Kingston for assistance. Bishop Horan replied on September 13, 1865, and offered to go to Saint John and do his best to persuade Bishop Sweeny to change his attitude. In time this had some effect; and an indication of a further change occurred in November when Anglin resigned from the New Brunswick Cabinet.

The most influential person in this field, however, and the closest to D'Arcy McGee, was Archbishop Thomas Louis Connolly of Halifax. His early life gave no indication of his later role. Born in 1814 in Cork, Ireland, he entered the Franciscan Order and studied in Italy, where his contemplative years among the laurels and the timeless olive trees of Frascati were far removed from the turmoil of practical life. After his ordination in Lyon, France, he came to Halifax as a missionary in 1842. Ten years later he was Bishop of Saint John, New Brunswick, and then in 1859 he became Archbishop of Halifax.

His were the natural qualities of a leader, with warm sympathies and open, independent views. His work among the poor and his interests in education led him into public affairs. With tact and common sense, he was able to create a new feeling of friendliness between the Protestants and the Catholics in Halifax, which was unusual for those sectarian days. The Archbishop was one of that fervent, patriotic class of prelates, impetuous and persevering, who extended his directions openly into the political field. Here the quality which served him best was his capacity to make lasting friendships, as he did with the Duke of Newcastle as Colonial Secretary, John A. MacDonald and D'Arcy McGee.

On December 18, 1865, Archbishop Connolly wrote an important letter to Lieutenant Governor Gordon of New Brunswick on British North America and the Fenians, which was made public. It was not simply an expression of loyalty on behalf of the Catholics. What made it unusual was his statement based on his experience of a quarter of a century, that Irish Catholics were better off and better represented in British North America than in the United States:

> Our people have nothing to expect from change of any kind but increased taxation, diminished incomes, a decided fall in the social scale, the scathing contempt of their new rulers, as was ever the case in New England, and with these, perhaps the horrors of a devastating war.
>
> The great Government of the United States has nothing more tempting to offer.
>
> And what have we to expect from the so-called Fenians? That pitiable knot of knaves and fools, unable to degrade themselves, are doing all in their power to add another Ballingarry to the history of

Ireland, and to make the condition of our poor country more deplorable than before.

He described his recent visit to the United States, where he met "many of these poor deluded people who talked flippantly of taking all British North America in the course of this winter and holding it as if they already had the title deeds in their pockets":

Two millions of Protestants and one million eight hundred thousand Catholics, who have mothers, wives and daughters, happy homes and free altars and a Government of their own choice, will meet them as they would the freebooter and the assassin.

These were remarkable declarations coming from an Archbishop, and indicated a sense of crisis in the political situation. His letter carried an air of patriotism for a new land, independent of the American Republic and maturing on its own with British ties. Such a spirit was bound to be considered as exaggerated and would be disputed, because whatever the differences were, Catholics were not that much better off in British America and that much worse off in republican America as Archbishop Connolly, like McGee, made them out to be. But the important point was that both the Archbishop and McGee felt strongly that they were better off and were publicly asserting it.

It seemed that Archbishop Connolly's letter was no sooner published than several bank managers in Saint John, New Brunswick, received a strange warning which, reminiscent of the St. Albans raid, hinted that the Fenians were about to rob their banks along the waterfront. Actually there was no Fenian Circle in Saint John. But a state of nervousness spread as the HMS *Pylades* arrived overnight to guard the Saint John Harbour, and a few extremists promoted a demonstration against the Irish and the Catholics.

By this time a turn in public opinion was underway, and it seems that by March 1866 the tide was no longer flowing in New Brunswick away from Confederation. The determination of the United States to end Reciprocity was hardening into an economic partition of the continent between republican and British America. And Great Britain's refusal to take New Brunswick's earlier electoral rejection of Confederation as final combined with it to turn New Brunswick back into the path which Tilley had first projected.

With the surprising approval of the Smith Cabinet, the Speech from the Throne at Fredericton on March 8, 1866, contained this statement:

I am further directed to express to you the strong and deliberate opinion of Her Majesty's Government that it is an object much to be desired that all British North American colonies should agree to unite in one Government.

There were cheers from the gallery when this was read. But in the debate which followed, when it was argued that military preparations were too weak to resist any serious Fenian attack, anxiety deepened. The great change came in April. The Smith Government resigned, a Confederate Government took over, and a new general election became imminent in New Brunswick. In Nova Scotia, Tupper gained strength and put a resolution through the House favourable to Confederation. All these remarkable shifts in public opinion occurred in the nervous conditions produced by the Fenian scare.

This Fenian scare is badly misread by those who would read its history backwards. When any scare is over and its real insignificance is known, all its motives and atmosphere have vanished, because the frightful force of any scare, however unreasonable, resides in the unknown. What was most unknown and causing most of the fear about the threats from the Fenians was the uncertainty as to what the American Government might do when the Fenians attacked. What, for example, did the New York *Herald* mean by these words written in March?

It will only be necessary to utter a word of encouragement to the thousands of Fenians who are eagerly awaiting an invitation to invade Canada, for our government to settle the question of a Canadian monarchy with an English Guelph upon the throne, promptly and forever.

The decision for the Fenian raids was made against the wishes of John O'Mahony, for he had privately written:

The Fenian circles of the Canadas are not organized for the purpose of making a revolution in those provinces.

Here he had the strong backing of James Stephens who wanted all the money he could get from America to arm the Fenian rising in Ireland. But talk of invasion persisted and kept reaching him in Paris. So Stephens decided to come to America, and ordered that no such plans should be made until he had arrived and discussed them.

It was Bernard Doran Killian, the former assistant editor to McGee in the days of his *American Celt*, who promoted the raid into New Brunswick. He had sounded out Secretary of State Seward and President Johnson on the plan, and reported favourably on these meetings to O'Mahony. Killian argued that O'Mahony had to do something before the dissident Fenian wing moved into action under Roberts and Sweeny. O'Mahony was thus pushed into military action in America by the impatience of his followers, who otherwise were tempted to leave him. So he adopted Killian's project to capture the island of Campobello, a British possession in the mouth of the St. Croix River which had been in dispute on the boundary between New Brunswick and Maine. Killian's idea was to occupy it, reopen the American claim upon it and foment an international dispute, using it at the same time as a base for preying upon British shipping.

Early in April of 1866 about four hundred unarmed Fenians in civilian dress gathered in the town of Eastport, another four hundred in Calais nearby and others scattered through the northeast corner of Maine. Killian was in command. The *Ocean Spray*, a ship chartered by the Fenians, left New York Harbour loaded with arms and ammunition bound for arrival at Eastport on April 17. But within three days of the decision taken so secretly by O'Mahony and Killian on March 17, "Red Jim" McDermott had sold the information to Edward Archibald, the British Consul in New York.

On April 10 three British warships, with steam up and gun ports open, moved quietly into the mouth of the St. Croix River, two others rode at anchor nearby, and a third left for the scene from as far away as Malta.

In Maine, Killian stated in a speech at Calais that his purpose was to obstruct the Confederation of British North America. This was widely reported. Then, as a quick diversion, on Saturday April 14, five Fenians made a sudden crossing to Indian Island, pointed their revolvers at the customs officer and made off with the British flag. That night as rumours of war spread, people gathered in their night-clothes and watched the gun drill on the HMS *Cordelia*. But no action followed.

The American Secretaries Seward and Stanton were very chary about interfering with the Fenians. But the American gunboat *Winooski* steamed up the coast, followed by another.

There was a tense silence for five days. Not a move was made. But on Thursday, General George G. Meade, the victor of Gettysburg, arrived at Eastport in Maine, with a battalion of three hundred troops under order to prevent any breach of the Neutrality Act. Then General Meade acted. And there was no resistance whatsoever when the American forces boarded the *Ocean Spray* and removed all the arms of the

Fenians. The Fenians were dispersed, and that was the end of Killian's plan to capture Campobello.

The Fenians had wasted $40,000 in the fiasco. O'Mahony was discredited; physically worn out, he became very dispirited. The Roberts-Sweeny faction ridiculed the venture as the "Eastport Fizzle." And so it was in a military sense. But its commercial and political consequences in the Maritimes were far reaching.

Business along the border had been at a standstill for two months. Michael Murphy, O'Mahony's Centre for Toronto, and six others were arrested on their way to Eastport at Cornwall. The quick election called in New Brunswick was barely a month away, and the speeches about the need for union and common action with Canada acquired an urgent meaning.

When the Fenian issue was injected, the political campaign took on a racial and religious tone. Some of Tilley's arch-supporters charged that those who opposed Tilley wanted Annexation to the United States and dismemberment of the British Empire; and the accused were "the whole Fenian fraternity and nearly all Irish and French Roman Catholics." Up in the Miramichi region, when the Catholic Bishop of Chatham, James Rogers, was confronted with this accusation, he decided to reply by making an open declaration that it was the duty of the people of New Brunswick to support Confederation. But Anglin continued to fight Confederation in his Saint John *Morning Freeman,* so Bishop Rogers made a further statement which recognized Anglin's personal worth but clearly disapproved of his policy. The influence of Archbishop Connolly was beginning to prevail, for about the same time, Bishop Colin MacKinnon of Antigonish, Nova Scotia, wrote favourably to Tupper and stated in a pastoral letter:

> Current events and all reliable sources of information within our reach, point to one conclusion, that British aid and protection in the hour of danger and emergency can be secured on one condition only. And that condition is the Union of the North American British Provinces.

In Canada the Coalition Cabinet had learnt its lesson when it stood aloof in 1865 and watched Tilley go down to defeat in New Brunswick on the issue of Confederation. This time when Tilley appealed for help in April 1866, John A. MacDonald arranged through Alexander Galt to send $50,000 to Portland, where it was privately handed over to Tilley's emissary, who returned by boat to Saint John with "the needful." The very first results of the New Brunswick election in the last week of May showed the effects. When all the votes were counted, it was clear that those in favour of Confederation had won thirty-three of the forty-one seats. New Brunswick, the Province indispensable to Confederation, was now ready, or at least resigned, to enter it.

It may well be doubted if this would ever have been the result without the Fenian scare. Timothy Anglin had ruefully summed up this external influence when he recalled Killian's speech to the Fenians in Calais against Confederation:

If Mr. Killian were in the pay of the Canadians and Mr. D'Arcy McGee himself wrote his speech for him, he could not have said anything better suited to the purposes of the Canadian party.

General Thomas Sweeny went right ahead with his own plans for a Fenian invasion of Canada. In fact, his whole plan of operations had been established in March of 1866 and "secretly circulated." It was elaborate and bold, but it was not the work of an amateur. As the former commanding officer of the 16th United States Infantry, he knew how to wage a campaign. Yet it was weak because its secrecy was not guarded. Most of it was sold to both the American and British governments.

Columns moving from Chicago and Milwaukee were to converge with others north of Lake Erie which would compel a concentration of forces about the meridian of Toronto and uncover Montreal. Fenian auxiliaries in Canada were then to destroy St. Ann's bridge where the Ottawa joins the St. Lawrence on the Grand Trunk railroad. While diversions from several points distracted and disguised the main point of attack along the line of the St. Lawrence, troops would be massed at Malone in New York and St. Albans in Vermont and strike northward. Such was Sweeny's plan; and John A. MacDonald and D'Arcy McGee knew of it.

In response to a Canadian order of March 7 calling for ten thousand volunteers for active service, more than fourteen thousand Canadians responded. And one who notably responded was Bernard Devlin, the president of Montreal's St. Patrick's Society. Devlin received the rank of lieutenant colonel in command of the 1st Prince of Wales Rifles and was assigned to guard the border from Huntingdon to Hemmingford. But by the end of the month a sign of slackness appeared, as the force on active service in Canada was reduced from fourteen thousand to ten thousand. When word came in April of O'Mahony's miserable failure at Campobello, it was foolishly assumed that Sweeny would show a similar military incapacity. John A. MacDonald as Minister of Militia began to act with a false sense of security. Though McGee continued to warn him of the dangers, other advisers, for some inexplicable reasons, lulled MacDonald almost to sleep.

Gilbert McMicken, head of the Canadian Secret Service, with full reports from spies and informers before him, wrote MacDonald on May 17:

> I cannot conceive it within the bounds of a reasonable probability that Sweeny will attempt any demonstration upon Canada now.

Two days later the British Consul Hemans at Buffalo, which by now was the chief base of operations for the Fenians, confirmed McMicken's opinion:

> I quite agree with you that Fenianism may be considered as virtually dead.

No Minister of Militia can afford to be a dawdler. As a politician John A. MacDonald had the luck and the knack of turning procrastination to good account. But if there was any need to show that he was not in his right position as Minister of Militia, it was revealed by a letter he wrote on May 19:

> Many thanks for your amusing letter as to the proceedings of the bold Fenians.
> I think that the row between Stephens and Sweeny puts an end to the whole affair. Still it may be the policy of both sections of that renowned body to keep up a spirited irritation and uncertainty along our frontier, and therefore they must be watched.

But the man whom Sweeny had placed in command of the Fenians at Buffalo was a soldier to be watched without amusement.

Colonel John O'Neill, at thirty-two, was a veteran who had seen eight years of active warfare. Well built, not quite six feet tall, with good carriage and military bearing, O'Neill was a Monaghan man, with fair short hair, a light moustache, an arched nose and a broad forehead. In his voice there was a ring of competence, which was borne out by his record in the Civil War as one of General Sherman's best military leaders. Brave and skilful, he possessed something more, which marked him as a professional. He was steady under fire. His talents, achievements and fine physique contributed, however, to his pride, which was his chief weakness. This did not show in his military life, which has more than its share of vain men. But this defect in O'Neill came out later as a leader of the Fenians as a racial and political movement. He was also open to flattery, and right after the Civil War, in Nashville, Tennessee, he had formed what he thought was a friendship with a man with a pointed moustache and flashing black eyes who pleased him with his praise. This artful person, who was never far from O'Neill, was the English spy Thomas Beach, alias Major Henri Le Caron.

In Upper Canada, General Napier was in command of the British forces under Sir John Michel. But by the end of May 1866, so lax was the attitude that the Niagara border, although it had attracted invading forces in 1812 and 1814 and had served as a classic battleground in 1837 and 1838, was now left almost undefended.

Towards midnight of Thursday, May 31, strangers in Buffalo were gathering in groups and moving with a show of nonchalance towards Black Rock about two miles northward on the Niagara River. Waggons were seen moving in the same direction. In the river two strong tugs and some canal boats were drifting quietly with the current to the same spot. The rallying point was Pratt's Iron Furnace Dock, where the river was barely three quarters of a mile wide. Muffled military commands could be heard as the men marched on to the waiting barges, which were soon moving across the river towed by the tugs. They made up one brigade of eight hundred Fenians under Colonel John O'Neill. Most of them were from Buffalo; others came from Ohio, Tennessee, Indiana and Kentucky.

Before dawn, at 3:30 A.M. Friday, June 1, they reached the Canadian shore at the Lower Ferry Dock about a mile below the village and old Fort Erie. The first invader to land was Owen Starr, a colour-bearer from Kentucky, who jumped ashore and unfurled the green Fenian flag of the Harp and the Sunburst.

O'Neill immediately posted guards, threw out pickets and without resistance captured Fort Erie. In the village the American Consul promptly put out the American flag, and O'Neill stated he would do no personal harm to private citizens but wanted food and horses; which he obtained.

Telegraph wires were cut, railway tracks torn up, and Sauerwine bridge was burnt which connected Fort Erie with Ridgeway, seven miles to the west. O'Neill then marched the main body of his men down the Niagara River road to Frenchman's Creek, and encamped in an orchard in Newbiggin's farm about a half mile north of the Lower Ferry where they had first landed. There they dug a line of trenches that afternoon. When their work was done, they rested, and they could hear through the quiet evening air, a good day's march away, "The Thunder of the Waters," which the Iroquois called "Niagara."

Mounted scouts were sent out about ten miles northward to reconnoitre around Chippawa, and others were dispatched in all directions, distributing this proclamation signed by General Sweeny:

We come among you as the foes of British rule in Ireland.

We have taken up the sword to deliver Ireland from the tyrant. Here the enemy is most vulnerable.

We do not propose to divest you of a solitary right you now enjoy. We are here as the friends of liberty against despotism, of democracy against aristocracy.

To Irishmen throughout the Province we appeal in the name of seven centuries of British iniquity and Irish misery.

We offer the honest grasp of friendship. Take it, Irishmen, Frenchmen, Americans. Take it and trust it.

We wish to meet with friends. We are prepared to meet with enemies.

We shall endeavour to merit the confidence of the former. The latter can expect from us but the leniency of a determined though generous foe, and the restraints and relations imposed by civilized warfare.

Late that Friday evening the Fenian scouts returned with reports that the nearest British or Canadian troops were still almost twenty miles away; one column had formed under Colonel Peacocke at St. Catharines to protect the northern end and the main locks of the Welland Canal, and was now marching towards Chippawa; another column was forming at Port Colborne at the southern end of the Welland Canal.

O'Neill was expecting his own reinforcements, but for a reason which he did not know then, none came, except a few Fenians who crossed in rowboats. When he heard that there were two divided columns marching in upon him, he decided to make a quick dash against one of the columns before the two had the time to join and overwhelm him. So at ten o'clock that same evening he quietly roused his men and marched through the night. So quietly was it done that the Newbiggin family did not know they had gone until the next morning. They moved forward three miles to the south bank of the sluggish Black River where it joined the Niagara River. It was a strategic site, an angle of high, dry land protected by an unfordable river with a low, marshy northern bank. There they bivouacked under the stars and awaited further reports.

About three o'clock in the morning, before Saturday dawned, O'Neill learned that Lieutenant Colonel Booker had placed his forces on railway cars at Port Colborne, with evident intentions of moving soon towards

Fort Erie through Ridgeway. O'Neill calculated that Booker must have heard by then that Sauerwine railway bridge between Ridgeway and Fort Erie had been destroyed, so that Booker would likely disembark at Ridgeway and make a forced march northeast along the Ridge road to join Colonel Peacocke's column moving southeast from St. Catharines towards Chippawa. O'Neill also estimated that Peacocke's force was stronger than Booker's. It was an accurate appreciation.

By daybreak Saturday, June 2, after a brief sleep, O'Neill was pushing his Fenians westward through an old bush trail until he struck the Ridge road, which he then followed southwest towards Ridgeway. It was a cloudless, still morning. There were wild flowers and fir, alder, peach, pear and plum trees on all sides. But there was not a breath of air stirring; it promised to be an oppressively hot day.

About 6:30 A.M. the Fenian mounted advance guard were a couple of miles from Ridgeway station when they heard a train whistle and a bugle call. Booker's troops were arriving. A scout raced back with the message; and O'Neill closed his column and prepared for battle.

He selected Lime Ridge as his site, about three miles north of Ridgeway station. It was an admirable choice. The Ridge was about thirty-five feet higher than the surrounding country, and a half-mile wide, with patches of bush and clumps of trees alternating with open fields. So the Fenians could command extensive views on all sides from hidden positions. Earth and fence rails were quickly thrown up into breastworks and barricades. Then outposts and sharpshooters were dispersed well in the front and along the flanks. There, cool as steel, O'Neill waited for Booker to arrive.

In the meantime some British regular forces and Canadian volunteers had been massing and advancing under a loose command.

As O'Neill had heard, Colonel Peacocke had left St. Catharines with his forces in the north on Friday noon, June 1, and was heading for the quiet village of Chippawa. When he arrived there, Peacocke was told that O'Neill was entrenched ten miles to the south at Frenchman's Creek.

At 1:30 A.M. Saturday, Booker received his orders at Port Colborne from Peacocke then at Chippawa. They were simple and were based on the assumption that O'Neill had cautiously dug in to fight it out at Frenchman's Creek, where he could keep close to his expected reinforcements from Buffalo. Booker was told to entrain his troops without delay; leave at 5:00 A.M. Saturday by train for Ridgeway station, and then march northeastward along the Ridge road to meet Peacocke at Stevensville, about seven miles southwest of Chippawa. Peacocke himself undertook to leave Chippawa at 6:00 A.M. and to reach Stevensville with his stronger forces by 10 A.M. Saturday.

But Lieutenant Colonel Dennis, who ranked under Booker at Port Colborne, prevailed upon Booker to propose a change in Peacocke's plans and telegraph it back to Peacocke. Booker and Dennis believed, wrongly as it turned out, that they had better information on the position and condition of the enemy than Peacocke. They were relying on a flimsy report that the Fenians were only 450 strong, drinking freely and still encamped at Frenchman's Creek. (By this time Peacocke had just heard that O'Neill was moving on towards Black River.) Nor did Booker and Dennis even know that Sauerwine railway bridge leading into Fort Erie had been destroyed.

The alteration they proposed was that Booker should transport his troops directly by railway to Fort Erie (which was impossible); and Dennis would immediately muster his men on board the armed tug *William Robb* and go by Lake Erie to Fort Erie (which the Fenians held); from there Booker and Dennis would proceed north to attack O'Neill south of Frenchman's Creek (where O'Neill no longer was); while Peacocke would attack from the north. And on the assumption that their new plan would be adopted, Dennis left on the *William Robb*, without awaiting Peacocke's reply. Peacocke did reply by a curt telegram, ordering them to follow his original plan. But by that time Booker was alone and Dennis had sailed away in the dark.

So at seven o'clock Saturday morning, Booker found himself at Ridgeway station facing an exposed march along the Ridge road to meet Peacocke at Stevensville within three hours. He had expected food, stores, horses and waggons to be there awaiting him. But none were there. Worse still, in that sweltering heat some of his troops were still wearing their padded winter uniforms. His strength was 840 men, consisting of the Queen's Own Rifles, the 13th Battalion and the York and Caledonia Rifle Companies.

Farmers nearby told Booker that some Fenians were hiding just ahead, but Booker was inclined to disbelieve them and to rely on his official reports that O'Neill was entrenched at Frenchman's Creek. So ahead they went, hungry and somewhat jaded, along the dusty Ridge road under a brassy heat.

The Queen's Own skirmishers had crossed the Garrison road and were fanned out in front, approaching the Concession road. Suddenly they were met by rifle fire flashing from an orchard on their right. They returned the fire, but they could not see the sharpshooters. So they deployed and sought cover wherever they could. From the smoke curling up from the trees, an estimate was made of their positions. Booker was under the impression that about four hundred Fenians opposed him, and not, as there were, some seven hundred. So the Queen's Own charged forward.

"The line was well formed and their advance was brave," O'Neill wrote later. And for over an hour there was some fierce fighting through a wheat-field. The outposts of the Fenians were repulsed step by step until they withdrew behind their main breastworks among the thickets on Lime Ridge, three miles south of Stevensville.

It was now 9:30 A.M.; and two telegrams were handed to Booker. Both were from Peacocke. The first message said that Peacocke had left Chippawa two hours late. The second ironically warned Booker to "be cautious in feeling his way, for fear obstacles should prevent a junction." Booker was discouraged, as he could not expect help that morning from Peacocke. Yet unknown to Booker, a similar feeling was spreading among the Fenians, who calculated that they did not have ammunition enough to hold out much longer before retreating. Then the battle took a quick, surprising turn.

Suddenly some of the Queen's Own advance guard saw a Fenian in a green uniform racing a sorrel horse behind the trees along the road. Then a glimpse was caught of another mounted man. Instantly a cry came down the road: "Cavalry! Look out for cavalry!" And Booker saw some of his men doubling back down the hill on his right. Booker was inexperienced and took the alarm for a fact. Had he paused to reflect on his own information, there was nothing to show that the Fenians had any cavalry available for a charge. Impulsively he gave the fatal order. The bugle was sounded to retire and prepare for cavalry. Squares were formed on the road, and perfect targets were offered to the Fenians.

By the time Booker realized his error, it was too late. Some of his troops on the flanks mistook the bugle call to retire for a general order to retreat. A few broke ranks and confusion led to panic. Meanwhile the exposed side of the main square on the road was dissolving under steady fire. Booker tried to correct his mistake, and issued new orders. But the situation was beyond recall. The men had heard that most disheartening of sounds, of nervous orders quickly reversed. So he finally ordered a full retreat.

The Fenians pursued them to Ridgeway station. It was a rout, and Booker's depleted ranks reached Port Colborne at three o'clock that stifling Saturday afternoon.

Nearby, at the crossroads in Ridgeway, was Hoffman's Tavern, known as Smuggler's Home. Here the Fenians ran up their flag and brought the wounded in from both sides. Here, too, someone found a keg of old rye whisky.

During this respite Colonel O'Neill was vigilant. He had defeated the southern wing of his foes. But serious difficulties faced him on his next move. His scouts reported that Peacocke had left Chippawa after a late start and for some unknown reason was following a roundabout route to Stevensville. With no cavalry to scour the countryside, Peacocke appeared to be uninformed of what had happened to Booker. But O'Neill also learned that American military forces had intervened at Buffalo and were preventing any further Fenian crossings. So O'Neill was cut off from his own reinforcements and Peacocke was threatening his line of communications. He decided at once to fall back to Fort Erie by marching the seven miles eastward along the Garrison road.

It will be remembered that several hours earlier Lieutenant Colonel Dennis had left Port Colborne for Fort Erie. With him, on the armed tug *William Robb*, were Captain King and 108 men from the Welland Canal Field Battery and the Dunville Naval Brigade. As the *William Robb* approached the Fort, the American man-of-war *Michigan* was seen over the glassy surface of Lake Erie, flying friendly signals.

The American naval officers informed Dennis what they knew of the approximate strength of the Fenians, and also that their reinforcements had been cut off. But Dennis was unaware of the battle at Lime Ridge, and still assumed that Booker and Peacocke were following his amended plan and converging on Fort Erie. Near noon that Saturday Dennis was disturbed when he received a report that a battle had been fought, that Booker was retreating and that the Fenians were on their way back to Fort Erie, moving rapidly. But he did not act on this, and decided to treat it as a rumour until it was confirmed. From then on, his orders lacked consistency.

Two hours later Dennis himself saw the Fenians coming over the hill and descending on Fort Erie in increasing numbers. Dennis' men were better equipped and had more firing power than the Fenians, but were outnumbered. So he ordered them to board the tug, then rapidly reversed this by commanding them to take up whatever defensive positions they could along the wharf. When the Fenians charged with fixed bayonets, Dennis gave the command to retreat, each man for himself. Dennis did much less than distinguish himself. In disguise, he escaped. And at three o'clock Sunday morning he came upon the tardy Colonel

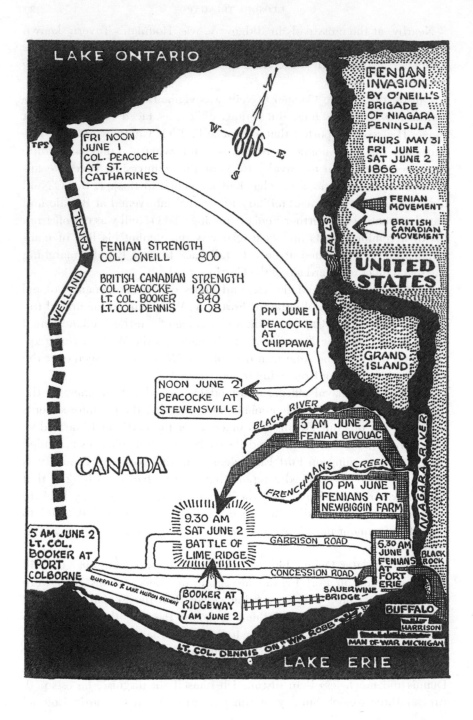

Peacocke and his forces bivouacked for the night at Bowen's farm, a bare three miles north of Fort Erie.

The one man to hold on was Captain Richard King. After Dennis escaped, he remained. Behind a pile of cordwood on the dock, where the tar was blistering in the heat, with one leg shattered by a bullet, King fought it out. Only when he had emptied every chamber in his revolver did he roll back and over the side of the wharf into the river. The current swept him under the next dock. There he caught hold of a truss and hid for several hours, barely holding his head above water. Finally he was rescued; but later his leg had to be amputated below the knee. In that patchwork of blunders on the Niagara Peninsula the one bright spot among the Canadian volunteers was the courage of Captain King.

The Fenian victory was fleeting. Five hundred of them were still encamped at Fort Erie that Saturday night, cut off from food, ammunition and reinforcements. By this time there were twenty thousand men under arms in Canada. So at one o'clock early Sunday morning, June 3, with a soft wind stirring from the southeast, two tugs crossed from Black Rock with their canal boats. The Fenians broke up camp and most of them boarded the boats to return to Buffalo. But halfway across the Niagara River the American man-of-war *Michigan* intervened and ordered the Fenians to surrender.

The order was at first resisted. But a shot across the bow of one of the tugs brought them to a stop. An American armed tug, the *Harrison,* appeared, and the *Michigan* came alongside. O'Neill submitted. At a point opposite Black Rock, the *Michigan* dropped anchor, and some four hundred weary Fenians were taken as American prisoners.

That was the end of the episode. From the start it had slender prospects of success in a military sense, but it drew most of its power from the threat of American political backing. What actually happened was the contrary of what was expected. The American intervention, belated as it was, cut the Fenians down. But as a military engagement, it was a victory for the Fenians, due to O'Neill's superior skill with the weapons of surprise and swift daring.

From something to ridicule, the Fenians once again became a source of vague fears. O'Neill's military success was minor, but it was striking and enough to re-create an air of apprehension about the unknown dimensions and allies of the Fenians as a conspiracy. As in all conspiracies, it had some startling effects. Suspicions were breeding both within and without. And those wrongly suspected of being traitors were quite as likely to become the victims, as were the genuine traitors.

Earlier, D'Arcy McGee had been troubled by a contemporary, unreliable writer, John Rutherford, who had spread a story that in 1858 James Stephens had sought to appoint McGee as a better leader of the Fenians in America than John O'Mahony. Then Rutherford added this insinuation:

> It is stated that McGee hesitated for a while and barely refused to take part in the plot.

Such a weird suspicion returned in a wilder form with the abortive Fenian raid on Campobello. On April 17 British Consul Archibald in New York reported to the Earl of Clarendon in London that John O'Mahony suspected that Killian was secretly in league with McGee.

Fortunately the British Government received much sounder views than that. In his official report Governor General Monck stated that the invasion of the Fenians in early June had at least done one thing: it had demonstrated "the absence of all disaffection amongst any portion of the people of Canada." Disraeli was not satisfied, however, and made this comment:

> If the colonists cannot as a general rule defend themselves against the Fenians, they can do nothing. What is the use of these colonial deadweights which we do not govern?

In fact, the Fenians had unwittingly done something of lasting value in the colonies. They had stirred up a new national fervour in Canada. American and Canadian newspapers concentrated almost completely on the news of the invasions as war, and the excitement became greater than that of the *Trent* crisis. The New York *Tribune*, for example, had a front-page headline on June 2: WAR—REVOLUTION IN CANADA. The Toronto *Leader* described the Niagara invasion as "the covenant of our new nationality"; and the *Globe* wrote:

> The autonomy of British America, its independence of all control save that to which its people willingly submit, is cemented by the blood shed in the battle of June 2.

Almost overnight the people in Upper Canada were abruptly faced with the real dangers of their isolation. Excited charges brought on two military inquiries. Why, the newspapers asked, had Canada been caught off guard, and the military preparations so poor? And why, they asked with more anxiety, had the United States Government delayed for five long days after the Fenians had crossed the Niagara River before it issued a declaration of neutrality? United Empire Loyalists in the Niagara Peninsula shared their fears with the Loyalists in the Eastern Townships and in New Brunswick. Minor freedoms of sectional independence now appeared as luxuries which no colony could afford alone. And from out of the old fragmentary feelings there grew a renewed desire for the strength of unity.

The unexpected had happened. In a refractory manner and as an alien force operating from both extremities outside the country, the conspiracy of the Fenians had strangely strengthened the work of Confederation. And within the country less noticeable perhaps but more salutary, fresh currents of opinion were now flowing, bringing new hope for a Northern pioneer among Federal nations.

In the lumbering town of Ottawa, where eighteen thousand inhabitants were huddled in their shops and shanties, the new Parliament had been built on a scale of magnificence. Below this expensive Gothic revival, the river flowed on as before out of the backwoods and over the "Big Kettle," turbid with sawdust. But above, high on their serene site, the buildings rose superbly, planned to serve far beyond the timber limits of this contentious capital of an inland colony.

When the Members were notified of the opening of Parliament on June 8, 1866, it was their first call to Ottawa. They met in an air of

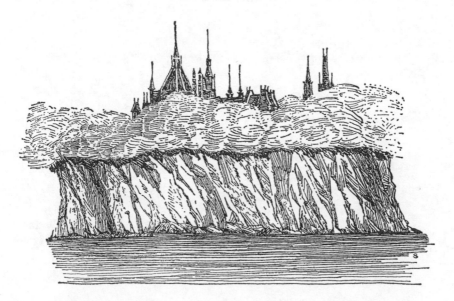

nervous excitement, as everyone sensed that this first Session in Ottawa would be the last Session for the old colony.

George Brown was pleased with the new buildings but was not in a mood to praise them. He criticized their acoustics and called them cavernous. Alexander Mackenzie complained that they were too costly. John A. MacDonald thought that the Tower in the West Lock looked "like a cow bell." A Quebec member found them impressive, but cold. Lord Monck said they were "handsome," and the Assembly halls "infinitely superior to those of Westminster." Anthony Trollope stopped on his travels and commended their "excellence, beauty of outline and nobility of detail." And D'Arcy McGee, seeing the pinnacles of the seven towers through a lifting haze, thought of the opening words of "The Deer's Cry":

> I arise today
> Through a mighty strength,

as a fine, warm rain fell upon Canada's new House of Parliament and the rubble all around.

# 18

## STRENUOUS MINORITIES

The great inspiring principle of national life as well as of
the Christian creed is charity and forbearance with one
another.

It is in that spirit I will seek to play out my political career
on this soil, be it long or short.

*Thomas D'Arcy McGee*

TO HIS FIRST ELECTORS

Throw confusion into the speech they use there so that they
will not be able to understand each other.

GENESIS XI: 7

If a certain point were to be designated as the watershed in the course of the history of Confederation, it would be the month of April 1866. From then on, the currents began to flow towards a union of the colonies. But these currents towards Confederation were not towards a common pooling of opinions or a merging of identities. Any attempt to form the new country in that manner at that time would have dissolved it and let it flow into the melting pot of the United States.

What gave character and the promise of a distinctive culture to this new nation forming on the North American continent were its minorities. If minorities have bothered the faint-hearted as the unending problem of Canada, they were, nonetheless, one of the reasons for its creation, and remain as the test of its worth as a living, plural nation.

Such different ways of life, to be able to survive adversity together, needed a climate of active tolerance. But there was another way out. There was the efficient way of intolerance which could stamp out the identities of minorities. And for those who recognized no duty to respect the values which smaller groups were handing down within themselves, and who saw no meaning in the sacrifices minorities were ready to make in order to do so, their solution could have been the ruthless one of obliteration. This might have been an escape. McGee had seen, as he expressed it, "magnates stifling their thoughts like slaves," and a general preoccupation with riches was enough in prosperous times to hide the emptiness faced elsewhere by the downtrodden. But sooner or later, McGee realized, such illusions about the enforced benefits of uniformity would vanish.

McGee, like anyone, was harnessed to the daily business of earning a living; but, to use his words, "beneath the mute, cold spirit" of making money, each person was aware "in the offing of his soul" that he was pledged to some inner finality of his own, whether it was known as devotion, the need to endure pain or perhaps the summons to sacrifice. It was this spirit which McGee felt gave heart and a lasting life to a minority.

In his views on governments D'Arcy McGee repeatedly made a marked distinction between the form of republican democracy which he saw in the United States, as it developed and was almost shattered by the Civil War, and the form of constitutional monarchy which he experienced in Canada and the Maritimes, as it grew with some hesitancy around the principle of responsible government in North America.

In a republican democracy, he reasoned, where the numerical majority of voters would be in fact the sovereign power, a minority had to cope with the consequences of a potential absolute power vested in people who were merely counted as units. And such a quantity would tend to grow unchecked unless qualities like tradition or justice were venerated deeply enough by the citizens to act as restraints.

So the central question for McGee was: Where did the supremacy reside? Was it in the law or in the will of the people? In a republic the claim was that it resided in both. Yet, with time, one was likely to dominate or subvert the other.

A monarchy could likewise be absolute; and the sovereign could be either a despot or a constitutional ruler. In the latter case, however, sovereignty would be shared by the constitutional checks and customs which resist and balance the monarch's power. In McGee's view, a constitutional monarchy was organically healthy when its powers, opinions and interests were usefully opposed to one another. But in a popular republican democracy this healthy antagonism of forces could be submerged by its uniformity.

McGee derived his views on political theory mainly from Edmund Burke; and with Burke, he expected that a constitutional monarchy would, with vigilance, grow more free in a disciplined sense, while a republican democracy would more easily grow towards freedom in an arbitrary sense. A republican democracy might carry the internal antagonisms it required within the ranks of its opposing political parties; but these differences would usually be economic and not cultural. A majority made up of numbers only would tend to become more homogeneous; and when that happened, a variety of cultural values among minorities would be considered as hindrances to the majority's notion of progress.

The history of minorities was there to support McGee's argument. And in the founding days of the United States, James Madison had given a similar warning:

In all cases where a majority are united by a common interest or passion, the rights of the minority are in danger.

A minority, it was argued, cannot survive without liberty, and liberty is unavailing without the authority to protect it. A minority needs the assurance that it will be protected in doing what it believes to be its duty, against the prevailing influences of the majority and their power to reduce everything to a sameness. But what force was there to stand up against the demagogue when all he needed was a simple majority of votes to gain the power that can corrupt and crush? Dorion shared Mc-Gee's concern when he said: "Experience shows that majorities are always aggressive"; and Cartier, in preferring a constitutional monarchy to a republican democracy, had a similar attitude.

McGee was not a blind believer in the age of progress. "Patriotism is in political life what faith is in religion"; and if faith crumbled, liberty would eventually crumble with it. Civilization, McGee said, really consisted not so much in "the subjection of matter to mind" as in establishing a higher "morality amongst mankind":

> He who says religion has nothing to do with politics if he means party politics, I agree with him; but if he means those maxims of right and wrong, which should govern states as well as persons, I totally disagree with him.

It was McGee's conviction that a government which is reluctant to tolerate differences and to do justice to the peculiar character of its various races would for the same motives interfere in the internal affairs of the religion of the minorities composed by such races. That had been McGee's experience in Ireland, where the emancipation of the Catholics and the movement for Home Rule were two aspects of the same struggle for liberty. It had also been his experience in the United States, as he described it when he first came to Canada; in a republican democracy the Anglo-Saxon race can be unrestrained in its "passion" for "levelling and despotic uniformity"; and in this sense, McGee held to a liberal philosophy:

> I do not mean the false liberality which is zealous for nothing, but the true liberality which desiring to enjoy equal rights, is always ready to extend them to others.

And he showed this from his earliest years in Canada by his respect for the rights of the French Canadians. "We are here two nations equally represented," he stated in his first year in Parliament, and added that it was incorrect to refer to 1759 as the "conquest" of Canada: "As long as French Canadians keep their language they are unconquered."

What D'Arcy McGee held most deeply in his view of Confederation

was the need for a proper balance, for fair practise and for daily resistance to the temptation to despise. To play it false with minorities
would be treason to the founding of the new nation. That, he held, must
be the pact and the burden of the treaty. To try and escape from that
burden would only be the wrong way out.

The timing in 1866 of the whole movement towards Confederation
was intricate and delicate. And John A. MacDonald approached it with
his peculiar calculating ways, which sometimes seemed to be nimble and
at other times desultory or merely dilatory. He insisted on awaiting the
final results of the election and the approval of the Union in New Brunswick, which in the end postponed action until June 30. As for Nova Scotia,
he did not want to draw attention to the differences between the Quebec
Resolutions and the rather evasive terms of the resolution passed by Tupper in the Nova Scotia House in favour of the Union.

But there was yet another reason why June, as a working month,
was practically lost. John A. MacDonald was drinking steadily, and so
was D'Arcy McGee. There were days in the House when MacDonald's
words were so muddled and his knees so wobbly that it was all he could
do to talk or walk. On those days, McGee simply did not appear. But
their nights at the Russell House were uproarious. After one hilarious
evening, when MacDonald had taken to his bed, McGee rambled off
on his own. Later that night, with one shoelace broken, McGee turned
up ready for more revelry at the office of a morning newspaper. He no
sooner had "all the lads in kinks of laughing" than he disappeared. He
was found at dawn, his small figure curled up behind the editor's desk
on a pile of old newspapers, deep in slumber.

All this was so widely known that even their own supporter, the Ottawa
*Citizen,* reluctantly conceded that "at times" they were indulging "a little too freely." There was so much talk that it came up at a Cabinet
meeting. "This sort of thing is a disgrace," someone said. MacDonald,
looking like "an ash tree in its palest hour," faced McGee:

Look here, McGee, this Cabinet can't afford two drunkards, and I'm
not quitting.

Through a large part of June, MacDonald and McGee had reduced
themselves to a state of jovial incapacity, and the chief work to be done
at that Session lay dormant. The powers of Upper Canada and Lower
Canada still had to be separated to make them into distinct Provinces.
This entailed the division of their assets and liabilities, which did not

promise to be too difficult. But it also involved the sensitive and complex question of education and the rights of minorities, which could ensnare the most experienced, and was, of all problems, the most sobering. McGee settled down.

As July opened, time was running short on the schedule which required the Canadian delegates to leave for England by July 21. On July 19 the Maritime delegates sailed. But, with Tupper and Tilley waiting impatiently in London, the Canadian delegates did not even leave Canada for another four months. The surprising story of what happened must be told.

The discussion about the two separate Provincial Legislatures was ruffled when John A. MacDonald made a plain statement that each clearly would not be a "sovereign legislature" but a "subordinate legislature." Still, Cartier did not directly join issue with him on this description. Instead, the debate on the Provincial Constitutions was postponed for two weeks, to allow the Government to fulfil its informal promise to introduce its Education Bill for the Protestant minority in Lower Canada.

The heat in Ottawa that July was almost suffocating, and when the ventilating system in the new House of Parliament failed to work, tempers became touchy. Certainly it was not the cool atmosphere needed to consider the inflammatory matter of schools for minorities.

Then, as always, it was a fiery topic; and an impatient majority could readily be persuaded to view the rights of minorities as a masquerade of pretensions and prejudices; and all the more so when the educational claims of minorities were based on language and religion. The Education Bill for Lower Canada had that special background.

Each interested minority had been quick to note that McGee's amendment to the resolution on education as adopted by the Quebec Conference in 1864, allowed for future legislation granting further "rights and privileges" to "the Protestant or Catholic minority in both Canadas," which would be protected by the guarantee of the Constitution, provided such laws were enacted by the time "the Constitutional Act goes into operation."

One month after the Quebec Conference closed, Galt spoke to his electors in Sherbrooke on November 23, 1864, and promised that the Government would amend the school laws in Lower Canada in time to extend the privileges of the Protestant minority in Lower Canada. Little was said, but the Catholic minority in Upper Canada quietly prepared to make a corresponding move. And James O'Reilly, an Irish Catholic leader in Kingston, warned his leader, John A. MacDonald, in a private letter of February 8, 1865, that any changes in the educational privileges of the Protestants in Lower Canada would cause the Catholics in Upper Canada to claim similar privileges.

On March 7, four days before the Canadian Parliament adopted the Quebec Resolutions without change (including McGee's wording on the educational clause), Galt assured the Protestant members of Lower Canada at a caucus that a special status for the education of Protestants in Lower Canada would be established by law before the Constitutional Act went into operation. What Galt promised was an open secret. In fact, before that on February 22, and later on March 10, Cartier had twice indicated that future legislation would "secure to the Protestant majority in Lower Canada such management and control over their schools as will satisfy them."

At the same time, McGee and Clerk of the *True Witness* each wrote to Bishop Edward Horan of Kingston recommending that the Bishops should not make too open a campaign on the coming school question, but should prepare and await developments. In Toronto, however, Bishop Lynch was restless, and on May 31 he wrote to Bishop Horan saying that Protestants in Lower Canada were privately preparing a School Bill to gain yet more privileges, when as it stood they already had greater privileges than the Catholics in Upper Canada. Catholics, he urged, should attempt to obtain similar advantages. Ten Catholic Bishops then met in Montreal and sent a petition to the Cabinet formally expressing Bishop Lynch's view.

As the Session advanced, George Brown, no longer a member of the Cabinet, adopted a peculiar position. He opposed the Government's financial policy advanced by Galt, and he repaired his broken friendship with Luther Holton and Aimé Dorion to join the Opposition's attack upon it. But he disassociated himself from the Opposition when he supported the Government in its determination to bring about Confederation. Then as July closed and the debate on the rights of minorities in education opened, Brown reverted to his old and passionate position against Catholic Separate Schools.

Hector Langevin, the Solicitor General, introduced the Protestant School Bill for Lower Canada on July 31 which asked for a Protestant Deputy Superintendent of Education to represent that minority and an increased share in taxes and grants for their schools. Being close to Cartier, and a French-Canadian Catholic with strong clerical influence through his brother the Bishop of Rimouski, Langevin was the tactical choice as the man most likely to disarm opposition and obtain a swift passage for the Bill.

But the very next day Robert Bell, the member for Russell, a county in Upper Canada south of the Ottawa River, gave notice that he would introduce a corresponding Bill to obtain equal privileges for the Catholic minority in Upper Canada to those granted to the Protestant minority in Lower Canada. During the following two days, Thursday and Friday, Bell's Bill was debated with great heat. Brown led a strong, sharp attack. Crossing swords with McGee, Brown surprisingly asserted that at the Quebec Conference in 1864 he had fought against all guarantees in educational matters for any minorities. There was no public evidence available to support Brown's statement. The record of 1864, scanty as it was, simply showed that McGee's amendment, which guaranteed existing rights and privileges to Protestant and Catholic minorities in education, had passed with unanimity.

Brown now took the simplest of all positions. Let the majority, he said, be free to act according to its own sense of what was right and just. But the simplicity seemed specious when he added that this was the best way to protect minorities. It permitted McGee to retort with equal simplicity:

> It is not a matter of honest intentions. A majority may be honestly wrong as well as honestly right.

Much was made in the debate of a point that when Scott's Bill for Separate Schools had been passed in 1863, the Catholics had accepted it as a "finality." Here, however, McGee had the reservation he made in the Confederation Debate in 1865 and earlier declarations to rely on:

> I would say this, as I said in 1863, that if any special guarantees were given to the minority in Lower Canada, I should insist, whether in government or out of government, that equal privileges, neither more nor less, be granted to the minority of Upper Canada. And I would like to see the man who could put forward a reasonable objection to the stand upon that question.

Brown was not the man to pass up a challenge, and he quickly cut in: "Do you wish to raise the point now?" McGee did; and so the debate went on.

McGee contrasted the position of the minorities. The Protestant minority in Lower Canada had a normal school, grammar schools and industrial colleges already supported out of the educational funds. The Catholic minority in Upper Canada had none. The Protestant minority in Lower Canada was represented in the Council of Public Instruction by five members, McGee continued, whereas the Catholic minority in Upper Canada in 1861 was represented by only one. Yet the Catholic minority of Upper Canada in 1861 numbered 258 thousand, while the Protestant minority of Lower Canada were 162 thousand; and the Catholic minority received less than one fifth of the amount granted to the Lower Canada minority out of the public funds.

Dorion supported McGee. So did John A. MacDonald. But all the other Ministers from Upper Canada opposed him as party lines were crossed. In numbers and as ratios, the two minorities could be compared. But there was a great difference between the scattered, underrepresented and economically weak minority of Catholics in Upper Canada, and the concentrated, strongly represented and economically powerful minority of Protestants in Lower Canada. No government could afford to ignore the latter, as it could the former.

When the debate spread to the newspapers, the Toronto *Globe* could find no word more apt to describe Catholic Separate Schools than "wicked." Then some *Bleu* journals, like *Le Journal de Quebec* and *Le Courier du Canada,* which had been drowsily supporting Cartier's earlier neutrality, were roused. They now objected to granting any privileges in education to Protestants in Lower Canada which Catholics could not obtain in Upper Canada.

Matters were getting out of hand. And George Brown revealed why; at the end of his short supply of patience, Brown was very frank in a letter to his wife on Monday, August 6:

John A. was drunk on Friday and Saturday, and unable to attend the House. Is it not disgraceful?

This time, by exception, McGee was not drinking with MacDonald. Early the next day, Tuesday, McGee was preparing for the work ahead as he wrote a long letter to his friend James Sadlier:

We are in the last days of the Session here, winding up the last Parliament of Canada under the old Union, with a Coalition Government, and majorities for Ministers of nearly 3 to 1.

It is possible I may have to cross the Atlantic again this fall, as one of the delegation to perfect the new Confederate Constitution, which we expect to go into operation somewhere about May or June

1867. There will of course be a general election, but I believe Montreal is quite safe.

We are to have the School question before us again this week, and I will send you the debate if it is a good one.

But there was no debate to send on. That night two Ministers rose in the House to make startling announcements.

John A. MacDonald, looking pale and wearied and speaking in a low, husky voice, described "the unfortunate spectacle of a majority in Lower Canada in conflict with the majority in Upper Canada on the eve of Confederation."

He then announced that, after consultation, the Government had decided that both School Bills, for Lower Canada as well as Upper Canada, would be dropped, and there would be no further legislation on the school question prior to Confederation:

> The minority in both Upper and Lower Canada will be obliged to throw themselves on the justice and generosity of the majority.

Alexander Galt then made his announcement. Because he had pledged himself to the Protestants of Lower Canada that the Government would pass an educational measure to protect them and because this was not being done, he was resigning as Minister of Finance and as a member of the Coalition Cabinet. The news of Galt's resignation was stunning. Following upon Brown's resignation seven months earlier, many wondered if the Cabinet could survive such another heavy shock. Whatever went on behind closed doors will never be known. But this much is now evident. Galt was disturbed; yet he did not make his move without a sense of tactics, and he designed it as a transitory measure. The Sarnia *Observer* suspected as much, when it wrote:

> It is some sort of Shuffle performance, either double or single.

In any event, Galt admitted privately that he parted on the best of terms with his colleagues, and it would not prevent him from going over to London, and taking part in the final drafting of the British North America Act, and particularly the section on Education.

The last day of that Session was Tuesday, August 14, and it was a bad day. Sandfield MacDonald started it off by renewing an old accusation that John A. MacDonald was baiting his hook with promises of political jobs. John A. MacDonald suddenly flared up and retaliated by resurrecting a buried episode. He recalled the strange appointment of

Judge Sicotte to the Bench, and turning on Sandfield MacDonald, he said flatly:

You bought him.

You withdrew his vote to make a majority of two a majority of one. You gave him office, and degraded justice, and the Bench.

The blunt accusation shocked the House, and after three years it seemed needless to haul it up.

Three days later, on Friday, the Toronto *Globe* published an editorial, headed "Scandalous." It was high time to speak out, the *Globe* declared: the only explanation for John A. MacDonald's inexcusable conduct in attacking a judge of the Superior Court was notorious; when he did it, John A. MacDonald "was not sober."

Really there was no denying it; and the newspapers supporting the Government would have been wiser to say very little, but some of them took it up and contested the charge as unfounded in fact. So on the following Wednesday, August 22, the *Globe* returned with more charges and incidents. Speaking of facts, the *Globe* asserted, John A. MacDonald had actually not been sober for the last ten days of the Session—"with his utterance so thick as to be almost incomprehensible," he had been obliged to hold on to his desk in the House to prevent himself from falling. And, what was more grievous, the *Globe* continued, during the two weeks leading up to the Fenian invasion of Niagara, MacDonald, as the Minister of Militia, was "drunk."

It was a painful scandal. And it grew worse, particularly when the religious newspapers picked it up. George Brown disclaimed any personal animosity in the *Globe's* disclosures, adding that the first editorials had been written without his knowledge, but now that the facts were out, he concurred in all that was said and held that, in the light of public interest, they had to be said. Then within two months came a rapid sequence of events which affected McGee's influence.

As the Session closed and rumours increased of further and stronger Fenian raids, McGee was drinking freely again. So on his way home to Montreal he stopped off for a rest "to take the water cure" at Caledonia Springs, north of Prescott, known for the medicinal qualities of its sulphur springs. It gave him a chance to think things over, and to express his views in some confidential and candid letters to Sir Narcisse Belleau, John A. MacDonald and Alexander Galt, which he summed up in a letter to Galt on August 24:

Considering here the situation most attentively, it occurred to me: 1st, That our militia administration proper does not give satisfaction; 2nd, That it sadly needs a head; 3rd, (not entirely new) That it costs a great deal, and is therefore as much a financial department as any other.

On these, and some other grounds, which you might possibly suspect were flatteries, I took the liberty of urging, from myself alone, that His Excellency ought to ask your services at the head of that Department, to organize and put it in shape. At first, I confined the suggestion to Belleau, but yesterday it occurred to me, I should make it direct to MacDonald. Hoping that you will hear of it formally and see your way to accept; at all events, that you will not think me meddlesome or officious, I remain, my dear Galt,

Yours very truly,<br>Thos. D'Arcy McGee

P.S. I am here emptying the wells, and hope to sally forth in a few days like a giant refreshed with mineral water.

However well meant his advice may have been to John A. MacDonald to leave the portfolio of Militia, McGee's political sense of tact had failed him. MacDonald received McGee's suggestion as a personal affront and became angry. With Brown publicly attacking him for being "drunk on duty" as Minister of Militia, MacDonald was in no mood to take a lesson about his behaviour, least of all from a person with such competence in that pastime. Yet it was just like McGee to have written directly to MacDonald, telling him what he thought. Whether it did MacDonald any good can be doubted. In any event, he never completely forgave McGee for his gratuitous frankness.

Four days later McGee was still at Caledonia Springs when he wrote another revealing letter to James Moylan, the editor of the *Canadian Freeman* in Toronto:

I am here since the close of the Session, drinking water with a strong savour of rotten eggs, which, I am told, however, is the very thing I want, with rest and quiet.

I suppose you know the secret of Brown's fury against John A. Notwithstanding his factious conduct last Session, he still expected to form one of the Delegation to England (which by the by, all rumours to the contrary, has not yet been decided, but upon which I have been invited to serve). Before he left Ottawa he understood unmistakably that he would not be asked to go to London. His ambitious dreams of a local governorship in some part of British

America, or the Premiership of the new Kingdom, goes with that
prospect, and hence his savagery.

This ought to be brought out in some significant manner, and sent
marked to all your exchanges. The last Session of the last Parliament
of Canada was such a scene of reunion and general jollification that
I was nearly *hors de combat*. But I am almost all right again, and
will defy the devil to catch me again, till we have another peaceful revolution.

Hoping to see you about the time of the Provincial Fair, the 24th
*proximo*. . . .

On September 6, in order to offset the attacks of the *Globe,* the citizens of Kingston gave a dinner in honour of John A. MacDonald; and
D'Arcy McGee, aiming to make amends for his suggestion that Galt
should take over as Minister of Militia, spoke in glowing terms about
his leader as the staunch defender of Canada against the Fenians and
the author of most of the Quebec Resolutions:

Of the seventy-two propositions agreed on at Quebec, at least fifty,
either in substance or in form, owe their origin to your honourable
guest, while some of those who are now crying so loudly as to his
inattention to public business never enriched our conference with
an idea, a suggestion or proposition; never contributed to our councils anything better than a few wild and declamatory objections
abandoned almost as soon as they were made.

McGee's eulogy brought a reaction in two quarters. The *Globe* recognized his insinuations as directed against George Brown and immediately widened its attack by including McGee. What, it asked, did McGee
know about how the original Resolutions were prepared at Quebec? How
could McGee remember, when he was so frequently intoxicated himself?

When the newspapers reached Joseph Howe in England, he decided
to make full use of them in his campaign against Confederation. He
showed them to Lord Carnarvon, the Colonial Secretary. It was his duty,
Howe said, to draw attention to the "impropriety and peril" of placing
the defence of the Maritimes in the hands of John A. MacDonald, "whose
habits and gross neglect of important public duties have been thus rendered notorious." Assuming D'Arcy McGee's statement to be true, Howe
went on, if MacDonald had drafted fifty of the Quebec Resolutions, then
"the inveterate habits" of MacDonald explain "the incoherent and de-
fective character of the whole scheme." Carnarvon was disturbed enough
to forward Howe's charges back to Monck and ask for an explanation.

If Monck gave a candid reply, it was obviously commended to oblivion.

All the while McGee's strenuous efforts for the protection of minorities within the Provinces did not dislodge him from his position that the Federal Government needed a strong central power. He put this plainly in his speech on September 20 at the Provincial Fair in London of Upper Canada:

> The minorities east and west have really nothing to fear beyond what has always existed, that is to say, the local irritations produced by ill-disposed individuals.

Nine days later, on a Saturday, McGee received a shock. An Order in Council was passed naming the Canadian delegates to the London Conference for the final discussion with the Imperial Government on the terms proposed for Confederation. Six were named: MacDonald, Cartier, Langevin, Howland, McDougall and Galt. McGee had been excluded.

All elements were represented in the delegation, except the English-speaking Catholics, and James Moylan expressed their disappointment:

> No one was better qualified and had the entire confidence of the Catholic community than the Hon. Thomas D'Arcy McGee.
> Suffice to say that the Catholic Bishops, clergy and Catholic laity were also amazed and unsatisfied.

Since two French Canadians and two Reformers had been appointed to the delegation, McGee insisted on his right to be included. But Lord Monck and John A. MacDonald put McGee off with an explanation that more than a simple quorum of the Cabinet would be needed to remain in Canada in case of an emergency, at least until the end of 1866; then, they promised, either Langevin or McDougall or Howland could return and permit McGee to leave and participate in the discussions and the final drafting of the British North America Bill in London.

Beneath that, there was another and probably the real reason. The fact that Galt, though no longer a member of the Cabinet, had been included in the delegation while McGee as a representative Cabinet Minister had been excluded was linked with McGee's determination to obtain the same rights in education for the minority of Catholics in Upper Canada as Galt was pledged to obtain for the minority of Protestants in Lower Canada. John A. MacDonald was still nursing a personal pique against McGee over the Militia portfolio, and knowing that he needed Galt in England, probably saw an opportunity to get out of the impasse on education, with Galt present while McGee was absent.

Throughout that fall the whole question of the protection of minorities under Confederation was vigorously debated. Some desired and others feared the insertion of a new section in the proposed Act of Confederation which would permit an appeal to the Central Government whenever the educational privileges of a minority in a Province would be endangered. And what appears to have been an authentic report of this proposal was circulated as a test of opinion in Canada. It was argued that this was a necessary means to control the arbitrary power of a majority which otherwise could be vested irrevocably within a Province; and it was also the proper way to avoid that very excess of State rights which had, it was claimed, wrought so much mischief in the American Federal system. In brief, it was the right of appeal for a minority against the decision of a local majority, and should be guaranteed in the Constitution.

This was Galt's argument for the English-speaking Protestants of Lower Canada, who were outnumbered in a ratio of one against three French-speaking Catholics. As to the future of that Protestant minority, Principal William Dawson of McGill University had been downcast ever since Galt had resigned from the Cabinet. In November he wrote to his old friend Joseph Howe:

I hardly know where to turn to escape out of the hands of the Confederationists, Fenians, French priests, American Democrats and all other enemies of British institutions.

In the previous month Dorion and nineteen other French-speaking Members from Lower Canada, who were dismayed by the prospect of a "subordinate position," had signed a protest called a "Remonstrance" against Confederation, and had sent it to the Colonial Secretary, Lord Carnarvon. The newspapers took it up, and some doubts about the future rights of French minorities were expressed in Cartier's journal, *La Minerve*. On October 30, at a dinner held in his honour at Montreal, Cartier felt it necessary to say:

I also solemnly give you my word that the Catholic minority of Upper Canada will be protected like the Protestant minority in Lower Canada. All apprehensions upon this subject are as absurd as they are false. Do not listen to them. I tell you all will be well.

And *La Minerve* was pacified and seemed to be reassured by this solemn declaration.

The Premiers of New Brunswick and Nova Scotia were restless. Both Tilley and Tupper were anxious to complete the work of Confederation in 1866 before the British House of Parliament adjourned in August. But the summer Session at Ottawa had dragged on to exasperate both of them until it became apparent that it would be impossible to have an Imperial Statute adopted that year.

In the independent tradition of Nova Scotia there were strong currents of seafaring self-interests still flowing against Confederation, and the influence of that strange genius Joseph Howe was growing. Yet Tupper maintained a majority in the Nova Scotia Legislature which he had won in the general election of 1863, and which could, with political astuteness, see him through until 1867. Archbishop Connolly of Halifax was most active in supporting Confederation and would, in fact, travel twice to England about it in 1866. Guarantees to all minorities should be a basic principle in Nova Scotia and New Brunswick, he maintained in a letter to Tupper in October of that year.

By this time a written petition had gathered forty thousand names to support Howe's campaign against Confederation. Howe made Maritimers fear that their whole Maritime community could be extinguished as a minority; the disparity in size, resources and wealth between Canada and the Maritimes, he argued, would leave them without protection against ultimate absorption in the scheme of Confederation where Maritimers were about to be "swamped."

Howe was so successful that by November 1866 he had almost reduced the matter to one popular question: Should Nova Scotia have Confederation forced upon it without its consent? Indeed, the Imperial Government was quietly considering the possible necessity of doing this.

The split among the Fenians in America had unnerved James Stephens. When he arrived in the United States he still felt that he was capable of healing the breach by his own presence and authority, and one of his first acts was to depose John O'Mahony on June 9. But it soon became clear that the real strength had passed to Roberts and Sweeny, and over them Stephens had no control.

Throughout the summer and autumn of 1866 there were scares and threats of new Fenian invasions of Canada under Roberts and Sweeny, and they were serious enough to make John A. MacDonald delay his departure with the Canadian delegation for London. The *Habeas Corpus* Act had been suspended and a stronger Felony Act had been adopted at the summer Session of the Canadian Parliament; this had helped to quieten the uneasiness, yet the dread of a secret invasion persisted.

At an Irish concert in Montreal on November 14, McGee made a passionate reference to some Fenian prisoners who had been sentenced to be hanged, when he said: "These men deserve death."

Hisses rose from the back of the hall. Stepping forward to the edge of the stage, he paused and spoke again:

I repeat deliberately, these men deserve death. But I will add, the spirit of our times is opposed to capital punishment.

As to the handful who hissed just now in the far corner, if I had not stood between them and the machinations of these men and their emissaries, some of them would be sharing today the fate of those condemned.

I have had in my hands evidences of your criminal folly, and I could have put some of you where you could not hiss much, but you were not worth prosecuting.

This impetuous declaration made a sensation. But what followed was almost incredible. George Brown picked up an unverified letter from a Montreal correspondent which accused McGee of disloyalty; and Brown published it in the Toronto *Globe*. McGee showed how deeply he was hurt when he answered Brown:

If there is any ground on which an honest Canadian journalist ought not to have attacked me, it is precisely the ground of Fenianism.

At a time when I have had to risk even my personal safety in doing battle against the miserable delusion; at a time when the secret enemy has tried every resource of secret intimidation against me; at such a time, you, with whom I have acted for many years as a friend, you choose this time to throw your testimony against me, as being untrue to Canada on the subject of Fenianism.

On the eve of my leaving this city for three or four months, you run me down, rather than lose an opportunity of damaging a person, whom you happen just at present to consider a political enemy.

Actually D'Arcy McGee did not leave Canada until the end of January 1867. How that delay happened and what effect it had will be told later. But before his departure McGee's reflections on public life were remarkably free of illusions:

In public life in this country, the bitterness is real, the hardships are real and the rewards chimerical. The public man gives up his domesticity, is banished from his family for six months in the year, until even his children only recognize him as an occasional visitor.

Is this not a sacrifice? He exposes his character to be traduced, and his motives to be aspersed, while he undertakes the heavy load of public business. And how is he rewarded?

Where is the kindly interpretation of any doubtful act? Where the kindly throwing of the veil over that which cannot be defended? A people who gives no titles, no great rewards nor decorations may at least throw the mantle of charity over the conduct of their public men.

# 19

## ROCK MAPLE

If we are a generation worthy to organize a nation, assuredly the materials are abundant and are at hand.

*Thomas D'Arcy McGee*

Creation is full of expectancy.

ST. PAUL TO THE ROMANS VIII: 19

John A. MacDonald was tired and lonely. Almost ten years had passed since his wife's death. And one evening late in October of 1866, leaning on an elbow and pausing now and then to run his hand through his bushy, tufted hair, he wrote to a friend:

> I have been working night and day to get ready for England, and scarcely know how I shall be ready in time. The Fenian prisoners and their fate may perhaps keep me for a while, but this is strictly *entre nous*, for I am supposed to sail on the seventh without fail.

Confederation was at last on the horizon of practical politics. Although Newfoundland and Prince Edward Island would not join, everything was ready for the final Conference in England where the delegates from Upper and Lower Canada, Nova Scotia and New Brunswick would meet with the Imperial authorities in London.

But the problems of the Fenians did detain MacDonald, as he had feared, until November 14, when he finally sailed with Cartier and Howland from New York. Galt went on his own. Meanwhile, as planned, Langevin and McDougall left on November 7, sailing out of Boston for Liverpool at fourteen knots on the first Cunard single-screw iron steamer, the fast and economical *China*.

When the *China* stopped for passengers at Halifax, Bishop Rogers of Chatham and Bishop Sweeny of Saint John were on the dock to see someone off—a prelate with a level, scrutinizing look about his eyes, steady rather than sharp, the firm, well formed mouth of a fluent man ready for a contest, and the large, square hands of a worker. He was Archbishop Connolly of Halifax. He had just been to England to see Tupper and Tilley, but now, returning on the *China*, he would have the opportunity he sought to urge upon Langevin and McDougall the justice of protecting the educational rights of minorities under the proposed Bill for Confederation.

The subject was one of lively discussion. That month Lord Carnarvon, the Colonial Secretary, received two formal petitions concerning the Bill for Confederation. One came from the Bishops of Lower Canada on the needs of the Catholic Separate Schools; the other presented the grievances of the Protestant Teachers Association of Lower Canada seeking special protection for their educational interests as a minority. In effect, these two petitions revived what the abandoned Bell and Langevin Bills had sought for Upper and Lower Canada at the last Session in Ottawa. Egerton Ryerson, the Superintendent of Education for Upper Canada, had also arrived in London to advance his firm views for a uniform and centralized organization of schools, as against any Separate School system; and he was prepared to argue his carefully documented case with all his ardour as a Methodist preacher.

A flurry of debate had arisen in Canada when the Toronto *Globe* published a report (which proved to be well founded) that the delegates at the London Conference intended to insert a new clause permitting a minority with a grievance on education in any Province to appeal to the Federal authority. But there was little more to be said, because it was immediately announced that the London Conference would proceed in strict secrecy, and there would be no information released until the Bill for Confederation was ready to be presented to the Imperial Parliament early in 1867. Yet one thing was clear. The subject of education would be a key issue at the London Conference.

The Conference opened in London on Tuesday, December 5, 1866, with MacDonald, Cartier, Galt, Tupper and Tilley as the leaders. D'Arcy McGee was not there. Much against his wishes, he had been obliged to accept the decision of the Cabinet and remain in Canada. Two weeks went by, and McGee became uneasy about the lack of news from London. On December 19 he wrote from Ottawa to John A. MacDonald:

> So far we have heard only of your arrival and of your presidency of the Conference, on which accept my congratulations.
>
> Lord Monck left this day week in a style and manner not quite to my taste. I should have wished a good deal more heartiness and popular *éclat*, but he discouraged everything of the kind, and so it was.
>
> As to the Fenians, we still continue to receive the average number of *startling rumours*, but no one seems to put much faith in them. It may be that we are in danger of running into the extreme opposite to credulity; and when you write Campbell you might give him a fillip on that score. Inertia is all very well in its way, but it may be carried too far.
>
> As to myself, I am only anxious to reach London before the Bill is introduced, in order to save my promises to my friends. With this view I hope to get off some time in January, and will trouble Bernard to bespeak me a room at your hotel.

If you see Archbishop Connolly at any time or place, I beg you to be specially attentive to him.

Important developments had happened quickly at the London Conference. On their second day, Wednesday, December 5, the delegates reached the troublesome topic of Education. By Section 6 of Resolution 43 at Quebec, Education had been placed under the jurisdiction of the Provinces, subject to one exception which limited the Provincial power:

Saving the rights and privileges which the Protestant or Catholic minority in both Canadas may possess as to their denominational schools at the time when the Union goes into operation.

How that simple exception, phrased in thirty words by D'Arcy McGee at the Quebec Conference, was transformed during the twenty days of discussion at the London Conference and the seven succeeding drafts of the Bill for Confederation was a curious adventure in legal history. Eventually, when it reached its final form in Section 93 of the British North America Act, it was six times as long and incredibly subtle.

The way it happened is worth following not only for its own sake, but because it served as a barometer for the changing fortunes of Provincial rights in the crucial months of December 1866 and January and February of 1867.

McGee's original wording did not, of course, cover the Provinces of Nova Scotia and New Brunswick; so this seemed to invite a change. Outside the Conference, Archbishop Connolly of Halifax was leading a movement to obtain for the Catholic minorities in the Maritimes the same protection in education which the Protestants enjoyed in Lower Canada. But the critical point was this. Whatever rights Catholics possessed in education, particularly in Nova Scotia, had been obtained through usage and practise and were not secured by law. So the Archbishop's move was resisted by most of the delegates.

On December 5 Galt proposed his own amendment. It dealt with the right of an aggrieved minority to appeal to the Federal authority, much as the Toronto *Globe* had rumoured, but it went further than that. Galt moved that these two paragraphs be added to McGee's proviso:

And in any Province where a system of Separate or Dissentient Schools by law obtains, or where the Local Legislature may hereafter adopt a system of Separate or Dissentient Schools, and appeal shall lie to the Governor in Council of the General Government from the acts and decisions of the local authorities which may affect the rights or privileges of the Protestant or Catholic minority in the matter of education.

And the general parliament shall have power in the last resort to legislate on the subject.

By its last sentence it really shifted the final jurisdiction over education from the Provincial to the Federal power.

Galt's amendment was discussed and adopted; and in the lower left-hand corner of Galt's original manuscript, John A. MacDonald noted in his own hand the results of the vote thus:

Nova Scotia + Yes

New Brunswick + Yes

Canada   Yes

Judging by the different manner in which MacDonald recorded the vote by leaving the plus sign out after "Canada" and the fact that discussion on education was renewed two weeks later, the Lower Canada delegates were probably not unanimous.

But what exactly happened was never clearly recorded. The minutes kept by Colonel Hewitt Bernard as the Secretary of the Conference were very brief, and they did not extend beyond December 14. The question of jurisdiction over education must have been discussed in some circles of London outside the Conference, because Archbishop Connolly expressed his opinion that he was in favour of that part of Galt's amendment which provided for an appeal to the Federal Government. As to what happened after December 14, Galt's letters to his wife are practically the only source of information. The first was written on Wednesday, December 19:

> The Education question came up today and I am thankful to say our Canadian delegates all stated that no change could be permitted in what we proposed on behalf of Canada, which however they might extend to the Lower (Maritime) Provinces if they wished. They have taken till tomorrow to decide and I therefore hope before I close this letter to tell you so far as the Delegates are concerned, the matter will be settled.
>
> I much apprehend that I shall have to be one of those who remain to see the Bill through Parliament. MacDonald cannot remain. And I feel sure that he will insist on my staying, as our friend Cartier devotes himself so much to Society that we do not get much work out of him. This is, however, for your eye only. Howland, McDougall and Langevin will go back.

This note was added late on Thursday:

> I have nothing to add to the foregoing, except that the Education question stands till tomorrow. The difficulty now is as regards the Lower (Maritime) Provinces, not with us in Canada.

The London Conference closed on Christmas Eve. Then after a brief note on Thursday, December 27, assuring his wife that all had been settled as he desired, Galt wrote the following day at greater length, stating that the report to Lord Carnarvon had been unanimously approved, and adding:

> I am very much pleased to be able to say that the Education question is all right, and has been extended to and agreed by all the Provinces. So that there is now, I may say, no fear of its going wrong in the Imperial Parliament.
>
> My enemies at home will not have the satisfaction they have hoped for.
>
> The Quebec scheme is adopted; very few alterations, and none that I regard as at all impairing it.

Meanwhile John A. MacDonald, who had impressed the Colonial Under-Secretary with "his power of management and adroitness" and his "cool, ready fluency" as the "ruling genius" of the Conference, had lost no time. On Christmas Day, although confined to his room by severe burns suffered in an accident, MacDonald managed to write to Lord Carnarvon:

> The Delegates who have sat steadily from the 4th to the 24th of December have arrived at a satisfactory conclusion, and have adopted by the unanimous vote of the Provinces, a series of resolutions which I shall transmit tomorrow morning.

With this desire for speed, MacDonald added a request for strict secrecy.

But in the text of the Resolutions which MacDonald sent to Carnarvon, a small but vital change had appeared in the original wording of McGee's proviso on Education. Inserted were two new words, "by law." The effect of these two words on denominational schools was to restrict "the rights and privileges which the Protestant or Catholic minority in any Province may have" to those which they had "by law."

How or when this restriction was made was not recorded. McGee's original wording had left the matter open, and whether the rights and privileges existed "by law" or merely "by custom," they were safeguarded.

But the new wording made a real difference. Maritimers were to experience the difference quickly, and the next generation would witness the decisive role played by the words "by law" in the Manitoba school question.

Nothing was known in Canada at that time about these changes in the text on Education. McGee was straining on the leash awaiting permission to leave for London, as he indicated in a letter from Montreal on January 6, 1867, to John A. MacDonald marked "Strictly for yourself":

> My position here is becoming an extremely irksome one in consequence of protracting my departure repeatedly, and for which I cannot give the reasons either to my constituents or the Western Catholics who write me on the matter. I need not repeat to you all or any of the explanation of my own position I gave at Ottawa, and which led you to draw the Minute for my departure after the close of the year '66. That was the second best thing that could be then done under all the circumstances; and I accepted therefore as you put it.
>
> But Lord Monck withheld his signature, as you know, to the Minute, lest Sir Narcisse should be left short of a quorum by any accident to the one or two other Ministers, at the same time assuring me by letter and personally that he would endeavour on reaching your side to hasten Langevin's return. To this I also yielded. But this also I could not publicly explain.
>
> I don't know whether Lord Monck will trouble his head much on my account or on any one else's but his own, after he gets over. And I do not want to ask Cartier to hasten the return of the only other French Canadian on the delegation. But if he, Langevin, Howland, or McDougall, or both, should be able to leave England by the 20th at latest, I may yet save my position in one material respect: by having seen the Bill and being able to satisfy my friends I have seen it, before it was introduced.
>
> I put so much stress on this point that I should consider myself sacrificed by my own colleagues if I am not able to make it.
>
> I put my case in your hands, and beg you to make it your own. I shall be miserable till I hear from you. And so vital is it to me, I would beg you to send over the wires at the earliest moment to Sir Narcisse or myself, this or something like it:
>
> "*Blank* is leaving, or has left, McGee may start at once."

At last D'Arcy McGee was off for London. On Sunday evening, January 27, he left Ottawa by special train, stopped briefly at his home in Montreal and then went on to Boston. There he heard a report that four days earlier, some Fenians had seen James Stephens sail from New York for Europe on a secret mission. McGee left Boston on Wednesday, January 30, on the Cunard wooden-paddle steamer the *Asia*. She was no mean ship. Just eight years after McGee's first crossing of the ocean in forty-two days on the old brig *Leo*, the new *Asia* had made a record eastward crossing from New York to Liverpool on the Atlantic Mail Run in ten days and eleven and a half hours.

When the *Asia* stopped at Halifax on Thursday, McGee was privately received at Government House by Sir William Fenwick Williams, a supporter of Confederation in his own blunt and crusty manner; and then publicly welcomed by the mayor at the Halifax Hotel, where he responded to an address, as the Halifax *Evening Express* reported, "briefly and eloquently, speaking on the Federal Union and the Fenians."

The Federal Union and the Fenians were, indeed, two of the main points which McGee had in mind as he crossed the Atlantic. But he also had to present a petition in Rome on behalf of St. Patrick's Church of Montreal, and then to return to Paris as the Canadian delegate for the opening of the World's Fair on April 1. So his voyage on the *Asia* was the start of several months of travel and business.

In the meantime the Bill for Confederation was rapidly taking shape in England, and McGee had not seen it. Based on the Resolutions of the London Conference which the delegates had reduced to sixty-nine in number, a first rough draft of the British North America Act was started early in January 1867. This draft was then completed by an Imperial law officer, F. S. Reilly; and by January 23 a few copies were distributed confidentially for discussion.

Earlier, Governor General Lord Monck on his arrival from Canada had discussed the new Constitution with Lord Carnarvon, and both had agreed that if a Legislative Union could not be had, then a strong central government with weak local governments would be the next best thing. So on Saturday, January 26, when the Canadian and Maritime delegates gathered at Lord Carnarvon's house on Grosvenor Street for their first formal discussion of the Bill, it quickly became evident that the influence of Carnarvon, Monck and other centralizers had been felt.

In fact, on January 26, the federal character of the proposed Constitution could not be recognized.

The very word "Federal," which had been used ten times in the Quebec Resolutions to describe the nature of the Union as a "Confederation," had been completely eliminated. The highest officer in each Province was called, not a "Lieutenant Governor," but a "Superintendent." A Provincial Assembly was empowered to pass, not "laws," but "ordinances." Most important of all, the residuary clause, which placed unspecified subjects within the general powers of the central government, had been widened and strengthened. At this stage, the powers of each Province were at their very weakest.

But protests were so strong that drastic revisions had to be made. When the next complete draft of the Bill was ready for renewed discussion on February 2, the word "Federal" unobtrusively reappeared. "Lieutenant Governors" were restored to the Provinces with power to enact "laws," and the Provinces regained much of their lost autonomy.

This restored autonomy was particularly noticeable in the field of Education, with a special section devoted to it. The previous draft had contemplated that a Provincial Assembly would merely make "ordinances" on education, under reserve of the power of the central government to make "laws" on education which would be overriding and, if need be, unrestricted. But the revised draft of February 2 was very different. A section allotted the power to make laws on education to the Provinces, and restricted the Federal right to intervene to those circumstances where "remedial laws" would be required.

It was in this draft of February 2 that "Kingdom of Canada" first appeared as the proposed official name. There was no time to be lost, as the British House of Parliament was due to open on February 5. Yet two further drafts of the Bill were made, and each one indicated a further strengthening of the powers of the Provinces. The second of these, known as the final draft, was dated February 9. At the last moment the name "Kingdom of Canada" was dropped for fear of irritating the United States, and replaced by "Dominion of Canada"; and in this form the Bill was sent to Queen Victoria for her consideration.

Such was the state of things when D'Arcy McGee arrived in London. As he quickly learned, the important discussions and revisions of the British North America Bill were practically finished, and the Bill was due to be read for the first time in the House of Lords on Tuesday, February 12. As it turned out, however, little was done that week.

Disappointed by what he had missed, McGee joined John A. MacDonald and the other delegates from Canada at the Westminster Palace Hotel. It was built in the wedge formed by Victoria and Tothill streets, on a site once occupied by the Almonry where William Caxton, the first English printer, had proudly shown his new press to King Edward IV. Overlooking Westminster Abbey, it was right in the centre of the historic sites which had fascinated McGee twenty years earlier when he had served as the Parliamentary correspondent for the Dublin *Freeman*.

To the surprise of McGee, and indeed of almost everyone, John A. MacDonald, who had all the habits and humours of a confirmed widower, announced that he was about to marry again. On Saturday, February 16, D'Arcy McGee was at the wedding. It was celebrated at St. George's Church on Hanover Square, where the poet Shelley had re-married his unhappy Harriet. There, John A. MacDonald, fifty-two years old, married Agnes Bernard, in her early thirties, the poised and pious sister of Colonel Hewitt Bernard, the Secretary of the London Conference. Galt described it to his wife:

> We have today married MacDonald to Miss Bernard. All went off most agreeably; the day was beautiful; and all were happy as possible.
>
> The Bishop of Montreal performed the ceremony, and we afterwards lunched at our hotel, since which the happy pair have started for Oxford to spend two or three days.

Then in his hurried handwriting Galt added what books have always repeated thus:

> There were rather a large party, four bridesmaids—Misses Mc-Dougall, McGee, Tupper and Archibald—and about seventy guests.

But neither of McGee's daughters was with him, and a study of the original letter shows that the second name, if undecipherable, is not "McGee."

In any event, that unknown bashful bridesmaid and the very cheerful guests had hardly stopped talking about the wedding when John A. and Agnes MacDonald were back in London. The second and important reading of the British North America Bill, which MacDonald could not miss, was set for Tuesday, February 19.

McGee was one of those who had maintained in principle that the Quebec Resolutions were in the nature of a treaty, to be accepted or rejected as a whole, but not to be amended. But the amendments made to the original Seventy-two Resolutions of the Quebec Conference by the Sixty-nine Resolutions of the London Conference and by each succeeding draft of the British North America Bill made it plain that the theory of an inviolate treaty had, under these tests, been discarded.

Moreover, movements were still afoot for more changes to be made in the Bill as it moved through the House of Lords and the House of

Commons. And there remained the fear that the whole Bill could yet be blocked, because Joseph Howe had been working hard in London with his formidable petition of opposition from Nova Scotia.

By Section 80 of the Bill, the Protestant minority of Lower Canada had already secured special protection for twelve electoral districts where they were strongest, mostly in the Eastern Townships; and they were now seeking to modify the Bill further during the sitting in committee of the House of Lords. But Lord Carnarvon disposed of the latter proposal in his brief letter of February 21 to John A. MacDonald:

> I understand that the amendment, which it is desired to introduce in committee in the Bill with regard to the Protestant minority in Lower Canada, is a provision to the effect that such minority shall have the same relative representation always secured to them in the federal and local Legislatures as now.
> I conclude that this would be a grave infraction of the terms agreed to and embodied in the Bill.

The next day McGee was in the House of Lords to listen as Lord Carnarvon guided the Bill through committee and carefully explained Section 93 on Education in this manner:

> The question which really divides the Protestants and Catholics is that of public instruction. Article 93 was adopted following a long discussion during which all opinions were expressed.
> The object of the Article is to protect the minority against all abusive pressure on the part of the majority. It has been drafted in a manner to place all minorities, no matter to what religion they may belong, on a footing of absolute equality, whether these minorities exist in fact or in a possible state, *in esse* or *in posse*.

As an expression of its spirit, perhaps Carnarvon's statement was as clear as the long, loose wording of Section 93 could allow; but in later years the courts would not find its complexities that simple, nor would their judgements concur with Carnarvon.

In its final form, Section 93 of the British North America Act stated that each Provincial Legislature could exclusively make laws in relation to education. But this general statement was subject to four exceptions; and the wording of these four exceptions illustrated how an excess of caution had clouded their origins.

The first exception was substantially the same as the stipulation inserted by McGee in 1864 at Quebec, but for the addition of the two narrowing words "by law."

By the second exception, the legal powers and privileges of Catholic Separate schools in Ontario were extended to apply to the schools of both the Protestant minority and the Catholic majority in Quebec. This was new, and originated in the forty-second Resolution adopted at the London Conference. While nothing was recorded in the minutes, this change had been attributed to Galt. Significantly, the reverse did not apply, that is to say, the powers and privileges of the Protestant minority schools in Quebec were not extended to the Catholic Separate schools of Ontario.

The third exception was based closely upon the first part of the amendment drafted by Galt and adopted on the second day of the London Conference. It permitted an appeal to be made to the Federal Cabinet from any decision of a Provincial authority affecting any educational right or privilege of a minority. It was so worded that the minority could appeal without the necessity of showing that the decision had "prejudicially" affected their rights or privileges.

Two generations later when the history of Section 93 was studied by the Privy Council, it was recognized that the subtlety of the wording in this third exception had not yet been fully explored. Yet this much seems clear. The change from McGee's wording had narrowed down the first exception to "legality." In this third exception a move had been made into a different area, that of "administrative propriety." This was intended to remove the danger that a group, which would be a minority in the whole country but a majority within one Province, might not respect the rights of another minority within that Province. For such a case, this exception promised a solution outside the precise region of the law, in what the courts have called the elastic one of "administrative fairness." In practise, this merely shifted the grievance of a minority from the domain of the courts to the sphere of the Cabinet. But Cabinets are political, and experience has confirmed that their sense of "fairness" cannot easily be detached from the number of votes involved.

The fourth exception completed the intricacies of Section 93 on Education. Galt's amendment at the London Conference had finished with a sweeping sentence:

> And the General Parliament shall have power in the last resort to legislate on the subject.

But the broad scope of Galt's wording had been cut down by each succeeding draft of the Bill. What was first recognized as an "unrestricted" power of the Federal Parliament to make laws in education was in the end whittled down to the power to make "remedial laws, as far only as the circumstances of each case require."

In time it was to be pointed out by the courts that the power of the Provincial Legislature to make laws on education was not unrestricted and that, within the special ambit of the fourth exception, the Federal Parliament of Canada did retain a degree of final authority. But this timid enunciation of Federal authority was to prove far too weak to be used in the world of pressures where politicians moved.

Such is the story of how words can increase and multiply to the point where intent and meaning are almost lost. The change from the simplicity of McGee's thirty words to the multiplicity of Section 93 illustrates in miniature how the British North America Act was conceived in compromise. It also illustrates what the ancient philosopher wrote when he lifted his text-worn eyes from his close study to see his white cat, Pangur, pounce upon his prey:

> He is master of the work
> Which every day he does,
> While I am at my own work
> To bring difficulty to clearness.

After so many delays and strange detours, John A. MacDonald, George Etienne Cartier, Alexander Galt and D'Arcy McGee had reached the end of the long road to Confederation, together. And they were relieved when the British North America Act finally received its third and last reading in the British House of Commons on Friday, March 8, 1867. Of the five men from Canada who were chiefly responsible for Confederation, only one, George Brown, was missing. But Brown was not deprived of a minor victory: his Toronto *Globe* obtained a scoop by printing the complete text of the British North America Act before it. even reached the Government in Ottawa.

The exact nature of the new Constitution of Canada remained vague in many minds. It was called, of course, "Confederation." Yet the framers of the British North America Act throughout all of its 147 sections, had deliberately avoided any use of the word "federal." In fact, the word appeared but once, in an intriguing opening phrase of the preamble expressing the desire of the four colonies to be "federally united."

On the whole, aside from some reservations, Brown was satisfied with the terms of the Act. Confederation was an achievement due in no small part to him, and he considered it a complete justification for his initiative in bringing about the Great Coalition of 1864. He was now busy around

Toronto, rebuilding the strength of the Reform Party. In Brown's view, the British North America Act had done some damage to the original Quebec Resolutions, and some of its changes he considered unjust. But he maintained that the remedy lay with the people; they had it in their power to reject the appeal for a political party truce, and to return his Reform Party to power in the coming general elections under the new Constitution. News of Brown's aggressive attitude reached England as the delegates prepared to disperse. They did not hide their displeasure. And John A. MacDonald was further disappointed by the indifferent manner in which the Members of the British Parliament had passed Canada's new Constitution. They failed to mark it, he wrote later,

> as an epoch in the history of England. The Union was treated by them much as if the British North America Act were a private Bill uniting two or three English parishes.

Joseph Howe's immense effort to block the passing of the British North America Act came to nothing. Yet, from his opposite point of view, he was also distressed by the indifference which he observed in England:

> I am not surprised at the indignation felt by our friends at the utter indifference shown in Parliament to our interests or our remonstrances.
> The fact is they think here only of themselves, and having made up their minds that the Provinces are a source of peril and expense to them—the prevailing idea is to set them adrift, to gradually withdraw British troops from them—to have no quarrel with the United States on account of them, and to leave them to defend themselves if they can, or to pass into the Union if they prefer that solution of their difficulties.

Galt was similarly disturbed, which he explained to his wife in a letter written from London:

> I am more than ever disappointed at the tone of feeling here as to the Colonies. I cannot shut my eyes to the fact that they want to get rid of us. They have a servile fear of the United States and would rather give us up than defend us, or incur the risk of war with that country.
> Day by day I am more oppressed with the sense of responsibility of maintaining a connection undesired here and which exposes us to such peril at home. I pray God to show me the right path.
> But I much doubt whether Confederation will save us from An-

nexation. Even MacDonald is rapidly feeling as I do. Cartier alone seems blind to what is passing around us.

But Galt underestimated Cartier's acuteness. No one was more realistic than Cartier, as he demonstrated in his explanation of the British North America Act to his compatriots of Quebec on his return:

It was the only means to escape Annexation by the United States. Confederation was a compromise and it still preserves today that character.

"At Westminster the twenty ninth day of March in the thirtieth year" of her reign, "the Queen herself Signed with Her own Hand" the Letters Patent of the British North America Act for her "trusty and well beloved citizens." On another continent, later that same Friday night, as D'Arcy McGee would soon point out, William Seward, the sagacious American Secretary of State, moved to prevent the spreading of the Confederation of Canada throughout the West. Seward's move recalled the old cry on the Pacific of "fifty-four forty or fight," as he purchased Alaska from Imperial Russia for seven million-odd dollars.

# 20

## THE BLUE RIM

The euphonious word, Canada, has three vowels, not an unpleasant incident for either tongue or pen. It is as old and quite as historical as the name, America.

Like the ice-shove in the St. Lawrence before the magic breath of Spring, so will cold sectional antagonism dissolve and disappear in the genial currents of our great new State, generously administered.

*Thomas D'Arcy McGee*

Poetry was the maiden I loved,
but politics was the harridan I married.
*Joseph Howe*

Bold and dangerous Fenian outbreaks started in Ireland as early as 1867.

In February, when a report came of a Fenian riot in Kerry, D'Arcy McGee wrote two letters from the Westminster Palace Hotel in London— one to the Prime Minister Lord Derby, and the other to Benjamin Disraeli, who was then Chancellor of the Exchequer. Signing both of them as Minister of Agriculture and Immigration for Canada, McGee made an urgent plea for a more generous policy towards Ireland. McGee gave Disraeli this opinion on Irish influence in America:

> Uneducated, as most of the Irish settlers in the United States are, passionate and prejudiced as they are against everything English, it is to be remembered they hold an immense mass of votes in a democratic society, and they are, for good or evil, a power.
>
> If it suited the United States Government to seek a quarrel with Great Britain, they might easily have from one to two hundred thousand soldiers of this origin, without bounty. Every year's immigration adds almost an army to the number; and the disaffection, disbanded in Ireland, is reformed and armed anew in America.

For "this ever-open source of Irish disaffection," McGee offered his remedy to Disraeli:

> At present, I dare to say, there is no large body of the Irish in Ireland who have a natural confidence in Imperial Statesmen. How, then, is it to be supplied? By patronage? No. By class legislation? Never.
>
> You should refer the whole state of Ireland to a Royal Commission of seven or nine Irishmen of the first character; men resident all their lives in the country; men of local popularity; so that the confidence felt in the men might be, by a natural effect, transferred to the Imperial Government.
>
> This would be placing the case of Ireland, in the hands of Irishmen, not by repealing the Union, but by Imperial initiation. From the President to the Doorkeeper, none but Irishmen should be connected with the Commission. And the Royal letters should hold out the hope that if their recommendations were such as could so be adopted, they would be made a basis of future Imperial legislation.

There is no evidence of the effect McGee may have had on Disraeli, who became Prime Minister for a brief period the following year. McGee's suggestion lay dormant for fifty years, when it was belatedly tried out by the Plunkett Commission meeting under the Dublin Rotunda. But there can be no doubt about the immediate impact made upon the mind of Gladstone, who succeeded Disraeli as Prime Minister. As Gladstone admitted later (to be blamed by many for his candour), the Fenian conspiracy and McGee's pleas influenced him strongly in making the English policy on religion and the tenure of land in Ireland more liberal.

But in 1867, McGee had time only to write these letters and make a brief visit to Dublin. There he saw his literary friend Samuel Ferguson once again. Then, early in March, he left for Paris and Rome.

On his way to Rome, McGee stopped briefly in Paris at the Irish College; and the history of that college prompted the poem "The Old Soldier and the Student," which he wrote on March 14 at Nice overlooking the Mediterranean.

On Saturday, March 16, McGee, weary yet excited, arrived in Rome for the first time in his life. He entered that great and complex centre of Christendom simply as a member of his parish. In Canada, St. Patrick's of Montreal was well known as the most populous English-speaking parish in the country. Its existence was now in jeopardy. But what could that mean to Rome? It is worth an explanation.

Bishop Bourget of Montreal was a devout and saintly priest. As an administrator, he was a rigid man of logic and consistency; and this, to the English-speaking Catholics who were 90 per cent Irish, meant uniformity.

St. Patrick's had developed over twenty years into an autonomous English-speaking branch of the single and ancient French-speaking parish of Montreal under the Sulpicians. But in 1865 Bishop Bourget decided to dismember the historic Sulpician parish and to erect instead two new parishes, one of them as a bilingual parish retaining the name of St. Patrick's. He obtained a decree from Rome dated December 22, 1865, as his authority, and in 1866 he announced that he would carry it into effect. Father Patrick Dowd, the pastor of St. Patrick's who was also a Sulpician, resisted the Bishop's move with all his vigour and influence.

There were then some thirty thousand English-speaking Catholics in Montreal, who were very conscious that they made up almost one third of the total population of the city. Organized in their two churches of St. Patrick's and St. Ann's, they were pressing, notwithstanding the Bishop's opposition, to create their third church. But by the Bishop's new plan, St. Patrick's jurisdiction would be smaller and reduced to three thousand persons, and only one twentieth of the English-speaking Catholics in Montreal would belong to it; the rest, outside of St. Ann's, feared they would become minorities in new bilingual parishes.

Bishop Bourget, in his single-minded pursuit of system, did not expect it to turn so quickly and so humanly into a problem of race and language. It came to a head on the last Sunday of November 1866, when the Bishop's proclamation was read at St. Patrick's. Father Dowd received an order to read it without comment from the pulpit, and it was said that, as he did it, he entoned it like a warrior's dirge. Toward the rear of the Church on the pulpit aisle, in a pew with a black leather cushion and the number 240 on a white enamel plaque, D'Arcy McGee understood his pastor's call and decided to act.

The following Sunday on St. Patrick's grounds, D'Arcy McGee addressed a meeting of 6000 people with these words:

> We have contended with many problems, with poverty and with prejudice. Now 30,000 strong, we stand in danger of disorganisation, division and prostration.
>
> It is a question of self-preservation. The most natural administrative boundary to our parish is language.

As a Romanist, Bishop Bourget relied on a strong central authority and a docile diocese. For the English-speaking people in his diocese to interpret his policy as a French melting pot, was something he never anticipated. But what he attempted to do simply made the English-speaking Catholics more homogeneous and more conscious of themselves as a minority within a minority. They recalled and reinterpreted the disputes of the past; how the Bishop had arranged in 1858 to close up St. Patrick's Hospital in exchange for two English-speaking wards in *Hôtel Dieu*, right down to the recent refusal by George Clerk to publish their protests in the *True Witness*, which they called the "Bishop's newspaper."

In December, the people of St. Patrick's appealed to the Archbishop of Quebec; but he declined jurisdiction and stated that the proper authority was Rome. So, on St. Patrick's Day 1867, D'Arcy McGee was in Rome with a petition to the Pope for the preservation of St. Patrick's Parish.

The principal men to see were Cardinal Barnabo and the German Cardinal, Carl von Reisach. For McGee, it was much more than a parish matter; he aimed to show that it would set the pattern for all bilingual areas across the new nation. His position was strengthened by the Sulpician Order which also opposed Bishop Bourget's policy on grounds of civil law, maintaining that it deprived *la paroisse* of Notre Dame of its acquired rights on the island of Montreal; and Cartier had just presented the Sulpicians' appeal in Rome against the Bishop's decision.

St. Patrick's Day, falling on a Sunday that year, was a very active day for D'Arcy McGee; and late that night in Rome he described it in a letter to Mrs. James Sadlier in New York, making a passing reference to possible political trouble:

I have great hopes of seeing you in New York, en route for Montreal, as political exigencies arising out of the recasting of parts, consequent of Confederation, will oblige me to return about the first week of May.

Then McGee recounted his own activities of that memorable day in Rome:

I have had a great day. I got here yesterday, very tired, but was up at seven this morning.

Took two hours to Saint Peter's; a cup of coffee; heard grand Mass at the Irish College. Dined there with Cardinals Barnabo and Reisach, several Monsignori, the heads of the Greek, English, Scotch, and some other foreign Colleges, Rev. George McCloskey of New York, Bishop Rogers of Chatham, New Brunswick, Rev. M. O'Donnell of St. Hyacinthe, Hon. Thomas Ryan, Mr. Donnelly of Harbour Grace, Newfoundland, and the students.

After dinner, I drove to San Pietro of Montorio and knelt at the grave of the O'Neills and O'Donnells. When I return to Paris, once the business of the opening is over, I shall send you for the *Tablet* two or three papers entitled "Irish Episodes of a Continental Tour." I don't want any other recompense but your good will; but as I owe the firm a bill for books, you may tell Sadlier he must put something to my credit for his contribution.

Then he added this note: "Last evening on the Corso, the Central Park of Rome, I pencilled down these lines," and he enclosed the poem which the Sadliers published, "Sunset on the Corso in Rome."

Five days later McGee had an audience with Pope Pius IX. The seventy-five-year-old Pio Nono, deeply disillusioned by the excesses of Young Italy, received this former rebel of Young Ireland graciously and promised to consider his petition on St. Patrick's with care. Rome moved slowly; in fact, McGee did not live to hear that years later Rome granted his petition. At the time, McGee felt he had done all he could, and he left Rome hopefully and deeply impressed, as he wrote:

I shall never be able to get this city out of my memory and imagination.

D'Arcy McGee returned to Paris, to represent Canada at the official opening of the *Exposition Universelle* on April 1. The day was superb, clear and bright, and the chestnut trees were in blossom. The wide slopes of the Trocadero were thronging with people when they heard the clatter of a hundred horses crossing the Pont d'Iena. It was the mounted guard of Emperor Napoleon III and his Empress Eugénie.

The Imperial carriage stopped at the spot where Gustave Eiffel would build his tower twenty years later. Napoleon emerged in civilian dress, followed by his elegant wife wearing a simple hat and shawl. It was the Emperor's sober gesture to democracy. Then, as the cannons from Les Invalides saluted, he declared the Paris Expo open.

The forty-one acres of Champ-de-Mars were replete with rich and exotic displays. There were replicas of a Pharaoh's temple, Turkish baths, Chinese gardens, the Catacombs of Rome, the Suez Canal and the Aztec monument of Xochicalco; a bazaar in Cairo, an Alpine village, a Russian izba, mosques, kiosques, strange snakes and camels.

In contrast, the American exhibit was modest, consisting of a typical farm, a red schoolhouse and a log cabin; and it was not yet completed. Neither was the British Imperial exhibit, described as the greatest of all; its Indian temple and towering lighthouse were still hidden by their scaffolds. Over in the corner, however, nearest the Quai d'Orsay, Canada's own small exhibit was ready. It displayed the natural and finished woods of Canada; and some specimens of sugar maple, red pine, white ash and wild cherry were being shown in Europe for the first time. But the displays of five hundred Canadian industrial exhibitors were not yet in place.

D'Arcy McGee was appointed an Examiner of Prizes. And at that Expo of 1867, which was visited by the Czar of Russia and his two sons, the Kings of Prussia, Portugal and Sweden and the Prince of Wales, and reached a record total attendance of seven million, his committee awarded a gold medal to a new marvel, the sewing machine.

Those were the daring days of Baron Haussman. By his bold, vast loans, he was building new bridges, intricate sewers and water systems, cutting and clearing out wide boulevards and spacious parks, and with his ruthless drive transforming the beautiful mediaeval town of Paris into a brilliant modern city.

D'Arcy McGee was living in the centre of Paris at 71 Champs Elysées on the south side, half way between Place de la Concorde and L'Arc de Triomphe, not far from Rond Point. Surrounded by so much enterprise, wealth and excitement, he found himself among the crowds growing very lonely; all this, he reflected was a "taper made but to be burned out." Easter was approaching, and he was writing home. To his wife, his days of "existing alone" were "as grass on an unsunned stone, bright to the eye but unfelt below, as sunbeams that lie over Arctic snow." Then he wrote to Fasa *Asthore* recalling their frisky black dog Tiny, and the kitten, the colour of maple syrup, with her bright red ribbon. His third letter was to his nine-year-old Peggy, dated April 19, Good Friday:

Dearest Peggy:

As I am writing today to Mamma and have already written to Fasa, I remember I have another daughter, who is not as yet a very good correspondent but will be one, no doubt, in due time.

I am very glad to hear from Mamma that you mind your lessons so well and that you are greatly improved in your reading.

I hope to be able to bring you some nice little present to show you how pleased I am that you are so good and docile a girl. I hardly know what very young ladies like best, but I think I will try a nice pair of ear-rings, or something of that sort.

You know from your geography how great a country France is, and that Paris on the river Seine is its capital.

When you come to study history, you will constantly meet with mention of Paris which is not only one of the oldest but also, in its improvements, one of the youngest and most beautiful cities in the world.

It has not the solemn grandeur of Rome, nor the immense size of London, but it really looks as if it was sitting for its picture, and that every day the sun shines was a holiday of obligation.

Give my love to all your little playmates, and the dog and the dolls and the cats and the two Maries.

Believe me always, dearest Peggy,

Your affectionate
Papa

Trouble which McGee had previously had with one leg recurred, but he continued to lead an active life in Paris. Finally ulceration flared up again, which confined him to his hotel room. In the middle of March, Lord Monck had confidentially asked John A. MacDonald to be Prime Minister and to form the first Cabinet under the new Constitution. Rumours of political manoeuvres and a remaking of the Cabinet were reaching McGee. So on April 9 he wrote from Paris to John A. MacDonald in London:

I am glad on public grounds—though sorry we are not to see you here—that you are to be in Canada so soon. There seem some rather embarrassing symptoms of old party warfare getting up again, before Confederation has even had a trial. Theoretically, it is true, the work is done; but, practically, it is only beginning. At such a real crisis, personal and mere party politics might afford to "bide a wee."

You observe in your last letter that my own "political future is at stake." I feel the whole force of that remark, and will not lose a day in returning that I possibly can spare.

As to Montreal West, I do not fear any issue which I may have to meet there with any one. But the other two seats in that city can only be secured by the active co-operation of those I can influence, as was shown to Cartier's and Rose's satisfaction last time and the time before. Whatever I can do westward, will be as it always has been, at your service, ever since we have acted together. I recognize no other leader in Parliament or the Country; and I only ask in return that you will protect my position in my absence, till I am able to mount guard over it myself.

I certainly have no desire to embarrass future arrangements which will naturally be under your discretion, but in a Confederation Government, founded on principles which I have always zealously advocated, I will, if in Parliament, give way neither to Galt, nor to a third Frenchman, nor any other man.

When John A. MacDonald received this letter, he wrote this note on the back of it:

My dear L Cartier
Read the enclosed and burn.

Both Langevin and Cartier were still in London at the time, and the capital L before Cartier's name would indicate, supported by other evidence, that McGee's letter was read by both Langevin and Cartier. Then, as usually happens to such a request, the letter was carefully preserved.

Later that month McGee began working on an exceptional document. While it was carefully composed, it was unusually candid for a Cabinet Minister. It was written as a letter to his constituents, dated "May-day, 1867, Paris," and reflected his "considerations on the true policy of the new Dominion of Canada." Before dealing with internal affairs, McGee made two acute and advanced observations on external relations.

The people of all Canada, McGee cautioned, had reason to look with suspicion on the sudden and secret acquisition of Russian Alaska by the United States:

> The motive is obvious enough. It extends their territory to the end of the continent. This purchase of a wilderness is an attempt to outflank our fellow countrymen on the Pacific. But if it should have (as it ought to have) the effect of hastening the Union of our countrymen there into the new Dominion, Mr. Seward and Baron de Stoeckl will have placed themselves involuntarily among the number of our benefactors.

McGee then made a remarkable forecast of the future autonomy of nations within the British Commonwealth:

> The less we trouble Downing Street hereafter, the more we shall be respected by all parties in England. We have passed forever, by our own act, out of the condition of colonies. And if we still desire to perpetuate the connection, it must be in the new and as yet to be created, character of Allies.

But what, McGee asked, are "our domestic duties arising under our new Constitution?" He observed with regret that an attempt was being made in Ontario "to resuscitate old party lines and party cries." This was "a reckless experiment," for it could "kill the Union in its very cradle":

> Parties must arise under the operations of the new Constitution itself. Then they will be wholesome because they will be natural.
> But do not let us pelt each other with old nicknames.

He dealt in turn with what he saw as the four leading internal affairs in the new nation. The first problem was "the increase and employment of our population," notwithstanding the "abnormal drain on the natural, native increase of our population, both east and west, by the enormous inflation of wages" in the United States since the Civil War. Borrowing capital for public works had sometimes, McGee observed, been made into a reproach. But it lay not so much against the borrowing as against the abuses in the spending. So McGee urged, as an equitable policy for the succeeding generations who would benefit from them, immediate borrowing to construct the Intercolonial Railway.

Turning to Galt's domain as Minister of Finance, McGee said he did not want legislation simply for the sake of a protective tariff. What he wanted was "a tariff which will not press unfavourably on our growing manufacturers." Here he took pains to mention, however, that a remark made by Galt in 1866 that proposed reductions in the tariff were "steps in the direction of Free Trade" should still be considered as an expression merely of "Mr. Galt's personal opinion." McGee expressed the hope that Canada should at least "commence the twentieth century with an industrious and prosperous population of twelve million souls."

On the second internal affair, and undoubtedly influenced by what he had seen in Europe, McGee was brief and to the point. Canada, he wrote, needed a standing army; the days of volunteers, however noble they had been in the past, were, for an adult nation, "over and gone."

The third was the important matter of education. Here McGee declared that he might "differ from the majority of Canadians":

But I would have no schooling without morals, and I believe there cannot be morals without religious training.

We have, however, secured the principle of the rights of minorities in all the Provinces to control the education of their own children.

The fourth and final matter was one, McGee admitted, which made him anxious. It concerned the future "harmony and unity of our whole people."

One thing is especial. We, who hitherto have monopolized the name Canada, must forever bear in mind that that general designation must rise, envelop and settle kindly down on territory and population not previously Canadian.

In all future arrangements with the Maritimers, who lived with the fear that their rights would be disregarded, McGee asked not merely for "a liberal but a generous attitude."

Then he mentioned two threats to national harmony, the first briefly and the second at length.

Fenianism, McGee said, could "at a few exposed points be an element of discord amongst us." But the second and "great danger to our unity which remains to be guarded against is sectarian animosity." There were special dangers from this source in each of the three main divisions of Canada:

> In the Maritime Provinces, under the lead of the wise and noble hearted Archbishop of Halifax, whose vast services to the Union cause can never be forgotten, the Roman Catholic minority have still to establish locally the liberties guaranteed to them in general terms, in common with the rest of us, by the Constitution.

In Lower Canada (now called the Province of Quebec), McGee noted that the Protestant minority would enjoy enviable privileges in education and politics:

> Apart from their wealth and their other acquirements, they have secured forever, twelve cautionary constituencies, and their due share of the superior education fund, drawn from the confiscated Jesuit estates.

No similar fund could conceivably be created now for the benefit of their opposite minorities in Ontario (the former Upper Canada) or in the Maritimes, McGee explained, and it would be absurd to make a grievance out of an historical disparity:

> So far from begrudging our Protestant friends in the Province of Quebec the strong political and educational ground they occupy, I, for one, in the interest of union and good neighbourhood, cordially rejoice in their good fortune.

Then, turning to consider the position of the Catholic minority in Ontario, he added:

> I am sorry I cannot speak with equal satisfaction of their position. They have and could have no constituencies secured to them. They, in point of wealth, cannot for a moment compare with our minority.

Here, McGee said, "the electioneering spirit of Mr. George Brown augured ill for mutual concession and good will":

> I have watched the proceedings of those candidate-cutting machines called "County Conventions," which have reached us here to the April 15th, and I have yet to find one Roman Catholic candidate, nominated either for the local or general Parliament by what are called "Conventions of Reformers." This won't do. And it is time that open issue should be taken on such shameful prescription.
>
> If the battle of toleration, long since decided elsewhere, must still be fought on in Ontario, then it must be—that is all.

This was frank talk. And McGee added this counsel: it would be a "fatal mistake" for the Catholic minority in Ontario politically "to combine together as a religion." The "true remedy" was to extend their hand to their fellow countrymen of every creed and rely "freely and fearlessly on the sense of justice of the majority of their neighbours."

McGee then concluded:

> Gentlemen, my anxiety for the successful operation of the new Constitution must be my apology for the length of this letter. I see the God-given opportunities and the man-made obstacles; all we have to lose by error or incapacity or faction; all we have to gain by wisdom, unity and toleration.
>
> Let no man say the work of the Colonial Coalition ended in England. Nothing can be considered done till the instrument framed by the few takes up its abode in the hearts of the many.

This strong and stirring letter was published on May 18 in the Montreal *Gazette*, its thirty-five hundred words extending over four columns, and was reprinted in the Ottawa *Times* and other journals. It was not, however, a message from a Minister who was sensitive about Cabinet solidarity, for it took a clear and vigorous stand on several contentious matters such as external affairs, armament, public works and Separate Schools which were not related to his portfolio of Agriculture and Immigration.

It was the first statement from a Cabinet Minister to reach Canada after the passing of the British North America Act. The Reform press pounced upon it as "the joint handiwork of the illustrious quartette, MacDonald, Cartier, Galt and McGee" and criticized it heavily as a bold promise of "jobbery and extravagance, increased customs, fresh excise duties, new stamp taxes and enormous deficits." But there is no evidence that McGee's May-day letter had even been seen by any other Cabinet Minister before it was printed. In fact, McGee had intended to follow it up with a second letter, but when the second letter never appeared, the silence was an adequate explanation of why it did not.

Such straightforward dealing with thorny questions was typical of McGee's independence. But the open expression of these views, as patriotic as they were meant to be, did not serve him well, particularly with the old Upper Canada Tories or within the cautious circle of the Cabinet.

McGee was anxious to get home. On May 6, he met with Lord Cowley, the veteran British Ambassador in Paris, and that evening attended the *soirée* of Napoleon III and Empress Eugénie in *Les Tuileries*. Then he left France for England, and on May 8, he sailed for Halifax on the *Africa*.

"Sir, a ship is worse than a jail," Samuel Johnson had said. But not D'Arcy McGee. The tang of the air, the zest of the deck games, the fiddler

after dinner in the evening and even the dangers of life at sea stimulated him.

The *Africa*, like her sister ship the *Asia*, was a wooden-paddle wheeler with a clipper bow and a good spread of canvas; but she was somewhat slower. She weighed 2226 tons, was 266 feet long, had a single funnel and three masts and could carry 160 passengers. Churning the water with her huge side-lever action and burning seventy-six tons of coal each day, she could reach, with the aid of her auxiliary sail, a speed of twelve and a quarter knots. The *Africa* had also been designed to serve in an emergency as an armed merchant cruiser, and the next year after 120 round voyages she was fated to become a floating barracks in Ireland during the Fenian raids.

This crossing was slow for the *Africa;* and McGee spent most of his time on deck, his bad leg propped up in front of him, gazing at the peaceful blue rim of the horizon. "The days were all sunshine and the nights were all stars." One evening, "as the late sun lay on the water like mellow cream," looking aft towards Ireland, he was dreaming the dreams of the blind: "in the trance of childhood once again, with gleanings of purple upon the rocks in the wild freshness of the morning, and blackberries by the dark blackthorn by the side of the cold, pure water."

But on the twelfth day of the voyage McGee was listening to the troubles of an angry sea, as the rising wind grew colder. It was "Bank weather," and they were nearing Newfoundland.

At midnight Sunday, May 19, the alarm sounded. The ship slowed down almost to a stop. At latitude 46.55 north, longitude 52.30 west (which McGee noted with care) a "fearful fleet" of icebergs was en countered. Hours later, when the danger had passed and the special night watch had been lifted, McGee was in a pensive mood as he wrote these lines:

> Lonely in nights of summer
> Beneath the starlight wan
> A way-worn berg is met with
> Sad featured as a man.
>
> All softly to the southward
> Trailing its robes of white
> It glides away with the current
> Like a hooded Carmelite.

The next day the sea was clear and the passengers were called on deck "to smell the land." As he looked out to the west D'Arcy McGee felt his heart lift. On that blue rim of the ocean he sighted "the strong sea wall of Newfoundland, the outwork of the New World."

# 21

## FOOLS EXPECT MORE

What if the dream come true? And if millions
unborn shall dwell
In the house that I shaped in my heart, the noble
house of my thought?
"THE FOOL": *Padraic Pearse*

Politicians are generally cunning fellows.
*Edward Whelan*

It was raining when D'Arcy McGee returned to Montreal. At half past nine Friday morning, May 24, the patient mayor and a few hundred drenched supporters were waiting on a soggy scarlet carpet at Bonaventure Depot to welcome him home from London, Dublin, Rome and Paris. The train was late. But something more than that was wrong. His friends had made elaborate preparations; but his enemies were also at work spreading reports that he would not stand for re-election and would be dropped from the Cabinet.

If the reception was dampened by bad weather and some discord, McGee's spirit was not, which he showed when he responded to the mayor's address:

> You have referred to the great event of a "new nation"; and the phrase has been fathered on me. In passing through Halifax, however, I perceived by their newspapers that some were going into the election as the "Nova Scotia Party." While in Paris, I also observed by some Montreal and Toronto papers that others were getting up an "Ontario Party." To sectional agitators at each end of the Confederacy, to Brown in the West and to Howe in the East, let me say this. These gentlemen must not be allowed to remain out of harness and out of doors, making mischief. Come into this partnership; advance to the table of the House of Commons; and take an oath of allegiance to the Dominion of Canada.

Turning then to the general election which was expected to follow the Confederation of Canada on July 1, McGee spoke openly about his personal position:

> If you wish to have me as I am, personal faults and all—and God knows I have my share of them—I am ready to serve you. And if you do not wish me, I am prepared to make my bow in good humour, and go and look after—what would have been better perhaps had I minded more—my own personal affairs.

Two days later, in a letter to the Sadliers, McGee revealed more of what was on his mind:

I got back again day before yesterday, quite well but rather tired, having left Paris only sixteen days before. News of electioneering and Cabinet-making intrigues from Canada, induced me to hasten my return three or four weeks, and will start me off to Ottawa to-morrow, Monday morning, where I shall be for a fortnight at least. As you may suppose, passing out of one state of political existence into another, there is no end of intrigue and compromises and re-arrangement. About my own position I have no anxiety.

But that last optimistic note was not what McGee had heard in Paris nor what had prompted him to write to John A. MacDonald on April 9 that he would "give way neither to Galt nor to a third Frenchman nor any other man." What McGee then added had the very salt of realism in it:

I feel that I shall get just what I am able to command, as is usually the case in politics. And the man is a fool who looks for more.

The reports of impending shuffles in the Cabinet were so urgent and upsetting that McGee, although he had been away from his family for al-most four months, decided to spend but a brief week-end at home and leave at once for Ottawa. So on Monday morning, above the rapids of Ste. Anne which had inspired Tom Moore's "Canadian Boat Song," Mc-Gee boarded the *Queen Victoria* (the same ship the delegates took to the Charlottetown Conference) and sailed up the Ottawa River.

That evening about seven o'clock as the steamer approached the land-ing in Ottawa, the wharf and the road sloping up to the crest of the hill were crowded with people. It was a larger and more enthusiastic recep-tion than that in Montreal. Again the mayor spoke, and again he used McGee's phrase of ushering in "a new nation on this continent." As Mc-Gee started to reply, the *Queen Victoria* interrupted to blow off steam; McGee said he could take a hint and would try to reserve his; but he did want to extend a welcome to Prince Edward Island, Newfoundland, Brit-ish Columbia and the Northwest Territories to join Confederation soon:

We should aggrandize the kindred colonies. But we should not enter on the acquisition of territory by any aggressive measures. The Con-stitution of Canada should be made attractive to those who have not yet come in under its influence. And we must qualify ourselves to fulfil the spirit of toleration and forebearance. It is our only means to make a great nation of a small people.

Excusing himself "for having been betrayed into making something like a speech," he then stepped down to accept a bouquet of flowers from some orphans.

George Clerk did not miss the significance of what was going on, as he made these entries in his diary:

> May 28: McGee had a reception at Ottawa, a display to keep him in the Ministry.
>
> June 1, Saturday: Many rumours as to the formation of the new Ministry. McGee's friends and enemies both excited.

For anyone who had not yet learnt what McGee called "the ABC of politics," there could be no better lesson than the promises, shifts, and sacrifices of that month of June in Ottawa. The task of forming that first Federal Cabinet was far from simple; and to appreciate the difficulties, the elements of the problem should be stated.

First, the number of Ministers had to be decided. There had been twelve in the Coalition Cabinet, and MacDonald was convinced from the outset that and any number larger than that would be unworkable.

Next, the new Cabinet had to be a coalition in character, that is to say, divided as equally as possible between the groups loosely called the Conservatives and the Liberals. In fact, there was little enough held in common among the Reformers or Clear Grits of Ontario, the *Rouges* of Quebec and the Liberals of New Brunswick and Nova Scotia; but all could be called "professional liberals"; and MacDonald knew the political value of a semblance of unity.

Then, the Cabinet had to be representative; and nothing involved more complexities than that third requirement. Traditionally, Upper Canada had been represented by six Ministers, and Lower Canada by six. Now that the House of Commons would be based upon Representation by Population, and the Senate avowedly appointed to protect sectional interests, it was felt from the start that an adequate and fair balance would be four Ministers from Ontario, four from Quebec, two from New Brunswick and two from Nova Scotia to make up a Cabinet of twelve. But the arguments merely began there. For within each Province (and particularly in Quebec) the dividing lines of language, religion and geography ran crooked and conflicting paths, cutting up the population into a multitude of separate communities, each seeking representation in the Cabinet. Then, as between the Provinces themselves, one Province was not content to be treated simply as the equal of another, and this was particularly so in the case of Ontario towards Quebec.

The final consideration was the most important and delicate. The personal requirements essential to any Cabinet Minister had to be weighed. And here, the individual merits and experience of each candidate invariably raised special problems.

Early in March, while still in London, John A. MacDonald had started to discuss the make-up of the Cabinet. At that stage it was taken for granted that MacDonald, Campbell, Howland and McDougall from Ontario, Cartier, Langevin, Galt and McGee from Quebec, Tilley from New Brunswick and Tupper from Nova Scotia would be ten likely appointments. Such an assumption did not leave much room for further speculation. If politics were that uncomplicated, there merely remained the selection of two more, one from New Brunswick and another from Nova Scotia. But if politics were that simple, McGee would not have been obliged to spend the whole last week of May, as he did, at a series of meetings behind closed doors with his colleagues.

All the while John A. MacDonald was busy writing letters, and McGee had received one promising him his seat in the Cabinet. Alexander Campbell, his close associate, was also asked. By Thursday, May 30, MacDonald indicated in a letter to Tilley that he had already made preliminary arrangements for the Ministers from Quebec and Ontario, and asked Tilley to recommend a second Minister from New Brunswick, suggesting Mitchell, Fisher or Wilmot. Meanwhile Peter Mitchell had written MacDonald pointing out that the North Shore of New Brunswick was a section which should have a seat in the Cabinet as distinct from the City of Saint John; and on June 1 MacDonald replied encouraging Mitchell's hope to represent the North Shore interests.

On May 30 MacDonald also wrote to George Archibald definitely offering him a post to join Tupper as the second Minister from Nova Scotia. So by Thursday, June 5, it seemed to be settled that the four Maritime Ministers would be Tupper and Archibald from Nova Scotia and Tilley and Mitchell from New Brunswick.

But on that same Thursday, McDougall made two demands in writing on behalf of the Ontario Liberal Reformers. First, because Ontario had more people and paid more taxes than Quebec, Ontario must have one more Minister than Quebec. Second, because more Liberal Reformers than Conservatives had previously been elected in Upper Canada, the Liberal Reformers must have one more Ontario Minister than the Conservatives. Blair was now proposed as the third Liberal Reformer to join McDougall and Howland and thus outbalance MacDonald and Campbell as the two Conservatives.

This threw everything out of joint. Cartier responded immediately. He insisted on an earlier stand that three of the four Quebec Ministers must be French-Canadian. In previous Cabinets, he argued, there had been four French Canadians out of twelve Ministers; if now there were to be thirteen Ministers, the proportion of French Canadians would be further reduced; so if Ontario was to have one more, raising the total to thirteen, the minimum number of French Canadians must be three.

Within these new rigid lines, there was no effective answer to Cartier. But it meant that if Chapais was added to Cartier and Langevin, as Cartier proposed, that would leave but one Quebec vacancy, and then either Galt or McGee would have to go. And neither the Quebec Protestant minority nor the Irish Catholic minority would yield on their respective representatives. So everything was reopened. The claims of each Province, section, race, religion and party were challenged and reasserted with more passion than ever.

An alternative was suggested to increase the number in the Cabinet to five from Quebec, six from Ontario, three from New Brunswick and three from Nova Scotia, making a total of seventeen. But this would again reduce the ratio of French Canadians to three out of seventeen. Strange to say, no one seems to have suggested the device of adding one or two Ministers without Portfolio to the Cabinet.

In any event, John A. MacDonald was completely opposed to any such increase as a solution. The Cabinet would then become too unwieldy, he insisted, and rather than tolerate an increase, he would resign. This resulted, not in resignation, but in deadlock.

In order to strengthen his own position, McGee returned to Montreal, where he met with his advisers and supporters on Monday, June 10, at Mechanics Hall on St. James Street. That Thursday in the same place he addressed the mayor's committee which was preparing Montreal's celebration of Canada's first national holiday on July 1. McGee was careful to say that he did not appear "as a member of the Government of Canada as it is and as it is to be on the 30th of June next," and he hinted at his own political troubles when he added that he had been "distracted by other and more immediate and more exciting interests during the last few days." With that said, he turned to the subject of Confederation:

I believe no day, not even the day of discovery of this Continent, nor the day of the landing of the Pilgrim Fathers, nor the fourth day of July, will be more marked and more memorable for the people of this country than the first day of July.

In Toronto, meanwhile, George Brown and his *Globe* were concentrating on politics and a rise to power. Brown was determined to bring about the downfall of John A. MacDonald. He was working closely again with Luther Holton in Montreal, and doing all he could to induce his old colleagues Howland and McDougall to quit MacDonald and return to the Liberal Reformers of Ontario, who were about to hold their convention in Toronto near the end of June. Drawing on his own bitter experiences with MacDonald, Brown warned them:

> John A. MacDonald is a very astute man, and knows well how to play one colleague off against another.

McGee's May-day letter from Paris, which had called for a truce in old party warfare, stood in Brown's way, and he attacked it. The Montreal *Gazette* rallied to the defence of McGee. But some Conservatives felt that McGee had somehow fomented the Fenians, and they were also irritated by the independent tone of his May-day manifesto from Paris; so they renewed their own criticisms. McGee was caught in this crossfire between the Grits and the Tories.

When McGee returned to Ottawa on Monday, June 17, for that crucial week of final discussions about the Cabinet, he sensed, as others did, that he was a magnet of controversy. Holton, for example, wrote on June 21 to Brown, making some innuendoes about McGee's sprees and Irish sympathies:

> There is a good deal of uncertainty about McGee's position. It is whispered that owing to his conduct here last autumn and in England, Lord Monck may voice objections to his being made a Privy Councillor. I have not much faith in His Lordship taking so creditable a stand, but his name may be used to do what others desire done but will not venture to do directly.
>
> We are doing nothing in McGee's division until we see what is done with him on the 1st of July. Many of his countrymen are anxious to have him opposed.

Tupper, Tilley, Archibald and Mitchell had also arrived from the Maritimes. As the week wore on, John A. MacDonald showed all his resourcefulness, but to no avail. At the end of the week Cartier spent two long mornings in discussions with McGee.

The best evidence indicates that the crisis was reached on Saturday, June 22, when a long and fruitless session of the Cabinet ended with John A. MacDonald threatening to resign and let Brown be called in to form a Government. After that Cabinet meeting Tupper went to McGee and, as Tupper recalled it, said this:

> The union of the Provinces is going to end in a fiasco unless we give way. We are the only two men who can avert that calamity.

As they talked McGee recognized Galt's position as stronger than his, because Galt represented the Protestants, who were a minority unique to Quebec, and their wealth could not be ignored, whereas the Irish Catholics were a minority in all the Provinces. With that said, Tupper then suggested that the Irish Catholics could still be represented if McGee was replaced by, say, an Irish Catholic from Nova Scotia.

CHARLES
TUPPER

Tupper then made this proposal to McGee:

> If you will stand aside in favour of Edward Kenny of Halifax as the representative of the Irish Catholics, I will likewise surrender my claims to a portfolio.

It was a generous offer, and it was generously answered. McGee readily agreed to Tupper's proposition.

That same Saturday evening Tupper called on John A. MacDonald, who repeated that he had given up as Prime Minister and was calling his colleagues together on Monday to announce his failure and have Brown summoned in his stead. Tupper then told him he had a solution and immediately explained it.

But what are you going to do, Tupper? Will you take a governorship?

To MacDonald's question Tupper replied:

I would not take all the governorships rolled into one. I intend to run for a seat in the Dominion Parliament.

On Sunday, MacDonald probably told Cartier, who saw McGee privately when McGee surrendered MacDonald's original letter which had offered McGee a portfolio. Otherwise it was kept as a secret, and Galt, McDougall, Howland and the others knew nothing of what had happened. In fact, that Sunday evening Galt was so dejected that he wrote to his wife:

I have never before had so much worry and anxiety about political arrangements as on this occasion at Ottawa.

The Upper Canada Liberals in the Cabinet have insisted on every sort of concession to them. Cartier has resisted, and I think with good reason. McGee has been a great difficulty.

A final proposition was made on Saturday to the Liberals and rejected by them. But at Mr. Tilley's request they have taken till tomorrow, Monday, to reconsider their decision. It was proposed to meet today, but I positively refused to consider such matters on Sunday, and all acquiesced.

MacDonald at one moment says he will go on without the Grits; the next, he says he will throw up the cards and recommend the Government to send for George Brown. Things are turning out fast as I told you I feared would be the case; and I am so thoroughly disgusted that if it were not for the fear of deserting my friends in such a crisis, I would shake off the dust of my feet on political life.

Monday morning at eleven o'clock the Cabinet met in the Council Chamber. McDougall and Howland appeared in a perfunctory manner with their coats on their arms, determined to make the meeting brief. They announced they were still holding out for a larger representation from Ontario than Quebec and, in fact, were about to catch a train for Toronto to attend the Liberal Reform Convention called for Wednesday by Brown. MacDonald listened quietly and then said: "Tupper has found a solution."

He explained it. Tupper and McGee nodded. And within fifteen minutes John A. MacDonald had formed his first Federal Cabinet.

The Cabinet was to be sworn in on July 1 and it was clearly understood that the names of the members would not be announced by anyone until that day. But on Thursday, June 27, the Montreal *Gazette* published this complete list of the thirteen new members:

John A. MacDonald, Prime Minister and Minister of Justice;
Alexander Campbell, Postmaster General;
William McDougall, Minister of Public Works;
William Howland, Minister of Inland Revenue;
Fergusson Blair, Privy Council President;
    as five Ministers from Ontario,
    the first two Conservatives,
    and the latter three Liberals;
George Etienne Cartier, Minister of Militia and Defence;
Alexander Galt, Minister of Finance;
Narcisse Belleau, Minister of Agriculture;
Hector Langevin, Secretary of State of Canada;
    as four Ministers from Quebec,
    and all Conservatives;
Leonard Tilley, Minister of Customs;
Peter Mitchell, Minister of Marine and Fisheries;
    as two from New Brunswick
    and both Liberals;
George Archibald, Secretary of State for the Provinces;
Edward Kenny, Receiver General;
    as two from Nova Scotia,
    the first a Liberal and the
    second a Conservative.

The *Gazette* stated that its information was reliable; which it was, except for one error in printing the name of Narcisse Belleau instead of Jean Charles Chapais. The *Gazette* then added this comment:

The absence of the names of men so prominent as Dr. Tupper and Mr. McGee will cause remark on the part of the public. But political exigence governs the situation.

That was putting it mildly. There was public consternation. That evening George Stephen (who later resigned as president of the Bank of Montreal to become the first president of the Canadian Pacific Railway) wrote a note of congratulations to Galt and added this postscript:

T. D. McGee's friends do not seem to know what to say finding his name conspicuous by its absence from the list in today's paper.

Hardly anyone in Canada knew who Edward Kenny was. In Halifax he was known as "Papa" Kenny, a jovial man of sixty-seven from County Kerry who came to Halifax in 1824 to establish a firm with his brother as wholesale dry-goods merchants. Having served for nine years as president of the Legislative Council of Nova Scotia, he had previously been a Liberal and was now a Conservative. This at least permitted the Cabinet to be described as made up of Conservatives and Liberals as equally as the odd number of thirteen would allow. Kenny was also one of the high number of five Senators in the Cabinet. The other four (whom Brown ridiculed as "the old ladies") were Campbell, Blair, Chapais and Mitchell.

Indeed, no one was more surprised than Edward Kenny himself when he was singled out to replace, in effect, both D'Arcy McGee and Charles Tupper in Canada's first Federal Cabinet. Unwittingly he became the classic example of the dark horse in that hazardous steeplechase to the Cabinet.

It was far from easy, but D'Arcy McGee kept silent.

Canada's first national holiday on Monday, July 1, 1867, was celebrated across the land with good weather everywhere. But it would be too much to say that popular enthusiasm was general.

As the day dawned in Toronto, George Brown was working like a man possessed. From Sunday midnight to seven o'clock Monday morning, in the heavy, hot air of his *Globe* office, his coat and collar off, Brown was writing unceasingly at the incredible rate of twenty words a minute. It was his version of the whole movement of Confederation. Working right through that night and drinking several gallons of water, he produced the *Globe*'s leading article for the first of July. His nine thousand ardent words ended with a wish for "blessings of health, happiness, peace and prosperity," and Chaucer's archaic phrase "so mote it be."

To avoid embarrassment at the celebrations in Montreal, D'Arcy McGee, at the request of John A. MacDonald, did not appear. Instead, he went directly from Ottawa to fulfil a speaking engagement in Cornwall, and then spent the first of July quietly with his wife in Toronto.

In Montreal the celebrations which McGee had helped to organize began at dawn with a royal salute from St. Helen's Island, and continued gaily until midnight. The day was described as a great success, but not by everyone. Dorion and the *Rouges* who opposed Confederation, not only as a cultural threat but also as a geographical absurdity, remained unmoved. And George Clerk made this entry in his diary:

> Monday, July 1, 1867: Today was kept as a holiday on which the Union Act came into force. In forenoon, turnout of troops. In evening, fireworks. No great thing. As usual at office and read proofs. Weather fine.

He confined his editorial comment on Confederation in the *True Witness* to a crabbed nine words.

In Halifax there were expressions of mixed feelings, and black crepe appeared on a few public buildings. In Fredericton the Anti-Confederate *Headquarters* commented:

> The future may be full of hope, but it is useless to shut one's eyes to the fact that in New Brunswick there is discomfort smouldering in many places.

Over in Charlottetown, Edward Whelan wrote sadly in the *Examiner:*

> Here, alas, the great public of Prince Edward Island treat the thing with feelings akin to contempt.

In the capital city of Ottawa, Lord Monck, the Governor General, did not rise to the occasion. He nonchalantly appeared in civilian clothes, swore in the Cabinet and then, without any prior consultation with the Canadian Cabinet, announced that honours would immediately be conferred: the Prime Minister would become "Sir John A. MacDonald"; and Cartier, Galt, Tilley, McDougall and Howland of the Cabinet, as well as Tupper outside the Cabinet, would be Companions of the Bath.

It was a blunder. Cartier and Galt, far from feeling honoured, were hurt by the implication that their rank should be less than MacDonald's, and they declined to accept. The next day Cartier wrote a sharp letter of protest to Monck for the affront he felt as the recognized representative of the French Canadians by the offer of an inferior title. In a letter to his wife Galt was no less explicit:

> It is an ungracious and most unusual thing to refuse an honour publicly conferred, but if Lord Monck is an ass, I cannot help it.

The Colonial Office aggravated the feelings already injured by mishandling the announcements; and it would take two years before ways could be found to make amends and award new titles acceptable to Cartier and Galt. Meanwhile Cartier and Galt never quite believed that

John A. MacDonald knew nothing beforehand about the proposed awards to be made through Lord Monck. From then on, Cartier and Galt developed a coolness towards MacDonald. In politics, rank and honours are never minor matters, as Napoleon recognized when he exclaimed:

Toys? You call these decorations toys? With such toys we govern men.

McGee, still plain D'Arcy, had his own bitter cup to take. Being dropped from the Cabinet meant a severe loss of income for him at that time. But that was not a new experience. What weighed most heavily upon him were the desolate feelings of a castaway. These were expressed in his own words:

You ask me why I speak forever on this theme of life, as if it were the only care of man, instead of being a rope of slippery strands, full of vile accidents, vexations, dreams, or, like the diver in the secret sea who opens his eyes and sees it all revealed, quicksands, currents, monsters, weeds and shoals.

Desolate as he felt on that first day of July in Toronto, he did not take it as "the wreck of lofty expectations." And it was due in generous measure to the gentle strength of his wife beside him. Once again it was her "patient charity" which "colonized his moral wilderness." But it took all the courage he had been taught in the hard life of politics and a faith beyond his own merits to put Confederation above himself and remain staunch, as his verse attested:

> In the night time, I groaned on my bed,
> I felt, O my Father, thy rod.
> I felt all thy beauty and truth.
> In the morning I rose and I said:
> I will go to the altar of God,
> To God who rejoices my youth.

The Ottawa *Times*, as the feature for its Confederation issue, selected the speech which McGee had just made at Cornwall on "A New Policy for Canada." Speaking before the mayor and a thousand persons, McGee said he felt "a due sense of responsibility and" he added wryly, "of freedom." But not many knew of his inner struggle, as he spoke with such hope:

Dead issues cannot mould our future politics. Mighty waters have swept over the weak patterns of the past. It is not a question of men, nor even a question of policy, so much as a meeting of a new state of affairs.

The people of Canada number nearly four millions, and we are strong enough and should be wise enough to meet our new duties. One of these is the opening up of the West as a field of emigration to those of our own people who now go to the United States.

A few days later McGee heard sad personal news from the Far West. It concerned McGee's old comrade from the days of Young Ireland and the leader of his younger brother, James McGee, in the Civil War, General Thomas Francis Meagher. On that memorable first of July, General Meagher, as the new Governor of Montana, rode in the heat with twelve horsemen through hostile Indian country from Sun River to Fort Benton. That night, fatigued, he boarded a battered river boat, chatted with the pilot about his new mountain home where he and his wife were "as happy as two thrushes in a bush" and then climbed to the upper deck to retire. Somewhere in the dark, "Meagher of the Sword" tripped over a coil of rope and fell overboard, striking a guard-rail below as he plunged into the swift black waters of the Missouri. His body was never found.

It appeared incredible to many that D'Arcy McGee, who had been hailed as the prophet of Confederation, could have been excluded from the first Federal Cabinet. And it was of special interest to the Opposition.

Luther Holton had opposed the new Constitution, but now that it was adopted as law, he expressed his view through the Montreal *Herald* that "it is the duty of all to give the system a fair trial." Meanwhile he was attempting to spread some appearance of unity over the very different groups who happened to use the same name of "Liberal" or "Reformer" but who turned away from one another in their separate attachments to Dorion or Brown or Sandfield MacDonald. On Thursday, July 4, reporting the results of a long discussion he had just had with Sandfield MacDonald, he closed a letter to Brown with this observation:

Sandfield is specially pleased at McGee's exclusion. I suspect McGee will soon be in Opposition from what I hear of the talk among his friends.

It was true that McGee's political friends in Montreal were not only talking, but disputing and dwindling. There were signs of an ebb tide. But McGee in no way recognized that his popularity was running out, and gave no indication of any turn towards the Opposition. On Saturday, July 6, McGee called a meeting of his general committee. It had to be postponed to Monday, however, as a later announcement admitted, "because bad weather and poor advertisement resulted in a small attendance." McGee promptly went to the right people, his workhorses, and on Monday so many showed up that they had to accommodate two hundred curious electors.

The chairman, Walter MacFarlane, came right to the point. McGee's friends, he said, had naturally expected him to be in the Cabinet and were disappointed:

> We are very sorry you are not there. Yet we understand you intend to explain that it was your own wish to remain out for the present.

McGee then rose and did something which no one recalled ever seeing him do before. He took a prepared statement from his pocket. Because of the confidential nature of the events which had occurred in Ottawa and which he could now disclose "as far as he was allowed to do so," he announced that he intended to read what he had to say.

His statement began with a recital that, to form his first Cabinet, MacDonald had first approached those who had taken part in the Conferences, and among them, McGee had been asked to join; but before these arrangements could mature, difficulties arose which were so serious that they threatened to deprive Canada of a Government by July 1. He then went on:

> Those difficulties left only three solutions open. Either for Mr. MacDonald to resign the whole business; or to make the number of the Cabinet larger than would probably meet the sanction of Parliament or the wishes of the country; or for some two or more gentlemen by their own action to avert both these results.

Throughout the whole course of the proceedings, McGee added, the conduct of MacDonald and his former colleagues had been personally gratifying and no one could have been "more upright and straightforward" than Cartier. Then McGee explained what he did, stressing that it was the result of his own voluntary decision:

> My friend Dr. Tupper and myself determined between us in a sort of Committee of two that we would both decline seats at the Council, Dr. Tupper proposing in the handsomest manner to substitute Honorable Edward Kenny of Halifax for himself, and at the same time to preserve the proportion agreed on by all as desirable.
>
> In this proposition I heartily concurred.

McGee, describing Kenny in magnanimous terms as "a man and a merchant of high standing," confirmed how Kenny had accepted this duty in order to complete the first Federal Cabinet:

> To this Union Cabinet, gentlemen, I propose, should I again repre-sent you, to give hearty and zealous support.
>
> Some of my best friends, and some others whom I have not lately known in that character, have expressed many decided opinions that I ought to take another course.

Here McGee said he wished to be very frank. The interests were too vital and too vast, he declared, for any act of his to embarrass or impede the Government in any way:

> The Government should have a full, fair and generous trial.

McGee then read extracts from an exchange of correspondence which he had just had with *Sir* John A. MacDonald. The first letter, written by McGee on Tuesday, July 2, from Toronto was read in full, except for its first paragraph which he omitted:

> Bay Street, Tuesday morning
>
> My dear MacDonald:
>
> Agreeably to your request I returned from Cornwall, and re-mained over till today, but it would be a very great convenience both to Mrs. McGee and myself if we could leave this afternoon for Montreal. I am sure, however, that on presenting myself there I shall be beset by good and kind and constant friends, as well as by the curious generally, for political explanations, which, without your concurrence (or rather perhaps I should say His Excellency's per-mission), I do not feel that I have any right to make.
>
> What I should be able to say to my friends, does not so much concern myself as the general interest of the class to which very many of them belong, namely the Irish Catholics of the Dominion. Mr. Kenny's appointment to office ought, in my opinion, to be a guarantee to them that they were, and are to be fairly considered in the Executive Councils of our Common Country. But, unfortunately, all men are not equally reasonable, and I fear that the appeals lately made to this large and important body, by designing demagogues who have no particle of real regard for them at heart, are produc-ing a mischief, which even in my own constituency, I shall find my-self powerless to correct.
>
> Now I think you know that there is one sort of power I am very ambitious of, namely, to hold the good opinion of my friends. What I want you, therefore, is, with His Excellency's permission and the

concurrence of your colleagues, to provide me with such a memorandum of the proposed policy of the new Government, as will enable me to fight the Union battle, not only at Montreal, but anywhere else where I may be of use, with advantage to the vast public interests at stake. For I will add frankly that I should deplore as the greatest calamity that could now befall us, a sectarian, in addition to a sectional organization. I would do anything possible to one man to avoid such a state of things, and I hope you may see your way to arming me with such a memorandum of facts and intentions, as will help me to do so.

P.S. I add with great pleasure to your address, those marks of honourable distinction which you and my other ex-Colleagues have so honorably achieved.

MacDonald's reply was an artful letter, and dated the very same day. Although it attempted to explain away the generous nature of McGee's withdrawal as impetuous, McGee did not comment. As he read it he seemed to be studying it anew:

After I had offered you a seat in the Cabinet, you should, I think, have consulted with me before taking the course you did.

I quite appreciate the generous feeling which induced you and Tupper to throw yourselves into the breach. The difficulties of adjusting the representation in the Cabinet from the several Provinces were great and embarrassing. Your disinterested and patriotic conduct, and I speak of Tupper as well as yourself, had certainly the effect of removing those difficulties.

Still, I think you should have first consulted me. However, the thing is done and cannot be undone for the present, but I am sure that at a very early day your valuable services will be sought for by the Government.

Mr. Kenny will be received in the Lower Provinces as a most fitting representative of the Irish Catholic body in the Cabinet; but in Upper Canada he is unknown, whilst the name of D'Arcy McGee is there a household word. I need scarcely say to you, that as an individual, I valued your assistance in the Government ever since we have been colleagues. Nor need I assure you of my desire as a statesman to give full representation in the Government to the Catholic body.

I see that George Brown, after vilifying them and all they hold sacred for years, is now endeavouring to secure the support of the Catholics by the shallow device of getting some half a dozen of them nominated by Grit Conventions. This is, however, too flimsy a trick to catch your co-religionists. They are too wise to make such a bad bargain as to give the Catholic vote to Grit candidates, in exchange for the nomination of six or seven in constituencies where they have no chance of being elected. It is an exchange of substance for shadow.

Having read from the letters, McGee concluded without ardour:

It will be seen that Sir John A. MacDonald and the Union Party are thus publicly pledged in favour of the doctrine of the representation of minorities, in Ontario and in every other Province. In fact, we are the authors of the doctrine of the representation of minorities, embodied, in spite of all the efforts of Mr. Brown, in Section 93 of the British North America Act.

As he finished reading, McGee's rich voice had faded to a monotone and his last words sounded like a lifeless echo. He sat down in silence. His hearers were uncertain whether to applaud or not, and some did. But that was lost in the rumble of talk that arose from two hundred bewildered followers.

When McGee had entered Mechanics Hall, he had been handed a telegram informing him that Edward Kenny had left Ottawa that morning, and was then probably across the street at St. Lawrence Hall. A deputation was sent to ask Kenny to join the meeting, but word finally came back that Mrs. Kenny had suddenly taken ill which prevented Kenny from visiting them.

While they were waiting, someone in the audience asked McGee if he knew when the next election would be held. McGee paused, put his prepared statement back in his pocket, and stepped forward. He was himself once again:

I don't know. But for my part, the sooner the better. If the writs are sent out tomorrow, I am ready.

# 22

## NO FEEBLE FIGHTER

It ought to be the glory of a representative to live in the
closest correspondence with his constituents. Your representative owes you, not his industry only, but his judgment.
And he betrays instead of serving you, if he sacrifices it
to your opinion.

*Edmund Burke*

And be the drink I drink
Clear water from the mountain stream.
"THE SONG OF THE HERMIT,"
FROM THE IRISH, NINTH CENTURY

D'Arcy McGee was not what a political chieftain would call "a manageable man." Yet he was in many ways a practical politician. Though still retaining the yearnings of a writer (with more than fifteen books to his credit) he practised the trade of a politician skilfully, if recklessly.

The formation of the first Federal Cabinet of Canada, improvised around the generous withdrawal of McGee and Tupper, was in effect a harsh political setback for him. Yet it was part of his resilient temperament to meet this adversity by striving to regain the lost ground in his own way. John A. MacDonald knew McGee well enough to realize this, and was not too sure just what McGee might do as a private member.

McGee had never lost an election, and he was now facing his fourth. In 1857 he was elected on his own as an Independent. In the general elections of 1861 and 1863, being more immersed in organized politics, he was returned with clearer commitments to political parties. But he had never fully shed his independent attitude. Nor was McGee lacking in advisers, whether gratuitous or interested. There were those who were so embittered by McGee's exclusion from the Cabinet that they were urging him to leave John A. MacDonald and revert to his original independent position; there were others in the wards who foresaw a loss of patronage and were losing interest in supporting him merely as a private member; and there were the usual number of fair-weather friends and wiseacres with political gossip.

Irish Catholics had traditionally been Liberal Reformers in Upper Canada. Moylan of the *Canadian Freeman* had quit their ranks under the influence of Bishop Lynch of Toronto to support John A. MacDonald. And by another path McGee had reached the same position. This had happened mainly because the stand of the Reformers against Separate Schools had cut the Catholics off from hope. But now that this was no longer an issue and Confederation was achieved, George Brown was busy rebuilding the Liberal Reform Party and felt the need to win the Catholics back. In fact, some two hundred Catholic delegates were about to meet in Toronto on July 9 as a special political convention in order to repudiate the Conservatives and reassert their former ties with Reform.

Brown was delighted and expressed it in a letter of July 5 to Luther Holton in Montreal:

> The fun of it is that there was not one word passed nor a demand been made nor any inducement sought or offered that might not be cried from any house top in the country.

John A. MacDonald showed his concern by a telegram to Moylan, followed by a letter, urging him "to checkmate and counteract the movement of this Catholic Grit Convention"; and there was just a trace of uneasiness in the remark which he added:

> McGee proposes to go to Toronto on the 9th, but I suppose will not attend the Convention.

On July 10, in a letter to MacDonald, Senator Alexander Campbell went so far as to offer to resign from the Cabinet, if any urgent need arose, in order to make room for McGee.

Bishop Lynch addressed a letter to the delegates at this Catholic Convention, stating that the Catholics of Ontario would do well to support the Coalition Government as it was constituted in Ottawa and give it a fair trial. Then on his own, McGee confirmed in public that his withdrawal from the Cabinet was a voluntary act on his part, and that he would remain loyal to his former Cabinet colleagues.

Against the advice of his friends and his doctor, McGee decided to run in two constituencies in 1867. The first was, of course, his own riding of Montreal West, where he would be a candidate for the Federal House of Commons. The second was the riding of Prescott, where he would run as a candidate for the Ontario Provincial Legislative Assembly.

This was a brave departure, but not so novel then as it may seem now. The first elections for the Federal House and for the Provincial Assemblies were being held concurrently as Canada's new Constitution came into effect on July 1, 1867. A system of dual representation then permitted the same man to sit in the Federal House and the Provincial Assembly, and a number were to do it, such as Sandfield MacDonald, Pierre Chauveau and Joseph Howe. At that time, too, the elections were open and staggered; that is to say, polling extended over two days with the results of the first day's voting announced before the polls opened for the second day; and different days were set for the elections in different constituencies extending over a period of about two weeks, so that, for example, the results of the Federal or the Provincial election in Kingston could be known a good week before the polls would be open in Montreal.

McGee was convinced of the need for more English-speaking Catholic representation in the new Ontario Provincial Assembly. He knew the county of Prescott, and he felt that with twelve hundred Protestants and nine hundred Catholics on the electoral list, he had a fighting chance; so he made up his mind to run there, too. It was a decision taken without too much thought for political success, and none at all for his own health.

In Montreal West, McGee joined forces with Alexander Ogilvie, a prominent miller and grain merchant who was running at the same time and in the same riding for the Quebec Assembly.

McGee's Federal opponent in Montreal West was the forceful, colourful lawyer Bernard Devlin, running as an Independent Liberal. Devlin and George Clerk, it will be recalled, were the two delegates from Montreal at the Buffalo Convention in 1856, where they first met McGee; and the following year Devlin was the man who nominated McGee as candidate for Montreal West. But rivalry rather than friendship had soon developed between them. "Barny" Devlin, as everyone knew him, gained prominence in the trial of the St. Albans raiders; and his practise in the criminal field was lucrative. Temperate speech was not one of his characteristics.

Devlin's plan for his political campaign against McGee was simple and ingenious. Montreal West was then made up of three wards: St. Ann's, which was predominantly Irish Catholic; St. Lawrence, predominantly French Canadian and St. Antoine, predominantly English-speaking Protestant.

French-Canadian voters looked either to Cartier, who was lukewarm about McGee, or to Dorion, who opposed McGee. English-speaking Protestants generally supported McGee; and the Montreal *Gazette* was entirely in his favour. Devlin felt he could make lateral attacks through Luther Holton and the Montreal *Herald,* and sensed that many of McGee's speeches were going over the heads of the people. So he decided to concentrate on local issues and exploit McGee's weaknesses.

What made McGee unbeatable in the past was the complete support he obtained from the Irish. But this was now open to question. Ever since the controversy about McGee's speech at Wexford, the atmosphere was heavily charged with emotions about Fenianism, and there were sections of McGee's support which were obviously unstable. Many Irishmen felt that McGee had said too much; and others accused him of abandoning the cause of Ireland's freedom and condoning England's oppressive policy for the sake of his own personal advancement.

Devlin was not a Fenian. In fact, he had served as lieutenant colonel with the volunteers mustered to resist the Fenians. But Devlin was one of those who considered that prudence was a calculation rather than a quality, and it was expedient now to say nothing about the Fenians. If the battle-cry in the campaign should become Fenianism, which Mc-Gee could easily be led into accepting, then Devlin reckoned McGee would quickly become the centre of a passionate issue and at the right moment Alexander Ogilvie might be induced to withdraw from McGee as too controversial, and to follow his own path towards a quieter success.

Devlin opened his campaign ahead of McGee at a well-attended meeting on Thursday, July 11, at Mechanics Hall on St. James Street. He made it clear that he was chiefly concerned with local issues; and he asked to be sent to Ottawa to represent the Irish of all opinions, in order to advance their interests without reserve.

McGee spent the first ten days of July working on his dual organization for the coming campaigns in both Montreal West and Prescott. This naturally broadened his approach; and on the same day that Devlin held his opening meeting McGee wrote to John A. MacDonald with these observations:

I found the feeling in Montreal more unsettled than I could imagine.

Rose's retirement had emboldened the enemy; and besides there were local causes of irritation both in Cartier's quarter and my own, which were being artfully fomented.

Being on the spot for a few days, I think I have done some good for Cartier, and I'm sure I have for myself.

My explanations have, I think, satisfied every real friend that I have in the city, and, I have even heard, made converts. I have seen Mr. Kenny and introduced my principal friends, upon whom he has made, as I was sure he would, a most favourable impression.

On full reconsideration, I did not go to Toronto, and I am glad I did not. The Grit-Fenian clique in that vicinity would not have asked better than to offer me personal affronts, and as these things are epidemic, the whole tone of my election tour would be spoiled at the start. I go to Prescott tomorrow and shall oscillate between Prescott and Montreal for the present week or ten days. I shall have contests in both.

Devlin is really canvassing hard, with the Holton-*Herald* clique in the background, but I shall beat him easily by 1000 votes. Of Prescott I am not as sure up to date.

D'Arcy McGee opened his Montreal election campaign of 1867 for Montreal West in a remarkable manner. His first meeting was held jointly with Ogilvie on Wednesday, July 16, at Mechanics Hall; and long before the candidates appeared it was so crowded that hundreds had to be turned away. In terms rarely heard from a practical politician, McGee expressed his attitude:

If I am to be again elected for this division, I shall go into the House of Commons as one of the members for the whole country of Canada. Halifax and Saint John so far as I understand their wants, shall be as near to me politically as Montreal or Toronto.

This tone was maintained throughout his speech. Speaking of sectionalism, he denounced the false politics of George Brown and Joseph Howe in preferring "the part as greater than the whole"; both were "great partisan leaders," McGee conceded, "and able, but they are mistaken men." Even the Toronto *Globe* was describing Howe's course as "reckless and indefensible," but McGee was just as much concerned about the disruptive effects of Brown's *Globe*. Here McGee found his ground for unqualified support of the administration under Sir John A. MacDonald:

They comprise the best talents and the largest experience of public affairs existing in these Provinces, and no true patriot will throw one straw of impediment in their way. Let personal passions and personal politics be suspended for a season.

After an aside in which he confessed that he had "a dislike for the word, Dominion," McGee spoke of the British North America Act in a way that seemed to spring from his concern about the increasing sectionalism, and his fears that the new young nation could easily be torn asunder:

Assuredly I look forward to the day when the people of this country will go to the polls, not as British or Irish or French, not as Protestants or Catholics, but as Canadian subjects and fellow citizens.

This was an ideal. But in the next breath he brought it down to earth with the touch of a military strategist:

But in order that we may reach that day, and reach it soon, it is needful to conduct our detachments of population by already frequented ways and easy inclines to the general *rendezvous*.

The best basis for Canadian achievement, he continued, was a system of government so framed as to supplement the weakness of individuals, and so balanced as to adjust, so far as human foresight could provide, against the frailties common to all men; and this found its solid footing in firm guarantees to minorities:

> Canada has already played an important part in the history of civil and religious liberty, in the emancipation of the Catholics, in the enfranchisement of the Jews, in the liberation of the Negroes.

Describing Section 93 on Education as "This glorious peculiarity of our new Constitution," he added:

> It guarantees the right of the minority to educate its own youth in its own way, extends a protection never before secured, so far as I know, to any minority in any Constitution, European or American. This is fair dealing and wisdom which, I trust, may in time come to be accepted by all men, for it embodies the golden rule itself.

It was a speech worthy of a statesman. But it did not touch on local issues, and a whispering campaign was easily started. How did all this enter into the ordinary lives and the daily work of the people in the wards of St. Ann's, St. Lawrence and St. Antoine?

It was not long before the campaign fell from its high level.

No two months in McGee's entire political life were more arduous than those of his double campaign in Montreal and Prescott through the heat of the summer of 1867. Those days were crowded with hard work, travelling, intrigue, surprises, abandonment, reversals, illness, drinking, violence and almost everything except quitting.

Early in the campaign a desperate attitude showed among the Opposition. When Luther Holton heard surprising news about Sandfield MacDonald, he became, as he wrote to George Brown, despondent. The surprise came about in this way.

Holton and Dorion had previously met with Sandfield MacDonald and were left with the impression that they would co-operate together, particularly in the triangular area marked by Kingston, Ottawa and Montreal, often called Central Canada, where Brown had no strength. All the while Sandfield was quietly awaiting a proposal from John A. Finally John A. made his offer: Sandfield would form his "Patent Combination" made up of Old Reformers and a few Grits and Tories, with an appearance similar to John A.'s Coalition; John A. would support Sandfield as the first Premier of Ontario in return for Sandfield's support of John A. in the Federal field; and the two MacDonalds would "hunt in pairs." Sandfield accepted, and the deal was made.

In one brilliant stroke John A. had cut Brown's movement back to a limited area around Toronto and the western section of Ontario; the *Rouges* under Dorion had been isolated, and the recalcitrant Liberals in New Brunswick left leaderless.

On the last Sunday in July, Holton spent a good part of the day preparing a long and confidential report to Brown. His discouragement was passing away, but it left a residue of bitterness. No words were strong enough for Holton to describe Sandfield; he was "despicable," "disgusting," "unprincipled" and guilty of "the last great treason." Holton was himself a candidate in Châteauguay, where he was meeting serious opposition from T. K. Ramsay. So he took comfort in noting every sign of dissension in the ranks of John A. MacDonald:

> There is a strong disposition to check Cartier's dictatorship; his conduct and especially his recent appointments have disgusted many of his more judicious friends; and Galt is very unpopular.

Then Holton had this to say about McGee:

> Matters begin to look as if D'Arcy would get hoisted in Montreal West. We are not identifying ourselves very closely with the Devlin candidature. But at the proper time we shall give him all the assistance we can. D'Arcy's personal conduct which is as bad as ever is disgusting everybody.

Holton was not the only one who was upset by Sandfield MacDonald. D'Arcy McGee and Sandfield MacDonald were running both as Federal and Provincial candidates and, as it turned out, in neighbouring ridings of Prescott and Cornwall; so both, though still inveterate adversaries, found themselves looking to John A. MacDonald for help and direction. How John A. MacDonald was able to succeed in keeping the support of two such opponents, while holding one apart from the other, was revealed in three letters.

On July 13, while McGee was canvassing as a Provincial candidate in Prescott, he wrote in plain terms to John A. MacDonald in Ottawa about Sandfield MacDonald's Federal opponent in Cornwall:

> I am bound, with your full approval and consent, to support Duncan Lachlin McDonald for Cornwall. I, therefore, while willing to swallow Sandfield (disagreeable as he is) as your selection for an

Ontario Premier, wish you to tell me frankly in return, if this includes making that man the ministerial candidate of the Federal Government for Cornwall.

Please answer this in some words I can understand. For sooner than desert my friend, Duncan Lachlin, whom I led on in your name and my own, I will withdraw from this contest and from every other, but my own old constituency.

John A. MacDonald replied at once by telegram and promptly delivered a reassuring note to McGee, which McGee acknowledged the following day:

Thanks for your kind letter before going west and for your telegram about Cornwall, which completely relieves my anxiety. I was most anxious not to give Duncan Lachlin McDonald any cause of complaint. He is an excellent man and a true friend.

With the open support of John A. MacDonald, Sandfield MacDonald was running in Cornwall at the head of his Patent Combination for Premier of Ontario. Since he was also the Federal candidate for Cornwall, he was looking to John A. for similar, if less open, support. So when Sandfield heard that Duncan Lachlin was coming out with the pledged support of John A. to contest the Federal seat in Cornwall, and to oppose Sandfield, he naturally protested to John A. Without the least sign of disturbance, and in his own easy, sloping hand, John A. MacDonald replied one Saturday from Toronto, August 24, with this leisurely explanation:

My dear Sandfield:

I intended to have written you ere this as to your letter of the 19th with respect to Duncan Lachlin, but in the hurry of matters I neglected it.

The facts are simply these. Shortly after the last election it was represented to me that Duncan Lachlin could run against you with a prospect of success and would spend money for the purpose. I, of course, had no objection to get up an opposition to yourself, and encouraged it.

The thing had faded away almost from my mind when I got a letter from McGee, written, no doubt, at the instigation of Duncan Lachlin, in which he states (this of course is strictly between you and myself) that he was obliged to swallow you as Premier for Ontario, and that was a bitter pill enough, but that it was my affair and not his; that he had, however, at my instigation, encouraged Duncan Lachlin to come out, and that if he were going to run that he, McGee, must support him; and that if I should use my influence against Duncan Lachlin, McGee would feel himself bound to come out strongly against us and to run on opposition principles for Montreal West.

This was written at the time when the Catholic Convention in Toronto gave us so much anxiety.

My answer to McGee was simply that you had not even asked me to support you in Cornwall or elsewhere, and that, therefore, I had made no engagement of any kind with you relating to your running for the General or the Local Legislature.

This as you know is exactly the fact, and it was quite sufficient to keep McGee in the traces.

I have never had any correspondence with Mr. Duncan Lachlin that I remember in my life. I certainly have never written him about the elections that are now going on, and you have my full permission to state that I have had no communication with him on the subject.

I really forget the terms of my letter to McGee. Most likely I have a copy of it at Ottawa. At all events, I can get for you, from McGee, a copy of it. I don't suppose, however, that it would interest you much just now, inasmuch as Duncan Lachlin has not filed an appearance against you.

No sooner had McGee left Montreal to campaign for a week in Prescott than Devlin opened his attack on McGee. That was Monday, July 22, at an open-air meeting in Chaboillez Square before three thousand people. If anyone was responsible for Fenianism in Montreal, it was McGee, Devlin charged; in his youth McGee was a fiery Irish rebel and the equivalent of a Fenian, and now by continually attacking what he himself once was, McGee was simply stirring up anger, providing grounds to be called a turncoat and provoking the Fenians to conspire for revenge. Devlin promised that as president of St. Patrick's Society he would support and not attack his own people; as far as McGee was concerned, let him be condemned by the extravagances of his speech at Wexford.

The next day McGee wrote an open letter from Prescott, challenging Devlin:

I invite you to meet me face to face with the electors of Montreal West every day next week.

But Devlin knew what he was about; he had nothing to gain in debating national issues, and the small local grievances, on which he was counting, festered most when ignored. Devlin did not take up McGee's challenge.

Suddenly the spotlight was cast on larger issues. On Thursday, August 1, an unprecedented intervention occurred. The Montreal *Gazette* published a letter from Archbishop Connolly of Halifax written ten days before to Henry J. Clarke, Q.C., the secretary of McGee's election committee, in which the Archbishop openly supported McGee in this tenour:

Thomas D'Arcy McGee as an individual may have his faults and shortcomings, from which no mere human being, however great and good, can be entirely exempt. But as a public man, whose career I have narrowly watched with deepest interest since he first touched the soil of Canada, I unhesitatingly say that he has earned for himself a loftier public character, and has done more for the real honour and advantage of Catholics and Irishmen here and elsewhere, than any other I have known since the days of the immortal O'Connell. I would add one other quality. Amid the rubbish of popular claptrap and at the risk of the displeasure and clamour of the crowd, he has sought all that was sound in policy with a high-souled patriotism.

This letter had an electric effect on the campaign, and a week later the *Rouges* made a formal declaration that internal evidence showed that the letter attributed to the Archbishop was a hoax. A hoax it was not; it was extraordinary but it was genuine.

That critical period for Canada was marked by major ecclesiastical statements. In June of 1867 the four Bishops of Quebec, Rimouski, Trois Rivières and St. Hyacinthe had issued pastoral letters calling on the people to accept Confederation. But Bishop Bourget of Montreal remained silent. His personal feelings towards McGee and Cartier were strained when they opposed his policy on St. Patrick's and the Sulpicians in Rome; and George Clerk in the *True Witness*, who spoke unofficially for Bishop Bourget, remained adamantly opposed to Confederation. Yet even Bishop Bourget in a pastoral letter of July 29 finally submitted and in passive terms asked the people to accept the Federal Government. In Ontario, Bishop Lynch of Toronto had openly discouraged Catholics from organizing themselves into a political opposition to the first Government under Confederation and in August, John A. MacDonald received two letters from the Bishop of Hamilton offering his support, as well as two similar letters from the Bishop of London.

As these statements became generally known, they hurt the chances for success of both Dorion in Quebec and Brown in Ontario. Yet none of the Bishops entered into any election so openly as Archbishop Connolly did in the political contest between McGee and Devlin in Montreal. Archbishop Connolly left little room for speculation about the meaning of his reference when he added:

> Until Mr. McGee set a new and fearless example of leadership in Canada, it was commonplace for a politician to earn any amount of Irish popularity by a process similar to that adopted by the Fenian leaders, and deal largely in Irish grievances with fire and thunder and vengeance as his stock in trade, but prudently hold his tongue and carefully keep his own person away from danger while sense-less and rabid men took over and led the people blindly down to disaster.

The Archbishop of Halifax was just as deeply concerned as McGee about the undermining effects of the Fenians, particularly because of the recent changes which had galvanized them into a greater action.

The reputation of James Stephens in Ireland as a Fenian man of action was fading fast. John Mitchel had broken with the Fenians, quit his post in Paris and returned to the South in the United States to write a history of Ireland. After the dismal failure of the Fenian raid on Campobello in New Brunswick, John O'Mahony declined, a heart-heavy, desolate man; losing influence everywhere, he lived on in poverty in New York; and there, years later, he died in a garret, the toothless, dreamy old lion of the Comeraghs.

With the decline of O'Mahony and Stephens and the arrest of Michael Murphy, their chief supporter in Canada, the centre of gravity for Fenianism in Canada shifted from Toronto to Montreal. The new wing of American Fenians under Roberts, Sweeny and O'Neill was evidently gaining in strength; and about the time that McGee's election campaign opened, the Fenians in Ireland abandoned Stephens and recognized the new American Fenian wing. This wing was more outspoken and more bitter towards McGee than O'Mahony had ever been, and also much more influential. In fact, its members were so articulate that it was almost taken for granted that the Irish in the United States were opposed to McGee. Yet this was far from the case.

There were many Irishmen in the United States, men of achievement and influence like General Philip Sheridan, who understood McGee's position and quietly supported him. However, they said very little in public. There was no better example of that than Thomas Francis Meagher. His private papers would reveal how favourable he was towards McGee in the last years before his death on July 1; but most people thought he was opposed to McGee, and his private papers were not published until years later.

The committees for McGee and Ogilvie announced that as soon as McGee returned from Prescott, they would hold three joint public meetings on Thursday, Friday and Saturday evenings, the first three days of August, with one meeting in each ward and speeches in English and French.

The meeting of August 1 was fiery but without incident. On August 2, however, the meeting was held at Jolicoeur's saloon at the corner of St. Catherine and St. Lawrence Main, and just as McGee got to his feet an organized gang rushed at him, throwing eggs and other missiles to drive him outside. Ogilvie worked his way down among the crowd, trying vainly to restore order, but the gang shouted they would hear him only if he broke away from McGee and spoke on his own. This Ogilvie refused to do.

During the course of Saturday, August 3, McGee received further threats. But that night he was on hand for the third meeting. It was held at Bull's Head in Point St. Charles. Heavily guarded with police, the meeting had an ugly beginning. One of the speakers, Chapleau, tried four times to talk in French, and each time he was howled down. But McGee persisted until he got a hearing for himself, and he headed straight for the issue:

> As to Fenianism, I have strangled it when it first attempted to concentrate in Canada, and I am not going to be annoyed by its carcass.
> If it is necessary to face a domestic conspiracy, I will do so. I will not temporize with the introduction of fire-brands and foreign schemes for the destruction of the Government. I have been told that if I would let the Fenians alone, I would be let alone. But I drove the man from me.

Suddenly there was a disturbance, and McGee was stopped. He waited until it was almost subdued. Then, raising his voice above the noise, he made a startling announcement:

> Next week in the Montreal *Gazette* and the *Daily News* documents will be published on the attempts of the Fenians to form Circles in Montreal. These documents have been in my possession for two years.

That was as far as he could get. The meeting at Bull's Head broke up in wild disorder.

It did not show that night, but it was too much for McGee. Too much strain, travelling and fatigue had been coupled with too many threats and too many opportunities to drink. He suffered an acute attack of ulceration in the leg and was ordered to bed. There he had to stay for a full week, from the sixth to the twelfth of August. All his meetings for that critical period had to be cancelled.

While McGee was ill, Holton appeared publicly and spoke at a meeting for Devlin, belittling McGee:

Confederation would have been carried, whether McGee advocated it or not.

And that, he said, was emphasized when McGee was shut out of the first Confederation Cabinet. Then Holton made a direct charge:

Cartier excluded McGee from the Cabinet.

The charge was widely reported, but Cartier remained silent. This caused the Opposition to draw attention to the strange behaviour of Cartier, who, up to this point in his campaign, had never once mentioned McGee and McGee's French-Canadian support in St. Lawrence ward began to weaken. A week later, however, McGee's committee had the *Gazette* publish a denial of Holton's charge which was signed by Cartier:

I was very desirous to have Mr. McGee as one of my colleagues. His withdrawal was entirely owing to his own act.

This slow and somewhat cool statement of co-operation from Cartier did little else but draw attention to another curious fact. Sir John A. MacDonald was also holding himself aloof; he never entered McGee's riding and never spoke in his favour throughout the campaign. There was something else, too. It had been noticed very early, and by those among whom it counted, that there were no Government funds available for McGee's campaign expenses. This cautious withdrawal of most of his former colleagues had started from that day in late June when McGee was dropped from the Cabinet, and it was weighing more heavily than ever upon him as he recalled what Brown had said ten years earlier:

Politics, I believe, hardens men's hearts worse than anything else.

One person who stood by McGee, however, was Brown Chamberlin of the Montreal *Gazette*. He backed McGee completely, and almost daily, in his editorial comments. If anything, his support was too partisan, for it provoked Holton and Penny of the *Herald* to make sharper attacks on McGee.

On Wednesday, August 14, on one of his first appearances after his illness, McGee was hobbling with his cane to visit one of his committee rooms, at the corner of Ottawa and Duke streets in Griffintown, when he was pelted with stones. It became almost impossible for McGee to hold a meeting in Montreal. Then he heard that Devlin would be speaking at a contradictory meeting in Holton's riding of Châteauguay on Tuesday, August 20. So he arranged to be one of the speakers, aligning himself with Ramsay (Holton's opponent) and Cartier, as against Holton, Dorion and Devlin. It was an old-fashioned political meeting in Ste. Martine, with charges, promises, denials, heckling, retorts, insinuations, direct frontal attacks and everything to excite the electors until the early hours of the morning. McGee was back in form, in rare good humour and hitting hard, too, particularly at Holton. Everyone joined in except, as the chairman announced "due to circumstances beyond control, Mr. Devlin is unfortunately unable to be present."

The voting in Prescott was then only ten days away, so McGee left for the official nominations at L'Orignal, a small mill town on the Ottawa and the principal seat of the county. There he met his opponent, Boyd, a tall, slim man with sharp features and long greying hair combed into a dramatic knob on the top of his head; he had a good voice, and an irresistible fondness for gestures. Here again McGee was faced with a shrewd campaigner. Boyd had started his campaign much earlier than McGee and was constantly on the go, moving through the county. As a local merchant with a number of customers in his debt, he did not lack for helpers. He tried to entice Devlin to come up to Prescott, but "Barny" replied that he had more work than he could handle. So Boyd's slogan for his campaign became "No outsiders wanted."

McGee spent four busy days, filled with meetings, in Prescott and then returned home on August 26 to find that Montreal (not to his surprise) was in a turmoil. In the week that McGee was sick at home, he received an anonymous letter, illustrated with a gallows and a coffin, warning him that if he dared to say anything about the Fenians in Montreal he would be assassinated. McGee immediately had the *Gazette* publish the letter, along with his reply that he was then working on a report which would appear as soon as his health would permit, as a detailed account of "The Attempts to Establish Fenianism in Montreal." By the time McGee returned from Prescott, this account had appeared in thirty-three short, sharp chapters, stating places, dates and names, and filling fourteen columns of the *Gazette* on August 17, 20 and 23.

In it McGee charged that the first signs of Fenians in Montreal had appeared when some of them came up from Vermont during the *Trent* crisis in 1861, and tried by systematic interruptions to break up the meetings called to raise Canadian volunteers. Five years later they had infiltrated the city police to a small extent, and had persuaded eighty or ninety employees of the Grand Trunk to refuse to defend the railway lines which the Fenians threatened to cut at the western end of the Island of Montreal. And now, McGee added, the Fenians had infiltrated St. Patrick's Society. This, of course, implicated Devlin, without mentioning him, because Devlin was well known as its president.

Such statements, bristling with names and including a few prominent ones, could not escape the fate of being completely exploited by all the anger, exaggerations and sly slanders of an election campaign. There was a hard core of fact in what McGee revealed. But there was also a good part of it which was unprovable or unfounded. The threats, the violence and the fever of the campaign (and the connivance of some with ulterior motives) had pushed McGee off balance.

Then, as others joined in the excesses, matters got out of hand. For example, on the eve of the election the Montreal *Gazette* published a story charging that Devlin had just received Fenian money from Richard O'Gorman of New York. O'Gorman had belonged to the Young Ireland movement with McGee, and had escaped from Limerick to Constantinople and then made his way to the United States. But this time he was a prominent member of the New York Bar. Far from being a Fenian he was then so outspoken against them that James Stephens called him "that miserable hybrid." It was shown later that the cheque which Devlin received from O'Gorman was simply a payment of trust funds for his niece in an estate. The *Gazette* finally apologized that it "had falsely accused Devlin, but that was on September 18, when the election was over.

Such incidents were highly inflammable. McGee was burnt in effigy in Quebec City, and the atmosphere in Montreal was rising to the explosive point.

Finally the official day of nominations for Montreal West arrived. On Thursday, August 29, at Victoria Square, each candidate was called upon to speak. When McGee's turn came, a large gang made so much noise that he could hardly be heard. He tried for half an hour but it was impossible. So he adjourned to his committee rooms a block away at Mechanics Institute on St. James Street; and there from a window he spoke to the crowd in forceful terms:

> The denial of the right to free speech is a more important matter to Montreal than the selection of its representative,
>
> Attacks or threats upon my person I do not intend to notice here. But I am bound to condemn those acts whereby some of my friends have received messages threatening to burn their places of business if they venture to record their votes or use their influence in my favour.

McGee had asked John A. MacDonald to set the dates for voting in his own constituency of Montreal West (where he felt more secure) a week ahead of those to be set for Prescott (where he was venturing into a relatively unknown riding). But the dates were established in reverse order: the polls would be open in Prescott on Friday and Saturday, August 30 and 31; and in Montreal West on Thursday and Friday, September 5 and 6.

Under this arrangement, McGee suffered the disadvantage of having the results of an election where he was weaker announced before voting took place where he was stronger. And it happened as it was feared.

McGee lost in a close contest to Boyd in Prescott. This was his first defeat in an election. So on Monday, September 2, he returned for the last few hectic days of his campaign in Montreal without that greatest of electioneering *mystiques:* the myth of the undefeated politician.

On the eve of the election, Devlin spoke from the balcony over Cutler's tavern on Victoria Square, and earlier at five o'clock McGee hobbled up to sit at the window of the Mechanics Institute and address the crowd on St. James Street.

Speculation was widespread. By this time it was known that George Brown had been defeated in Southern Ontario, while John A. MacDonald had been re-elected in Kingston; and these returns helped McGee.

The polls opened in Montreal West on Thursday, and that evening the results of the first day's voting showed McGee leading by 511 votes. But this did not hide a disturbing fact. In St. Ann's Ward, which was almost solidly Irish, Devlin had received 16 more votes than McGee.

That evening, Devlin called an urgent meeting on Victoria Square where he made an impassioned plea to his followers to reverse the tide in the other wards the next day; and special preparations went forward throughout the night. From the moment the polls reopened on Friday, it was apparent that a new trend had set in for Devlin. Whether it would be strong enough to overcome McGee's dwindling lead was the question.

At five o'clock Friday evening the polls closed, and the results started to come in from the three wards. In St. Lawrence, McGee's lead of 162 from the first day was shaved down by a few votes. In St. Antoine, where McGee's advantage had been 365, Devlin cut it down by 87. So the crucial ward was St. Ann's, where Devlin had won on the first day. As the crowds milled around the polls, the first counts showed Devlin gaining, and this continued until Devlin's lead for the second day's ballot in St. Ann's reached 137.

Finally the last returns were in. The official count for the two days' voting in the three wards was made, and there was wild excitement when it was announced. Devlin had 2478 votes, and McGee 2675. So McGee was elected by a majority of 197.

It was a victory with a warning. For D'Arcy McGee's command over the solid Irish vote in St. Ann's had been broken. And most people recognized it. One old Irishman, eighty-two years old and bedridden for months, who had been carried to the poll by two friends to cast his ballot, could still smile: "I voted for McGee. All praise to him."

That night, as the final results were confirmed above the clamour, the darkness was charged with that blind force which an impersonal crowd can quickly generate. It flared into a riot. A mob surged up St. James Street and converged on the Mechanics Institute. Furious attempts were made to break into McGee's committee room, but the doors were blocked by McGee's supporters, as fighting broke out and spread rapidly. All the windows of the first two storeys of the Mechanics Institute were smashed and nearby houses were sacked. Bludgeons appeared, sling shots were used and revolvers were fired. No count was made of many minor injuries, but one man was reported seriously wounded. It was a reign of terror, though of short duration. For the police soon brought it in under control.

Evidently, the leaders of the mob had been under the impression that McGee was in his committee room in the Mechanics Institute. In fact he had met his friends briefly at St. Lawrence Hall and had retired to his home early, and very ill. Throughout that night and the next day the police kept a guard around McGee's home.

Right across the new nation it had been a rough and rowdy election. Up in Ontario the Lambton "lambs" were wilder than ever. Alexander

Mackenzie vainly tried twice to speak in a country schoolhouse, had his meetings broken up and barely escaped serious injury. Down in Yarmouth, Nova Scotia, a mob had suddenly gathered one quiet Sunday in the middle of July and burnt Charles Tupper in effigy; and the next day the only regret expressed by the anti-Confederate newspaper was that "he was not burnt himself."

In Ontario, George Brown was a victim of his overconfidence. Rather than stay in his own relatively safe seat, he had moved eastward to contest the riding of South Ontario where he was defeated by the Conservative sitting member, Gibbs, 971 to 875. As this was one of the earliest elections, the announcement of the result had a discouraging effect on his Liberal Reform Party in Ontario, but his chief lieutenant, Alexander Mackenzie, managed to win in Lambton.

In Quebec, Cartier was re-elected, but his majority, like McGee's, was substantially reduced. Galt was returned by acclamation; and Holton and Dorion were elected.

Through an unusual combination, Sandfield MacDonald was elected as Premier of Ontario and a Federal member as well. Similarly Pierre Chauveau was elected as Premier of Quebec and as a Federal member too.

THOMAS
D'ARCY
M^CGEE

Over all, it was a decisive victory for the government of Sir John A. MacDonald and his Cabinet. The Clear Grits would no longer concede that it was a "Coalition Cabinet"; in Alexander Mackenzie's biting phrase it was "a Cabinet of Tories and mongrels." But whatever it was called, it clearly controlled a safe majority of the 181 members of Canada's first Federal House of Commons.

Prime Minister MacDonald had won a clear majority of Ontario's 82 seats, swept most of Quebec's 65 seats and obtained slightly better than half of New Brunswick's 15 seats. But in Nova Scotia the result was alarming. There Joseph Howe on his platform of outright opposition to Confederation won all of the 19 seats, except one which went to Charles Tupper. More than that, in the Provincial elections of Nova Scotia all members elected were opposed to Confederation, except two.

Otherwise, the Opposition to MacDonald was fragmentary. Thirty-six Liberal Reformers were elected in Ontario and 20 *Rouges* in Quebec, but they had no working arrangement between them. The one, real and great danger came from Nova Scotia.

Four days after his election was over, McGee wrote a letter from his bed to the *Gazette*, reflecting on his views about violence:

> Riot has its charms for riotous natures, as peace for peaceful men. Let no man be deceived. A mob unpunished is a fatal precedent.
>
> Every time you permit it to act unpunished it will become stronger and the law weaker. A month ago its weapons were stones and rotten eggs. Last week it had armed itself with axe handles and revolvers.
>
> A mob is a compound crime against all society.

McGee's illness was more serious than it had ever been before. His doctor told him that he would have to be confined to his room for a lengthy period, and he resigned himself to an enforced rest with the memories of three bitter months in his heart. There was something else of a private nature which had wrought a lasting change in him. What happened was recalled later when time and tragedy had placed the endurance of his resolve beyond question. On Sunday, September 8, two days after the election, McGee said to his wife:

> Tell the grocer tomorrow to come and take the wine and liquor out of the cellar. I've made up my mind to have nothing more to do with it.

# 23

## A DREAD LIGHT

I am Raftery the poet,
Full of hope and love,
My eyes without sight,
My mind without torment,

Going west on my journey
By the light of my heart,
Tired and weary
To the end of the road.

Behold me now,
With my back to a wall,
Playing music
To empty pockets.

FROM THE IRISH OF A BLIND FIDDLER,
*Anthony Raftery*

Here is but a small part of his doings,
here is but the whisper of his voice.

JOB XXVI: 14

The autumn of 1867 and the severe winter which followed were marked by the painful and recurring illness of D'Arcy McGee. The controversies between Devlin and McGee continued after the election, and the Montreal *Gazette* and its opponent, the *Herald,* kept up their dispute about the violence in the election. But their sharpest comments concerned the charges of Fenianism in St. Patrick's Society. And these brought more anonymous threats to McGee to aggravate his illness. The circulation of blood in his foot was very poor, and the ulceration was worse. But he was far too tense and wrought up to relax and remain in bed as his doctor had ordered.

Instead of remaining at home, McGee left Montreal on September 26 for Ottawa. The newspapers explained his trip as "a matter of private business," and this renewed an earlier rumour that he was about to retire from politics, because of his broken health and bad financial condition, to accept "a lucrative Government position," probably as Queen's Printer. The prospect of another political campaign enflamed the controversies, which did not subside even when McGee denied the rumours.

The Montreal *Herald* made a vicious attack on McGee, calling him a "common drunkard," a "hired and false informer," a "scoundrel" and a "liar." Before he returned to Montreal, McGee replied in kind, with an exasperated open letter holding Edward Penny and Andrew Wilson of the *Herald* responsible for libel. In his scornful counter-attack McGee said he had never charged the *Herald* with Fenianism as they had implied; but he would now assert that they had connived with Devlin, and had played the silent game of compliance by tolerating the underhand work of Fenians in Montreal for their own political advantage. On the other hand, Devlin had reason to be angry with the *Gazette* because of its false attack on him that he had received Fenian money from Richard O'Gorman of New York.

The bitterness between Devlin and McGee, each egged on by the *Herald* and the *Gazette,* came to a head when McGee returned to Montreal. As McGee stepped out of Moretti's Shop on St. James Street he met Devlin face to face; what happened was recorded that night by George Clerk in his diary:

October 2, Wednesday: A row betwixt Devlin and McGee on account of letters of the latter in today's *Gazette*. Devlin spat in McGee's face near Post Office. Much talk.

The rest of the month of October was a trying period for McGee. This time he obeyed his doctor and remained at home. In fact, there was no choice, for the disease in his foot had become acute. His low spirits were reflected by the lines he wrote at the time:

> Where Age has no regret and Youth no passion,
> Know you that sunless land?

As the tone of his writing showed, the suffering he experienced had a probing and purging effect upon him. In those recesses where philosophies never enter, pain made some things plain to him. He drew upon his faith for strength and read at length, particularly from the Old Testament.

In a few weeks he was well enough to return to earlier interests. He wrote a paper to the Lower Canada Protestant Teachers' Convention urging the development of "evening schools for adults, apprentices and others during the six months of winter," which was read in his absence by Principal Dawson on October 19. The *Gazette* recalled how in 1844 McGee with a few citizens of Boston had succeeded in opening five adult night schools, and five years later in New York had started a similar project which had grown, as the New York *Evening Mail* attested, into a high school, two coloured schools and thirteen male and eleven female schools, with twenty-one hundred scholars being in attendance.

Towards the end of October, with the short, golden days of Indian summer, McGee's spirit brightened and he wrote to the Sadliers in New York:

> *A propos* of your coming, we are all anxiously expecting you. Do not come on us like the Gospel "thief in the night." And come before the 6th of November, on which day I am summoned with the rest of the wise men of the Dominion of Canada, to advise Her Majesty what she is to do with the said Dominion.
>
> At present the weather is most exquisitely lovely, and if it should last two or three weeks, you will be charmed with your old city and its surroundings. If you could come up with me to Ottawa, the opening of the first Parliament of the new Confederacy will be worth seeing; and the voyage up the Ottawa itself will certainly be pleasant, if the weather is good.

But James and Mary Sadlier were unable to join D'Arcy and Mary McGee as they prepared to leave for Ottawa.

On the day before they left, more than ordinary interest was stirred at the Montreal Literary Club by the fact that the speaker was D'Arcy McGee. It was his first speech in public since his election. Still unable to walk, he was obliged to sit throughout his talk, as he spoke on "The Mental Outfit of the New Dominion." It proved to be one of his best addresses. As he concluded by urging youth to read the Bible, there was a touch of nostalgia:

> If we wish our younger generation to catch the inspiration of the highest eloquence and noblest patriotism, it will be found in the sadness beyond the solace of a song which bowed down the exiles by the waters of Babylon.

Wednesday, November 6, 1867, in Ottawa, was a clear, crisp day, resplendent with colour and ceremonial. The first Parliament of the Dominion of Canada was opening, and D'Arcy McGee had made a special effort with his wife to be in attendance.

The dead leaves had been swept from Parliament Hill, and all was ready for an ancient ritual in a new land. The most fetching figure was the Gentleman Usher of the Black Rod. He was gotten up in superb style, spreading lace ruffles, closely moulded coat, tight knee-breeches, silk stockings, pumps, sword and full coat regalia, lacking only the powdered wig to make him perfectly uncomfortable.

Yet the rites so solemnly performed that day had their meaning. For they enshrined the highest attainments of liberties in the past and now embraced a new experiment of different cultures as a new nation. Confederation in Canada was both a novelty and a marvel in political architecture. Constructed, so to speak, in defiance of the strong slope of the land to the south, this new political edifice was built and balanced on a remarkably slender base, stretching from unsteadiness in the East towards uncertainty in the Far West. There were racial, religious and regional strains within it, and economic movements in the soil beneath it, all to be withstood in order to endure. Among many bonds holding it together, two can be mentioned. There was the railroad, which would push its way both east and west to become the spinal column of continental Canada. And of a different nature entirely, generally invisible, weak in some spots but strong in the critical areas, there was the magnetism of the ancient Crown.

The Members of the House of Commons assembled amid talk that

McGee would be elected as Speaker; but his health would have prevented it, in any event, and the rumour was groundless. McGee was assigned to a seat on the Treasury Bench, and looking unusually serious and sallow, he limped to his place in the front row on the Government side.

Sitting two seats to his right was Galt. Resourceful and independent, Galt had promoted the principle of Confederation as steadily as McGee. Yet Galt came to Ottawa one day earlier in order to resign as Minister of Finance, which he did. Sir John A. received the blow with an outward show of nonchalance and a thoroughly uninhibited remark:

Galt is as unstable as water. He has the characteristic of a chameleon, and can't be trusted because of his drinking habits.

MacDonald had no choice but to accept Galt's resignation, but he soon found a seat for John Rose in Huntingdon, who became the new Minister of Finance.

Five seats to McGee's left was Cartier, Minister of Militia and Defence, and the one man in the House who had worked for years without a break with John A. MacDonald. Now, because of the quarrel over titles, a coolness had developed between them, and intimacy would never really return to their political partnership.

Yet sitting right beside Cartier and appearing as friendly as ever, with his lounging, patient and pleasant air which hid everything except a shade of dissipation, was Sir John Alexander MacDonald. In open waters and out on deck, he could be a doughty fighter; but it was in the shifting sands of coalitions, the cross-currents of suspicion and the sudden squalls that blow up among politicians that he showed himself to be the cool pilot. There was no doubt that John A. with his vagrant hair, slightly bulbous nose and intelligent eyes, possessed that rare blend of tact, procrastination, toughness and practical wisdom to make him the Prime Minister.

On the Opposition benches, sitting side by side as desk mates but belonging to different worlds, were Antoine Aimé Dorion, olive-skinned, cultured, supple and intelligent, and Alexander Mackenzie, rigid, untrained, blunt and courageous. Yet the man who had been temporarily assigned by the Government to the seat of Leader of the Opposition, to the consternation of everyone, was John Sandfield MacDonald.

There was a twist of irony in this. Sir John A. MacDonald was the first Prime Minister of Canada under Confederation, and Sandfield MacDonald, as the nominal Leader of the Opposition, had also been elected (with the aid of Sir John A.) as the first Premier of the Province of Ontario. Yet three years earlier the two MacDonalds were the chief men who had voted against Confederation in the House Committee on the Constitution which had been sponsored by Brown and McGee.

Now, as Confederation began its life in Parliament, Brown had been defeated in his bid to be a Member of the House, McGee had been dropped from the Cabinet, Galt had suddenly resigned as a Minister and Cartier, like Galt without his title, was angry. The best organized force among the Opposition was the compact power from Nova Scotia, under the command of "that pestilent fellow" (as Sir John A. called him) Joseph Howe.

The baffled genius of Joseph Howe came to haunt that Session. Two

JOSEPH
HOWE

days before Parliament opened in Ottawa, Joseph Howe as the member for Hants of Nova Scotia, and Timothy Anglin as the member for Gloucester of New Brunswick, on their way through Montreal, attended the annual concert of St. Patrick's Society, where Howe spoke. The Montreal *Gazette* was quick to remark the peculiarity that Bernard Devlin as president did not ask D'Arcy McGee as a guest, and in inviting Howe and Anglin, Devlin had selected the two most outspoken opponents of Confederation.

Howe's reputation as a tribune had travelled ahead of him, and Ottawa was curious to hear him. Hearty and expansive, he was instinctively disposed to support a vast project like Confederation; and perhaps, if Tupper had not promoted it, Howe might well have been the one to do so. But Tupper, in the jealous eye of the aging Howe, was young and his advocacy of Confederation was too aggressive and cocky to suit Howe, who was ready to sum it up in a sentence:

The game of brag played by Tupper has lasted long enough.

Those who disliked Howe described his style of speaking as "all sail and no anchor." He was not superficial, however, and his past accomplishments for responsible government were there to prove it.

At the age of sixty, Howe was a sad figure. A man of tantalizing promise and sensitive pride, he found himself fighting a courageous, disappointing rear-guard action, which someone described with heartless accuracy:

His day has gone by, and he babbles of the past as if he were fighting over again the battles of self-government.

His pride in his past achievements, which were no longer very relevant, betrayed his frailty; and the Halifax *Morning Chronicle* wrote on February 25, 1867: "The old man is vanity struck." For him Confederation became "preposterous and absurd" as he carried both his audience and himself away with his rhetoric:

I would not be such an idiot as to embark in this crazy Confederacy with a mongrel crew half French and English and certain to be sent to the bottom at the first broadside.

Lately his hair was thinning and his open countenance showed signs of worry. He had personal financial difficulties, and at times he admitted he was "lonely, weary and vexed." Despite his natural buoyancy, he had become the chief exponent of negative, sectional views; so he comforted himself in the role that he "was fighting the battles of Nova Scotia."

Indeed, what Howe was saying in such forceful phrases appealed to Nova Scotians, because most of them half believed it themselves. The Maritimes, they felt, would be swamped by the Canadians; they would be immersed in racial and religious quarrels not their own; they would have to pay for the most expensive of all possible forms of government; their sea trade would be neglected; and they would have to bear their share of enormous military costs to defend endless open miles of boundaries that were really indefensible.

A full week went by and McGee could make only an occasional appearance in the House. But on Thursday, November 14, word spread that he would speak that evening in the debate on the Speech from the Throne. As the galleries filled up, special interest was added when it became known that McGee, though ill all day, had left his bed, determined to fulfil his first engagement to speak in the House of Commons under Confederation.

It was a speech of admonishing eloquence, delivered under physical difficulty; more than one reporter remarked that McGee, supporting himself with a chair, appeared to suffer considerable pain as he spoke of the lesson to be drawn from the American Civil War:

> We were taught that the days of colonial comedy of government were over and gone, and that politics had become stern and almost tragic for the New World.

Although he participated sparingly in the opening work of the Session, McGee rose a few times to counterbalance the effect Howe was making upon the House of Commons. Everyone remarked a new restraint about McGee and an unusual air of gravity, which was intimated by the Montreal *Gazette:*

> Limping badly, worn out and evidently shattered in body, not handsome by any means, but gifted with noticeable eyes, he is still the fascinating, easy, graceful, elegant and brilliant speaker. To us, he seems more intellectual and far better read than Howe.

During the next four weeks McGee was ill and again confined to his room. His wife remained with him in Ottawa, nursing him back to health, and their friends Alderman James Goodwin, an Irish contractor, and his wife were very helpful. But the time was long, and they missed their home and the children, as Mrs. McGee showed in her letter from Ottawa on November 25 (enclosed in an envelope addressed in D'Arcy's own hand to "Miss Agnes Clara or Sweet Peggy"):

> My dear old Pet:
>
> I hope you and Miss Colgan are enjoying yourselves and that your dogs, birds and cats are quite well, not forgetting the dolls. I have a nice little doll dressed as a sailor and another in a cradle given to me for you by Mrs. Goodwin.
>
> I saw little Lily. She was asking for you. She played the piano for me and is greatly improved.
>
> I hope you learn your catechism every day, and your lessons and

reading, and that you amuse Miss Colgan by reading to her. I hope
Mary attends to the birds every day and that you feed Fido.

I am longing to be home again with my poor beauty. Papa joins
in love and kisses. From your affectionate

Mamma

P.S. I feel very lonesome without you.

On Tuesday, December 17, McGee was able to resume his place in
the House, and that evening he was cheered as he entered to take his
seat. His purpose in attending was to congratulate the Government on the
adoption of the final resolutions for the construction of the Intercolonial
Railway. He returned to the House the next day and spoke briefly on
the need for unity among the people of Canada, predicting that

> The next six months will be the most critical six months through
> which Canada has ever passed.

Two days later he took an independent stand when the Government
proposed to increase the postage on newspapers in the Maritimes, which
McGee opposed as "a tax upon intelligence, and an unfair burden which
would fall more heavily upon small newspapers or new ones struggling
into existence." On this particular issue, McGee cast his vote against Sir
John A. and with Alexander Mackenzie. But it did not affect his general
allegiance to the Government.

In Montreal something strange had developed. It seemed to find its
centre in St. Patrick's Society. Ten years earlier, in November 1857, the
representative membership of this Society had sponsored McGee's entry
into Canadian public life. But in the last few years it had undergone
some subtle changes which were not so easily traced in their causes as
in their effects. Developments began when Bernard Devlin became
president for three years starting in April 1865.

At a regular monthly meeting on May 1, 1865, with fifty in attendance,
twenty-eight members resigned. No reason was recorded. But a few
months later a sharp note of antagonism was shown towards D'Arcy Mc-
Gee. And it developed in a curious way.

It started in 1865 with the shooting of an Irish immigrant named Felix
Prior, who had been keeping company with a maid in a prominent residence on Drummond Street. One evening he set out to see her, but he
met some friends on the way and took a long time in getting there. Finally
he arrived alone, somewhat intoxicated. Unfortunately he decided to go
in by the back way, and in his confusion he tried to enter the wrong

house. This neighbour mistook him for a burglar and grappled with him in the dark. What happened was never made clear, but in the tussle that followed Prior was shot and killed.

The coroner's jury exonerated the neighbour who was a wealthy English-speaking Protestant, and rendered a verdict of justifiable homicide. But the case did not die there. Prior's friends felt that the investigation was too brief and that justice was too summary. They voiced their protests at a meeting of St. Patrick's Society, and gave the case a racial interpretation. In September 1865, two anonymous letters appeared in the Montreal *Gazette* signed "A member of St. Patrick's Society," criticizing the Society for permitting a racial question to be injected into the administration of justice. Replies, protests and resolutions followed; the case became controversial, and the newspapers kept it alive for a full year. Yet no new facts were uncovered, and it merely degenerated into bad feeling. Pressure was then exerted on Cartier as Attorney General to reopen the whole case.

Near the end of October 1866, at a dinner tendered to Cartier just before he left for the London Conference, McGee made a passing reference to the Prior case:

> I had thought we had got the demon of class discord pretty well laid in our own city till I saw a crazed attempt made to make a national question out of a late deplorable homicide, and to coin the blood of a slaughtered countryman into the small currency of political intrigue.

The officers of St. Patrick's Society took this as a clear attack upon them, and at the next meeting on November 12 the forty members in attendance charged McGee with making "false, unfounded and calumnious accusations," and called upon him to reply. McGee did not help matters by treating the charges with scorn.

Then on January 14, 1867, a mysterious fire occurred at Nordheimer's Hall, where St. Patrick's Society had just held a meeting, and (so it was said) some of its books and correspondence were destroyed or disappeared. McGee claimed that these lost documents included the minutes of a meeting held in Montreal for John O'Mahony, the Fenian Head Centre, and an exchange of letters with him and other Fenians. This was hotly denied, and it remained unproved.

One week after the fire, Father Patrick Dowd intervened, and as chaplain of the Society wrote a firm letter to its members warning them of "internal dissensions which could lead to fatal divisions in the Society."

St. Patrick's Society promptly met and replied to Father Dowd, formally denying such rumours as false:

They are propagated solely by a few individuals who, unable any longer to use this Society for the advancement of their own social ends, have resorted to such contemptible means.

The next development occurred on October 7, one month after Devlin was defeated by McGee in the Federal election. A formal notice of motion was given at the regular monthly meeting of St. Patrick's Society to expel D'Arcy McGee as a member. There was no discussion. Everyone awaited the motion and debate at the subsequent meeting.

In Ottawa the next month, on November 14, McGee remarked that only ten days before, while Joseph Howe and Timothy Anglin were present as guests in Montreal, a group within St. Patrick's Society had unexpectedly taken advantage of this meeting to honour some Fenian names. Because of this renewal of Fenian activity, McGee added that it would be unwise to allow the suspension of the *Habeas Corpus* Act to expire. Anglin, who twenty years earlier had been with McGee when the Young Ireland movement was crushed by the English Government's suspension of the *Habeas Corpus* Act, rose from the Opposition benches and rebuked McGee for his remarks:

He is casting a slur on the Irish in Montreal for the sake of building himself up.

On December 2 St. Patrick's Society met in Montreal and adopted a resolution thanking Anglin for his speech and condemning McGee as a calumniator. This resolution was published in the Montreal *Gazette* on December 13. But no action was taken on the proposal to expel McGee as a member of the Society.

Two days later, though confined to his room in Ottawa, McGee wrote an open letter to the Ottawa *Times* declaring that, while he was still a member of St. Patrick's Society, it was his duty to reveal how it had been diverted from its original purposes and was allowing Fenians to work in hiding behind its good national name. McGee made these explicit charges:

John O'Mahony had come to Montreal in 1864 and had spoken as the Fenian Head Centre on the invitation of F. B. McNamee, one of the present officers of St. Patrick's Society.

At dinners held by a small set of seventeen people on St. Patrick's Day in 1864 at the Exchange Hotel and again in 1865 at the St.

Louis Hotel, the speeches were sympathetic to the Fenians. Among those present were F. B. McNamee, O. G. Devlin, Daniel Lyons, W. B. Lenihan, J. J. O'Meara and J. McGrath, all of whom (except the last) had lately become prominent in the activities of St. Patrick's Society.

As for J. McGrath, he attended the Fenian Convention at Philadelphia in 1865 as "a delegate from Canada."

Michael Murphy, then the Fenian Centre in Toronto, accompanied by F. B. McNamee, had taken up a collection among members of St. Patrick's Society, exploiting their good faith by telling them the money was "for the relief of Ireland," without disclosing that it was destined for the treasury of the Fenian Brotherhood in New York.

Fenian names and mottoes had been displayed at the St. Patrick's Day dinners of the Society during the past three years, without any word of objection from Bernard Devlin who was presiding.

And other such circumstantial evidence indicated that a small set of designing people were trying to get hold of persons and positions of influence where the conspiracy of Fenians could be sheltered.

As soon as D'Arcy McGee published these sensational accusations, the motion pending before St. Patrick's Society for his expulsion was pressed. Through the intervention of some influence (whose it was never became clear), the motion was not put to a vote. It was deferred until January 1868. But the handwriting was on the wall.

As 1867, the first year of Confederation, came to a close, D'Arcy McGee wearily left Ottawa, where, after undergoing some painful surgery, he had spent most of November and December in bed. The train from Ottawa was badly delayed, and he was worn out when he reached Montreal at five o'clock Sunday morning, three days before Christmas. On December 27 McGee sent Alderman James Goodwin, "as a slight New Year's gift," the two volumes of his *History of Ireland*, adding a note about his health:

The foot, you will be glad to hear, continues to improve, though slowly. I suppose I am in for another month or six weeks' room-keeping; and shall be well content to cry quits with the doctors then.

In McGee's political survey at the end of the year 1867, the chief cause of concern for the future of Confederation lay in the Maritimes.

Nova Scotia, in particular, now dominated by Joseph Howe, was threatening to secede. On the last day of December Sir John A. MacDonald, confiding his own worries to Archbishop Connolly in Halifax, admitted that Joseph Howe and his solid bloc of anti-Confederate members from Nova Scotia were exasperating him:

> I must say that they tried our patience extremely. Howe talked a great deal of nonsense and some treason, but we bore with it all.
> There must be an end to this kind of thing, however, and language of the same kind will not be permitted when we assemble again.

McGee had clung to the hope that Prince Edward Island would soon join in Confederation. But unlike all the other Provinces, from its earliest days, it was well settled and under cultivation, and had little feeling left for the empty spaces or any adventures of expansion. Lately, bad news for the cause of Confederation had come from the Island, with the loss

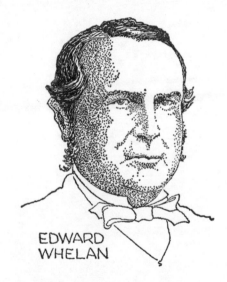

EDWARD
WHELAN

of one of its most consistent supporters. Edward Whelan died on December 10 at the age of forty-three. Among the Fathers of Confederation, it was an early death, and it intimately affected McGee. On December 30, the Montreal *Gazette* published these lines written by D'Arcy McGee in memory of his ardent friend:

> By this dread line of light,
> Rises upon my sight,
> Borne up the churchyard white,
> The dead, mid the bearers.

# 24

## SHADOWS AT NOON

In the time of my boyhood, I had a strange feeling
That I was to die in the noon of my day,
Not quietly into the silent grave stealing,
But torn, like a blasted oak, sudden away.

*Thomas D'Arcy McGee*

I remember so clearly the last words my father said to me,
as he was leaving for Ottawa. We were living on St.
Catherine Street two doors east of Drummond Street. I
stood at the top of the stairs to watch him go. I had a toy
stuffed dog that I called Fido under my arm.

My father said "Well, God bless you, Peggy. Take good
care of Fido and the dolls while I am gone."

*Agnes (Peggy) McGee,*

ON AUGUST 6, 1935,

HER SEVENTY-EIGHTH BIRTHDAY

It was a cold Monday night in Montreal. A chilly group of men were assembling for the adjourned monthly meeting of St. Patrick's Society at half past seven on January 27, 1868. Bernard Devlin, the president, was absent, so the first vice-president took the chair. There was a perfunctory air about the proceedings because the only item of real business had already been prepared in a written report.

This report from a special committee, appointed three weeks before "to investigate the charges brought against the Society by the Hon. Mr. McGee," was immediately read. With that done, it was then proposed that:

> in accordance with the notice of motion given on the seventh of October last, the Hon. T. D. McGee be now expelled from the Society.

What discussion followed was not recorded. The minutes merely relate that the question was put; a show of hands was taken, and, there being only one member voting against, the motion was declared carried. And Thomas D'Arcy McGee was no longer a member of St. Patrick's Society of Montreal.

Twenty new names were then nominated as future members, and the meeting terminated. But when the committee's report, signed by the acting president J. E. Mullin, and the corresponding secretary William B. Lenihan, was published the next day in the newspapers of Montreal (and repeated in Toronto, Ottawa, Halifax and Saint John) it was much more instructive, notwithstanding its selective phrasing, than the actual minutes of the meeting.

The published report began by stating that McGee had charged that St. Patrick's Society was implicated in "the attempt to establish Fenianism in Montreal," and in a suspicious fire of a year ago "the books and records of the Society" had been burned, when "the O'Mahony correspondence and some less direct evidence of Fenianism were blotted out forever." The committee added that the Society itself had asked for a judicial investigation into the cause of the fire, but Judge Coursol was busy on another inquiry, and it was "unavoidably postponed." McGee had also charged that this judicial investigation was purposely avoided, and the report explained that after the long delay the public had lost interest, and there was nothing to be gained by pursuing it. McGee had, however, repeated the charge. So the committee had been appointed to act.

The committee's report then cited the guarded text of a certificate dated four days before the meeting. It carefully certified that "the Books of record of St. Patrick's Society dating from February 21, 1856, to this date, containing the minutes and proceedings of each meeting of the Society during that time, and bearing the signatures of each Secretary for the period, had been submitted to the mayor of Montreal and the presidents of the St. Jean Baptiste Society, St. George's Society, the New England Society and the German Society"; and the mayor and these officers had signed this certificate.

The report then declared:

> With so incontrovertible a statement before the public, this wanton accusation of Mr. McGee was not only false but malicious and vindictive; and all other charges made by Mr. McGee would be treated as mere accusations which have already been met, until such time as Mr. McGee controverts the above and explains his criminal conduct.

This public statement from St. Patrick's Society went on to conclude:

> Under these circumstances we must take leave of Mr. McGee.
>
> We have not the time nor the desire to enter into further discussions with him. We regard him as a public slanderer, and it is with the public he must now settle the question of his conduct. St. Patrick's Society will treat any further statements from him with contempt.
>
> At this meeting, which was one of the largest and most influential since the annual meeting in April last, Mr. McGee was expelled from the Society.
>
> Only one member dissented, who explained that while in favour of the expulsion of Mr. McGee, he merely thought it should be deferred to a future meeting.

The following week the assertion about the number of persons present at this meeting was contested. It was not "one of the largest and most influential" of meetings, the *Gazette* stated; only sixty members were present, and it published their names. The *Gazette's* list did not indicate men of any special standing or influence, and many were recognized as workers for Devlin in the last election. Among those present were Daniel Lyons and William B. Lenihan, who were both mentioned by McGee in his charges; but F. B. McNamee was not present. Nor were there any friends or supporters of McGee. The *Gazette* also reported that "the meeting was very violent," and two members, F. M. Cassidy and Miles Murphy, had left the meeting and did not vote.

Later, when a rumour circulated that members of St. Patrick's Society were thinking of revoking this expulsion, D'Arcy McGee made a public statement:

> Under no circumstances, short of a thorough reformation of the Society as recently conducted, could I consent to my name being inserted on the new books.

Far off on the Atlantic Seaboard, matters were rapidly coming to a head to affect McGee in a very different way. Most people in Nova Scotia believed they had been cheated by Confederation. Joseph Howe told them bluntly they had been bribed and bought by rich Canadians:

> At eighty cents a head! That's the price of a Nova Scotian as well as a sheepskin.

An angry desire was aroused to get out of Confederation. Then, with eighteen of the nineteen Federal members and thirty-six of the thirty-eight Provincial members in Nova Scotia all elected in September 1867 as Anti-Confederates, Howe, it seemed, made a tactical error by going to Ottawa that autumn.

Howe was so prominent among the Opposition that his very presence appeared to be an implicit recognition of the binding power of Confederation. He took sharp stands on many questions, opposing, for example, the Government's policy of Western expansion. Such a matter was essentially a concern of Confederation, and once involved in it, Howe could not resist stating his reasons and making a comment which merely made Nova Scotians appear as timid:

> Nova Scotians fear the future, the afterbirth of Confederation.

This sort of talk from Howe did not suit their sturdy independent character. And many of them, who had watched Howe fail the year before in England, when he opposed the adoption of the British North America Act, sought a new escape. During Howe's absence in Ottawa, they began to talk of Annexation to the United States as the real alternative. By coincidence, the American movement for Annexation of Canada had been revived, particularly out west around St. Paul, by the acquisition of Alaska. And in fact, within a few months, the Legislature of Minnesota adopted a resolution in favour of Annexation as its solution for the future of the continent.

This talk of Annexation alarmed Howe. So when he returned to Nova Scotia, he decided to take a bold and direct course. In January 1868 he organized a delegation of four, and under his leadership they left for England to make an urgent demand that the British North America Act be repealed for Nova Scotia. Howe succeeded in enlisting the support and the passionate voice of John Bright to expose the grievance of Nova Scotia in England. Yet in so doing, he could not prevent a colour of Annexation to slip in, because Bright tolerantly conceded that it was the Manifest Destiny of the United States to control the whole North American continent under one government.

The Canadian Government was disturbed by the Secessionists of Nova Scotia and the compulsive propaganda of Howe. Yet John A. MacDonald refused to send a member of the Cabinet to England on the ground that it would raise the Nova Scotia Repeal movement to the level of official importance. He maintained that Repeal was not even a matter for discussion. Meanwhile Howe was making headway, assisted by depressed economic conditions.

That winter some ten thousand fishermen in Nova Scotia were suffering severe hardship. The trade in dried cod on the historic triangle of Nova Scotia, the West Indies and England had declined. Iron steamships replacing wooden sailing ships introduced refrigeration with new methods and new species of fish into other areas. And the ending of the Reciprocity Treaty had hurt the market for fish in New England. In adapting themselves to these new conditions, the fishermen of Nova Scotia were either too slow or not free to change. For many had placed themselves in the hands of the large houses that would make advances of food and goods to them during the winter and fit them out in the spring, as against a mortgage on their future season's fishing. That winter their plight was desperate. And with talk of a new tariff, more taxes from Ottawa and a general economic lethargy, Confederation became the scapegoat.

D'Arcy McGee did his part to try and offset this. Working from his room at home, he devoted a great part of his time in January 1868 in organizing a committee in Montreal to raise funds for the relief of the fishermen in Nova Scotia. Their distress was acute, and in some cases it was approaching starvation. On January 18, McGee took the initiative and made an appeal through the Montreal *Gazette*. This resulted in a well attended public meeting twelve days later at Mechanics Hall. McGee was too ill to attend, but his message, accompanied by a gift of twenty dollars, was read by the mayor. In the month that followed, with the help of Montreal Workingmen's Mutual Benefit Association and other charitable societies, more money was raised. Still hoping week by week to get out, McGee could not be present to speak at any of the meetings and had to content himself with written addresses on behalf of the cause.

If McGee had not been ill, it would have been natural for him to go to Nova Scotia where he had long maintained a special interest and had a strong personal influence. But even under the handicap of his illness, he managed to remain active, as shown by his letter of February 15 from Montreal, marked as "Confidential," to Sir John A. MacDonald in Ottawa:

> Mr. Haliburton (son of the old Judge) spent a couple of hours with me yesterday. Topic (refreshing and novel) Nova Scotia. He goes to Ottawa and mainly, I think, to see you. He is well worth hearing.
>
> As to the Repealers I suppose you have taken all due means to have them properly understood in England.
>
> But if anything could be done, by commercial legislation or otherwise, to bisect the mass of downright disaffected down there, it should be done.
>
> There is little doubt Annexation motives are at the bottom of it.
>
> I have been trying in the *Gazette* to keep up the true Constitutional doctrines, on which even many of our friends are at sea. I am to be out in a week, and to give on the 28th an address to the English Workingmen on the "New Nation and the Old Empire." It will contain a strong and pointed appeal against personal politics.
>
> An article on what the country expects from the Minister of Militia will appear in the *Gazette* of Monday. It may not be amiss that all you gentlemen should feel, that public, not personal interests are expected to be in the ascendant next Session.
>
> P.S. Don't let A. C. Buchanan's office be disposed of in a hurry; no need to be filled before the opening of navigation.

The postscript referred to the position of Chief Immigration Agent held by Buchanan up to his recent death at $4000 per year. The talk then was that the department would soon be moved from Quebec City to Ottawa, and McGee would be appointed to this vacant position.

That McGee was badly in need of money was shown by a slip of paper inserted separately in the same letter to MacDonald, marked "Strictly Confidential":

I am pestered and penniless, and want about $1000 to gain time and save my credit. Could you let me have half, "payable on demand," which I hope would mean during this present year.

I am really ashamed to bother you; but there are only two or three here I should like to know my exact circumstances, and they are pretty deeply in for my Election.

Three days later, McGee wrote to the Sadliers in New York:

I am going to trouble you to act for me in a little matter.

Not having been in receipt of an income for near a year, you can imagine, now that I feel "the wine of life," as the poets call it, rushing back along my veins, that I am anxious to be doing as well as up.

I owe the *Catholic World* among other smaller and larger obligations, some two years subscription. Will you give Mr. Kehoe the enclosed ballad, never before published, in fact just written, and ask him to offset my account.

In England they order these things better. The Laureate gets £100 for seven doggerel stanzas. But I shall be content with a receipt in full.

There are only two things on earth I fear—death and debt.

We are all laid up here with colds and coughs; except myself, who hop about troubling the house and waiting for the first fine day to go out.

On Thursday, March 5, D'Arcy McGee wrote another letter to James Sadlier in New York which he also marked as "Private":

I am off tomorrow for Upper Canada and Ottawa, where the House reassembles on the 12th. This is my last Session in actual legislative harness. That arrangement, which I mentioned to you and Mrs. Sadlier as on the tapis, of a life office worth $4000 a year, will be completed, please God, before June.

It will be right welcome and sore is it needed. It will enable me, too, to return to literature, which was my first and at all times my favourite line of exertion.

My foot I flatter myself is now finally cured. And otherwise I never was better—or poorer, indeed, for that matter.

Tell Mrs. Sadlier I have been twice at my duty since New Year's, and that I mean, with the blessing of God, to let no second month pass me again. This is sacredly for yourselves.

But his health was still uncertain and he had to delay his departure

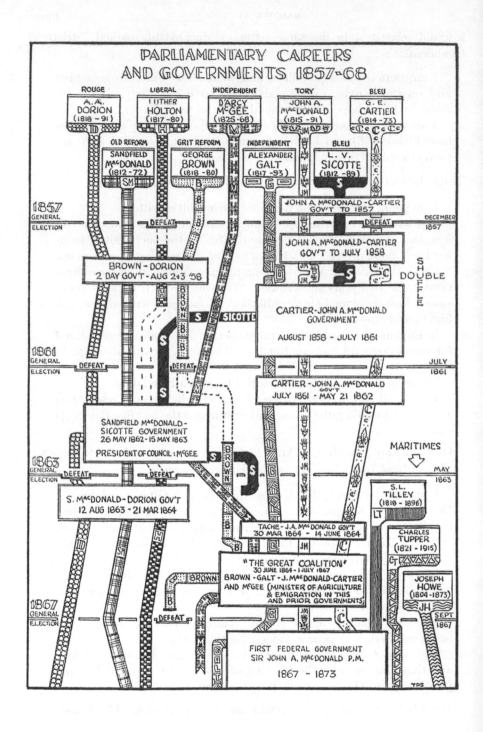

to Ottawa for a few days. Money had always been a chief source of worry for him, and he had hardly ever been able to make ends meet. It was the seamy side of his carefree and open-handed manner. Debts, which he always seemed to have, did not give McGee too much concern when he was healthy. Like John A. MacDonald and Howe, he had grown accustomed to impecunious straits, and in a way they propelled him to work. Before he entered public life, he wrote and lectured to make a modest living; yet when he saw the cause as worthy, he was improvident enough or easily persuaded to work for nothing. That winter McGee's letters were filled with plans of writing and lecturing for whatever money he could get as soon as his health would permit. He had agreed to lecture in Toronto on March 4 on "Revolutions in English Literature," which would have brought him a small fee. But it had to be cancelled, and he gave the talk a few days later at the Montreal Literary Club. That was in fact his last appearance in Montreal, on Monday, March 9, when he expressed the wish before a large attendance of his literary friends:

> I do hope next season, if Providence allows me better health, to be much more with the members than it was in my power to be this last winter.

As March opened, McGee was saddened by the death of one of his closest friends in Montreal, Lawrence Devaney. Four years before to the very day, on March 3, 1864, Mary Ann Devaney, his twelve-year-old daughter, had lost her life while trying to save two of her playmates who were skating when the ice gave way on the Welland Canal at St. Catharines. The tribute which McGee then wrote had contained these lines:

> Little we know when morning skies
> are clearest,
> What tempests may engulf the closing
> day.

The father died on March 3, 1868, and was buried three days later on St. Victor's Day, which moved McGee to write one of his best and most solemn chants, ending each of the seventeen stanzas with the same supplication:

> Saint Victor's Day, a day of woe,
> The bier that bore our dead went slow
> And silent, sliding over snow.
> *Miserere Domine.*

With Villa Maria's faithful dead
Amond the just we made his bed,
The cross he loved to shield his head.
*Miserere Domine.*

Well may they grieve who laid him there,
Where shall they find his equal. Where?
Nought can avail him now but prayer.
*Miserere Domine.*

There was more than sickness, debt and misfortune weighing upon McGee's heart. The threats against his life were becoming more insidious. Ever since his speech at Wexford in 1865 he had been receiving anonymous letters, which became more violent as he intensified his stand against Fenianism. They called him "a traitor" and a "turncoat," told him he had "sold his soul" and "to prepare for death." Often he was called (what he had called Dr. John Gray when he left the Dublin *Freeman* twenty years earlier) "a trimmer." But of all the accusations the worst was "informer." Some of these letters were mailed from Ireland; a few indicated they were posted in Montreal; but most of them came from the United States. Were these what McGee described in the lives of others as "the dark lines of destiny"? His temperament would not let him admit it about himself—or so he imagined.

Among his friends D'Arcy McGee affected to shrug off these threats, and he even kept a scrap-book where he preserved the most extreme specimens decorated with skulls and cross-bones. Under such stresses he was stronger than most men would have been. In his youth in Ireland he had moved in and out of plots and conspiracies; in Canada he had been menaced by Orangemen with revolvers at Brantford in 1861; and up to a certain degree, he appeared to have developed an immunity to them. But Fenianism was a dangerous and peculiar poison because it could spread among some simple people under an alluring label as a kind of patriotism.

To his wife and friends McGee's favourite expression was "Threatened dogs live long." In recent months, however, the threats had taken on new forms, as was shown on New Year's Day.

It had passed quietly for McGee into a very pleasant evening at home with all his family. John, his half-brother, was with them. And Fasa played the piano; "you remind me of my mother," her father told her; and they all sang some of Tom Moore's melodies together. While D'Arcy McGee bounced Peggy on his good knee, Mary McGee brought up a cold stone jug from the cellar and served their favourite ginger beer with simmel cake. The children then retired with their mother, and he read until one o'clock, when he went to bed. Suddenly, about a half hour later, the whole household was disturbed by a loud ringing of the front door-bell.

When John McGee opened the door, he saw two men in the dark. One of them stepped forward and, in a hushed voice, said he had to see D'Arcy McGee about "something urgent." John McGee spoke to D'Arcy, who told him "to let the men in, but to stand by in case of need." When he went back, however, John only saw one man, so he brought him in, locked the door and led him upstairs. There the stranger took a chair in the centre of the library. When D'Arcy McGee entered, he asked John to bring the other man in out of the cold. So John returned and called outside for the second man. He saw a figure about twenty yards away, partly hidden by the snowbank at the corner of Drummond Street, but there was no response.

Upstairs, D'Arcy McGee asked the stranger for his name. He hesitated and then gave the name "Smith of the Grand Trunk." Without further preliminaries, he rapidly told McGee that he had just hurried from a dance where he had heard of a plot to attack McGee and to set fire to his home at four o'clock that very morning. McGee made him repeat what he had said, and studied him closely. He was a young man of agile build, probably in his late twenties, and well tailored in appearance. He noted his restless eyes and red whiskers. McGee then wrote out a brief note and asked the stranger to take it at once to the police and tell them what he had just heard. With that, the stranger with the red whiskers disappeared as mysteriously as he had arrived. The McGees spent the rest of the night sleepless, as a guard was set up around their home. But nothing whatsoever happened.

McGee was shaken further when Sir John A. MacDonald warned him to be particularly careful, and in the last letter which McGee wrote to MacDonald, dated February 25, 1868, he added this postscript:

Many thanks for your hint about my personal safety. I shall not forget it.

When the threats were extended against his wife and his two children, it was fiendish, and there were moments when McGee felt undermined, almost unmanned. "I should outlive the malice, if not the men," he told a friend. To face it, he recognized that it called for something higher than human courage.

On Tuesday, March 10, when he departed for Ottawa, Fasa was at school in Villa Maria. As he left his home for the last time he turned and waved to his wife and Peggy in the doorway. He did not notice, standing discreetly to one side, the plain-clothes man who had been guarding his home and his family for the past few months.

PART FOUR

# MURDER

These bloody short-cuts to forbidden ends.
*Thomas D'Arcy McGee,*
ON THE ASSASSINATION
OF ABRAHAM LINCOLN

# 25

# THE HOUSE ADJOURNS

For all the past, read true, is prophecy.
*Francis Thompson*

By and by never comes.
*St. Augustine*

"Confederation is artificial and aloof, like a child trying to walk on stilts. What Nova Scotia needs is to come back down to earth." With such rough and tumble arguments, Howe had won the popular vote of Nova Scotia. To gain official support in England was a very different matter. But as Howe and his delegation kept on working in London for the repeal of Confederation, the Canadian Government grew uneasy and decided to send its own unofficial delegation, selected outside the Cabinet, to counterbalance whatever weight Howe was exercising.

Galt, who had resigned from the Cabinet three months earlier, wrote to Prime Minister MacDonald on February 10, 1868, expressing his alarm about Howe's movement:

> The crisis is, I think, a very serious one, as the failure to retain Nova Scotia voluntarily in the Union will not end with her secession, but practically paralyzes all our efforts to build up a nationality independent of the United States.

This prompted the Cabinet to ask Galt to go to London with Tupper and uphold the case for Confederation against Howe. When Cartier asked Galt officially in March, Galt answered that although he was disposed to accept, he did not wish to go with Tupper, who, he said, was badly disliked by Howe. But MacDonald insisted that Tupper should accompany Galt, so Galt refused to go.

Later in March, after that bad start, Tupper as the Federal member for Cumberland and the only Confederate representative from Nova Scotia, left alone on his special mission, with "delicate instructions" to oppose any move by Howe to harm Confederation, and yet to remain "conciliatory towards his Nova Scotia friends." Delicacy was a difficult assignment for the "war-horse of Cumberland," who had his own direct way of doing things, as he explained:

> On reaching London the first man I called on was Howe. He was not in, but I left my card.
> Howe returned the call, and on greeting me, said: "Well, I can't say that I am glad to see you, but we have to make the best of it."

Shadows of political intrigue moved across that month of March. Sir John A. MacDonald had been suffering from headaches for several weeks and was not well. Before Parliament reassembled he had talked again with his old law partner, Campbell, about retiring. What was really going on among his supporters, and even within the Cabinet, was difficult to ascertain, but there was discord and disaffection. Later Tupper wrote to MacDonald:

> I think I have ascertained Mr. Galt's difficulty in coming with me. General Doyle tells me that Howe and his friends confidently relied upon Galt effecting with them the overthrow of your government, and I assume that Mr. Galt was too deeply committed to present himself in London with me to counteract Mr. Howe's efforts.

An intermittent feud was known to exist between Galt and Cartier. But it was a closely guarded secret that Cartier, assumed to be the indissoluble partner of Sir John A. MacDonald, was still embittered because he had not received his equivalent title, and was then pursuing his own intrigue with Brown in Toronto. Brown revealed it privately on March 19 when writing to his wife in Edinburgh:

> Cartier sent me a letter suggesting a political alliance and my return to Parliament.

But these passing attempts to "ditch John A." came to nought. What remained was the feeling, which Brown expressed and passed on to others, particularly to Dr. T. S. Parker, the member for Wellington Centre of Ontario, that MacDonald had made a serious mistake by sending Tupper with his "clever fashion" to London.

That year, St. Patrick's Day fell on a Tuesday, the day after the House reassembled in Ottawa, and there was a festive dinner at the Russell House to do honour to D'Arcy McGee. Cartier made some brief, friendly allusions, and MacDonald was more expansive:

> I share the regret that Mr. McGee is not a Minister of the Crown. Yet never was he greater or more esteemed in the affections of the public than at the present day. He had surrendered his position in the Government unselfishly, from an anxious desire to allow all classes their fair share in starting the new order of things.

In response to a glowing toast and a great ovation, McGee spoke on his felicitous theme of Union. Mayor Friel, who was presiding, had referred to the success of McGee's *History of Ireland,* and in thanking him for his kind reference to his "labour of love," McGee added that "no one is more sensible of its many deficiencies than I am. If I live, I hope to remedy some of them."

> May I thank you for allowing me to say a word in season on behalf of that ancient and illustrious Island. On the seventeenth of March, its mere mention warms the heart of every Irishman, wherever the day may dawn or the stars look down upon his political destinies or his private enjoyments.

The work of the House went forward slowly in March, and D'Arcy McGee intervened in the debates a few times. He answered A. W. Savary, the Member for Digby, Nova Scotia, who had protested anew against Confederation; and due to the urging of McGee, the House resolved that the Maritimes should receive their proper share in all future openings in civil service and distribution of public works. He joined in the debate on election riots, and recommended that further prosecutions against "some mere boys" who had been arrested in his own riding should be dropped, "because the real authors of the crime were not among them."

But there was one motion which McGee was watching like a hawk. It was marked in the name of Dr. Parker of Wellington, asking for the immediate recall of Dr. Tupper from his mission in England.

April came and brought with it yearnings for recess and home, as McGee wrote from Ottawa to James Sadlier in New York:

> I hope to get home Easter week for a few holidays, and by that time a letter from you or Mrs. Sadlier would reach me at Montreal.
>
> I continue to gain in strength, though slowly.

Awaiting his return, his friends had commissioned John Bell-Smith, the founder of the first Society of Canadian Artists, to paint a life-size portrait of McGee which they planned to present to him on his forty-third birthday, which was Easter Monday, April 13.

On Friday evening, April 3, in the course of a long conversation which he had with Charles Clarke and Dr. John Howitt of Guelph, McGee mentioned how tired he was of those leaders who were shirking discussions on basic issues, and leaving the door open merely to have the chance to escape in whatever direction the wind happened to be blowing. As an example, he cited Dr. Parker of Wellington, who, he claimed, was privately aspiring to rise as a leader of public opinion under the very Confederaton which he would neither condemn nor approve in public:

If the opportunity arises on Monday, I intend to disapprove strongly
of Parker's refusal to commit himself.

Luther Holton in a letter to George Brown described Parker as "reliable," but Sir John A. MacDonald found other words for him: "that sneak
Parker" was his description in a letter to Tupper.

McGee's conversation that Friday evening then turned from politics
to literature and his own personal prospects. He mentioned that he had
just made an arrangement with some American publishers, notably
Harper, which promised some permanency:

I think I have trodden a few things underfoot which have hindered
me in the past, and I am looking forward to a new phase of life for
myself and my family.

The next evening, Saturday, at Speaker James Cockburn's sixth dinner
in the Parliament Buildings, McGee was in good form and enjoyed himself, "floating along very nicely on cold water, thank you!"

McGee spent Sunday, April 5, at the Ottawa home of his friend, Alderman James Goodwin, and Irish affairs were on his mind. "Don't exasperate the Fenians any further," Goodwin advised him. Before lunch
McGee began two letters, completing and dating both the following day
when he mailed them. The first was to Dr. Charles Tupper in London:

I delayed writing you till we should have had the debate on Dr.
Parker's motion for your "recall" from England. He will, of course,
take nothing by his motion but a good drubbing, which he richly
deserves. I had arranged with Sir John to administer the castigation
to the Doctor, and waited to send you the result; but the motion has
gone over from day to day.

Our friends in the Cabinet seem to be getting on very well together; Cartier's Militia Bill gives general satisfaction, and to no one
more so, than its author. The breakers ahead have gone down, and
all is plain sailing at present. Of course there are and will be rumours
a plenty; but there seems no truth whatever in any report which indicates a change.

The temper of our House, except an odd *mauvais* subject, like
Parker, is extremely good. Mackenzie is playing up to his part well,
taking a strong national tone, on all leading topics. Galt has returned in better humour than he left, and even Holton is tolerably
pacific.

All the Nova Scotians, but one or two, are again in their places,
and less querulous than in the first part of the Session. Savary, who
seemed bidding for "anti" leadership three weeks ago, has been much

modified and mollified by an item of $5000 in the Estimates for re-building the Digby pier. On such trifles do such convictions depend. Rose is doing all he can to conciliate the members *vis à vis* and *tête à tête;* and Sir John manages the House with admirable tact.

If we had conclusive news from you, the heart of every true Union-ist would be content.

McGee then asked Tupper if he would call on Hurst and Blackett, the publishers, to try and arrange for the publication of a new novel he was writing called *Cyrus O'Neill,* and also look after the issuing of a pamphlet in London on Fenianism, which, he added with new-found caution, "for obvious reasons must be published anonymously."

Sixteen days later on the arrival of the letter in London, Dr. Tupper would write on the back of it in his own hand:

Hon. T. D. McGee. Rec'd at the Colonial Office at 12 noon April 22nd 1868. Requiescat in pace. C. T.

McGee's second letter that Sunday was a plea to Lord Mayo, the Sec-retary of State for Ireland:

Settle for our sakes and your own, for the sake of international peace, settle promptly and generously the social and ecclesiastical condition of Ireland, on terms to satisfy the majority of the people to be governed.

Brute force has failed. Proselytism has failed. Anglification has failed. Try, if only as a novelty, the miraculous agency of equal and exact justice for one or two generations.

Then came a sign of something ominous stirring within him beneath the conscious surface, like a current which first appears as a ripple on smooth wide water before the rapids are reached. After luncheon that Sunday at the Goodwins', McGee lay down on the sofa and fell asleep. As Mrs. Goodwin was passing through the room later, she noticed Mc-Gee awakening in great distress, and it took him several minutes to re-gain his composure. Then he told her of a troubled dream he had just had:

I dreamed that I stood on the bank near the Falls of Niagara where I saw two men in a boat, gliding towards the Falls. I rushed to the brink and shouted to attract their attention. Then they picked up their oars and rowed up the stream, and I went over the Falls.

It was a quiet Monday afternoon in the House. The Speaker, James Cockburn, took the chair at three o'clock. Two Bills received routine readings, indifferent replies were given to minor questions, and Prime Minister MacDonald evaded one on the law of bankruptcy.

The Order Paper for that day, April 6, 1868, showed a number of motions. Several were called and allowed to stand. Among them was that of Dr. Parker asking for the immediate recall of Dr. Tupper from London; but when it was called Parker was absent. A few minutes later, however, he entered and asked for special leave to speak to his motion. McGee objected on the ground that it was not designed to contribute to the peace of the country and did not merit preferred treatment. The point of order was maintained, and Parker's motion could not be heard.

Business then turned to a series of questions about a recent issue of government bonds and the role played by the Bank of Montreal, which bristled enough to carry the discussion through into the evening sitting. During the evening recess McGee returned to his room at his boarding-house on Sparks Street and picked up his notes on Parker's motion.

About ten o'clock that night the member for Antigonish, H. McDonald, speaking on his own motion, asked for the tabling of the address of the Nova Scotia Assembly seeking the repeal of Confederation, with all correspondence of the Canadian Government on the matter. Sir John A. MacDonald replied casually that the address had already been transmitted to England through the Governor General, and he doubted if a copy had been retained.

With this, Parker saw his opportunity to revert to his point. He protested strongly against Tupper's appointment, asserting that Tupper was the last man who should have been selected for such a mission to England. Tracing the causes of Nova Scotia's discontent back to the Quebec Conference of 1864, he argued that Tupper's actions all through had been distasteful to the people of Nova Scotia, that the Government had closed the door against conciliation and that no Canadian delegate should have been sent to England to interfere with Nova Scotia's mission seeking repeal of Confederation. Dr. Parker then moved, seconded by Luther Holton, that the motion be amended by adding that in the opinion of the House the appointment of Dr. Tupper would increase discontent in Nova Scotia and that he should be recalled.

D'Arcy McGee was on his feet to reply. Pausing, he looked around the House. He was obviously ready. But as word spread that McGee was about to speak the members started to come in from the smoking-room to listen, and a large number of about five hundred spectators were gathering in the galleries.

He was a short man, his clothing almost shabby, and his skin was pale and pitted. His tangled black hair and wispy beard had thickened and turned somewhat grey during his illness. While waiting for the noise in the House to subside, he hardly moved, except for his hands, which were unusually fine and delicate, rearranging his notes.

There are at least five good photographs of D'Arcy McGee, some portraits and a creditable statue of him standing in an oratorical pose near the Library on Parliament Hill. None of them portray, nor could they capture, his two most winning traits, the two things that everyone who knew him always recalled: his voice and his smile. There was a run in his voice and a leisure in its cadence, a silvery tone and a rich and flexible range. And there was his sudden sally or merely the half-said thing brought to fullness by his genial smile.

McGee began quietly. Usually this was a signal that the spark of debate was about to strike. Those who knew his style could expect an easy unassuming start, then the feint before a final flash of skill and the thrust home. His first words were spoken softly yet so distinctly that they were easily heard throughout the House. McGee had turned slightly to his right to face Dr. Parker across the House, as he reminded him of his pledge to his electors "to give Confederation a fair trial":

> If he had been earnest in his desire for the success of Confederation, he might have said: "I do not think Dr. Tupper was the best choice for this mission, but since he has gone, I wish him all success for the sake of the welfare of the Union."
>
> He knows well that if it were possible for it to be adopted, the recall of Dr. Tupper would have no appreciable effect in the conciliation of Nova Scotia. It would only be the abstraction of a thimble full from the bucket of her discontent.

McGee's words were beginning to flow like fast waters as he rapidly raised a series of questions. How now is Dr. Parker fulfilling his pledge for a fair trial? Is he seeking for subjects of irritation? Is he striking below the belt?

In his earlier years McGee's facility of expression sometimes became too sardonic. He excelled in repartee and could exult in it. But experience had tempered that gift. There was nothing flippant now in the character of his speech. What McGee said next was spoken slowly:

> Dr. Tupper's character has been assailed. And it would show but a base spirit to sacrifice the man in his absence who had sacrificed himself for Confederation.

Here, as a contrast to Dr. Parker's destructive attitude, he paid a tribute to Alexander Mackenzie as the leader of the largest section of the Opposition, for his "moderate, large-minded and truly national spirit" in supporting the achievement of Confederation. As McGee went on, it recalled something of his best speeches in the old House, where passion had often moved him and his words had lashed out like driving rain, and then, moments later, seemed to float in the air like snowflakes.

McGee shifted his weight and rested the knee of his weak leg on his chair as he continued:

It may be that there are some grounds of complaint. In such minor matters as the newspaper postage and certain impositions of the tariff, Nova Scotia may have reason to remonstrate. But Nova Scotia need only ask us to consider these subjects from a broad national point of view, to deal with her, not with exceptional partiality, but in the same spirit of even-handed fairness extended to Quebec, Ontario or New Brunswick.

He held up a small book just written by R. G. Haliburton, the son of the famous judge from Nova Scotia, on *Intercolonial Trade:*

What I hold in my hand shows beyond doubt or cavil that Union is not to be consolidated by any temporary, conciliating concessions to evanescent popular prejudice, but by our earnest and unremitting care of the commercial welfare and progress of the Province.

What we need above everything else, is the healing influence of time. It is not only the lime and the sand and the hair in the mortar, but the time which has been taken to temper it. And if time be so necessary in so rudimentary a process as the mixing of mortar, of how much greater importance is it in the work of consolidating the Confederation of these Provinces.

Time will heal all existing irritations. Time will mellow and refine all points of contrast that seem so harsh today. Time will come to the aid of impartial justice.

Referring then to E. M. McDonald, the Member from Lunenburg, he added that he would not despair, with the assistance of time, of seeing such a staunch opponent of Confederation himself converted, by and by, into its heartiest supporter:

For such a precedent can be found even in the history of Nova Scotia herself.

When Cape Breton was annexed to Nova Scotia, the people were so strongly opposed to the Union that they almost threatened re-

bellion. That took place as lately as 1820. And already time has brought its healing operation. There is no question raised now of the advantages of that Union. There is no such question because there has been no consequent injustice. And I have every confidence that we will similarly wear out Nova Scotian hostility by the unfailing exercise and exhibition of a high-minded spirit of fair play.

That Monday night as it approached midnight the Members and the spectators had been fascinated for over an hour by the lustre of McGee's words. His coat was crumpled and his hair was tousled. Leaning over the back of his chair, he let his gaze travel beyond the bounds of the House as his voice, with its lilt from another land, carried his thoughts to the level of his vision. And while they watched and listened, from some phantom recess, or so it was fancied, something psychic seemed to flow, which a reporter spoke of as a presentiment. Imagined as it may have been, those in the House felt strangely moved. Their attention was now absolute. Yet they scarcely knew that as old men they would so often say, "I heard him that night."

McGee was now concluding:

Our friends need have no fear but that Confederation will ever be administered with serene and even justice. Its single aim from the beginning has been to consolidate, with the utmost regard to the independent powers and privileges of each Province.

And I, Sir, who have been and still am its warm and earnest advocate, speak here not as the representative of any race or of any Province but as thoroughly and emphatically a Canadian, ready and bound to recognize the claims of my Canadian fellow-subjects, from the farthest east to the farthest west, as equally as those of my nearest neighbour or of the friend who proposed me on the hustings.

His great effort expended and his best achieved, McGee turned his chair back into its place and sat down, as the House broke out in a demonstration of admiration and deep affection. There were full-throated cries of support from the Government benches. Near-by members reached over to clap him on the shoulder or shake his hand. And from all sides came that thumping and pounding and all those solid sounds which men make to show their enthusiasm. At some point in that moving, buoyant scene, the final memory was fixed. Years later, in the twilight of parliamentary oratory, the memory of that spontaneous applause would warm many hearts, for it had caught the spirit and lit up the grandeur of D'Arcy McGee's last words in public.

About midnight Prime Minister MacDonald and Opposition Leader Alexander Mackenzie got into a wrangle. Neither would give way, and there seemed every prospect of a very late or even an all-night sitting. So D'Arcy McGee took a break and went downstairs to the restaurant. There he met a novice who had spoken after him and opposed him, James Young from Waterloo. "And so, my young friend," McGee said, putting a pleasant emphasis on the word *young*, "you undertook to go for me in your speech tonight."

They talked for a while, and Young noticed that McGee was in high spirits and very bright and cheerful. As McGee relaxed he had started to talk about literature, when to everyone's surprise the division bells began to ring, calling them back to their desks. A minor crisis had developed and a vote was threatening. Matters finally quietened down, however, and the need for a vote was avoided. So McGee was able to do some writing before the House adjourned.

In fact, that Monday, D'Arcy McGee wrote several letters. Probably the last one he wrote was to an old friend from the Young Ireland movement, the author of *The Fate and Fortunes of Hugh O'Neill,* and now a priest in Dublin. Whether it was the very last thing he wrote there is no sure way of knowing. Certainly it was his last serious letter. And it carried, unconsciously, the irony of a letter that would be read when the writer was dead:

Ottawa,
April 6th, 1868

*Private*
Rev. C. P. Meehan,
Dublin, Ireland
My dear Father Meehan:

Your very kind note reached me the day before yesterday, and our mail goes out today.

You will see in the *Catholic World,* Mitchel's article, and as soon as the New York edition reaches me I will write a newspaper notice and publish it either here or at Montreal, which you shall have by Monday, I hope. Next week we have a few days' recess from Parliamentary labour, and I will try my hand at a ballad as you suggest.

The "Iona to Erin" in the *Catholic World* is mine. If Sullivan reprints "blend," it should be "blent" in one of the middle stanzas. I hope this fall to issue a volume of ballads at New York. What say you to this title: *Celtic Ballads and Funeral Songs?* You know I am an old keener, and half my lays are lamentations. It could not well be otherwise in this age with an Irish Bard, if I am worthy to be called a Bard of Erin.

You will be glad to know that for now nearly twelve months I have been a firm teetotaller, and with God's blessing I intend to remain so for life. I also attend to other and more sacred duties monthly; this strictly to your own comfort.

His thoughts were turning back to friends of other days, as he recalled the two poets who had nominated him to the Irish Academy, Denis F. McCarthy and Samuel Ferguson, and the news of the latter's appointment as deputy-keeper of Irish records:

I want data for an article on McCarthy for the *Catholic World,* and if I thought there was a similar office to Ferguson's to be had for him, I would try, if the professions made to me by imperial statesmen of both parties had anything in them. Can you put me on the track of serving, or trying to serve that gifted old friend of both of us?

I send you a copy of a letter I wrote by this mail to Lord Mayo. It may serve Ireland to make it public. If you prefer to give it to the *Nation,* do so; or to any Dublin paper with some such paragraph, by way of preface, as the enclosed slip, marked A. I think I have earned the right to speak with authority on the Canadian view of Irish misrule, and I have endeavoured to do so plainly and to the purpose.

If the publication of my letter to Lord Mayo be so timed as to hit the resumption of the Irish question in Parliament, all the better.

It was late, and he had almost reached the end. His mind had moved back more than twenty years to the brightest days of Young Ireland, to the courage of James Duffy and his *Library of Ireland,* when its monthly shilling volumes on history, literature and the arts had popularized two of McGee's early books. Along with McCarthy and Father Meehan, McGee was still contributing signed articles to Duffy's *Hibernian Magazine:*

Is it not sad, this insane neglect of our native literature by this disintegrated generation? James Duffy alone is doing more for us and our descendants, single-handed, than all your magnates. May God bless him and lighten the load of life to him, is my sincere prayer.

Believe me, my dear friend,

Yours always truly,
T. D. McGee

# 26

## DEATH

A moon that sheds a needless light
On soulless streets in the far gone night.
"A FRAGMENT": *Thomas D'Arcy McGee*

There is no danger of my being converted into a political martyr. If ever I were murdered, it would be by some wretch who would shoot me from behind.
*Thomas D'Arcy McGee*
TO BROWN CHAMBERLIN, MARCH 1868

D'Arcy McGee had finished writing when the House of Commons adjourned very late that night. In fact, it was another day. It was then ten minutes past two, Tuesday morning, April 7, 1868. He was not too tired. The weariness which had weighed upon him that winter was lifting, and within a week he would be forty-three. He was back on his feet again, working with his usual warmth among his friends and with an extraordinary cool nerve among his enemies. His speech in the House that night showed much of his old power. It was hard-hitting and fair, and the fire of debate was still in him.

He walked down to the bar of the House, bought three cigars and lit one up with his chief, Sir John A. MacDonald. Then he chatted about Nova Scotia with Dr. J. F. Forbes, the Member for Queens of that Province, and waited while Robert MacFarlane, a younger Member from Perth, Ontario, had a whisky and water. In a few minutes they moved to the cloak-room in the west lobby. "Come, Bob, you young rascal, help me on with my coat," McGee said to MacFarlane. "Always ready to give you a lift," MacFarlane replied.

As they went out McGee asked Cartier to join them, but Cartier explained he was waiting to have a private word with Galt. So McGee and MacFarlane left together, relaxed and chatting easily. There were a number of Members leaving at that time, and some spectators were noticed near by. Going out the main door under the arches of the Tower among the Arnprior marble pillars, they passed the doorkeeper, Patrick Buckley, who had just seen Sir John A. off in his carriage to his home on Daly Street at Sandy Hill.

It was a clear, crisp night with a bite in the air. A full moon was high in the sky. Here and there were drifts of snow and puddles of water coated with thin ice, reflecting the moonlight. As the rattle of carriage wheels faded away, the distant roar of Chaudière Falls could be heard across the quiet city.

McGee was wearing an overcoat, gloves and a new white top hat. In his hand was his wheat-coloured bamboo cane with a silver handle and engraved band, presented to him five years ago by his friends in Montreal. Since the trouble with his leg, McGee had to walk slowly, so they took their time, McGee leaning on MacFarlane's arm, sauntering down the central path, across the broad terrace and out the front gateway to Wellington Street.

Veering to their left, they soon reached its intersection with Metcalfe Street close by. Keeping to the right side of Metcalfe, McGee on the inside, they walked one short block south to Sparks Street. Here, at the corner in front of Dwyer's Fruit Store, they had to part, MacFarlane to go east on Sparks, cross Sappers' Bridge and on to his lodgings in Lower Town, while McGee had merely to turn west and walk about a hundred and twenty-five yards to reach his room.

"Good night," said MacFarlane, and McGee replied: "God bless you."

As he turned, MacFarlane noticed the doorkeeper's brother, John Buckley, and three others whom he did not recognize, following behind them at a faster pace. MacFarlane crossed Metcalfe, waved to Cartier and Galt, who were walking down the other side of Metcalfe, and followed Sparks Street past the Russell House. As he was crossing Sappers' Bridge he noticed the cabdriver, John Downs, returning from Sir John A. MacDonald's home with his empty carriage and iron-grey horse.

Meanwhile McGee had crossed to the south side of Sparks and was turning west, when John Buckley called out: "Good night, Mr. McGee."

"Good morning." McGee answered. "It is morning now." And those words were remembered as his last.

It was unusually bright that night and Sparks Street appeared deserted. The gas street lamps were not lit; but that was customary, as the city's contract with the gas company called for service only "during the dull period of the moon." Telegraph poles and a series of hitching posts for horses were spaced along the edge of the unpaved road, and the fourth pole up the street marked his destination. It was the Toronto House, better known as Mrs. Trotter's Boarding House.

Limping slightly, his cane clicking on the frozen sidewalk, McGee walked on alone, the red glow and the blue smoke from his cigar spreading, so it seemed, an air of peace.

On his left he passed Hunton's Dry Goods Store, Crosby & Larmouth's Boot Shop and then an open gateway in darkness. Across the street to his right was a narrow lane leading back to Wellington Street. Beyond that, a light in a window indicated the Ottawa *Times* Building, where the printers were at work on the next issue. Next to that was Mrs. McKenna's saloon; then, an empty house; followed by a board fence six feet high, which enclosed a vacant lot for another fifty yards to the corner of O'Connor Street.

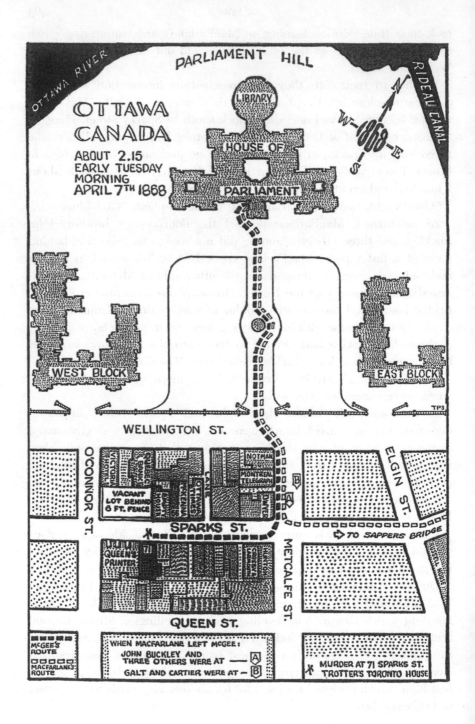

Opposite the *Times* Building, on the south side of Sparks Street, was another open gateway. Beyond was Trotter's Boarding House, four doors east of O'Connor Street. It stood in the Desbarats Block which housed the Queen's Printer, with its own recessed alleys.

Mrs. Trotter's House itself had three entrances, and McGee had the key to the middle one for the use of guests. So he passed the locked first door which led to the public bar, and then went by the large window. Then he stopped, took out his key and put it in the latch keyhole to let himself in.

At that instant the door was opened by someone from within. Simultaneously there was a sudden flash and the sharp blast of a shot right behind McGee. D'Arcy McGee stumbled to his right, shuddered, threw his head back high and fell flat on his back.

There was a commotion inside the Trotter House. Several people came running to the scene. But there was no sign of any assassin, no sign of any weapon. Nothing. No one but the victim.

He was on his back lying askew across the empty sidewalk. His legs were spread apart extending towards the door. They quivered slightly and then were still.

His body lay motionless, with his head towards the road. His right arm was stretched out, and the hand was gloveless. The left arm was extended at an awkward right angle and was hooked by his cane, pinned underneath his back. The glove was on the left hand, and the other glove was lying between it and the body. His new white hat was still on his head, but tipped forward. His face was distorted, and some froth had formed on his lips. A large pool of florid blood, oozing from his mouth and the back of his neck, had spread about four feet across the slightly warped planks of the sidewalk and was dripping into the gutter.

There was a latch key in the keyhole with two more keys tied to it by a red tape; and the lower panels of the door were spattered with blood. In the hall, inside the partially opened front door, about a foot from the lower sill, were broken portions of three or four artificial incisor teeth, with a base of gutta-percha attached to fit an upper jaw.

Dr. McGillivray was called and he arrived within minutes. The body was quite warm but pulseless, and he pronounced D'Arcy McGee dead. Then he told Constable McVetty to summon the coroner.

A bullet about the size of a pencil head was found partially impacted on the outside of the door about four and a half feet above the sidewalk and two inches above the keyhole. It had entered towards the west and seemingly had turned or twisted in the other direction. The conical end of the bullet was outermost and its hold in the door was not firm. Later it fell out and was picked up about a foot inside the door-sill. It was handed to Coroner Van Cortlandt as he arrived, and it was remarked that it looked like a lead bullet from a Derringer pistol.

Meanwhile someone had raced across Sappers' Bridge to Sandy Hill to tell Sir John A. MacDonald. He arrived about the same time as the coroner. The body was then lifted from the sidewalk with the Prime Minister supporting D'Arcy McGee's head, as they carried the body inside and placed it on a couch in a small front room on the ground floor of the Trotter House.

A careful examination followed. In McGee's pockets the coroner found two American silver half-dollars, a penknife and case, a likeness of Speaker Cockburn's son and another likeness, a Montreal *Gazette*, two or three other newspapers and pamphlets and a letter addressed to "George F. Hughes, Commissioner in B.R., Keenansville, Simcoe County, Ontario."

Noticeable was a strong smell of gunpowder and some burnt hair on the back of the neck. The wound was evident, somewhat oval in shape, on the back of the neck on the right side of the spinal column. There was a corresponding hole right through the back collars of the overcoat, the undercoat and the shirt. It was evident that the bullet had entered from the back and passed horizontally through the upper part of the throat, along the roof and out by the mouth. The upper plate of artificial teeth had been ripped out, and the remnants found were identified as matching those missing.

It was a piteous spectacle. The lower part of the face was mutilated, and the greying beard was clotted with blood. His overcoat was still on with the top button fastened, and his cane and loose glove were close to his head. Near by was his blood-stained white hat. On his feet were woollen socks, and someone had removed his shoes and replaced them with carpet slippers. His bare right hand was lying across his breast.

Outside, a curious crowd was gathering and asking questions in low tones. A ladder had been placed as a barricade to protect the area, and a policeman stood by. As Sir John A. MacDonald left Mrs. Trotter's a silvery dawn was breaking and a light snow was starting to fall around the pools of crimson blood. Lying there by the door-step was McGee's half-smoked cigar.

# 27

## AND DARKNESS FELL

Suspicions amongst thoughts are like bats among birds, they ever fly by twilight.

*Francis Bacon*

I remember being awakened early that morning. My mother cried and told me that during the night someone had killed my father.

*Agnes (Peggy) McGee,* AT EIGHTY-THREE, RECALLING APRIL 7, 1868

The newly invented Morse code was flashing the bad news everywhere in short stabs through the night, and the Canadian morning newspapers were very busy during the early hours of Tuesday resetting their front pages with a few stark phrases in their boldest type. Typical was the first proof from the presses of the Montreal *Daily News:*

SPECIAL TELEGRAM
ASSASSINATION OF THE HON. T. D. MC GEE
OTTAWA IN A FERMENT
THE ASSASSIN NOT DISCOVERED

Ottawa, 3 A.M., April 7

The Hon. Thomas D'Arcy McGee was shot dead at half-past two this morning, as he was on the point of entering Mrs. Trotter's, Sparks Street. The ball passed through his head. His body is now lying on the pavement.

The wildest excitement prevails.

Even in Ottawa, where all sorts of versions were spreading from mouth to mouth, the morning newspapers were not able to set much more into print for their first editions. But by the alert work of one reporter and a constant flow of telegrams, the Toronto *Leader* was filling its front page with the news in detail, and within five hours would outstrip every newspaper in Canada.

Amid all the baffling excitement Sir John A. MacDonald, from the moment he arrived at the scene of the crime, took charge with efficiency and remarkable tact. He sent telegrams to the railway stations and to the mayors and the constabulary in all the surrounding towns and the principal cities, alerting them to be on the lookout for the assassin. But there was very little to go on.

There was, of course, an immediate and almost unanimous assumption that the assassin was a Fenian. Here popular imagination had raced ahead. In some groups it ran close to panic. Rumours spread of an impending Fenian insurrection, of the burning of Parliament, of threats on the lives of the Prime Minister and some Cabinet Ministers, of guns and ammunition hidden in graveyards, of a large quantity of nitroglycerine obtained on a forged order from New York, and so on. As crowds gathered on Sparks Street near the Ottawa *Times* Building, and in front of other newspaper bulletins in Ottawa, these scares were inflated by the reports, for even the most irresponsible were posted up in the obscurity of that early overcast morning.

The neighbourhood was quickly searched. The dark alleys at the Queen's Printer, the two open gateways east of Trotter's, the narrow lane across the street leading to Wellington, the vacant lot with its six-foot fence across from Trotter's, all were searched in vain. But it was noticed that the doors to the empty house next to McKenna's saloon were unlocked.

There were no tracks to follow. To get away, an assassin simply had to race fifty yards westward on Sparks Street, turn south on O'Connor and, within a block, reach undeveloped areas where he could disappear to the southeast or the southwest into broken and wooded country.

Thomas Workman, the member for Montreal Centre, arrived to report that he had left the House of Commons about the same time as D'Arcy McGee and had encountered four men coming along Sparks Street, two and two, bearing such a suspicious appearance that he went out of his way to avoid them:

> They were wearing slouched hats and had a rowdy appearance. I would calculate that they must have passed Trotter's about the time of the assassination.

Some other members of Parliament, as they reached their lodging house, noticed a man loitering. When he saw them, he seemed to pretend he was intoxicated and rang the bell asking for a room:

> When he was refused, he paced off very briskly and without any sign of intoxication. We were not very far from Trotter's house. Probably this happened about ten minutes before the murder.

But the most persistent story involved a mysterious horse and a buggy. One woman in the neighbourhood said that she heard a shot, then a noise like a man running around the corner, and the sound of waggon wheels. A man named Myles and his wife, and a barrister named Keefer and his wife, who lived on Queen Street almost directly behind Trotter's, all said that they heard the noise of carriage wheels, and before any sound of a shot, a buggy or some other light vehicle was drawn up on the north side of Queen Street almost in line with Trotter's.

Back to town came a report that about five o'clock that morning a carriage, carrying three men, crossed Billings Bridge spanning the Rideau River about five miles south of Ottawa:

> They were driving fast and did not stop to pay the toll and soon were lost to sight. About fifteen or twenty miles off in that direction, there is a lodge of persons who have something to do, they say, with the Secret Society of Fenians.

Another version was that a buggy was on O'Connor Street, close to Sparks:

> Just after the sound of a shot, it drove off at a furious rate towards the country to the southeast.

But strongest of all was the report that a buggy was seen and heard driving off in another direction, to the east, that it crossed the Ottawa River at the Chaudière Falls Bridge and went up the Aylmer Road:

> And the police are on the trail.

Stranger and more anonymous tales appeared and disappeared leaving no traces. For example, there was a yarn that on the previous Friday night a pistol shot had been heard on Sparks Street soon after the House of Commons adjourned, and a scrape on the sill of one of Mrs. Trotter's windows was indicated as a possible mark of that bullet. And so the question was raised: Was there a previous attempt on McGee's life? Other stories just as vague were cited in support: and some went much further, adding that prior to the murder, shots had been heard nightly in the vicinity of the Ottawa *Times* Building on Sparks Street.

Sir John A. MacDonald was obliged to inform the widow, and the means he chose were rapid and delicate. He immediately sent a telegram to Father Patrick Dowd, the pastor of St. Patrick's in Montreal. In turn, Father Dowd asked two Grey Nuns to accompany him and they went directly to the McGee home on St. Catherine Street. Joseph H. Daley, McGee's close friend, the general agent of the Grand Trunk, was also informed and went to the McGee home. There, all met at the door.

It was shortly after four o'clock the morning of the assassination when Father Dowd broke the news to the widow. It was related that Mrs. McGee collapsed in grief; then her friends and prayers helped her to regain some calmness.

Someone drove out to Monklands for Fasa where she was a boarder at Villa Maria Convent, and the annals of Villa Maria for that day contain this entry:

The sudden death of Mr. McGee has affected all of us, who recognized in him a devoted friend of the house. They came for Euphrasia. What a scene!

Ten-year-old Peggy was still asleep in her room when her mother went in to tell her. Open on her desk was her last letter from her father. It was dated Friday, April 3, and had just arrived from Ottawa in the mail:

My dearest Peggy:

Mamma sent me all your kind messages and kisses, which I have counted up, and find you owe me in all 220. Remember that.

Fasa wrote me, since I came here, two very nice letters, and I hope next year to be able to have a few lines from you. I sent Fasa last week a little locket because it was her birthday; and as Easter Monday (April 13th) is mine, I propose to give you some little memorial of the day. What it is to be, I can't tell till I consult Mamma.

I hope Alley and Katy and you enjoy this beautiful weather, and that Fido and the dolls are all well, and dutiful as usual.

Don't forget your lessons, dear old woman, is the special request of

Papa

# 28

## THE EMPTY SEAT

But tell them not our sad complaints,
For if they dreamt our spirit faints
There would be fruitless sorrowing.

"IONA TO ERIN," THE LAST POEM OF
*Thomas D'Arcy McGee*

The morbid anatomy of nations, the causes of their decline
and fall, do not much interest me. What we in Canada
should study is their rise to greatness.

*Thomas D'Arcy McGee*
TO HIS ELECTORS, JULY 17, 1867

When Speaker Cockburn took the chair, a hush fell over the crowded House of Commons. It was ten minutes past three that same Tuesday afternoon, and a thousand people were crammed into the galleries. A shaft of silver light streamed downward through a cluster of small dark pillars to fall on a pier of greyish marble across the silent Chamber as the Prime Minister, Sir John A. MacDonald, rose to speak. He looked weary and pale and under heavy strain. After two brief hours of sleep he had returned to his office at seven o'clock that morning, and had been working steadily since, issuing a series of orders in an effort to cope with the emergency.

His opening words were low. He faltered and seemed to have difficulty in going on as he spoke of "pain amounting to anguish." The spectators could hardly hear him when he continued:

> He who was with us last night, no, this morning, is no more. If ever a soldier fell in the front of the fight, it was D'Arcy McGee. He deserves well of Canada.
>
> His hand was open to every one. His heart was made for friendship. And his enmities were written in water.
>
> Let me apply to Mr. McGee the words he used about another in his speech last night.

The Prime Minister glanced to his right along the front bench to an empty chair, where only a few hours ago under the flickering gas-light, D'Arcy McGee had paid his tribute to Dr. Charles Tupper. MacDonald then repeated what McGee had said:

> "I hope," Mr. McGee had wished, "that in this House mere temporary or local popularity will never be made the test by which to measure the worth or efficiency of a public servant.
>
> "It is, Sir, in my humble opinion, the leader who is ready to meet the tide of temporary unpopularity, who is prepared, if need be, to sacrifice himself, who is ready not only to triumph with his principles but even to suffer for his principles, he is the one who has proved himself, above all others, worthy of peculiar honour."

McGee's words, spoken earlier in his clear, melodious voice and now heard for a second time in this tragic sequence, seemed like a final flow from a generous soul. MacDonald completed the quotation, and went on, speaking with his head down and in broken tones:

> He was too good, too generous to be rich. Yet he has left us a sacred legacy, and we must look upon his widow and his children now as belonging to the State.

The light from the high window had faded away as the Prime Minister took his seat.

Then from the other side of the House, as the representative Leader of the Opposition, Alexander Mackenzie arose. His small blue eyes, usually so bright, had that day lost their sharpness. Holding his head erect and rather rigid, his neat greyish beard relieved the thin, set line of his mouth. His first movement was to gaze upwards, as if to search for some better words. Then he began very simply:

> It was my lot to oppose McGee. Yet I am able to say that through all our political warfare I have always found him generous.

He had never forgotten McGee's kindness in helping his late brother, Hope, when he was unsure of himself and so ill during his first Session in Quebec City. But Alexander Mackenzie was not a man who could express what he felt, and he made no attempt to share his sentiments. He went on to remark that this was the first instance in Canada when any of its great public men had been struck down by an assassin. There was a stir when he added:

> I think there can be no doubt that he has been assassinated by an alien hand.

George Etienne Cartier followed. He was short, compact and wiry, quick and vibrant in manner, with his voice pitched in a high key. Though he had had his *contretemps* with McGee, that afternoon Cartier was visibly moved:

> Mr. McGee was not an ordinary man. He was a man of impulse, of genius, of wisdom. And he joined with those gifts something rarer; he was so judicious.

Then Cartier turned towards the Speaker, and the massive cut of his lower jaw marked his purpose as he made a direct attack upon the Fenians:

> I speak now of that foreign organization in the land inhabited by

our neighbours, and of the hateful doings of that abominable institution.

His brush-cut hair seemed to bristle as he went one step further than Mackenzie, and added:

It is very likely that his death was the work of an assassin in that organization.

In the galleries, half hidden by the two great chandeliers, the faces of the spectators could be dimly seen, turning to one another, alive with excitement.

The tension eased with the next speaker. He was two years younger than D'Arcy McGee, new to Parliament as the Member for Missisquoi, but well known as the proprietor and editor of the Montreal *Gazette*. It was Brown Chamberlin, the man who had fostered early doubts about McGee in 1857. But he had become one of his strongest admirers, and this was apparent as Chamberlin started:

When profound grief weighs down men's hearts, few words are best.

Quietly and with a sense of intimacy, he talked of McGee as a fellow journalist, of his abiding love of letters as a lecturer, historian and poet, and of his diligence to promote the habit of reading among the young. As Canada knew him, Chamberlin said, D'Arcy McGee was a man of peace, labouring to allay strife, "one who thought as a statesman." It was an admirable and spare tribute of two hundred words, and his closing statement drew applause:

The press and literature of Canada must mourn today for their brightest light extinguished.

Timothy Anglin spoke next. Though he made no mention of it, his simple presence served as a final tribute from Young Ireland. Anglin was now the member from Gloucester, New Brunswick, the political foe of McGee and the fiery opponent of Confederation. But twenty years ago he had been a rebel schoolmaster in Cork, Ireland, clasped in union with McGee in the rising of Young Ireland. Now he was one of the few who survived from that ardent movement.

Those who had shared that spirit of McGee's youth were almost all gone. William Smith O'Brien had died in 1864 after a long exile gallantly endured. Two years later John Blake Dillon died, respected as a chivalrous Member of Parliament for Tipperary. A year had not yet passed since the tragic death of Thomas Francis Meagher, the Governor of Montana. As for the poets, Thomas Davis, so simple and spontaneous, and James Clarence Mangan, with a wildness in his pale blue eyes, they were no more, though their lines lived. It was Charles Gavan Duffy, as Prime Minister of Victoria in Australia, who would receive the news of McGee's assassination and recall him at the age of twenty, with his "rare intellectual gifts which were only partially developed, for he was still a boy. Ill-dressed and underbred, these were drawbacks which long masked the depth and range of his powers."

Anglin spoke that Tuesday afternoon with a sense of horror:

I feel peculiarly embarrassed on this occasion because it has been assumed, and I fear only too correctly, that this foul assassination has been the work of an organization of Irishmen not, I trust, of Irishmen belonging to this Dominion.

It is an outrage that will probably have a great effect upon the history of this country. Perhaps in the effects of his death, this will be the highest tribute paid to the man who has gone from among us.

The first Premier of the Province of Quebec, who was also the Federal Member for Quebec County, scholarly and sensitive Pierre Chauveau, then addressed the House in French:

The man who has just fallen was modest, affable and generous. He was often at gatherings for the poor. And only yesterday he presented a petition in favour of the family of a hero, Colonel de Salaberry. He told me himself what he proposed to say in coming to the aid of that needy family.

A few hours later, he fell as a hero, leaving his own family without support.

I recall the eloquent speech he made last night in a spirit of conciliation and concord. And we would search through it in vain for a single word that would wound the feelings of those he opposed.

He drew a parallel with the atrocities in the deaths of Caesar, Rienzi and Lincoln. Then he continued:

His patriotism, too, had taught him to disdain danger. And the fear of that danger never caused him to recoil in the struggle he had undertaken against those whose hand struck him down last night. But his death will mark the death of Fenianism.

Here Chauveau, a man of restraint, paused before he made his next statement:

There is reason to believe that the cruel monster was present at the last sitting of the House.

This was startling. For, aside from the Members, the five hundred spectators who had been present could probably be traced through the records of their admission passes.

The galleries hummed with the excitement of Chauveau's accusation while the last two speakers spoke briefly. Both were Anti-Confederates from Nova Scotia: E. M. McDonald of Lunenburg, to whom McGee had referred in his last speech, and Stuart Campbell of Guysborough. Though both were political opponents of McGee, each remarked on his genius for making friends. Now that his voice was a shade and his laughter an echo, they recalled "his genial nature and wide charity," his "eloquence, patriotism and kindness of heart." The worth of D'Arcy McGee's last plea for Confederation was demonstrated by what Stuart Campbell then added:

In the political philosophy which Mr. McGee displayed on the floor of the House last night, there was sound advice to the people of my Province of Nova Scotia.

He was the last of the eight speakers that afternoon, but none had approached the eloquence of the man they remembered.

A civil servant who had just managed to get in to a crowded gallery that afternoon recorded his critical impressions in his diary that evening. MacDonald, he wrote, "was inaudible," Cartier's voice was "harsh and unusual," Chamberlin's few words were "well chosen" and Chauveau spoke "with deep feeling." But he was most impressed by the behaviour of the Members:

Sitting in their seats, motionless, many with their heads down, some were in tears. Not a whisper was heard. The profound stillness of the House was indeed the most eloquent tribute to McGee.

And in that silence the House of Commons adjourned at five minutes past four until the Tuesday following Easter.

As the galleries emptied and the last persons left the quiet House they turned and looked down at the empty seat. It was an instinctive gesture to an unseen presence, as though they sensed that a glorious voice was still imprisoned among the echoes, and a soul had been released to rise beyond their reach.

Few were aware of a special group in the galleries that afternoon.

Sitting together and listening intently were "thirteen able and sufficient men of the City of Ottawa," the coroner's jury. At half past ten that morning Coroner Edward Van Cortlandt had sworn them in at Mrs. Trotter's Boarding House where they had heard the testimony of two doctors in their raw, clinical descriptions of the autopsy of D'Arcy McGee. When the jurors heard that the Members of Parliament were assembling that afternoon "to deliver speeches of condolence," they had passed a formal motion, with the coroner's consent, "to adjourn until 7 P.M. and in the meantime to attend at the House of Commons in a body, clad in dark clothes but not craped." So, in this irregular manner, the Members of Parliament, in referring to the crime and the suspected criminals, had, without realizing it, delivered unsworn evidence before the coroner's jury.

While it was still light, many of the spectators went back to the scene of the crime on Sparks Street, which became so crowded that the Queen's Printer Desbarats decided to remove the blood-stained planks from the sidewalk "to save them from desecration." As the shadows lengthened and the air grew very damp, people huddled together tense with anticipation of some sudden developments. Everyone felt sure that the assassin was a Fenian. Or almost everyone.

In Toronto that midnight George Brown read the latest reports received by the *Globe*, and then, with unusual detachment for such an outspoken enemy of the Fenians, made this cryptic comment in a letter to his wife in Edinburgh:

My dearest Anne:
A dreadful thing happened this morning. Poor D'Arcy McGee was shot dead at the door of his lodging house. It is supposed to be the work of Fenianism—but I am not certain as to that.

# 29

## FUNERAL

A very flimsy, miserable makeshift,
Neither an art nor yet a mystery?

Ah! Were there many rulers among men,
How fragrant in God's nostrils would become
This reeling, riotous and rotten earth.

"LIFE, A MYSTERY TO MAN"
*Thomas D'Arcy McGee*

How the mighty man has fallen who saved the people of
Israel.

TEXT FROM MACCABEES
FOR THE FUNERAL SERMON AT ST. PATRICK'S,
APRIL 13, 1868

At eight o'clock Wednesday morning, April 8, a great number of citizens, headed by the gaunt figure of Sir John A. MacDonald, assembled at Mrs. Trotter's Toronto House on Sparks Street to accompany the remains of D'Arcy McGee to the railway station in Ottawa. A procession a mile long wended its way to the Cathedral, where prayers for the dead were said, and then proceeded further north to a special train at the old depot on Sussex Street. Noted among the mourners walking behind the hearse were Patrick Buckley, the doorkeeper of Parliament, and his brother John.

The corpse was brought to Montreal by McGee's faithful friends Walter McFarlane, William O'Brien, James Donnelly, Luke Moore and William McNaughton. Leaving Ottawa at 9:40 A.M., the train followed the only route to Montreal, taking the St. Lawrence & Ottawa Railway for fifty miles to its junction with the Grand Trunk Railway at Prescott. Here, where he had suffered his only loss of an election, McGee's casket was opened for the public to view. From Prescott downward, flags were at half-mast at each station, where crowds gathered and stood in silence. The small station at Iroquois was completely draped in mourning. At Cornwall, the mayor headed a prominent assembly, and as the train stopped, church bells tolled and once again the face-plate was removed from the casket. At Lancaster the platform was lined by Captain Mc-Lennan's Volunteers. Finally the train approached Montreal. It was met at Lachine by another train which came out, filled with friends, to escort it in to Bonaventure station, where it arrived at 5:15 P.M.

An immense crowd waited at the depot. There were literally thousands along the route, as McGee's body was borne up Beaver Hall Hill and westward to his home on the south side of St. Catherine Street (now number 1198). There McGee's body was met at the door by his intimate friend Joseph Daley.

D'Arcy McGee lay in state for three days, in the dining room near the dark-panelled stairwell of his home. The coffin, known as a Fisk Metallic Burial Case, had an unusual shape, being deeply ridged along both sides and curving upward at each end to a point a few feet above the level of the body. Under a heavy glass fitted across the top, the body could be seen, clad in full dress, bearing a large brown scapular of the Order of St. Francis, and lower down a cross wrought in green leaves of myrtle, olive and cedar. On the breast amid some maple leaves was one pure white camellia.

Standing on a pedestal at the head was a crucifix in bronze. At the feet on a marble table were three alabaster vases filled with white lilies. Banked in flowers at the back were six massive silver candelabra from Notre Dame Church, with burning tapers all around casting a dim light through the room. In front on a white carpet was a *prie-dieu*.

Soon after the arrival of the body the public were admitted, entering by the front door and leaving by the rear. Solemn and official as it had to be, it was still a wake, in the manner beyond memory of the Irish. There were warm, soft words of affection, formal gestures of sympathy and elaborate phrases, but mostly humble and countless prayers as an unending stream of people entered, knelt, passed by the coffin and looked upon the face, so exceedingly pale, of D'Arcy McGee. The features in repose were recognizable, except where the strong line of his mouth had been mutilated by the bullet.

The line of people outside stretched for blocks: men with mutton-chop whiskers, close short coats and tight trousers, young women with bonnets perched high on their chignons and older women wearing shawls, patiently waiting. Amid the thousands passing through the home a lady, attired in deep mourning, unknown, stopped long enough to place a wreath of immortelles over the crucifix.

There was a flurry in the crowd when D'Arcy McGee's younger brother, obviously distressed and excited, arrived from New York. He was "Jimmy," now Colonel James E. McGee, who had won a reputation for bravery as an officer in Thomas Francis Meagher's Irish Brigade in the American Civil War.

Good Friday came and the grief was beginning to tell on Mrs. McGee. Her close friend Mrs. James Sadlier spoke of her sorrow as perhaps "too sacred for the public eye." So it was announced that the house would be closed after five o'clock that evening, to be reserved for the family and their friends over Holy Saturday and Easter Sunday.

Over the week-end special trains with crowded carriages ran in from Ottawa, Prescott and points in the Eastern Townships. It was decided at a large civic meeting that the funeral should be public, at the expense of the city, to be held on Easter Monday, April 13, which was proclaimed as a public day of mourning. It would have been the forty-third birthday of D'Arcy McGee.

Monday morning broke clear and cold. As early as six o'clock preparations were visible in almost every quarter of the city. For a mid-April day in Montreal it was a remarkably fine one, and as the day advanced it grew a trifle milder. The scanty snow on the ground had almost disappeared, yet the weather was cool enough to prevent a thaw, which could have made walking very unpleasant. The whole city was soon astir, and spectators had begun to assemble along St. Catherine Street. A visitor driving through the city at eight o'clock found it "already alive with mourners and the military."

By half past nine, the long procession had been marshalled and fully formed, winding from the McGee residence down Drummond Street, along Dorchester and around Dominion Square. St. Catherine Street was thronged. Many of the houses were draped in mourning, and all the windows were crowded, as were the roofs, where, it was remarked, there were mostly ladies.

The line of march had been carefully marked off. From the residence it was to proceed eastward on St. Catherine to Bleury Street, where it turned south to Lagauchetière Street and thence westward for two blocks to St. Patrick's Church. The streets were kept clear by a double scarlet line of soldiers from the home to the church.

At forty minutes past nine the funeral procession left the McGee residence. With the band of the Grand Trunk Brigade under the leadership of Horr Zeigler playing Handel's "Dead March" from *Saul*, moving slowly, six abreast, the police led off. They were followed by the fire brigade, officials, aldermen and the mayor of Montreal. The city of Ottawa was similarly represented. Next in order were the members of the Quebec Legislative Assembly and the Council; then the members of the House of Commons and the Senate. Foreign consuls followed. Next were the militia, the officers wearing crape on the left arm, and the men with their overcoats rolled up and fastened in cross-belts as a badge of mourning. Then there was a gap.

Walking in their robes of office came the judges, the Cabinet Ministers and the representatives of the Lieutenant Governors of Ontario and Quebec and the Governor General.

Then came the hearse. Six spirited dark grey horses, owned by James McGuire and well known in Montreal as the Grand Trunk Team, were drawing the funeral carriage of magnificent proportions. Specially built, the hearse itself was fifteen feet long and sixteen feet high. On an inside platform, eight feet from the ground and exposed to the view, rested the coffin. Over it was an open tent-shaped canopy, with drooping dark plumes of feathers at its corners and supported by eight twisted pillars from Irish designs. It was crowned by a golden cross in a circle.

On each side of the platform was a silver escutcheon, bearing the inscription in red lettering: "T. D. McGee, April 7th, 1868," adorned underneath with silvered shamrocks and four legends, one of them taken from McGee's memorial verses for Lawrence Devaney, *Miserere Domine.*

Directly behind the hearse were the chief mourners and the funeral carriages. Next were the clergy, the Bar, the notarial and medical professions and the representatives of the universities, followed by numerous students in law, medicine and arts from McGill. The cosmopolitan character of the city was shown in the subsequent sections, where all the national, benevolent and religious societies walked one after another in full membership.

Present were the Montreal Literary Club, proud to honour D'Arcy McGee as one of its most distinguished members, the Typographical Union to pay tribute to him as a newspaper man, several workingmen's benefit societies and all kinds of public and private bodies, joined by a vast body of citizens whose numbers were augmented by visitors from all parts of Canada. Bringing up the rear was an impressive contingent of the government police.

It was estimated that fifteen thousand people were marching. The organization of a funeral on such a vast scale was unique for Montreal, and any number of difficulties had to be surmounted. For example, there was the delicate matter of precedence. St. George's Society felt that it should walk ahead of the St. Jean Baptiste Society, but it was finally conceded that the French-Canadian body would rank first, "without however establishing a precedent." The ranking of St. Patrick's Society presented a highly emotional problem. Only ten weeks before, it had expelled D'Arcy McGee as a member, and it was now suffering posthumous contrition; but it was eventually settled by ranking St. Patrick's Society after the St. Jean Baptiste Society.

Drums and fifes were in attendance, and solemn martial music was taken up in turn by the different bands of the volunteer and regular regiments stationed along the route. As the procession moved slowly eastward the dust and the ruts in the broken gravelled surface of St. Catherine Street became somewhat muddy. All the while, Lieutenant Colonel Stevenson's field battery occupied ground near St. Patrick's Church and continually fired off two nine pounders at the rate of one a minute, firing two hundred times in all, throughout the proceedings.

As the rear of the procession was still passing Erskine Presbyterian Church at the corner of Peel Street, it stretched right along St. Catherine past the Crystal Palace and the recently completed Christ Church Cathedral, while the front section had already turned down Bleury Street. As it descended Bleury a bystander was overheard using some coarse language. He was immediately assumed to be a Fenian supporter and was knocked down by a volunteer guard, which was done, as the *Gazette* described it, "in a highly commendable manner."

As the cortège rumbled slowly down Bleury, passing St. Mary's College on the right, a particularly striking view could be had from the high steps of the Church of the Gesu. Bleury Street had been cleaned for the funeral, its uneven surface repaired by broken stones, and the old water-courses which ran down the hill, had been channelled into brick shafts and covered. Just below Dorchester one of the submerged streams swollen by an earlier thaw had overflowed, but a ditch had been dug and temporarily covered. The wooden footpaths on both sides of the street were jammed with spectators. Everyone remarked the home of Joseph Daley nearby. He had been like a brother to McGee, and the front of his house was now completely covered in black cloth.

Finally the hearse turned off Bleury Street, crunching its way westward over the rough gravel on Lagauchetière and coming to a stop where the front gate to St. Patrick's Church was then located, on Lagauchetière just west of St. Alexander Street.

McGee's widow, dressed in deep black, was directly behind the hearse in a mourning coach. Her pale face could be seen through the glass windows, and on each side of her, the bewildered eyes of her two daughters.

The war pipes of the 78th Highlanders played a dirge as the coffin was removed from the hearse and carried up the long, inclined walk and steps, lined with trees, to the arched front entrance under the Tower of St. Patrick's. The military presented arms as the coffin passed, and then as Mrs. McGee went by, holding her children by the hand, the officers saluted.

It was a solemn moment at the front door as the coffin of D'Arcy McGee was met by his friend, clad in rich vestments, Father Patrick Dowd. He gave three vigorous strokes of blessing, sprinkling the casket with water, and then broke the toneless silence by the opening words of the chant: "*Exultabunt Domino.*" On that signal, the vastness of the church seemed suddenly filled, as the choir and the organ broke forth, charging the air with sound, which rose above the muffled movements of the crowd surging in to fill all the pews.

The ladies were in the gallery. And they turned to watch the widow and her children quietly move up the side aisle to the front pew, there to kneel and to pray in the words of the liturgy for "fresh life."

Then, with the feet turned towards the altar, the mortal frame of McGee was solemnly wheeled up to the middle of the church and placed beneath a black pall flanked by a score of lighted tapers of unbleached wax. And so it rested, not far from his own pew, number 240.

Amid the grey, the green and the ivory of old St. Patrick's, in those years before it was decorated, the catafalque stood alone, relieved by deep purple on the sides and a single wreath of green on top.

Father Dowd began the sacrifice of the Mass for the Dead. Opening with that ageless greeting "To God who rejoices my youth" (which had moved D'Arcy McGee to verse a few months before his death) it was renewed in the Collect as the priest prayed with the people "to establish him in that bliss which knows no ending." The direct talk of the Epistle followed:

Make no mistake about those who have gone to their rest; you are not to grieve over them, as the rest of the world does, with no hope to live by.

As Father Dowd prayed silently before reading the Gospel the words seemed fitting as a remembrance of the fire of the orator:

Cleanse my heart and my lips, Almighty God, who did cleanse the lips of the prophet Isaias with a living coal.

The Gospel was read; then everyone sat as the choir sang that Franciscan hymn of such strange and solitary beauty the *Dies Irae*. The *Miserere* and the Offertory followed. In a quiet interval the Secret prayer was offered for the departed to go on to the land of the living. The Preface led to the *Sanctus,* and then the Canon, accented by incense and the ringing of the bell at the central act of adoration. The *Pater Noster* was intoned and the *Libera* was sung that "men will remember the just man forever." Then, rising with its marvellous quality of supplication and its perfect metaphor, came the *Agnus Dei*. Following Communion was the prayer to "give rest to his soul in green places." The Mass was ended with the mystical words of the Last Gospel. Then, like the pause of the pilgrim, there was silence.

The altar was empty, and the congregation sat with their thoughts. As always in the presence of death, the ancient unspoken questionings arose. Where now is earthly endeavour? Where is the vanity of earthly doings? Where the crowd and the tumult? And what lies beyond this dread mystery?

A vigorous young priest with a well-shaped head and clear eyes appeared. He walked down the altar steps and through the aisle to mount the winding stairway to the pulpit, which was placed higher then than it is today and one pillar closer to the middle of the nave. He was Father Michael O'Farrell. This young priest (who would later become the first Bishop of Trenton, New Jersey) was only thirty-five and had been chosen as the preacher because he had been specially close to McGee and shared something of his eloquence.

In a solemn and quiet opening he referred to "the poor relics of mortality" and "the silvery tones of the magnificent voice which passed so easily from the grave to the gay," how McGee had risen above local interests to act in the open field of honour and how he had worked to build a public spirit in Canada and "to diffuse a common spirit of charity."

Then came a flash of vehemence:

D'Arcy McGee loved everything about Ireland except the shortcomings of her people.

And he added:

If it be proved that his death was the result of his enmity to those secret societies, then I call upon every honest man to stamp out with horror every vestige of them among us.

With those words spoken, loud applause suddenly broke out in the church. Such an outburst, so unheard of, brought with it its own sense of shock and shame. No one knew quite where to look, as quiet returned. There was a long pause. Then in a low tone Father O'Farrell, half as a reminder to himself, added:

Remember this is the House of God.

The spirit changed, and the speaker rose to a higher level:

More than all, I loved and admired the humble Christian. In the last year during his long illness, he showed the firmest hope. From those lonely hours came a new view of things, and a resolve to apply himself more closely to his duties.

Praising McGee's unflinching courage, Father O'Farrell then added:

He had his faults as everyone knows.

That phrase from the pulpit was narrowed in the busy world of the gossips to mean one thing, his weakness for drink. But the priest saw deeper, yet did not indulge further than to use an oblique Victorian phrase:

> This change might also be seen in the resolution which he kept so inviolably until the day of his death, to abstain from those social excesses which would mar so considerably the effect of his talents.

He testified then to this truth about D'Arcy McGee:

> One thing was very remarkable in his character. It was the simple and unaffected way in which he was ever ready to aid in any cause of benevolence.

It was reassuring for the faithful to hear, as Father O'Farrell expressed it, that on the day before McGee had departed from Montreal to Ottawa:

> He had fulfilled his Easter duty in his church. As far as human knowledge can go, I believe that the deceased did earnestly strive to prepare himself for the great account.

By the time the Mass and sermon were over, it was almost one o'clock. In the cramped space outside St. Patrick's Church, heavily encumbered by the crowds, there was great difficulty in reforming the procession.

As his friends stood around in groups one of them pointed out a small house, just a stone's throw from the hearse. It was 37 St. Alexander Street, on the east side just below Lagauchetière. That, it was explained, was the home of a red-whiskered tailor who had just been arrested in Ottawa. On him had been found a Derringer pistol.

# 30

## LAMENT

Men cannot cast a dungeon
O'er the stars, and he's among them.
He, of his the liberal spender,
Of ours the stern defender,
The pillar of our power
Snapped in our trial's hour.

Chant slower, sister, slower.
'Tis the keen of Donnell More.

UNFINISHED FRAGMENT
*Thomas D'Arcy McGee*

Her sun is gone down while it is yet day.

JEREMIAS XV: 9

There was something immense about Montreal that Easter Monday. The population of the city was then one hundred thousand, but there were so many visitors for D'Arcy McGee's funeral that the population had practically doubled. Newspaper reporters who estimated the numbers marching and gathered along the long route wrote that a hundred thousand people participated in one way or another in the demonstration of mourning. The newspapers themselves doubled their sales, and the Montreal *Gazette* announced on its front page that the circulation of its special issue for the funeral had climbed to a record of 13,400.

After some delay outside St. Patrick's Church the funeral procession moved westward on Lagauchetière and turned down the hill into Victoria Square. Not as unkempt as it had been in its days as the Haymarket when McGee first arrived in Montreal, the Square now had some small trees and a new fountain for the warmer weather. On its east side at Craig Street, St. Patrick's Hall was just about completed, based on an Irish design inspired by Cormac's Chapel on the Rock of Cashel. The Square was densely crowded, particularly with Irish immigrants from Griffintown who stood with their heads uncovered while policemen, polished and burly in their dark blue uniforms, kept watch.

The funeral moved slowly east into Great St. James Street, where the small grey houses with tin roofs, shuttered windows and iron doors were gradually being replaced by new buildings of cut stone. The surface of the road was now laid with smooth wood blocking, with sidewalks of three-inch hemlock planks tied together and nailed to four-by-four-inch floats. For a short distance there were flagstones and bricks imported from England. But that day it was all hidden, for the street was choked with people. Windows were crowded; boys were perched on narrow cornices; and hundreds were leaning forward from the roofs, their forms cutting sharp silhouettes out of the brilliant sky.

Immediately on the left, at the corner of Victoria Square, draped in black, was the city's leading dry-goods merchant, Henry Morgan & Co. As the procession moved eastward it passed smaller shops on the north side, hairdressers, lace cleaners, haberdashers, saddlers, photographers, shoemakers, coal merchants, tailors and opticians, until it reached the

Montreal Club and then, covered in heavy mourning, the auction rooms of Lawrence Devaney, now operated by the widow of McGee's close friend who had died the month before.

On the south side were two particular haunts of D'Arcy McGee, the Ottawa Hotel and the Queen's Chop House, both in mourning for their merriest customer. Then came Dollard Lane, which led over to Notre Dame Street. There the Irish had their first parish church in the monastery of the Récollets; but this had vanished when the Récollet Church was torn down the year before, and with it went the last of the Franciscans' majestic elms which once shaded Notre Dame.

On the site now known as 360 St. James Street stood an ornate three-storey building in Italian style. This was the Mechanics Institute, which brought back vivid memories of McGee. Upstairs in its main hall he had delivered some of his finest lectures on Moore, Burns, Scott, Milton and Shakespeare. There, too, were his committee rooms during his last election, when he had spoken from a window to the crowds below; and just across St. Peter Street on the western wall of Molson's Bank (now the Bank of Montreal) was the mark of a bullet fired during the riot on the night of his victory.

East of St. Peter on the north side was Freeman's popular Oyster and Chop House, where for twenty-five cents McGee had often had a good lunch, sat long and laughed with his friends. Beyond that were the newspaper offices, so familiar to D'Arcy McGee, of Brown Chamberlin's *Gazette*.

Across the street, at the intersection of St. John Street, and much to the annoyance of the antiseptic, remained Tattersall's horse yards. At the southwest corner of St. Francis Xavier stood the deficient Post Office, which faced the leading hotel of the city, Henry Hogan's famous St. Lawrence Hall, the centre for the Southerners during the American Civil War, and the scene of McGee's eloquence at the closing of the Quebec Conference.

Just beyond Place D'Armes was the poorer part of the street, called Little St. James, where it continued eastward to the Court House. There in a square, three-storey stone building on the south side D'Arcy McGee had rented his modest office in 1863 as a lawyer.

When the hearse reached Place D'Armes, the larger part of the procession was stopped along Great St. James Street, and as the men waited in line, they told one another all the different stories they had heard about the assassination.

Arrests were being made by the hundreds, particularly in Ottawa, To-

ronto and Montreal, and many names were mentioned. But the most surprising of all to be arrested was the popular coachman to both Sir John
A. MacDonald and George Brown, the doorkeeper of Parliament, Patrick
Buckley. There was also a startling and gruesome report that an elderly
Englishman by the name of Dent, who had worked as a night watchman
for the Queen's Printer on Sparks Street, had committed suicide by blowing his brains out.

But few knew anything for certain about the suspected tailor with
the red whiskers and the Derringer pistol. He had lived in Quebec City
before coming to Montreal, it was said, and the shop where he had
worked was directly in front of them, on the south side of Great Saint
James Street just west of Saint Francis Xavier, where the sign read:

Gibb & Co.
Merchant Tailors and
Gentleman's Haberdashers
since 1775

He was in his late twenties, and his name was Patrick James Whelan.
But that was about all that was known.

After turning into Place D'Armes the funeral entered Notre Dame
Church for a second religious service, as a reminder that the autonomy
of St. Patrick's was not yet recognized. There the immensity of the
demonstration took on a special air of majesty. There were salvos of
cannon, tolling of great bells, martial dirges, the beat of muffled drums,
flags dipping at half-mast, banners furled and draped, the flash of swords
in the sun, the rattle of arms being presented, the thud of rifle butts
falling in unison on the flagstones, the military clink of metal, and everywhere the slow tramp of marching feet.

Rows upon rows of nuns, in their impeccable costumes of black and
starched white, were set off against the mottled colours of the crowd,
ranging from the subdued dress of the respectable resident to the bronze
face of a *voyageur* in his red-checked jacket or an Indian woman
wrapped in an olive-coloured blanket. And almost everyone, it
seemed, was wearing a badge or special emblem, a draped rose, a *fleur
de lis*, the cross of St. Andrew's or the shamrock tied with black ribbon.
Such were the signs expressing the sentiment of the people. Like most
demonstrations of official sorrow, it was awesome and profuse. Yet it did
not miss its mark. There was simple grief, too, and no one pretended
that it could be soothed by pomp. All in all, it was the way the city

took to protest against a crime and do honour to someone who had died with a touch of greatness upon him.

In the noble church of Notre Dame, where ten thousand people filled the nave and the double galleries, the great organ released its full power as a magnificent *Libera* was sung. Then a frail and venerable figure appeared. It was Bishop Bourget, an old opponent of D'Arcy Mc-Gee, standing on the lower steps of the altar and expressing his sorrow:

A unanimous sentiment has brought a whole population to the front of the altar of expiation. You will not regret the manner in which you have spent this day. It will give to our children a spectacle of loyalty, patriotism and confidence in God.

It was then half past two. The coffin was removed from its large cata-falque of black and gold and carried outside. Once again the pro-cession was reformed to march east on Notre Dame Street, where one of the insignia read:

We shall never look upon his like again.

The funeral turned from Notre Dame Street to go north and down St. Lambert Hill, now St. Lawrence Main. Troops again took up their po-sitions in open ranks and saluted as the slow-moving hearse came down the Hill and turned west on Craig Street. A horse suddenly reared up and kicked, breaking a woman's arm. In all the crowding of that day, this was the only accident reported.

Turning up Beaver Hall Hill, more volunteers joined the procession, marching with arms reversed as they mounted the hill of churches, pass-ing the Zion Congregational Church, then further up on the right the Unitarian Church of the Messiah, and across the way, at the corner of Belmont, the Presbyterian Church of St. Andrew with its stately spire. On Beaver Hall Terrace, the home of William O'Brien was draped with heavy black cloth; and nearby, the home of another of McGee's good friends, Walter McFarlane, carried the single word "Farewell."

Up Union Avenue at Burnside, the funeral crossed the *burn* which ran eastward from James McGill's farm. Here the creek had been cleaned and the crossing freshly covered with quarry chips. Then the last turn of the formal procession was taken to the west on Sherbrooke Street, where groups of schoolgirls with their bright faces stood in silence as the hearse went by.

Beyond the lacrosse grounds at Guy Street, the public demonstration was over. The militia were dismissed, and the Highlanders, "their bare knees blue with cold," returned in their kilts to their armoury.

But many continued on, plodding up Côte des Neiges Road as it wound its narrow way amid some boulders and a swollen stream, up the most concave part of Mount Royal. Even the toll gate carried a wreath of evergreens and a small flag at half-mast.

Reaching the summit of the road, and looking back, there was a splendid view of McGee's Montreal. Just below was the rich orchard country of apples, pears and choice plums. But it was too early for the blossoms. The early spring soil and last year's grass were washed in a fawn light, descending terrace by terrace to the level of the old stone city. With its tin roofs, steeples and spires, Montreal seemed reticent, but here and there its weathered grey limestone was touched by a whisper of green.

The cortège went on through a gap, as the April sun was declining straight ahead. Finally it reached Côte des Neiges Cemetery, which was spread out to the right and upward like an amphitheatre. Following a gravelled road, lined with elms, it passed a wooden cross, a chapel and a sombre square building called the dead-house. The procession then

turned to the left to go up an alley lined with black railings and marble slabs, until it reached a plain vault built into the side of a small hill like an ancient rath. There they entombed D'Arcy McGee.

Father Dowd said the final formal prayers of the Church. Then Mrs. McGee entered the vault with her two fatherless children, and they spent a few moments there alone. Coming out into the cold sunlight of that late afternoon, for it was now half past four, they entered their carriage, which wheeled around on that high ground to go down slowly towards the west.

Soon enough there would be flowers everywhere and in profusion, rich in perfume and wild in beauty, yellow, purple and berry-coloured, dog-tooth, twisted stem, lady's slipper, Indian pipe and snake's head. But the ground that day was barren. A few sparrows chirped and a grey squirrel scuttered across their path.

In the distance through the bare April woods, Mary Teresa McGee could see the grey waters of Lake St. Louis. Ahead of her, life stretched out as her husband had described it:

> The lone lake, like a lady, grieves
> Saddest in the long autumn eves.

# BIBLIOGRAPHY

## A NOTE ON SOURCES

In the course of his hurried career Thomas D'Arcy McGee wrote about twenty books, delivered more than thirteen hundred lectures and made countless political speeches. He wrote steadily for the newspapers: for the Boston *Pilot*, the Dublin *Freeman* and the *Nation* in his early years; for his own *New York Nation, American Celt* and *New Era;* and then for the *Canadian Freeman*, the *Tablet* and the Montreal *Gazette*. His poems, collected by Mrs. James Sadlier with her valuable comments, offer a special insight into his ideals and conduct. His many letters (a large part of which still remain uncollected) were written in an open and generous manner, and are unusually revealing. So McGee was the best of all sources for this book. This is covered by the first part of the Bibliography. It contains a list of his published works, which is probably complete (although his last manuscript, a novel called *Cyrus O'Neill*, was lost).

The second part of the Bibliography lists the books and articles written on McGee. Here the biographical works of Brady, Cameron, Clarke, O'Gorman, Phelan, Skelton and Taylor were the most useful.

In the third part, under the heading Archives, are the manuscripts, documents and contemporary newspapers which were constantly used. Excerpts from them have occasionally been paraphrased.

The fourth part, under the title General, contains those works which were most profitably consulted on those times. Instead of inserting footnotes in this book, the working papers and references to authorities have been deposited in the McGee Room of the Vanier Library at Loyola of Montreal, with collections of manuscripts, notes and correspondence on McGee.

## 1. BY THOMAS D'ARCY McGEE

*Historical Sketches of O'Connell and his Friends.* Boston, 1844.
*Eva Macdonald. A Tale of the United Irishmen and their Times.* Boston, Brainard, 1844. New York Public Library, 47 p.

The Irish Writers of the Seventeenth Century. James Duffy, Library of Ireland, v. 8. Dublin, Simpkins, 1846–47.

A Memoir of the Life and Conquests of Art MacMurrogh, King of Leinster, from A.D. 1377 to 1417; with some Notices of the Leinster Wars of the 17th century. James Duffy, Library of Ireland. Dublin, Simpkins, 1847.

Memoir of Charles Gavan Duffy. Dublin, 1849.

A History of the Irish Settlers in North America, from the Earliest Period to the Census of 1850. Boston, American Celt, 1851. 180 p.

History of the Attempts to Establish the Protestant Reformation in Ireland, 1540–1830. Boston, Donahue, 1853.

Political Causes of the Protestant Reformation. New York, 1853.

The Catholic History of North America, five discourses to which are added two discourses on the relations of Ireland and America. Boston, Donahue, 1855, 239 p.

The Life of the Rt. Rev. Edward Maginn (1802–49), Coadjutor Bishop of Derry, with selections from his correspondence. New York, O'Shea, 1857. 320 p.

Canadian Ballads and Occasional Verses. Montreal, Lovell, 1858. 124 p.

Sebastian; or The Roman Martyr. A Drama founded on Wiseman's Fabiola. New York, Sadlier, 1860. 52 p.

"Emigration and Colonization in Canada," a speech in the House of Assembly. Quebec, 1862. 25 p.

"On a Lately Discovered MS. of Samuel Champlain." Transactions of the Literary and Historical Society of Quebec, 1862–63, vol. V. pp. 35–41. Quebec, Hunter Rose, 1863.

A Popular History of Ireland, from the Earliest Period to the Emancipation of the Catholics. New York, Sadlier, 1863. 2v. 823 p.

"The Internal Condition of American Democracy," considered in a letter to the Honorable C. G. Duffy, M.P.P., Minister of Public Lands of the Colony of Victoria. London, 1863. 19 p.

"Two Pleas for British American Nationality." British American Magazine. Aug. and Oct. 1863, p. 338 and p. 562.

"The Crown and the Confederation." Three letters to the Hon. John Alexander McDonald, Attorney General for Upper Canada. By a Backwoodsman. Montreal, 1864. 36 p.

Notes on Federal Governments, Past and Present, with appendix. Montreal, Dawson, 1865. 75 p.

Speeches and Addresses, chiefly on the Subject of British-American Union. London, Chapman & Hall, 1865. 316 p.

Two Speeches on the Union of the Provinces. Quebec, Hunter Rose, 1865. 34 p.

The Irish Position in British and in Republican North America, a Letter to the Editors of the Irish Press, irrespective of Party. Second ed. Montreal, Longmoore, 1866. 45 p.

Poems, with copious Notes, also an Introduction and Biographical Sketch by Mrs. James Sadlier. New York, Sadlier, 1869. 612 p.

Thomas D'Arcy McGee Papers, mainly correspondence, 1848–68. Public Archives of Canada, Ottawa.

Unpublished Letters of D'Arcy McGee, his wife, his father and others. 44 original letters with notes in two volumes. McGee Room, Vanier Library, Loyola of Montreal.

Transcripts and Photostats of T. D. McGee Correspondence. McGee Room, Vanier Library, Loyola of Montreal.

McGee Letters. W. S. O'Brien Papers. National Library of Ireland, Dublin.

McGee Letters and Photographs. Antiquarian and Numismatic Society, Château de Ramezay, Montreal.

*American Celt.* Boston newspaper, Jan. 4–Dec. 27, 1851. Fraser-Hickson Library, Montreal.

*New Era.* Montreal newspaper, May 25, 1857–May 1, 1858. Archives of St. Patrick's Church, Montreal.

## 2. ON THOMAS D'ARCY McGEE

ANDERSON, J. R. "A Tragedy of Sixty Years Ago." Montreal, *Family Herald & Weekly Star Magazine*, March 21, 1928.

BRADY, ALEXANDER. *Thomas D'Arcy McGee.* Toronto, Macmillan, 1925.

BURNS, ROBIN B. "D'Arcy McGee and the New Era. The Political Career of D'Arcy McGee." Ottawa, Unpublished Papers, History Dept., Carleton University, 1966.

BURRELL, MARTIN. *Betwixt Heaven and Charing Cross.* Chapter on T. D. McGee. Toronto, Macmillan, 1927.

CAMERON, E. R. *The Memoirs of Ralph Vansittart,* a biography of D'Arcy McGee. Second ed. Toronto, Musson, 1924.

CLARKE, HENRY J. O'C. *A Short Sketch of the Life of the Hon. Thomas D'Arcy McGee, M.P.* Montreal, Lovell, 1868.

COFFEY, AGNES. Hon. Thomas D'Arcy McGee, A Bibliography. Montreal, McGill University Library School, 1933.

COLEMAN, JAMES F. R. *Bibliography of T. D. McGee.* Dublin, Falconer, Bibliographical Society of Ireland, March 26, 1925.

CONNOLLY, ARCHBISHOP THOMAS L. *Funeral Oration on Thomas D'Arcy McGee.* Halifax, Compton, 1868, 24 p.

COOPER, DR. J. I. "Journal of Opinion A Century Ago; McGee's New Era." *Montreal Star,* May 24, 1957.

―― "Thomas D'Arcy McGee, McGill's Father of Confederation." Montreal, *The McGill News,* Vol. 38 No. 4, 1957, p. 15.

DAWSON, REV. A. MACDONNELL. "Requiem Sermon at L'Orignal, Ontario: Our strength and their strength," with opinion of press. Ottawa, Times Office, 1870.

DOHENY, MICHAEL. *The Felon's Track,* with D'Arcy McGee's Narrative. Dublin, Gill, 1914.

DOYLE, M. "Sketch of Life of T. D. McGee." Ottawa, Women's Canadian Historical Society of Ottawa, Transactions, 1928, pp. 147–51.

FORAN, J. K. "T. D. McGee as an Empire Builder." Toronto, Empire Club Speeches, Vol. 1905–6, p. 155.

GRANNAN, R. L. "Thomas D'Arcy McGee and Confederation in the Maritimes." *Canadian Catholic Historical Association Reports*, 1953, p. 93.

GRIFFIN, WATSON. *An Irish Evolution.* Toronto, Ontario Press Ltd., 1912, 33 p.

HARVEY, D. C. "Thomas D'Arcy McGee; The Prophet of Canadian Nationality." University of Manitoba, 1923, 30 p.

—— "The Centenary of D'Arcy McGee." Halifax, *Dalhousie Review*, Vol. 5, pp. 1–10, April 1925.

HASSARD, A. R. "Great Canadian Orators, D'Arcy McGee." Toronto, *Canadian Historical Review*, Vol. 1, p. 114, 1919.

KEEP, G. R. C. "D'Arcy McGee and Montreal." Quebec, *Culture Magazine*, March 1951.

KIRBY, JAMES. "Hon. T. D. McGee." Montreal, Lovell, *Lower Canada Law Journal*, Vol. 4, No. 2, April 1868, p. 25.

MARKEY, JOHN. "T. D. McGee, Poet and Patriot." Toronto, *Canadian Magazine*, 1915, p. 67–72.

McCORD MUSEUM. D'Arcy McGee File, with articles, photographs and newspaper clippings. Montreal, McGill University.

McGEE, JOHN J. "Reminiscences," partial transcript of notes on Thomas D'Arcy McGee in J. J. O'Gorman Papers, Ottawa, Public Archives of Canada.

McGIBBON, ROBERT D. "An Address on T. D. McGee," before St. Patrick's Society in Sherbrooke. Montreal, Dawson, 1884.

MONAHAN, ARTHUR P. "A Politico-Religious Incident in the Career of Thomas D'Arcy McGee." *Canadian Catholic Historical Association Reports*, 1957, p. 39–52.

MORGAN, H. J. Biographical Files: McGee, pp. 5244–5308. Ottawa, Public Archives of Canada.

MULLALLY, JAMES E. "The Story of D'Arcy McGee." Montreal, *United Irish Review*, 1957.

MURPHY, CHARLES. *A Collection of Speeches and Addresses.* Toronto, Macmillan, 1937.

NEW YORK PUBLIC LIBRARY. Biographical material on T. D. McGee, not separately catalogued. AN (M) N.C. 2—No. 8. New York Public Library Annex.

O'GORMAN, REV. JOHN J. "Biographical Sketch of Thomas D'Arcy McGee," and four lectures. *The Catholic Record*, London, Ontario, April 1925–April 1926.

O'LEARY M. GRATTAN. "D'Arcy McGee." Toronto, *MacLean's Magazine*, April 1, 1925, p. 21.

—— "Assassination of D'Arcy McGee." Article with photograph. *Ottawa Evening Journal*, April 7, 1915.

O'NEILL, K. "Hon. T. D. McGee—Statesman, Journalist, Poet." *Catholic World*, March 1930.

PHELAN, JOSEPHINE. *The Ardent Exile.* The Life and Times of Thos. D'Arcy McGee. Toronto, Macmillan, 1951.

—— "D'Arcy McGee's Poetry: Its Place in his Biography. *Canadian Catholic Historical Association Report*, 1957, pp. 23–38.

SADLIER, ANNA T. "Thomas D'Arcy McGee, The Canadian Statesman." London, *The Month*, 1914, pp. 140–52.

SKELTON, ISABEL. *The Life of Thomas D'Arcy McGee*. Gardenvale, Garden City Press, 1925.

SLATTERY, PATRICIA. Chronology of Life of T. D. McGee, and Analysis of *Gazette* Files. Unpublished Manuscript, McGee Room, Vanier Library, Loyola of Montreal, 1966.

TAYLOR, FENNINGS. *The Hon. Thos. D'Arcy McGee: A Sketch of his Life and Death*. Montreal, Lovell, 1868.

TEEFY, POSTMASTER. Contemporary Scrap Book on D'Arcy McGee. Ontario, Richmond Hill, Edgar A. Collard.

THOMAS, W. K. "Analysis of McGee's Speech on Canada's Interest in the American Civil War." Halifax, *Dalhousie Review*. Vol. 39, Spring 1959, pp. 19–30.

WALKER, H. J. "Struggle for Canadian Unity recalled by McGee's Martyrdom." *Ottawa Journal*, April 4, 1942, p. 18.

WALLACE, WM. STEWART. "The Growth of Canadian National Feeling." Toronto, *Canadian Historical Review*, Vol. 1, No. 2, June 1920, pp. 136–65.

## 3. ARCHIVES

The following manuscripts were consulted in the Public Archives of Canada:

George Brown Papers

Brown Chamberlin Papers

Sanford Fleming Papers

Galt Papers

Gowan Papers

John A. MacDonald Papers

Sandfield MacDonald Papers

Mackenzie Papers

McMicken Police Reports

Meredith Journals

Morgan Papers

Moylan Papers

Murphy Papers

O'Donohue Papers

O'Gorman Papers

O'Hanly Papers

O'Reilly Papers

Sadlier Papers

Spry Papers

Tupper Papers

Copies of the relevant parts of the above Papers have been noted with comments for the McGee Room of the Vanier Library at Loyola of Montreal, and classified with the other materials used, including:

The Unpublished Diary of George Edward Clerk, K.S.G.
Minutes of St. Patrick's Society of Montreal

The following newspapers were consulted as indicated:

*Canadian Freeman*, Toronto (Public Archives of Canada)

*Citizen*, Ottawa (Public Archives of Canada)

*Gazette*, Montreal (Gazette Library)

*Globe*, Toronto (McGill Redpath Library)

*Herald*, Montreal (Library of Parliament)

*Leader*, Toronto (Public Archives of Canada)

*Mail and Advertiser,* Niagara (McGill Redpath Library)
*La Minerve,* Montreal (Montreal Municipal Library)
*Le Nouveau Monde,* Montreal (Montreal Municipal Library)
*Times,* Ottawa (Library of Parliament)
*True Witness,* Montreal (Montreal Municipal Library)
*Witness,* Montreal (Public Archives of Canada)


## 4. GENERAL


ATHERTON, W. H. *Montreal, 1535–1914.* 3v. Montreal, S. J. Clarke, 1914.

BECK J. MURRAY. *Joseph Howe: Voice of Nova Scotia.* Toronto, McClelland & Stewart, 1964.

BENJAMIN, L. N. *The St. Albans Raid.* Montreal, Lovell, 1865.

BOYD, JOHN. *Sir George Etienne Cartier.* Toronto, Macmillan, 1914.

BRAULT, LUCIEN. *Ottawa Old & New.* Ottawa Historical Information Institute, 1946.

BUCKLEY, REV. M. R. *Diary of a Tour in America.* Dublin, Sealy Bryers & Walker, 1886.

BUREAU, JOS. *Hand Book to the Parliamentary and Departmental Buildings, Canada.* Ottawa, Desbarats, 1867.

CALLBECK, LORNE C. *The Cradle of Confederation.* Brunswick Press, 1964.

CARELESS, J. M. S. *Brown of the Globe.* 2v. Toronto, Macmillan, 1959.

CARON, HENRI LE. *Twenty-Five Years in the Secret Service—The Recollections of a Spy.* London, Heinemann, 1893.

CARTWRIGHT, SIR RICHARD. *Reminiscences.* Toronto, William Briggs, 1912.

CHAPAIS, THOMAS. *Cours d'Histoire du Canada.* Quebec, Garneau, 1934.

CLARKE, CHARLES. *Sixty Years in Upper Canada.* Toronto, William Briggs, 1908.

COLQUHOUN, A. H. N. *The Fathers of Confederation.* Toronto, Glasgow Brook & Co., 1916.

COLLARD, E. A. *Montreal Yesterdays.* Toronto, Longmans, 1962.

—— *Canadian Yesterdays.* Toronto, Longmans, 1955.

CREIGHTON, DONALD. *John A. MacDonald: The Young Politician; The Old Chieftain.* Toronto, Macmillan, 2v. 1952, 1955.

—— *The Road to Confederation.* Toronto, Macmillan, 1964.

D'ARCY, WILLIAM. *The Fenian Movement in the United States, 1858–1886.* Washington, Catholic University of America Press, 1947.

DAVIN, NICHOLAS FLOOD. *The Irishman in Canada.* Toronto, Maclear, 1877.

DAVID, L. O. *L'Union des Deux Canadas—1841–1867.* Montreal, Senecal, 1898.

DEBATES. Parliamentary Debates on Confederation of British North American Provinces, Quebec, 1865. Ottawa, Queen's Printer.

DENT, JOHN CHARLES. *The Last Forty Years: Canada Since the Union of 1841.* Toronto, George Virtue, 2v. 1881.

——, AND OTHERS. *The Canadian Portrait Gallery,* Toronto, 4v. 1880–81.

DEVOY, JOHN. *Recollections of an Irish Rebel.* New York, Charles D. Young, 1929.

DRISCOLL, FREDERICK. *Sketch of the Canadian Ministry.* Montreal, 1866.

DUFFY, SIR CHARLES GAVAN. *My Life in Two Hemispheres.* London, Fisher Unwin, 2v. 1898.

EGERTON, H. E., AND W. L. GRANT, *Selected Speeches and Despatches Relating to Canadian Constitutional History.* John Murray, 1907.

EXPO 1867. *L'Exposition Universelle de 1867.* Paris, Illustré, 2v.

FAIRLEY, MARGARET. *The Selected Writings of William Lyon Mackenzie,* Toronto, Oxford, 1960.

GROULX, LIONEL. *Histoire du Canada Français.* L'Action Nationale, tome 4. 1952.

GUILLET, EDWIN C. *The Great Migration, The Atlantic Crossing by Sailing Ship, 1770–1860.* Second ed. University of Toronto Press, 1963.

HAMMOND, M. O. *Confederation and Its Leaders.* Toronto, McClelland & Stewart, 1927.

HARDY, W. G. *From Sea Unto Sea (Canada 1850–1910).* New York, Doubleday, 1960.

HARRIS, MRS. AMELIA. Extracts from Her Diary—1875–77. Montreal, McGill University, 149–11H24.

HAVERTY, MARTIN. *The History of Ireland.* Dublin, James Duffy, 1906.

HODGINS, J. GEORGE. *Legislation and History of Separate Schools in Upper Canada, 1841–1876.* Toronto, 1897.

HYDE, DOUGLAS. *A Literary History of Ireland.* London, Fisher Unwin, 1910.

JENKINS, KATHLEEN. *Montreal.* New York, Doubleday, 1966.

KEEP, G. R. C. "The Irish Migration to Canada." Montreal, unpublished thesis, McGill University, 280 M & K 25, 1948.

KENNEDY, W. P. M. *The Constitution of Canada, 1534–1937.* Second ed. Oxford, 1938.

KERR, D. G. G. *A Historical Atlas of Canada.* Toronto, Nelson, 1959.

LANGEVIN, SIR HECTOR. *Le Métier de Ministre.* Montreal, La Presse, 1886.

LASKIN, BORA. *Canadian Constitutional Law.* Toronto, Carswell, 1960.

LETT, WM. PITTMAN. *Recollections of Bytown and its Old Inhabitants.* Ottawa, Citizen Printing Co., 1874.

LONGMOORE, M. *The Canadian Handbook and Tourist Guide.* Montreal, Longmoore, 1867.

LOWER, A. R. M. *Colony to Nation, A History of Canada.* Toronto, Longmans, 1964.

LYNE, DANIEL C. "The Irish in the Province of Canada." Montreal, unpublished thesis, McGill University, 1960.

LYONS, CAPT. W. F. *Brigadier-General Thomas Francis Meagher, His Political and Military Career.* New York, Sadlier, 1870.

MACDONALD, CAPT. JOHN A. *Troublous Times in Canada. A History of the Fenian Raids of 1866 and 1870.* Toronto, W. S. Johnston, 1910.

MACNUTT, W. S. *New Brunswick, A History, 1784–1867.* Toronto, Macmillan, 1963.

McInnis, Edgar. *Canada—A Political and Social History*. Revised ed. New York, Holt, Rinehart, 1964.

Maguire, John Francis. *The Irish in America*. New York, Sadlier, 1868.

Mannay, James. *The Life and Times of Sir Leonard Tilley*. St. John, N.B., 1897.

Mitchel, John. *Jail Journal, or Five Years in British Prisons*. New York, Haverty, 1868.

Morgan, Henry J. *Canadian Parliamentary Companion*. Ottawa, Desbarats, Nov. 1867.

Morton, W. L. *The Critical Years; The Union of British North America 1857–1873*. Toronto, McClelland & Stewart, 1964.

—— *The Kingdom of Canada*. Toronto, McClelland & Stewart, 1963.

Pope, Joseph. *Memoirs of Sir John A. MacDonald*. Ottawa, J. Durie, 2v. 1894.

—— *Confederation Documents Hitherto Unpublished*. Toronto, Carswell, 1895.

Preston, W. T. R. *My Generation of Politics & Politicians*. Toronto, D. A. Rose Publ., 1927.

Reid, Msgr. M. P. "Mrs. James Sadlier." Canadian Catholic Historical Association Report, 1946–47.

Reid, McNaught and Crowe. *A Source-book of Canadian History*. Revised ed. Toronto, Longmans, 1959.

Roger, Charles. *Ottawa Past and Present*. Ottawa, *Times* Printing & Publishing Co., 1871.

Roscoe, Theodore. *The Web of Conspiracy*. New York, Prentice-Hall, 1959.

Ross, Sir George. *Getting Into Parliament and After*. Toronto, William Briggs, 1913.

Ross, A. M. *Memoirs of a Reformer (1832–1892)*. Toronto, Hunter Rose, 1893.

Rumilly, Robert. *Histoire de la Province de Quebec, Georges-Etienne Cartier*. Montreal, Valiquette, 1942.

Ryan, Dr. Mark. *Fenian Memories*. Dublin, M. H. Gill & Son, 1946.

Saunders, E. M. *The Life and Letters of the Rt. Hon. Sir Charles Tupper*. 2v. London, Cassell & Co. 1916.

Sissons, C. B. *Church and State in Canadian Education*. Toronto, Ryerson, 1959.

Skelton, Oscar Douglas. *The Life and Times of Sir Alexander Tilloch Galt*. Toronto, Oxford, 1920.

Smith, Goldwin. *Reminiscences*. New York, Macmillan, 1910.

Sullivan, T. D., A. M. and D. B. *Speeches from the Dock—Protests of Irish Patriotism*. 23rd ed. Dublin, T. D. Sullivan.

Sullivan, A. M. *New Ireland*. Philadelphia, Lippincott, 1878.

Thomson, Dale C. *Alexander Mackenzie, Clear Grit*. Toronto, Macmillan, 1960.

Tupper, Sir Charles. *Recollections of Sixty Years*. London, Cassell, 1914.

Varcoe, F. P. *Legislative Power in Canada*. Toronto, Carswell, 1954.

Waite, P. B. *The Life and Times of Confederation, 1864–1867*. University of Toronto Press, 1962.

WALKER, FRANKLIN A. *Catholic Education and Politics in Upper Canada, 1804–1867.* Toronto, Dent, 1955.

WALLACE, WM. STEWART. "The Growth of Canadian National Feeling." Toronto, *Canadian Historical Review,* vol. I no. 2, June 1920, pp. 136–65.

—— *The Macmillan Dictionary of Canadian Biography.* Toronto, 1963.

WEBB, ALFRED. *A Compendium of Irish Biography.* Dublin, Gill, 1878.

WHELAN, EDWARD. *Confederation of the Provinces.* Charlottetown, Haszard, 1865.

WINKS, ROBIN W. *Canada and the United States, The Civil War Years.* Baltimore, Johns Hopkins, 1960.

YOUNG, HON. JAMES. *Public Men and Public Life in Canada.* 2v. Toronto, William Briggs, 1912.

# INDEX

*To users of the Index:* note that dates are given as breakdowns in many major references; events occurring during these time periods may be found summarized in the Table of Contents.

## C